CW01186933

HORSE AND MAN IN EARLY MODERN ENGLAND

Horse and Man in
Early Modern England

Peter Edwards

hambledon
continuum

Hambledon Continuum is an imprint of Continuum Books
Continuum UK, The Tower Building, 11 York Road, London SE1 7NX
Continuum US, 80 Maiden Lane, Suite 704, New York, NY 10038

www.continuumbooks.com

Copyright © Peter Edwards 2007

All rights reserved. No part of this publication may be reproduced or transmitted in any form or by any means, electronic or mechanical, including photocopying, recording or any information storage or retrieval system, without prior permission from the publishers.

First published 2007

British Library Cataloguing-in-Publication Data
A catalogue record for this book is available from the British Library.

ISBN 978 1 85285 480 5

Typeset by Egan Reid, Auckland, New Zealand
Printed and bound by MPG Books Ltd, Cornwall, Great Britain

Contents

Illustrations		vii
Acknowledgements		ix
Preface		xi
1	The Horse and Society	1
2	Attitudes towards Horses	17
3	The Training and Treatment of Horses	35
4	Horse Riding and Status	69
5	The Racecourse	89
6	Preparation for War	119
7	The Cavalry and Early Modern Warfare	145
8	Work Horses	183
9	Coach and Horses	211
	Conclusion	235
	Glossary	245
	Notes	249
	Bibliography	297
	Index	325

Illustrations

Between pages 180 and 181

1   Detail from Hoefnagel's painting *A Fête at Bermondsey* (*c.* 1570).

2   Henry VIII rides with his retinue to meet Francis I of France on the Field of the Cloth of Gold near Calais in June 1520.

3   Wootton's portrait of the Bloody Shouldered Arabian exported from Aleppo by Nathaniel Harley.

4 and 5   Exterior and interior views of the Duke of Newcastle's riding school at Bolsover Castle in Derbyshire.

6   A. Sijmond's painting *Five of the Dukes of Newcastle's Managed Horses.*

7   A farm scene at Twyford in Shropshire in the early eighteenth century.

8 and 9   Loggan's engravings of a stage coach and packhorses at Oxford in *c.* 1675.

10   Charles II leaving Nonsuch Palace by coach.

Acknowledgements

The first person I would lie to thank is the anonymous referee who recommended that I severely prune the contextual chapter that opened my book, *The Horse Trade of Tudor and Stuart England* (1988/repr. 2004). By doing so, he or she made this book possible by prompting me to consider writing an account of the demand for horses to set alongside the one on supply. The swathes of deleted material also provided me with starting points for a number of chapters in the present book. Fortunately, several people stopped me from embarking on the project for a number of years. Principal among them was the late Professor John Kenyon, who originally wrote to me with a question about horses in warfare, explaining that he was thinking about working on the logistics of the British Civil Wars. He never did it, but he did stimulate my interest in the subject. In 2000 I published *Dealing in Death: The Arms Trade and the British Civil Wars, 1638–52*. When I returned to the task I was far better prepared to write this book, which bears little resemblance to the one I would have begun in 1988. Having attended conferences on animals in history and listened to the views of English Literature scholars, cultural historians and anthropologists, I became aware of different approaches to the subject. I am particularly grateful to Dr Kevin de Ornellas for loaning me his doctoral dissertation on literary horses in the Renaissance, which showed me how literary material could be used to gain insights into historical issues. A quick glance at the bibliography reveals that I remain a document-based, empirical historian but I have tried to incorporate some of the ideas I have picked up from other quarters.

Numerous people have helped me with this book. As ever, Dr Thirsk has been a source of inspiration, a person I could always turn to for advice and encouragement. She also provided material assistance when she generously donated her extensive archive on horses, saving me weeks of work. Professors Donna Landry and Malcolm Wanklyn, Dr Gary Marvin, and Dorian Gerhold have read specific chapters, usually more than one, and they have saved me from numerous errors. I would like to give special thanks to my 'technical adviser', Mrs Ann Hyland, whose practical knowledge of horses is unrivalled. I have read papers on specific themes at seminars in Bath, Cologne, London, Piacenza, Roehampton, Saumur and Versailles, and have benefited enormously from the ensuing discussions. The Marquess of Salisbury graciously gave me permission to reproduce a portion of

Joris Hoefnagel's painting, *A Fête at Bermondsey*.

Naturally, I could not have written this book without the support my wife, who for years has had to put up with the practical problems of academic research: books and papers everywhere; research widowhood; and an often distracted and overwrought husband. I am grateful for her patience and forbearance, which, if it is what I said in 1988, is just as true today.

University of Roehampton,
August 2006

Preface

Throughout history humans have exploited animals for their own ends. At first, in prehistoric times, man hunted them to survive, for they helped meet his basic need for food, clothing and shelter. The development of farming and the domestication of animals not only eased his task but also added to the ways in which he made use of them. By Tudor and Stuart times man's demands were much more complex and far more controversial. He killed for pleasure, enslaved domesticated animals and, with regard to horses, used them for frivolous as well as utilitarian purposes. Like other creatures, their role was to serve man. Indeed, many people in early modern society believed that the Earth's resources were completely at their disposal. In literature, with hardly a hint of satire, the animals were depicted as complicit in their own submission. As Ben Jonson wrote in 'To Penshurst',

> The painted partrich lyes in euery field
> And, for thy messe, is willing to be kill'd.[1]

If domestication of animals made the job of control that much easier, it did not imbue it with greater moral authority. Giving an animal a life before quickly dispatching it is a fallacious argument, for a non-existent animal would feel no sense of deprivation.[2]

Man's domination of the natural world raises important ethical questions about our right to do so and the way we treat our fellow creatures. Within the traditions of western civilization this discourse dates from at least classical times and, with the growth of animal rights' movements in the world today, it is still a contentious issue. It is certainly one that has begun to attract modern academic interest, the key publication being Keith Thomas's seminal work, *Man and the Natural World: Changing Attitudes in England, 1500–1800*.[3] Thomas sees the early modern period as a time of change, a bridge between the unabashed anthropocentric views of the middle ages and the theriophilic-influenced posture of the modern world. The nature of the relationship between man and animals did concern early modern thinkers and many writers at the time contributed to the debate. As a result, the period witnessed the growth in theriophilic opinion, even if it retained its anthropocentric bias. Writers not only advocated better treatment for animals but also began to dispute the basis of man's claims to superiority.

Recently, the basic principle that underlies Thomas's work has been questioned. Revisionists, while recognizing his sympathetic treatment of the plight of animals in early modern society, have criticized his anthropocentric stance. They want to place animals squarely in the centre of the discourse: to look at the past from the animals' perspective and to assess the degree to which they exercised agency, that is, an ability to influence their life and environment.[4] Moreover, when they examine the nature of the relationship between man and the rest of the natural world, they emphasize the degree of overlap, blurring the divide and casting further doubt on humanity's claims to uniqueness. Although hampered by a lack of evidence of the real experiences of creatures with no verbal or written means of communicating with us, this research, if successful, will enhance our understanding of the interaction of humans with other species and is therefore of interest. Even so, as a social and economic historian rather than an anthropologist, my approach remains determinedly anthropocentric. Whether I agree with it or not, early modern man did dominate his environment and disposed of its flora and fauna at will. When Fudge censoriously points out that the subtitle of Thomas's book betrays his purpose, namely, to examine changing human attitudes towards animals rather than to look at animals themselves, she provides an accurate appraisal of the aim of the present book![5]

1

The Horse and Society

In 1970 Michael Thompson categorized the Victorian age as a 'horse-drawn' society. The same was true of early modern England, even if horses were not quite so dominant at that time, as oxen and some mules and asses shared the tasks.[1] Many thousands of people earned a living directly or indirectly from horses, and horse-related industries generated huge sums of money each year. Farmers and gentlemen bred horses and grew hay and cereals for their fodder. Horse owners, according to circumstances, employed servants to tend their animals and paid blacksmiths, farriers and horse leeches to shoe them and cure their ailments. Masons, bricklayers, carpenters, glaziers, tilers and shinglers built and maintained their stables, and labourers hedged and ditched the closes in which horses grazed. Horse tack manufacturers included saddlers, harness makers and lorimers, and tailors and shoemakers fashioned a rider's wearing apparel. Horses pulled ploughs and harrows, as well as carts, wains and wagons, and provided an income for craftsmen such as cartwrights, ploughwrights and wheelwrights. Coaches, as luxury vehicles, offered an opportunity for coachbuilders and leathermakers, upholsterers, painters and carvers to exploit the interest of the gentry in ostentatious display. On the roads, packmen and carters distributed a wide range of goods around the country. Horse dealers provisioned the markets and fairs with stock and helped to integrate the nation's equine resources.

In a predominantly rural society most horses worked on farms, preparing the ground and hauling agricultural products. Oxen provided the main alternative source of power, though by the end of the period horses were replacing them even in areas where they had once predominated. The timing and pace of the change naturally varied from place to place according to such factors as type of soil, availability of feed and even the attitude of the farmers. Occasionally, farmers combined the two in a team with horses in front, in order to speed up the plough. They also employed horses to carry out other jobs on the farm. Horses worked in trade and industry too. They drove machinery that carried out a number of jobs, a particularly important one being the draining of water from mines. Horse mills were far more powerful than hand-operated ones and helped speed up an array of industrial processes. Mostly, they transported goods around the country. It is true that, wherever possible, cargoes moved by water but in most cases consignments still had to get to and from the river or port.

Possession of a horse enabled an individual to take a greater quantity of goods to market and to serve customers over a wider area. Horses certainly gave their owners greater mobility, allowing them to travel farther and do so more freely. In the seventeenth century a rider could cover thirty to forty miles a day, though much depended on his or her sense of urgency and the quality of the horse. An ambler reputedly could travel at up to six miles an hour, but only gentlemen would have possessed such a mount.[2] Literary evidence suggests that distances of forty miles in a day represented a creditable performance. In *The Recruiting Officer* (1706), Farquhar has Captain Plume declare,

> At ten yesterday morning I left London; a hundred and twenty miles in thirty hours is pretty smart riding.[3]

Masculine bravado also intruded, judging from the following quote from Shakespeare's Cymbeline.

Innogen	How many score of miles may we well ride
	'Twixt hour, and hour?
Pisanio	One score 'twixt sun and sun,
	Madam's enough for you; and too much too.
Innogen	Why, one that rode to 's execution, man,
	Could never go so slow

In her retort Imogen seems to be reacting to Pisanio's chauvinistic inference that a lady should take it easy when riding.[4]

HORSES AND STATUS

On the bottom rung of the horse-owning ladder were those with one animal, which they used to perform a variety of tasks, including, 'carrying turf and bracken in packs, panniers, and *nets*, slung across its back; in carting hay, corn, and wood; and in conveying the labourer's wife and neighbours to the nearest market town'.[5] Another significant dividing line separated owners who kept horses specifically for riding from those who used them as work animals as well. They could literally as well as metaphorically look down on those on foot. In the late sixteenth and early seventeenth centuries members of the 'middling orders' who profited from rising demand, acquired mounts. The fact that they owned saddle horses showed that they had surplus wealth and this gave them added prestige. Probate inventories list few of these animals and even if they under-record them, this reinforces the point.

Most people at the time, affected by rising prices and competition for jobs and land, experienced declining living standards and could not have afforded a horse.

For owners, the expense of maintaining a horse was particularly high. It was only when population pressure eased in the late seventeenth century that the horse-owning sector of the population increased. Probate inventories chart this rise, though they only record the possessions of selective groups of people, the ones for whom it was worth drawing up a list of their personal possessions.[6] According to the inventories, one-fifth of the householders at Yetminster in Dorset owned horses in the 1590s and three-fifths of them in the 1660s. At Horbing, a fen edge parish in Lincolnshire, the percentage of sixteenth-century inventories that include horses is just under three-quarters (73.9 per cent), falling to a little over one-half (54.3 per cent) in the next fifty years. For the post-Restoration period the proportion is up to six people in seven (86.2 per cent).[7] This trend is confirmed by a series of parish rates, based on the number of animals owned. Between 1636 and the mid eighteenth century, the proportion of ratepayers who had horses rose from three in five in 1636 (60.0 per cent) to just under three in four in 1701 (73.4 per cent), to over four in five in 1724 (81.1 per cent) and to six in seven at an unknown date between 1724 and 1742 (85.7 per cent).[8]

The upper classes, with their greater wealth, were able to indulge themselves to a much greater extent. Like others, they rode on horseback as a means of getting from one place to another. Nonetheless, they did not merely view horse riding as a utilitarian exercise but also valued it as a signifier of their status. Good horsemanship was deemed to be one of the essential attributes of a gentleman. The horses of the elite therefore stand out in terms of their quality and price. For whatever purpose, they wanted the best, that is horses of the correct size and conformation, from sought after breeds and in fashionable colours. For this reason, the stables belonging to the upper classes contained the largest and most varied stock. Local gentry might keep ten to twelve head but the nobility would have dozens of horses in their stables. The crown counted royal animals in hundreds. When Henry VIII died he left well over a thousand horses in stables and studs dotted around the country.[9] The number kept not only reflected the size of an individual household but also how much an owner wished to spend on horses as an item of conspicuous consumption. He could, for instance, employ horses for highly specific tasks and therefore required greater numbers. In 1691, Sir Richard Newdigate of Arbury Hall possessed sixty-one horses yet prefaced the list with the observation 'Keep few Idle horses'. He had ten for the coach ('3 too many'), eighteen for the cart ('at least'), eight for hunting ('few enough'), four for war ('too few'), five pads ('enough'), one stallion ('for breed'), six mares, eight unbroken colts and fillies and one black tit.[10]

If horses conferred status, they did so at a price. Owners had to house and maintain them and, above a certain number, employ people to look after them. At the top end, a string of valuable horses, kept in well-apportioned stable blocks and run by an army of servants, cost a good deal of money.[11] Numbers employed varied according to the size of the property, ranging from places where one or two men had responsibility for all husbandry matters to the crown estates, where the staff ran into the hundreds and they all had specific jobs to do within the stables. Gentlemen of moderate means might have stables that were little better than those of yeomen, but county gentry and the nobility built imposing stable blocks, the better to show off their prize horses.[12] Indeed the early modern period witnessed a number of striking developments in stable design that enhanced its status in the overall plan of house and ancillary buildings. Firstly stables were set apart from other outbuildings, their prominence being emphasized by the use of high quality materials. During the course of the seventeenth century the houses of offices, including a stable wing, often flanked the forecourt of the house, embellishing the approach to the home. Stable design may even have made use of innovative classical motifs. The most imposing stables resembled small country houses. At Chiswick, in the late seventeenth century, Sir Stephen Fox built a fashionable house with the proceeds of the paymastership of the army. According to John Bowack, writing in 1705–6, his stables and outhouses looked 'like so many Gentlemen's seats'. Finally, in the early eighteenth century, the stables evolved as a substantial separate block, arranged around a quadrangle, typically built to fashionable neo-Palladian specifications. While this arrangement did have practical value, its chief rationale seemingly lay in its aesthetic appeal. Hitherto, the plan had largely been restricted to royal stables.[13]

Horses' dietary requirements were high. In breeding areas grass and hay might suffice for ordinary horses, and many farmers with access to open commons kept horses there. Enclosed pastures provided better nourishment and were essential to a breeder who wanted to produce good quality stock. As Heresbach observed, 'He that hath a fansey too breede Horse, must first prouide himselfe of a good race, and then of good ground and plenty of pasture, which … in Horses there must be special care therof'.[14] The site was also important. In 1639 de Gray, reflecting the consensus of opinion, stated that the grounds should neither be too rich and rank nor too barren, short or mossy. Upland pastures were best, especially those with patches of stony ground, because they helped the wind, knitted the joints and toughened the hoofs.[15] Even so, horses, unlike oxen, did not look their best nor could they operate effectively if fed on grass alone. Farmers, gentry and others with access to land could grow their own crops, but they lost income by doing so, especially if the horses were underused or kept for non-functional purposes. In 1562 an official calculation set the cost of feeding a horse in service at 5s. a week, at a somewhat generous rate of fourteen pounds of hay, seven pounds of straw, one peck of oats and half a peck of peas a day.[16] When another official estimate was made in 1702 the rate had tripled, the daily ration, 15 pounds of hay and a peck of oats, working out at about 15s. 9d. a week.[17] The cost of 'cutting a dash' in the capital was even higher. In a statement entitled 'London and Middlesex inconveniences', written by Sir John Newdigate of Arbury at the beginning of the seventeenth century, he claimed that 'one horse cannot be kepte under £17 a yeare & a coache & tow horses not under £40 a yeare ... tow may be kepte at Erbury as cheape as one in Midlesex and London'. Sir John, like others, sought to avoid unnecessary expense by grazing his horses outside for as long as possible, advising: 'kepe them out as longe as I can give them pease strawe & chaffe onely till Candlemas and hay after with oates or pease'.[18]

There were also hidden costs. Horses had to be shod regularly and, as they were prone to disease and injury, money had to be spent on remedies such as drenching, bleeding and applying poultices. Horse owners therefore had to make use of blacksmiths, farriers and horse leeches, usually hiring them as and when required. Where the number of horses warranted it, they might employ such men on a permanent basis. Furthermore, when sick or otherwise incapacitated, a horse could not carry out the tasks for which it was employed and the owner lost money. Even if used for a social function, it could not fulfil its role. After a few years at its peak, a horse was a depreciating asset. According to a price series of individual horses on the Blomfield family estate at Stonham, values reached their highest point at about seven years old, held that level for a year or two, and then started to decline.[19] Finally, at the end of their active life, horses were almost valueless. Because of the long-standing aversion to eating horsemeat in England, they were only worth a couple of shillings for their hide and as dog meat.[20]

NATIVE HORSES

At the beginning of the period the bulk of the country's horses technically comprised ponies, that is, horses of fourteen hands and below. The best came from the outlying parts of Britain. Irish hobbies were the most sought after; they had some Spanish blood in them and, although not large, were well-proportioned with a finely shaped head. Contemporaries also prized the Galloways of south-west Scotland. William Camden wrote that 'their little nagges, which for being well limed, fast knit and strongly made for to endure travaile, are much in request and bought from hence'.[21] Hostility between England and Scotland hindered the trade in the sixteenth century but after the union of the crowns in 1603 the numbers crossing the border increased. At the turn of the seventeenth century John Spreull included the trade in Galloways with England as one of Scotland's main exports.[22] Borderers on both side of the line travelled to Dunbarton Fair to buy them.[23] In Wales, the merlins of Montgomeryshire were reputed the 'best nagges' in the country. These semi-wild horses, which roamed the vast open commons of the county, were rounded up at the age of three and, when trained, sold at Border fairs.[24] All three breeds were employed for work as well as for the saddle.

In England smaller horses roamed the commons and moors of the country, including noted breeds in the Peak District, the Pennines, the New Forest and on the south-western moors.[25] They were hardy, sure-footed and wiry animals, toughened by fending for themselves in a harsh environment. Dartmoor ponies, for instance, lived out on the moors all year round, foraging for their own food.[26] In his attempt to increase the size of the native stock Henry VIII tried to ban such horses from the commons. This was a mistake because the qualities of these animals made them ideal pack horses. As Carew said of Cornish ponies in 1602, 'they were hardly bred, coarsely fed, low of stature, quick in travel and (after their growth and strength) able enough for continuance, which sort prove most serviceable for a rough and hill country'.[27]

England did produce some larger horses, notably in northern and western vales, in fen edge parishes in Lincolnshire and Somerset, in Cleveland, and in the sandy soils of Norfolk and Suffolk. In 1512–13 the most valuable draught horses bought for the army came from Lincolnshire, Norfolk and Suffolk.[28] Agricultural developments during the course of the early modern period helped to extend the areas where farmers could breed or rear such animals. The rich pastures of drained fens nourished breeding herds of heavy horses, while greater emphasis on fodder crops in mixed farming areas encouraged the rearing and training of draught horses. Suffolk Punches specialized in the draught but specimens from other breeds, of the right size, gait and conformation, might serve as saddle mounts too. At about the age of four, mixed farmers bought colts for training in the collar and then, two or three years later, sold them on as cart, coach and carriage horses. Horses bred in pastoral areas moved to mixed farms elsewhere for training. Colts and horses from the Severn Valley in Shropshire, for instance, travelled to the felden parts of Oxfordshire, Warwickshire and Worcestershire. Conversely, some rearing areas, including the Southwell district of Nottinghamshire, Bedfordshire and Hertfordshire, bred their own stock. A collection of probate inventories for Bedfordshire for the years 1617–19 show a preponderance of mares, horses and colts on the farm.[29]

In Henry VIII's reign, therefore, the country produced a considerable number of light saddle horses and small pack ponies, together with some heavier horses suitable for the draught. What the king really needed, however, were horses that he could use in his military campaigns: large cavalry mounts and powerful draught horses to pull the baggage and artillery trains. He did not find them in sufficient numbers. Writing to the marquis of Mantua in 1511 at the beginning of Henry's reign, Polydore Vergil admitted that good horses were scarce in Britain.[30] In 1557, ten years after Henry's death, the situation had not improved much. In that year the Venetian ambassador declared that Britain possessed no heavy cavalry horses except for a few in Wales and in the royal studs. He also criticized the quality of the light cavalry horses, which, although 'mettlesome and high couraged', were weak and broken-winded because fed on grass alone.[31] There were insufficient numbers of suitable draught horses too. In the 1540s commanders reported critical shortages of draught horses in the Scottish and French theatres of war. Besides, those that they did have were ineffective. In 1544 Norfolk and others reported to the Privy Council that English horses proved to be very weak and could not pull heavy loads.[32] Ironically, Henry had set in motion a programme that would eventually improve the quality of native horses for the saddle and the draught, but in the short term the country could not cope with the huge demands that his military campaigns placed on the equine resources of the nation.

IMPROVEMENT IN NATIVE HORSES

Even before the end of Henry VIII's reign commentators were coupling the poor quality of native horses with a lack of interest in good breeding practice. In April 1540 John Uvedale, thanking Thomas Cromwell for a stallion he had given him, yearned for the day when such a horse would be available in each county. If this were to happen, he believed, home-bred horses, 'much decayed here for want of good stallions', would improve.[33] Similarly, in Elizabeth's reign Sir Thomas Chaloner, ambassador to Spain, declared that 'England had none but vile and ordinary horses', and recommended that his countrymen should pay more attention to breeding.[34] In 1565 Thomas Blundeville exhorted the queen to enforce statutes regulating the breeding of horses and to utilize deer parks as breeding grounds for horses for service 'whereof this Realme of all others at this instant hath great neede'.[35] The potential was there for, as the Venetian ambassador reported in 1557, Britain produced a greater number of horses than anywhere else in Europe.[36]

By the end of the seventeenth century commentators were reporting considerable progress. In 1686 Richard Blome wrote, 'In England several good breeds; our running horses, hunters and pads, and our horses for all manner of fatigue of whatsoever nature, are not matched in Europe; nor is any horse better for an officer in war, than one of our *Twelve-stone horses* (such as usually run for plates) if he is well-chosen and taken in time'.[37] Signs of progress were already apparent by 1600; in particular, a thriving trade was developing with France in spite of a ban on exports. Licences to export horses were readily obtainable and, if not, smugglers helped to cater for the demand. Foreign dignitaries from all over Europe were asking permission to ship out horses they had obtained in England. In January 1606/7, the emperor, having heard of the 'swiftness and excellence' of the great Irish hounds and English trotting horses, asked his emissary in England to obtain some for him.[38] Half a century later, in 1652, one of Samuel Hartlib's correspondents contrasted the scarcity of good horses in Elizabeth I's reign with the current state of affairs: 'at this time we are known to have many thousands of horse not inferior to the best in the world'.[39] This letter, written at a time when the British Civil Wars had hardly finished, indicates the extent of the advances made. Indeed, five years later the government felt confident enough to free the trade and to allow the export of horses on the payment of a duty.[40]

To a certain extent improvement occurred as a result of developments within the country itself. As more and more people came to appreciate the qualities of the various breeds of horses, and to use them for appropriate jobs, a specialist market grew. This encouraged farmers in horse-breeding areas to pay greater attention to the business, and output rose. At a higher level, the crown took the lead in improving the quality of the stock by setting more exacting standards at its studs.[41] After a hiatus in the reigns of Edward VI and Mary,[42] Henry's successors continued his policy. In furthering his plan, they made good use of their Masters of Horse, who were all keen horsemen themselves. For all his faults George Villiers, first duke of Buckingham, was a superb judge of horseflesh. James I thought so, expressing his gratitude for the work he had done in improving the quality of his horses in the following words, 'God thanke the maister of the horse for provyding me such a number of faire usefull horses, fitte for my hande; in a worde I proteste I never was maister of such horses'.[43]

Henry VIII encouraged members of the landed elite to follow his lead and, as a spur, promoted measures that ensured that they did so. An Act of 1535–6 ordered all owners of parks outside the four northern counties to keep two brood mares at least thirteen hands high. From May 1537 only stallions of at least fourteen hands could cover them. A further Act, passed in 1541–2, enforced owners, according to rank, to keep a certain number of trotting stallions of at least three years old and fourteen hands high.[44] It achieved some success for, as the French ambassador noted in his letter to his master in 1542, 'all the nobles are now making studs, for which they have great commodity in their great parks and good ground'.[45] Much remained to be done, but at least Henry VIII had made a start. Further legislation followed under Henry's successors. In 1580 Elizabeth I appointed a Special Commission for the Increase and Breed of Horses, with the brief to see that existing statutes were being observed, especially those relating to serviceable horses (that is, for the cavalry). The seriousness with which the queen took its work is indicated by the high rank of members of the commission, which included the lord admiral, the lord and vice chamberlains, the lords president of the North and Wales, the Masters of the Horse and Ordnance and the earl of Bedford.[46] Deputy commissioners in each county reported back to them. They were probably chosen for their own interest in horse breeding.[47] In Staffordshire Sir Robert Bagot was a member of a family that certainly bred good quality horses and continued to do so throughout the rest of the period. When in the First

English Civil War the Parliamentarians captured the favourite horses of Colonel Bagot, then governor of Lichfield, he offered a reward of £1,000 for them.[48]

Among the gentry the royal gentlemen-pensioners took the lead in promoting horse-breeding in the country. Indeed, the authors of three of the earliest books on horsemanship were members of this group and a fourth was the son of one.[49] Nicholas Arnold, for instance, obtained Flemish horses in Henry's reign, travelled to Italy under Edward VI, and subsequently maintained a stud of Neapolitan horses on his estate at Highnam in Gloucestershire. According to Harrison, he 'hath bred the best horses in England and written of the manner of their production'.[50] Other gentlemen became enthusiasts too. When Ninian Staveley, esquire, of Ripon Park died in 1559 he left forty-one horses, comprising five mares, six young horses, nineteen young colts, three foals, six nags and two geldings.[51] Sir George Reresby, who lived at Thrybergh Hall in the early seventeenth century, was another keen horseman. According to a descendant, his pastime 'was sometimes haukes, but his cheefest was his breed of Horses, in which he was very exact'.[52] Groups of horse fanciers might form a breeding ring and avail themselves of each others' stallions to service their mares. One who did was Edward James, a Staffordshire gentleman, who at the opening of the eighteenth century made use of stallions belonging to Captain Lane, Sir John Leveson-Gower and Mr Salt.[53]

To encourage an interest in breeding good quality horses, the authorities and writers alike stressed the prestige a gentleman would acquire not only from owning such animals but *a fortiori* from breeding them too. Writing in 1639, de Gray pointed out that good, able and serviceable horses could be bred as easily as 'Iades and Baffles, unusefull and unprofitable'. All that was needed was the inclination and certain basic facilities.[54] To aid them the gentry could read the books on horsemanship that appeared in increasing numbers in the period from the late sixteenth century. We know that they used them for they referred to them in their correspondence, recorded them in their accounts and added glosses in the margin. Among the papers of Sir John Gell, the Parliamentarian leader in Derbyshire, is a memorandum dated 29 March 1645 which lists the general rules to be observed in buying horses. It looks like a set of notes culled from a book, covering such matters as the breed, colour, pace and size of horses, and emphasizing the need to consider these factors in relation to function.[55]

Enthusiasts imparted their knowledge as well and in this way improved standards within their family and among their friends and neighbours. Because they had acquired their expertise through practical experience, their comments were particularly valuable. In 1691 Sir Richard Newdigate of Arbury Hall wrote down an annotated inventory of his horses for his son's instruction, prompted by criticism from his family that he spent to much time and money on his horses. After proving that others were asking much higher prices, he drew the obvious conclusion when he wrote, 'Make much therefore of your own breed my son'. Later in the document he reinforced this message by advising him to 'Value not selling. Wee breed to save buying'. Even so, he did not hesitate to sell horses in order to improve the breed, asserting 'Take care not to be overstockt ... Keep few idle horses'. He followed up his precept by earmarking twenty-two horses for sale in 1691. Constant weeding out of inferior animals raised the overall quality of his stock: 'Breed few but choice ... Sell the worst cart jades for any thing, & turn off some yearly to cart, even of the best breed.' He also differentiated between coach and cart horses on the one hand and better quality animals on the other. 'Be sure put no coach or cart mares tho they seem fine to a right bred horse. Beware a bastard breed.'[56]

The other aspect of crown policy was to cross-breed English stock with foreign horses. Once more, Henry VIII deserves credit for introducing the programme in a systematic way. To enhance the quality of his draught horses he imported Flemish mares, a breed renowned for its strength. In 1542 Andrew Borde noted, 'Great studmares we bring up in Flaunders, we sell them in England'. According to Blundeville, they 'wyll endure great labour, as is wel sene for that the fleminges do use none other drawght, but with those mares in their wagons, in the whiche I haue sene two or three Mares to go lightly away with suche a burthen, as is almoste incredible'.[57] The deterioration in Anglo-Spanish relations during the course of Elizabeth I's reign, caused, *inter alia*, by the English response to the Revolt of the Netherlands, then a province of the Spanish Empire, inhibited commerce with Flanders. Undoubtedly, this slowed down the process of improvement, but the situation was not as bad as it could have been. Flemish merchants continued to trade with England, braving both their government's wrath and attacks by Dutch privateers, an aspect of the ongoing struggle between Spain and rebels in the northern Netherlands. The Dutch and the English moved closer together and this opened up an alternative source of strong draught horses. In 1572, for instance, intelligence from London informed the Duke of Alva, the governor of the Netherlands, that the English had brought over four hundred brood mares to improve the breed of their horses. Northern European horses, in general, made suitable draught animals. German horses approximated most closely to those from Flanders, whereas Friesians were lighter than both of them. Danish horses were lighter still and those with the right conformation, size and action made excellent coach horses.[58] In Oldenburg, the counts developed a particularly fine breed of coach and carriage horses in the late sixteenth and seventeenth centuries. Johann XVI, who succeeded in 1563, began the process, crossing imported Barbs, Turcomans, and Danish and especially Spanish and Neapolitan stock, with readily available Friesian horses from East Friesland. Anton Günther made further improvements, to the extent of establishing a distinct Oldenburg breed.[59]

At the beginning of the period, military commanders regarded Neapolitan coursers as the cavalry mount *par excellence* on account of their strength and courage. The French, in particular, made use of coursers because of the prominence they gave to heavy cavalry.[60] Blundeville also thought that North European horses made suitable heavy cavalry mounts, if of 'convenient stature, well proportioned and suitable for the purpose'. He even included Flemish horses in this list, as well as similar German animals. The latter were commonly used as great horses but, because of their coarseness and weight, were better 'for the shock than to pass a cariere or to make a swift *manège*'. Hitherto, they had been 'gross and heavy' but through selective breeding had become lighter.[61] He also recommended Hungarian horses, which he described as large, good tempered, hardy and very swift. By the late sixteenth century, however, the military role of men-at-arms, riding on horses like these, was in decline and with them their mounts. This was due to a change in military tactics which increasingly emphasized firepower at the expense of the cavalry's role as a battering ram. When the mounted arm regained its role as an instrument of shock in the early seventeenth century its members now rode into battle on lighter, quicker and nimbler horses. Many of them had Spanish ginete, North African or Eastern blood in them. When Prince Rupert led the defeated Royalists out of Bristol on 11 September 1645 he was riding on a 'spectacular' black Arabian.[62]

The courser, on account of its size and conformation, made an ideal parade animal. In origin, the term 'courser', appears to have referred to tournament horses, those that ran at the tilt, and therefore denotes a type rather than a breed.[63] Even so, contemporaries generally associated the name with the large saddle horses bred in the kingdom of Naples. They were imposing animals, strongly built and comely in appearance, well-proportioned and with the sought after convex profile of the head. By nature they were gentle and tractable.[64] When the Spanish annexed Naples in 1502, they brought their own horses with them and the infusion of blood affected the Neapolitan breed. While the traditional courser continued to be be bred in the royal stud, a smaller, lighter version came into prominence. Known as *veneten del regno* because of their Spanish ancestry, they were virtually identical to the ginetes, from which they had sprung. The famed Mantuan stud contained coursers but ones that were lighter than the larger Neapolitan stock as a result of cross-breeding with Barbs, ginetes and Turcomans.[65]

For general riding, a ginete was preferred, on account of its conformation, lightness and speed. William Cavendish, the Duke of Newcastle, thought that it was 'Absolutely the best Stallion in the World'.[66] Ginetes originated in Andalusia, an area which in the middle ages had come under Moorish rule. With them, the Moors had brought Berber horses from North Africa, a breed which in prehistoric times had acquired Spanish blood via the land bridge across the Straits of Gibraltar. Some of the best ginetes came from the royal stud at Cordoba and

Henry VIII received horses from this stud as well as from that of the marquis of Mantua.[67] The crown also imported French, Polish, Savoyard, Sardinian and Corsican horses. In 1624 six stallions at the royal stud at Tutbury – two coursers, an Arabian, a barb, a ginete and a French horse – covered forty-seven mares, with names that reveal German, North African, Polish, Savoyard and Spanish blood.[68]

Some horses, as already shown, came into the country as part of the diplomatic process. Merely to be allowed to buy horses could be a sign of favour. Thus, as the emperor's ally against France in the 1540s, Henry VIII obtained Flemish draught horses. When in 1544 his agent there acquired two hundred mares without the permission of the regent, Mary of Hungary, it caused a diplomatic incident.[69] A gift of hackney horses, hobbies, greyhounds and mastiffs in March 1546 helped to restore good relations, the regent declaring that she was 'the gladdest woman in the world'.[70] In fact, gifts of horses often accompanied a round of diplomatic negotiations. To create an even better impression, donors spent lavishly on the trimmings. In 1605, James I paid £144 8s. 4d. for twenty-nine yards of velvet, silk lace and fringe, plus labour costs, to make saddle cloths for four great horses given to his father-in-law, the King of Denmark. This was hugely extravagant; a year earlier ten yards of cloth, two yards of cotton and labour for cloths for the colts had only cost Lord Willoughby 12s. 8d. A saddler would have sold one to a member of the general public for a couple of shillings.[71]

Of course, magnanimity was not the sole criterion. A valuable gift of expensive foreign horses, targeted to the interests of the recipient, was a useful diplomatic ploy. Henry VIII delighted in receiving fine horses, especially from Italian princelings, who used their studs to ingratiate themselves with foreign rulers and raise their own political standing. They were able to produce such superb specimens because their trading and diplomatic links with North Africa and the Near East allowed them to obtain high quality stallions and brood mares, in spite of a general ban on their export. The Mantuan stud was particularly impressive on account of the fineness of its horses and the scale of the enterprise. In 1516 it produced eighty-one colts, which, according to Marquis Francesco Gonzago, were 'the most beautiful that we've ever had'.[72] One consignment sent to England in 1514 so pleased Henry VIII that he remarked that he had never ridden better trained animals nor had he ever received a more agreeable present. The diplomatic effect was immediate, Henry avowing as a result of the gift that the marquis could rely on his support on all occasions. In return he sent Irish hobbies, much sought after in Italy, where their sprinting ability made them ideal *palio* horses.[73] The monarchs of the day continued to exchange horses throughout the period. In November 1611 the Savoyard ambassador gave James I four horses, 'the like hath never been seen in England'. A month later the Elector Palatine, James's future son-in-law, sent him six fine coach mares and two handsome saddle horses.[74] James's son, Henry, a lover of all equestrian pursuits, also encouraged such gifts. Donors included the count of Emden, the landgrave of Hesse and the count of Vaudemont. Above all, he admired Barbary horses.[75] Oliver Cromwell, another excellent judge of horses, acquired them in the same way. Among those who supplied him with horses was the count of Oldenburg, who could draw on the choice stock of his own studs.[76]

Unfortunately for the donor, presents did not guarantee the success of negotiations, especially if the stance of the recipient differed from his or her own. An essential element of James I's European policy was a match between a Spanish princess and his heir, and he tried for years to bring it about, first for Henry in 1611–12 and then for Charles. In 1614 he sent his Master of Ceremonies, Sir John Finet, to Madrid to discuss the matter. As a sweetener, he armed Sir John with a 'rabblement' of presents: hunting horses and nags, greyhounds, spaniels and water dogs, pied bulls and kine, cormorants, stone-bows and cross-bows, 'curious' pieces, trunks and 'many things els'. John Chamberlain, who reported on the gifts, noted with derision the Spanish response, which consisted of 'but a chaine of £200 value, and as much monie to distribute among his companie'.[77] Talks continued intermittently for another nine years but always foundered on Spanish religious demands, the scale of which indicates that they were put forward as a means of torpedoing the negotiations.

Such gifts only benefited the crown and a few courtiers and ministers. Most people had to pay for their imported horses. Because of the expense involved, they had to take particular care when choosing, for unscrupulous merchants and intermediaries exploited the gullible for their own ends. In 1609 Nicholas Morgan made this point when he ridiculed the idea that a horse was good merely because it came from a particular country. He condemned the uncritical attitude of many horsemen and breeders who 'doe much insist herein, so as if a Neapolitan, Arabian, Barbarie or such like bee brought into England, how inestimable hee is valued, prised, and solde, and how all men desire him, who can doubt'.[78] William Cavendish, who was a particularly discerning judge of horses, echoed this view. He believed in general that only inferior Barbs were imported into Europe because they were brought over either by French horse dealers seeking to maximize their profit or by merchants, who did not know what to look for. He recalled seeing twenty-five Barbs, nothing but skin and bones, being sold at Paris for twenty-five pistols each. Of these, he helped Lord Montague choose nine but, although one of them did win many races, he added, 'but truly, if I had a Million, I would not have bought one of them, for they were very ordinary Horses'.[79] Perhaps this statement is as much a comment on the refinement of the Cavendish's taste as on the quality of these particular animals.

The landed classes emulated the Crown; they imported foreign horses and used them for breeding purposes. In 1600 Lord Willoughby, hearing that Sir

Robert Cecil was setting up a stud, offered him a young ginete, 'rightly bred by both sire and dam'.[80] A horse like this could benefit other studs; foreign stallions were often the ones chosen to service another gentleman's mare. Accordingly, in 1639 and in the 1650s, Barbs belonging to the Earl of Northumberland, Mr Hewitt and Mr Masters covered Sir John Pelham's mares.[81] In time the blood of imported horses spread more widely through the equine population: a gentleman, for instance, might allow his tenant farmers use of his stallion in return for a consideration. In 1617 Richard Cholmeley of Brandsby obtained a horse foal from a tenant, William Young, paying for it by reducing the latter's rent and allowing his Turcoman stallion to service Young's mare. In Ireland in 1668 the duke of Ormond, having received advice that his Spanish stallion would not produce 'likely' colts, decided it to put it to more general use 'to help the neighbourhood to mend the ordinary breed'. He earmarked his large horse, Crop, for the same purpose.[82] Tenants might also receive, at a reduced price, an ageing or injured horse no longer in its prime and therefore valueless as a status symbol. If they did not obtain one privately on the estate, they might find one at a market or fair. The increasing prominence of black-coated horses in toll books in the late seventeenth century suggests that a number of farm and road horses had Low Countries blood in them.[83] Foreign genes demonstrably did improve the quality of the native stock, as Cavendish himself acknowledged. They were the 'best horses in the world for all uses whatsoever, from cart to *manège* and some are as fine as any bred out of all horses of all nations'.[84]

HORSE SALES AT MARKETS AND FAIRS

Apart from the ones that they bred themselves, most people acquired horses at markets and fairs. Many of them may have been happy to buy whatever they could find locally, but increasingly purchasers became more discriminating in their choice of animal. As specialization in function progressed, a national market developed, which ensured that surplus horses of particular types moved on to places where they were needed. Certain centres stand out for the sale of a particular type of horse. In the east midlands Market Harborough, Melton Mowbray, Northampton and Rothwell were the leading outlets for coach and carthorses, being stocked with horses that had been trained on the mixed farms of the region. In the north, Malton and Ripon benefited from the patronage of northern breeders and dealers who sold their choicest saddle horses there. Further south, Lenton was 'a great Fayr for all sorts of Horses', while Penkridge specialized in colts.[85] Some centres, located between pastoral and mixed farming regions, occupied a pivotal position in the trade. Derby and Nottingham, for instance, attracted horses from the Trent Valley and from noted breeding grounds in Yorkshire and Lincolnshire. From these fairs, some of the horses, according to purpose, moved to the breeding grounds of the west midlands or to mixed farms locally or in the east midlands.[86] Shrewsbury acted as a centre for both Welsh Border ponies and larger Severn vale horses. Leighton Buzzard Fair in Bedfordshire was, according to information given to an agent of the More family of Loseley Hall in 1693, 'the greatest fair for Geldings'.[87]

The widening of the market in horses, as in other commodities, led to the emergence of a specialist group of middlemen, horse dealers, who alone had the time and the expertise to integrate the equine resources of the country on a national scale. They are the ones who regularly appear in toll books, which, by law, preserved a record of all transactions involving horses, a measure specifically introduced to curb horse stealing.[88] Horse dealers lived and worked in all parts of the country but toll books reveal that they tended to bunch together in a handful of contiguous parishes. Detailed investigation of these districts indicates that they possessed good lines of communication with easy access to markets and fairs, and plentiful supplies of fodder: grass from commons and rentable closes in pastoral areas and oats and pulses in mixed farming ones. In spite of the invaluable work that horse dealers did, they did not enjoy a high reputation. Many of the dealers were undoubtedly reputable, with some standing in their community, but because of the growing importance of the trade in the economy, it also attracted a host of small-time entrepreneurs. These dealers had few scruples and often possessed openly criminal proclivities. Unfortunately, the population at large associated the horse trade with such dubious characters and this affected the reputation of honest traders. As a result, all dealers were viewed with even greater suspicion than were other middlemen.[89]

The gentry were not so dependent upon the fairs. Apart from the horses they bred themselves, they could obtain privately what they needed from others of their own class. This is not surprising, given the value of many of the horses they possessed and the scale of their network of personal connexions. Often the buyer took the initiative, offering a price for a particular horse, or asking a friend if he or she had a suitable one for sale. The genteel custom of naming a horse after the person who sold it to them reveals just how extensive the links could be. Estate accounts of Sir Thomas Pelham of Halland indicate that he obtained horses from the Akehurst, Ashburnham, Cotton, Goring, Howard, Leigh, Merriwether, Percy, St John, Shurley, Stapley, Temple, Walsingham, Wharton, Willoughby and Wyvill families. Many of these names belonged to members of the Sussex gentry and allied to Sir Thomas by bonds of friendship, political opinion and, in the case of Algernon Percy, tenth Earl of Northumberland, patronage.[90] Friends might be more honest but it still paid to take an expert along when viewing a prospective purchase. In 1677–8 Thomas Rowley, a prominent Shropshire horse dealer, accompanied Thomas Wickstead, the agent of Sir William Leveson-Gower, to

Benthall to inspect Mr Benthall's grey horse. After all, Sir William had to pay £57 for it.[91]

The elite, nevertheless, did buy and sell horses at fairs in spite of their fear of being duped and a distaste for the business of haggling over price with the rogues they assumed haunted such places. In any case, their agents were the ones who 'got their hands dirty'. Richard Blome pointed out the advantages. After discussing the breeding of horses for hunting, racing and the road in his book, *The Gentleman's Recreation*, he wrote, "Ti's needless to give directions for breeding any other sorts of horses; as for the coach, wagon, cart, servants and all manner of drudgery, because there is not that nicety required; and from the fairs and horse-coursers you may be supplied, and save the trouble'.[92] Naturally, they patronized the high-quality fairs, often sending their servants many miles to obtain a suitable animal or to dispose of another in the right place. In September 1697 Sir Anthony Chester of Chicheley in Buckinghamshire paid £37 10s. for a grey stallion (with expenses) at Penkridge.[93] Charges were a significant extra, especially on long trips. They included the cost of food and drink and accommodation for the men and horses; the purchase of halters and horse clothes; the fitting on of shoes; the payment of miscellaneous tolls and charges on the way; and the handing out of gratuities.[94] The gentry also did business at local fairs, especially when they wanted to sell their less valuable horses. In Staffordshire Edward James only sent his best horses to Penkridge, which ironically was his local fair, two miles away from his home. He sold most of his horses elsewhere in the county, at Lichfield, Rugeley and Stafford.[95]

Clearly, horse breeding can be accounted as one of the success stories of early modern England. From unpromising beginnings at the beginning of the sixteenth century the situation improved dramatically over the course of the following two hundred years. This was due to a combination of political, social and economic factors: the strategic concerns of the crown, the social pretensions of the upper classes and the demands of agriculture, trade and industry. Horses were able to fulfil the various roles allotted to them because of their flexibility and because the breeds varied so much in their physique: size, conformation, strength, speed and action. Breeders enhanced specific qualities by importing horses from abroad and over time the benefits of this practice spread through the equine population of the country. Ironically, Henry VIII, who had done so much to destroy the stock of native horses, was the person who began the process of recovery and improvement. The elite developed their own network of contacts, buying and selling horses off one another and using each other's stallions to cover their mares. For the population at large, access to the growing variety of horses was made possible through the emergence of specialist horse fairs and the activities of dealers who moved horses around the country.

2

Attitudes towards Horses

Christians believed that man occupied a unique position in the natural world and this was part of a divine plan. God had created the Garden of Eden as a paradise for humans and had given Adam dominion over all living things. At first, humans and beasts cohabited peacefully; Adam and Eve did not eat meat and animals were tame. Unfortunately, the Fall changed the relationship for ever: beasts became wild and aggressive and might attack humans. God did reaffirm man's ascendancy after the Flood, but the world was now a far more dangerous and intimidating place.[1] 'The fear of you and the dread of you shall be upon every beast of the earth, and upon every fowl of the air, upon all that moveth upon the earth, and upon all the fishes of the sea: into your hand are they delivered. Every moving thing that liveth shall be meat for you.'[2] Aristotle, writing in the fourth century BC, also believed in the primacy of man, which, he argued, derived from his special position in the natural world. While plants, animals and humans occupied stages on a continuous scale of being and all possessed souls, *homo sapiens*, as a species, was qualitatively different from plants and other living creatures. Plants' souls only had nutritive and reproductive faculties and those of animals sensory and in most cases locomotive, appetitive and 'imaginative' aspects too. Only humans possessed, in addition, a rational soul.[3] At the pinnacle of creation, they bestrode the natural world and, applying a teleological argument, received the whole of Nature's bounty.[4]

MAN AND THE NATURAL WORLD

In the search to justify man's claims to distinction, Aristotle's notion of the hierarchy of souls contributed to the medieval concept of the 'Great Chain of Being', which, like his belief in the four causes, depicted man as the end product of the process of creation.[5] Other qualities deemed to distinguish humans from animals were the power of speech; the practice of religion and the possession of a conscience; and the ability to exercise free will and moral judgement. In his *Discourse on Method* (1637) Descartes argued that animals' inability to communicate with humans proved that they lacked these qualities. He claimed that if they truly possessed a mind which could think about what they were saying, humans would be able to understand their utterances.[6] He therefore concluded that they functioned by instinct, 'which acts in them according to the disposition of their organs, just as a clock, which is only composed of wheels and weights is able to tell the hours and measure the time more accurately than we can do in all our wisdom'.[7] Descartes gained a good deal of notoriety for this concept of the 'beast-machine', which viewed animals as mere automata, governed by impulse, without souls and incapable of speech or reason.[8] Some of his followers went further, interpreting his comments to argue that animals did not feel pain. In truth, Descartes's association of thought with sensation is far more nuanced than the version pedalled by others: he later denied that animals could not feel any sensation. Unfortunately, the perceived link he had established, when publicized by his supporters, had a baleful effect, being used to condone the ill-treatment of animals.[9]

The issue of man's distinctiveness was a crucial one because, by emphasizing his superiority over the rest of the natural world, it validated his exploitation of animals. As Thomas observes, it could be used to 'justify hunting, domestication, meat-eating, vivisection … and the wholesale extermination of vermin and predators'.[10] Theriophilic writers like Margaret Cavendish, the marchioness (later duchess) of Newcastle, and Thomas Tryon criticized this view; emphasizing the existence of animal agency, they challenged the notion of anthropocentrism by pointing out that all species had a life of their own, independent of human needs. In 1653 Margaret Cavendish wrote,

> And is so Proud, thinks onely he shall live,
> That God a God-like Nature did him give
> And that all Creatures for his sake alone,
> Was made for him, to Tyrannize upon.[11]

She also questioned the morality of meat eating. In her poignant evocation of hare hunting, viewed from the animal's perspective, she asked,

> As if that God made Creatures for Mans meat,
> To give them Life, and Sense for Man to eat;
> Or else for Sport, or Recreations sake,
> Destroy those Lifes that God saw good to make.[12]

Theriophilic writers, moreover, might turn the point round, questioning the rationality and distinctiveness of man. It could be argued, for instance, that if the great chain of being were a continuum, humans were not unique but merely an animal that had done particularly well.[13] Some doubted that speech and reason were uniquely human attributes. An early pro-animal writer, Michel de Montaigne, criticized man for his arrogance in making the contrast, arbitrarily denying animals thought and intelligence. To illustrate the point, he posed the question, 'When I play with my cat, who knows if I am not a pastime to her more than she is to me'.[14] A century later, Margaret Cavendish argued in her poems and essays that mankind did not have a monopoly of sense and reason. In her poem 'Of Humility' she declared that she could not discern much difference between the minds of mankind and animals:

> Onely the *Shape* of *Men* is fit for use
> Which makes him *seem* much wiser than a *Goose*.[15]

In *A Discourse of Beasts*, she asked in a way reminiscent of Montaigne,

> Who knowes, but Beasts, as they do lye,
> In Meadows low, or else on Mountaines high?
> But that they do contemplate on the *Sun*,
> And how his daily, yearely Circles run.[16]

By the end of our period, in the middle of the eighteenth century, animal intelligence had become more widely recognized. In 1742 John Hildrop, rector of Wath, claimed that animals did possess understanding, at least to a degree that enabled them to fulfil their role in the natural world. He pointed out that the methods deployed to train horses and dogs only worked because the animals possessed intelligence. Explicitly rejecting the Cartesian beast-machine theory, he observed that had they been 'Creatures that had no Sense, Understanding, or Reflection … this Conduct would be as absurd and ridiculous, as it would be to caress and reward your Clock or your Watch for going well'.[17] John Lawrence, writing at the end of the century, went further: he thought that horses possessed a 'strong and retentive' memory and shared with humans the ability to reason, differing only in degree.[18] Today, to an even greater extent, experiments are helping to push back the boundaries relating to animal capabilities in relation to supposed human attributes of intelligence, memory and speech.

Language, or the perceived lack of it, among animals was the key issue. According to Aillaud, the animals' 'lack of common language, its silence, guarantees its distance, its distinctiveness, its exclusion, from and of man'.[19] Of course, the reverse could be true. In the 1570s Montaigne pointed out that animals might think that mankind lacked intelligence because they (humans) could not express themselves in language which they (animals) could understand.[20] A generation earlier, Des Périers in *Cymbalum mundi* (1537) had a horse claim that in the past animals could talk, adding that if they had not been deprived of speech humans would not consider them so stupid![21] In fact many birds and animals are physically capable of talking.[22] Several species of birds actually possess this faculty and, even if they merely mimic human speech, creatures clearly do communicate with others of the same kind. Surely, if humans cannot understand what they are saying, that is not the fault of the animals.

Even among early modern writers who accepted man's dominion of the natural world there were many who believed that he should not act in an arbitrary way. As humans only held their position on trust, they should exercise their stewardship with care and consideration. Indeed, it has been argued that at the time this was a common interpretation of the word 'dominion'.[23] On a practical level, too, it mattered: cruelty towards animals, it was argued, led down the slippery slope to the abuse of humans. Puritans, in particular, railed against the brutal treatment of animals. Calvin, for instance, pointed out that they were also God's creatures and should be managed with respect. 'If a man spare neither his horse, nor his ox nor his ass, therein he betrayeth the wickedness of his nature.'[24] For this reason, some writers condemned hunting because it entailed killing animals merely for pleasure. 'For myself,' Montaigne stated, 'I have not been able without distress to see pursued and killed an innocent animal which is defenceless and which does us no harm.'[25] In *Love's Labour's Lost* Shakespeare has the remorseful Princess of France admit,

> As I for praise alone now seek to spill
> The poor deer's blood, that my heart means no ill.[26]

Naturally, Margaret Cavendish criticized man's cruelty to his fellow-creatures, contrasting his claims to be temperate and compassionate with his real actions. In 'The Hunting of the Hare' she observed,

> And is Yet *Man* doth think himselfe so gentle, mild,
> When *he* of Creatures is most cruell wild.[27]

In *A Dialogue of Birds* she chastized man for his arrogance and brutality, while revealing a respect for animal agency,

> The Sparrow said, were an Condition such,
> But Men do strive with News us for to catch:
> With Guns, and Bows they shoot us from the Trees,
> And by small Shot, we oft our Lifes do leese,
> Because we pick a Cherry here, and there,
> When, God he knowes, we eate them in great feare.
> But Men will eat, until their Belly burst,
> And surfets take: if we eat, we are curst.[28]

Of course, while Margaret Cavendish's views were radical at the time, they are remarkably similar to modern criticisms of human anthropocentrism.[29] Even so, she lacked consistency, elsewhere stating that man alone possessed reason and was therefore unique. In *A Dialogue betwixt Man and Nature*, she argued,

> Though Beast hath Sense, feeles paine, yet whilst they live,
> They Reason want, for to dispute, or grieve.[30]

In the debate concerning the treatment of animals, the question whether they possessed souls or not became a matter of concern for people other than abstract philosophers. If animals were capable of achieving salvation, caring for them took on an extra meaning and warranted a higher priority. The issue had long been a matter of debate within the Christian Church and continued to divide theologians in early modern Europe.[31] Mainstream reformers like Calvin and Bullinger thought that animals did not have soul but others believed that they did. Of the latter, Richard Overton, the Leveller and General Baptist, argued for animal immortality in *Mans Mortallitie*, claiming that, if sinful men could be saved in spite of their faults, sinless animals should not be condemned to eternal darkness.[32] In the eighteenth century the Anglican bishop Joseph Butler and the Methodist John Wesley both thought that the evidence demonstrated that animals possessed souls.[33] Wesley wrote that brutes 'perform a thousand actions which can never be explained by mere mechanism ... so that we are constrained to own there is in them also some superior principle of a spiritual kind resembling the human soul'.[34] Similarly, Lawrence presumed that animals possessed a soul but was unwilling to speculate what happened to it after death.[35]

Humans, who abused animals, may have been worried about their own humanity, a consequence of their position in the natural world: above animals but below God. As they possessed reason and freedom of choice, they could aspire to the heavens but also plumb the depths. In *Gulliver's Travels*, Swift may have been satirizing (even celebrating) the duality of man's nature in his contrast of rational animals, the houyhnhnms, with the beastly humans, the yahoos.[36] When theriophilic writers started to question the basis of man's uniqueness too, they revealed traits that overlapped with those of animals. Ritvo suggests that humans recoiled from this possibility in horror, prompting them to reject the 'beast within' by downplaying or denying the link between man and other animals.[37] This point is further developed by Fudge, who points out that the erosion of the belief in human uniqueness, by heightening fears about the beast in man, provoked an opposite reaction. 'Anxious anthrocentrism', as she terms it, drove man to accentuate his superiority by demonstrating his control of animals in a variety of ways, including some that are relevant to this study.[38] The act of saddling and harnessing horses, for instance, signified man's domination of them. What is more, gentlemen emphasized their mastery over their mounts by honing their riding skills and by teaching them to perform a series of movements in the system of exercises known as the *manège*.

EARLY MODERN ATTITUDES TOWARDS HORSES

Early modern society certainly held horses in high esteem. In 1618 Michael Baret wrote that of all creatures man alone surpassed a horse: in terms of its disposition and qualities he deemed it little inferior to humans.[39] John Worlidge concurred, remarking in 1675 that the horse 'hath the pre-eminence above all others, being the noblest, strongest, swiftest, and most necessary of all the beasts used in this country for the saddle, for the plough and cart, and for the pack'.[40] This implies that their status rested on twin attributes: their nobility and their usefulness to man. The popular genre of the beast fable, in which animals were given recognizable human (or even other animal) traits, provides an indication of the attributes which contemporaries sought. In 1523 Fitzherbert pinpointed fifty-three qualities which a good horse shared with other creatures: twelve with men and women and forty-one with lions, badgers, oxen, hares, foxes and asses.[41] Their human attributes suggest that they allied the pride, resolution and hardiness of a man with the fecundity, tractability, liveliness and companionship of a woman. Some of the animal attributes are difficult to discern but the general gist is clear: horses had to be well-shaped, strong and with a sound constitution, nimble and sure-footed, and lively yet tractable. Baret wrote in the same vein, comparing a horse to an elephant for its strength; to a lion for boldness; to a roe or hind for speed; to a hound for smell; to an ox for toughness; to a serpent for understanding; and to a black swan for beauty. Just as Worlidge concluded later in the century, these traits made horses particularly valuable when employed in the service of man, 'not onely for pleasure, but also for necessity and profit'.[42]

In 1587 Leonard Mascall reported the view that horses and mules lacked intelligence (literally 'no braines'), the argument being that, 'if they had understanding no man should be able to rule them', on account of their great strength. Most writers, however, did not hold this opinion. Gervase Markham, a practical horseman and one of the most prolific writers on equine matters, believed that horses felt emotion and possessed understanding. To him, a horse was 'A Beast of a most excellent understanding and of more rare and pure sense then any other Beast whatsoeuer'.[43] In 1639 Thomas de Gray termed a horse 'a dumb creature' yet went on to claim that 'neither is there any creature created by the great Creatour of all things, which doth so perfectly understand and connive with the nature and minde of man, or that beareth a more inly love to man, as doth this poore creature the Horse'.[44] Their views chimed with those of people who worked closely with horses. Handlers naturally formed their own opinion about the intelligence of their charges, especially over the question of whether instinct or reason governed their horses' behaviour. Ironically, their views may well have been in advance of those of the theorists. Carters, ploughmen, farmers and the like, even while they exploited them, were well aware that their charges could reason, had a memory and learned from experience. Midgley emphasizes this point in relation to keepers of all kinds of animals, noting that, 'As far as I know, it is quite unknown for people with this kind of experience to endorse the psychologists' view of their animals as mindless, unthinking machines.'[45]

If the talents of the horse Morocco, which reputedly could talk, count and dance, were fabulous, horses clearly did possess a degree of intelligence.[46] While describing a visit to the earl of Bridgwater's house at Ashridge in 1682, William Griffiths commented on the actions of a horse which operated 'a gin to draw water from a well. He noted that, whenever the servant took hold of one of the two buckets to empty it, the horse turned round in the wheel 'without bidding or forcing' in order to lift up the second bucket.[47] With no hint of a pain/reward stimulus the horse seems not to have been displaying a Pavlovian response. Although not as impressive as the oxen in ancient Susa, which reputedly knew when they had drawn one hundred bucketfuls of water, the Ashridge horse did display powers of observation, deduction and memory. On the other hand, Roger North, a barrister, who rode around the Northern Circuit in post-Restoration England, noted some horses that did exhibit a learned response. North observed that his horse, along with others that had done the tour once or twice, 'would always brisk up' at the sound of trumpets, as it meant that they would soon reach their destination and be fed and stabled. Yet North's own horse recognized places too. When passing a by-lane leading to a gentleman's house, visited as much as a year earlier, it would 'proffer to go that way'.[48]

Likewise, horses readily acted on instructions, though whether this was due to learned behaviour or to innate intelligence is also debatable. Baret implied that man merely trained a horse to do what it was capable of doing naturally, the only difference being that he prompted the animal to do it at his command.[49] Tone of voice was important, as a number of writers recognized, and this suggests a learned response. In 1587 Leonard Mascall recommended that carters should keep their horses moving by 'fierce words more than with stripes'. Gervase Markham later wrote that words such as 'ha', 'villaine', 'cariko', 'Diablo', delivered sharply, were effective in getting a recalcitrant horse to conform. By the same token, intonating soothing words like 'holla', 'so boy' or 'there boy there' had a calming effect. Thomas Powell wrote that to make a horse move, stop or turn carters used words such as 'gee' and 'ree'.[50]

The upper classes did not work their horses, nor did they perform the menial jobs associated with their keep. Even so, they spent so much time in the saddle that, as North's comments show, they were aware of their mount's capabilities. The result of this close association was the forging of a special relationship between horse and rider. They were given a name, were known by their character and were often described in anthropomorphic terms. In his *Defense of Poesie* Sir Philip Sidney recalled that his riding master, Pugliano, had said, 'what a peerless beast the horse was, the only serviceable courtier without flattery, the beast of most beauty, faithfulness, courage, and such more, that if I had not been a piece of a logician before I came to him, I think he would have persuaded me to have wished myself a horse'.[51] The Duchess of Newcastle also noted that her husband's horses displayed human virtues. Whenever he came into the stable she observed their show of pleasure by their trampling action and the noise they made. She noticed as well that the horses performed much better in the *manège* whenever he was present and that, if he rode them, 'they seemed to take much pleasure and pride in it'.[52] In a passage reminiscent of the relationship between screen cowboys and their steed, Edward Lord Herbert wrote of his favourite horse, a Spanish ginete,

> no horse yet was so dear to me as the Genet, I bought from France, whose Love I had so gotten that he would suffer none else to ride him, nor indeed any man to come near him, when I was upon him as being in his nature a most furious horse ... This horse as soon as ever I came to the stable would neigh, and when I drew nearer him, would lick my hand, and (when I suffer'd him) my cheek, but yet would permit nobody to come near his heels at the same time; Sir Thomas Lucy would have given me £200 for this horse, which though I would not accept, yet I left the horse with him when I went to the Low-Countrys, who not long after died ...[53]

From these examples one might assume that horses shared a number of psychological traits with humans: nobility of mind, loyalty, faithfulness, pride, courage, a desire to please and even intelligence. Evidently, these animals did respond to their owner but they probably acted in a similar way towards their groom. As evidence, these comments cannot be taken at face value because the observer was too close to the subject. There is a certain wish-fulfilment inherent in them, a desire to boast about the control that the writer was capable of exerting over a powerful animal. In this respect they provide greater insights into the mind of the owner than that of the horse. Besides, owners, even if they perceived human qualities in their horses, did not seek to alter the essential relationship between man and beast. They remained in charge, a point emphasized in the list of attributes itself. Distance was retained even (or especially) with saddle mounts, by not calling them by a human christian name. From this perspective, Swift's choice of horses as the rational houyhnhnms makes the inversion of the normal order more believable, if a little uncomfortable.[54]

The names that owners gave their horses provide an insight into the relationship between man and horse and an idea of the qualities looked for. To name is to exercise power and, according to the Bible, man's domination over animals began in the Garden of Eden when Adam called animals by their names.[55] Among the upper classes it was common practice to identify a horse by the person from whom it had been acquired. Sir William Villiers made this point in May 1687 when in his capacity of Gentleman of the Horse to James II he paid the earl of Rutland 100 guineas for a colt. As he explained, 'When I buy any horse for the King, I am asked that he may be called after the name of the person who sells'.[56] This tradition, long established by this date, reveals the elite's interest in blood lines as well as in quality control: a Rutland horse would have been a fine animal. It also appealed to its members' strong proprietorial sense, since the breeder had his name affixed to the animal as a personal mark. As such, the convention gave members of genteel society a feeling that they were participating in an exclusive group activity. They also emphasized the quality of their stock by identifying some of their horses by their breed, in itself a mark of distinction and an indication of ancestry.

Workhorses often had more prosaic names, ones which were similar to those given to cattle. Like them, they were an integral part of human society in respect to the work that they did, but because of the low status of the two sets of animals, they were treated as objects (unlike the personal mounts of the upper classes). As Levi-Strauss points out, because of the metonymic relationship with man owners were loath to give them human names.[57] In the 1660s the Blomfields of Stonham called their horses Bale, Brag, Butten, Dobe, Brag, Duke (or Duck), Lock, Mock and Jack.[58] The inclusion of Jack in this list is interesting; not only is it a human name but it also conjures up clear but contrasting images of the anthropomorphic qualities of the animal: either a knave or the opposite, a stolid, dependable workhorse. The latter representation certainly fitted Nicholas Blundell's 'good old coach Hors Jack' that died on 14 November 1712.[59] Other concerns are reflected in the name 'Bonny Buttocks', given to mares on the Muncaster and Little Crosby estates.[60] Owners naturally valued fertility in their stock but such a name reveals the commoditisation of animals. When Robert Toobey, a Reading hackney coachman, died in 1694, the appraisers of his goods listed twenty-nine horses, with names that derived from various sources: descriptive (as Bobtayle Bay), origin (Irish Don), noun (Nose), seller (Curtis) and even personal and historical names (Dick, Ginny Pigg and Homer). Almost certainly, Toobey did not name all these horses himself, the diversity representing an accumulation of horses bought from a number of previous owners, including gentlemen.[61]

The names of racehorses stand apart from the above forms of address. Firstly, they were particularly numerous and diverse (table 1). This variety was (and still is) due to the demands of form, betting and the ascertaining of bloodlines, which insist on a unique identifier for individual horses. Bay Rutland would not do as a name. Admittedly, the system took some time to become fully operational, and records indicate that in the late seventeenth and early eighteenth centuries recycling of names did take place. In about 1707 a syndicate of two Yorkshire mercers and a gentleman bought a horse called Hopeless off Charles Stoutville esq.[62] Yet, a horse of the same name raced in 1739. As names, some are distinctly

TABLE 1: Names of Racehorses 1739

Category	Number	Per Cent
Personal Names	73	16.0
Quality	52	11.1
Erotic	45	9.6
Flora & Fauna	36	7.7
Abstract	36	7.7
Descriptors	34	7.2
Status/Occupations	33	7.0
Nouns	29	6.2
Location	28	6.0
Historical/Literary	25	5.3
Sayings	21	4.5
Objects	20	4.3
Racing	19	4.0
Foreign	9	1.9
Types	6	1.3
Owners	4	0.9
Total	470	100

Source: John Cheny, An Historical List of all Horse-Matches Run, 1739

odd, especially those which comprise phrases or sayings. Levi-Strauss argues that the characteristically inhuman names racehorses acquired resulted from their isolated position in relation to human society, presenting, as they did, 'the image of an anti-society to a restricted society which owes its existence entirely to them'.[63] Perhaps, but more obvious reasons spring to mind. Individuality in naming procedure had the effect of using up words and combinations of words at an alarming rate. Devising variations on a theme, a means of linking family groups, further taxed the ingenuity of owners. Nor were names randomly selected; in many cases they demonstrably related to function. Because racehorses had to project a potent image, not uncommonly they received distinctly erotic names. As expected, owners also made allusion to hoped for qualities, indicated in such names as Speedwell and Sprightly. If they tended to burden their charges with negative attributes, this does not suggest that they were by nature pessimistic but rather that they possessed a sense of humour and a delight in irony. The owners who named their horses 'Run Now or Hunt Forever' and 'Win and Deceive Me' surely possessed a sardonic wit. The comic aspect of many of names similarly reflects the essential nature of horse racing, a frivolous pastime for men of leisure, even if it was a serious business involving large sums of money. Elite punters had to be able to lose with style and this insouciance influenced their naming policy. The largest category of names, however, consisted of personal names or words like Lass or Miss that denote a human being, seemingly at odds with Levi-Strauss's observation.[64] While the names rarely consisted of an unadorned Christian name, the addition of an epithet denoting a human quality, as in Merry Tom and Sober John, enhanced the closeness of their relationship with man. Some of the names derived from historical characters, an obvious and fruitful source of material for the well-educated racing fraternity to draw on.

HORSES AS SYMBOLS OF POWER AND AUTHORITY

The upper classes valued horses as symbols of power and authority. Indeed, so close was the connexion that the art of riding virtually defined a gentleman. As an essential skill, fathers made sure that it formed an integral part of their sons' education, along with such accomplishments as dancing and fencing. In 1616 John Holles wrote to his son, John, then in Paris, 'For what makes a good horseman, but the practise of many horses, which according to their severall mouthes, natures, and abilities, exercise each, and all parts of horsemanship, wherein I hope you will prove a proficient ...'[65] Naturally, members of the royal family had to be proficient. As James I told his son, Henry, 'It becometh a Prince better than any other man to be a fair and good horseman'.[66] In a figurative sense the king was equating an inability to ride well with a loss of status: a prince would not be worthy of his station without that mark of distinction. In fact, Henry was an excellent rider, as was his brother, Charles. Of Charles, Sir Philip Warwick commented that 'his exercises were manly; for he rid the great horse very well; and on the little saddle he was not only adroit, but a laborious hunter and field-man'. Unfortunately, his equestrian skills did not compensate for other negative traits and during his reign the country was beset by civil war.[67]

To heighten the effect, young men were encouraged to learn how to ride and handle the 'great horse', an imposing animal of strength and stature. In his autobiography Sir Edward Herbert recalled learning to ride the great horse in his youth, an animal 'made above all others for the service of man, as giving his rider all the advantages of which he is capable, while sometimes he gives him strength, sometimes agility or motion for the overcoming of his enemy, insomuch, that a good rider on a good horse, is as much above himself, as his world can make hime ...'[68] When a gentleman or aristocrat demonstrated his control of a powerful horse like this, his action was as much a political statement as a social one. By showing his easy mastery over such a noble and puissant creature, the rider, as a representative of the ruling elite, provided a justification for aristocratic power and influence. Sir Thomas Elyot made precisely this point in *The Boke Named the Governour* (1531), a handbook for the nation's rulers: 'the most honourable exercise ... of euery noble persone is to ryde surely and clene on a great horse ... whiche ... importeth a majestie and drede to inferiour persones beholding him aboue the common course of other men'.[69] Over a century later, William Cavendish, duke of Newcastle, repeated the adage when he declared, 'to see so Excellent a Creature with so much Spirit and Strength to be so Obedient to his Rider, as if having no will but his, they had but one'.[70]

Great horses therefore played a prominent role in public appearances, which were stage-managed to achieve as great an impact as possible. In the mid seventeenth century William Cavendish, posing a rhetorical question, asked, 'What prince or monarch looks more princely, or more Enthroned, than upon a beautiful horse, with foot clothes, or rich Sadles, and waving plumes, making his entry through great cities to amaze the people with pleasure and delight?'[71] Although elegantly expressed, Cavendish was merely commenting on a long-established practice. Henry VIII, for instance, had been well aware of the value of being seen dressed in rich robes sitting astride a powerful horse, richly caparisoned. So was Francis I of France. Consequently, their meetings on the Field of the Cloth of Gold in June 1520 resembled theatrical performances in which the kings, as leading actors, strove to upstage the other. When they conferred on 7 June Henry VIII reportedly rode a very handsome bay courser, with trappings embroidered in gold. Unfortunately, Francis's horse was better, due, it seems, to his having acquired superior specimens from the Mantuan stud a year earlier.[72] According to the Venetian ambassador, Francis was riding 'A most beautiful bay horse, which, as it surpasses all the others in beauty, so did the apparel and caparisons of rider and horse exceed all others in magnificence'.[73] Estate records indicate that many members of the upper classes were also willing to spend considerable sums on a fine horse, one which when ridden in public would bring them renown. In 1585–6, the Earl of Northumberland bought a valuable great horse from Mr Francis Cholmeley, the entry in the accounts revealing that the £80 paid out was merely a part payment rather than the price.[74]

The effect was even more dramatic if the rider were accompanied by retinue of men dressed in matching livery and riding fine mounts. As a spectacle, the meeting of Henry VIII with Francis I in 1520 once more stands out. To ensure that he made the maximum impact, Henry had scoured Europe for the best horses. When the time came, he did make an impressive entrance, riding at the head of a procession that numbered 5,704 persons and 3,223 horses.[75] Even so, Francis I outdid him in all respects. Courtiers, among others, similarly aimed to create an impression. When in 1562 Thomas Howard, the Duke of Norfolk and the premier nobleman in the land, rode into London to take up residency there, a hundred horsemen attended him, dressed in his livery, with his gentlemen, clad in velvet, preceding him.[76] Howard's flaunting of his wealth and position was an act that was both political and personal. Ceremonies that accompanied various public events offered other opportunities for individuals to display their status. The entry of the judges of assizes into a county, for example, was a splendid affair, specifically designed to emphasize the majesty of the law. The sheriff was in charge of events and, though it cost a good deal of money, it gave him a chance to underline his local standing. When in July 1583 the judges came to Shrewsbury, they were escorted by the sheriff, Charles Fox, accompanied by forty-two riders, all his own men, well-horsed and dressed in his livery.[77] At times, the pretentiousness provoked an adverse reaction. Thus, Sir John Tempest's arrival in Durham in January 1669 with 150 horsemen was deemed a conceit because he was neither lord lieutenant nor a deputy lieutenant nor an office holder of king or bishop.[78]

The popularity of equestrian portraits among the upper classes similarly reflected their absorbed interest in self-promotion. They did not commission them merely to preserve the likeness of horse and rider. Naturally, the painting depicted the sitter riding a great horse and, for further embellishment, dressed for war. James I's teenage son, Prince Henry, was particularly aware of the value of creating the right image. When he became Prince of Wales in 1610 he commissioned Robert Peake to paint a full-size equestrian portrait of himself to commemorate the event and to establish a marker for the future. Henry, clad in full armour, looks coolly at the painter, while Time, depicted as a naked old man with wings, walks by the side of the horse, carrying the prince's lance. Henry leads the old man by his forelock, which is attached to his arm by a favour, signifying that the prince is taking the initiative by seizing the opportunity of the moment.[79] That the iconographical impact of a painting was carefully considered can be shown by reference to two equestrian portraits, one of Charles I and one of Oliver Cromwell. In 1633 Van Dyck painted Charles I, seated on a Spanish ginete, carrying a staff of office and resplendent in full armour. His old riding master, St Antoine, standing by his side, looks up at him in awe and the whole scene is framed by a classical arch. The picture, placed at the end of the gallery at St James's Palace, was approached along a corridor, on the walls of which were hung paintings by Italian masters, notably Titian's portraits of the twelve Caesars and Romano's smaller equestrian studies of them.[80] Demonstrably, the aim of the portrait was to magnify the king by depicting him in imperial splendour and associating him with the glory of Rome. In the 1650s Pierre Lombart used this painting as the basis of his engraving of Cromwell, which, if it recycled an old image, broadcast the same message.[81]

The archetypal 'great horse' was the Neapolitan courser, which continued to be used as a parade animal throughout the early modern period, even if it had fallen out of favour as a warhorse by the end of the sixteenth century. In 1694/5 the accounts of Henry de Nassau, William III's Master of the Horse, listed twenty coursers and managed (dressage) horses for the great saddle.[82] Those specifically employed on grand public occasions were known as coursers of state. This suggests that by then the term denoted any great horse used on ceremonial occasions. As noted above, Charles I was riding a Spanish ginete in the equestrian portrait of 1633. In terms of its attributes and appearance, the larger strain of ginete was an imposing creature and proved a suitable replacement for the Neapolitan coursers as the quality of the latter breed declined. Henry VIII received a gift of twenty-five ginetes from Emperor Charles V in 1520 in time for them to appear in his train on the Field of the Cloth of Gold.[83] Elizabeth I and James I kept a number of ginete mares and stallions at their studs: at Hampton Court in 1623 all the mares were being covered by either ginete or Barb stallions, choice being dependent upon the precise function of the resultant foals.[84]

EASTERN HORSES AS ICONS

For many, oriental horses represented the equine ideal. Markham, writing in 1599, described Arabian stallions as 'paerlesse, for hee hath in him the purity and virtue of all other horses'.[85] In public their mere presence excited admiration, even in the post-Restoration period, a time when increasing numbers were coming into the country. On 17 December 1684 John Evelyn wrote in his diary that he had gone to Hyde Park that morning to view three oriental horses that had just arrived in England. All were 'choicely shaped', though he remarked on the exceptional beauty of a bright bay valued at 500 guineas: 'Never did I behold so delicate a creature … in all reguards beautifull and proportion'd to admiration, spirituous & prowd, nimble, making halt, turning with that sweiftness and in so small a compasse as was incomparable, with all this so gentle & tractable'. All three horses moved with grace and dignity, trotting 'like does, as if they did not feele the Ground'. The spectators, which included the royal family and members of the court, endorsed Evelyn's opinion of the horses.[86] When in November 1711 Thomas Pulleine saw eastern horses belonging to Robert Harley, Earl of Oxford, at the same place, he thought them 'the most hopeful and beautiful he had ever set eyes upon. They have all the symptoms of good blood than [sic] can be required'. Of another of his horses, the Dun Arabian, Oxford later wrote that all who had seen it thought it the finest horse ever imported.[87] Present-day commentators can gain some impression of the esteem in which these horses were held in their own day by viewing the equine portraits painted by artists such as John Wootton. Although not without precedent, the genre was essentially an eighteenth-century phenomenon and reflected the interest that these creatures generated at the time.[88]

Apart from their beauty, contemporaries remarked on the nobility and intelligence of Arabian horses.[89] These were the qualities that Nathaniel Harley commented on from Aleppo in January 1719/20 when he informed his nephew, Lord Harley, of the dispatch of the Bloody Shouldered Arabian. He not only wrote about its fine proportions but also on his great spirit and glistening eyes, a sure sign of alertness.[90] The tractable nature of Arabian horses also seemed to denote a sensitive and rational creature, one that had to be treated with respect rather than beaten into submission. The horses certainly responded better to careful handling, a trait which the Arabs were aware of and acted upon.[91] As Markham observed, 'the Arabian is of nature mild and gentle to his Rider and Keeper, but to strangers most cruell: they will bite like Mastifes'.[92] To some, their whole demeanour suggested an active role in the process, as if, like a loyal servant, they had made an independent and rational decision to obey their master.[93] It therefore appeared inappropriate to treat them as one would other animals. Racehorses, in particular, were cosseted. Writing from Newmarket on 25 September 1681, Lord Finch informed his wife that he was 'pretty well lodg'd, though not so well as my horses, there being much better accommodation here for horses than men'.[94]

Notions about the nobility of such creatures and the way they should be treated fitted uneasily with the reality of horse racing and its attendant brutality. Yet contemporaries found nothing contradictory in this seeming paradox. The noble and uplifting image of these horses, as depicted in their portraits, together with the perceptions that underpinned it, were as much a part of the relationship as a description of the treatment meted out to the same animal engaged in a hard-fought race. So great was the impact that these oriental horses had on English society that it may provide an illustration of animal agency at work. In the eighteenth century the thoroughbred helped to define Englishness in a country obsessed with horse racing, at least among the aristocrats who bred and raced them. The breed, a happy amalgam of native and imported stock, mirrored the hybrid English nation, both (Englishmen would claim) being superior to their component parts. In this respect, the comparison prompted the country's leaders to see in these creatures a metaphor for the qualities they wished to see in themselves.[95] This feeling gave added impetus to the genre for equine portraiture, its inspiration derived from the sight of oriental horses and their progeny racing at Newmarket: man and horse working in perfect harmony in a demonstration of pure, effortless power.[96] Significantly, they indicate a process in which humans reacted to and were influenced by the innate qualities of the horses themselves rather than one in which they imposed their own cultural values on the animals.

In a wider sense, too, the feelings roused by exposure to such noble creatures undoubtedly contributed to the contemporary debate on the relationship between animals and humans. The horses depicted in the paintings appear to possess estimable human traits and, as such, transcended the customary relationship between man and beast. Clearly a breed apart, their nobility and intelligence shines through and raises their status to almost human level. In Wootton's portrait of the Bloody Shouldered Arabian, the horse stands, 'bright-eyed, intelligent and noble-looking, commanding the space around him ... He is the still point in a turning world, timeless equine perfection.'[97] Swift must have had these horses in mind when he invented the houyhnhnms, the race of rational and intelligent horses, who ruled over savage hominids. At the same time he may well have been making a social comment, satirizing a society in which a landed elite spent vast sums of money on creating a superior breed of horses while oppressing the mass of their fellow countrymen.[98]

ATTITUDES TOWARDS AGED HORSES

Owners greatly valued their horses for the social, economic and cultural benefits they brought them. Surely, therefore, at the end of their charges' working life they allowed them an honourable retirement in recognition of the valuable all-round contribution they had made to their well-being? Certainly, the suffering of a favourite horse and its subsequent death did cause distress; in 1686 Ralph Palmer told his sister that 'Mr Muns Bears ye loss of his Brother, better than I do ye death of my horse'. To assuage the grief owners might commemorate the animal in an epitaph and raise a monument over its grave.[99] Yet, in general, owners did not waste money on superannuated horses, tending to view them in an unsentimental light. Few people emulated Sir Matthew Hale, who put his old horses out to grass.[100] On the contrary, abuse of aged horses served as a simile for unfeeling behaviour towards old and expendable retainers. In a critical portrait of Robert Dudley, Earl of Leicester, written in about 1584, the author likened his conduct towards his old friends to the treatment given to a retired horse, left to graze on a ditch bank or sold for 40d. to a dogmaster.[101] The same lack of feeling was apparent In February 1597/8 when Sir John Holles complained to Lord Sheffield about the treatment of his nag by the latter's groom. The horse had died but this counted only as a lever to obtain a favour from Lord Sheffield. As he wrote, 'But it mattereth not there is but a jade out of the way and I hope for exchange one of these years to have a good breeding mare from you so as I am very glad of this quarrel'.[102]

Contemporaries plainly viewed horses that served a useful function differently from those that did not. Swift has Gulliver make this point when describing to the Houyhnhnms the condition of horses back home in England. He admits that, although gentlemen looked after their horses well while fit, they discarded them as soon as they could no longer carry out a designated job through illness or age.[103] Many ended up as dog meat for the hounds. As a preacher explained in 1655, 'better knock him on the head than keep him … His skin, though not worth much, is better worth than the whole beast besides'. On 16 September 1674 Thomas Edwards, an agent of Sir Thomas Myddleton, received 3s. 6d., the sum he had laid out for a horse to be slaughtered for his master's hounds. Daniel Eaton was equally unsentimental. In a letter to his master, the Earl of Cardigan, on 3 December 1726, he reported that attempts to cure the mare were proving ineffective and that, as she was suffering from glanders, as well as being broken winded, she was virtually worthless. He sealed her fate with the words, 'I fear the dogs must have her in a short time'.[104]

Unlike oxen, superannuated horses were not fattened up and sold to a butcher for a few pounds because of the long-standing aversion to eating horsemeat in England. This taboo may have developed due to the closeness of the relationship between man and horse, a view which Thomas agrees is a likely explanation.[105] Robert Meens also puts this point forward as a possible cause but offers other reasons too: association with pagan rituals; part of a civilizing process that came with the Romans; and the link between social status and stigma.[106] The notion that horses had been a totemic symbol in pagan Anglo-Saxon times, is suggested by an old field name in Fetcham where one of the shots of the pre-enclosure open field was known as Horse Head Furlong. As people living in totemic societies identify bodily with the totemic animal, eating its flesh would have been tantamount to cannibalism: hence the repugnance.[107] Leach makes the same point, observing that the English viewed horses (and dogs) as 'sacred supernatural creatures surrounded by feelings that are ambiguously those of awe and horror'.[108]

The taboo, although not a formal ban, acted as a powerful constraint even in times of crisis and hunger, such as, for example, sieges. It seems as though defenders only ate their horses as a last resort. Evidence that they were doing so was a clear sign to the besieging forces that their enemy would soon surrender. On 15 October 1644, during the Parliamentarian siege of Banbury, Sir Samuel Luke informed Lieutenant Colonel Oliver Cromwell that, 'Since your leaving Banbury several soldiers in the castle are come out with their arms and made the colonels believe of the great want they are put to, and say they are fain too eat horse-flesh already, which puts our friends in great hopes of speedy obtaining the castle'.[109] The aversion to eating horse meat is explicit in a joke which Sir Ralph Verney and his friend, Dr William Denton, played on the guests at a dinner party at Claydon in Buckinghamshire in July 1658. Sir Ralph had his cook prepare a savoury horse pastry, though the nature of the meat was a closely guarded secret. To have informed the diners what they had eaten would have precipitated an intense, if short-lived, reaction, whereas knowledge of the event was something the pranksters could savour over a long period of time. Two days later Sir Ralph wrote that 'Cooke Laurence's owne privy kitchen had noe such dish as colt pye, but noebody knowes what they have eaten as yet, noe not Harry, nor dare not tell because Lady Longavile was at the feast'.[110]

Contemporaries, as others had done before them, took an anthropocentrist stance on the question of the relationship between humans and animals. They justified their position as derived from God, who had put animals at the disposal of humans. To consolidate their claims to domination they emphasized their unique status in the animal kingdom, the only species which could reason. Nonetheless, in comparison with other animals, horses enjoyed a privileged position. They were by general repute deemed to be among the most noble and intelligent of animals. Theriophic writers emphasized the point and all those who had regular contact with horses were well aware of the fact. Saddle mounts, in particular, benefited because of the close relationship they had with their rider. The upper classes took pride in appearing in public astride a mettlesome steed or riding in a coach drawn by a team of well-proportioned, matching horses. Lower down the social scale merely riding a horse was a mark of distinction. However, owners were not really concerned about the horses *per se* but rather with their ability to do the job and with the image of themselves that they helped to project. Horses were normally viewed in a strictly utilitarian manner and once they could no longer carry out the tasks assigned to them, they were discarded without ceremony. Age and infirmity were great levellers, for two horses separated by tens of pounds in their prime were both sold for a few shillings when of no further use.

3

The Training and Treatment of Horses

In 1584, John Astley, a gentleman-pensioner and a writer on the management of horses, criticized the harsh methods employed by an earlier generation of trainers, including those of the celebrated Grisone of Naples. Horses, he stressed should be cherished rather than chastized, pointing out:

> Contrarie to these things herein thus shortlie passed over, as namelie nature, art, and reason: it is violence, which nature abhorreth; error, which art rejecteth; unrulie passion of mind, which reason alwaies withstandeth: and as they be contrarie in nature, so be they also in working, and therefore must needs bring foorth contrarie effects, as we may see by those horsses, that both without courage and comliness are ridden, with raw noses, bloudie mouthes and sides, with their curbed places galled, turning their bodies one waie, and their heads another waie, which things are brought to passe by the violent unskilfull use of a hand upon the chaine, Cavessan, musroll, and such like, which were first devised to save their mouthes; and not to marre theire noses and muzzels.[1]

As a result of the growth in theriophilic opinion, such as the one expressed by Astley, the treatment of horses gradually softened during the course of the early modern period. The question is whether this trend merely marked a shift in the views of theorists and intellectuals or was it one that affected the practice of people actually in charge of the animals. If England was, as the Venetian ambassador declared in 1557, a hell for horses, was the same true in 1750?[2] One might expect to find that conduct towards horses gradually improved among the elite at least, the target readership for theriophilic writers. Even if this were the case, the opinions of the upper classes did not necessarily affect the treatment of their horses, since they hired others to look after them and to use them to perform a variety of tasks. Employees did not necessarily share the views of their master: in particular, concern for the well-being of their charges might conflict with their desire to get a job done. Among the horse-owning population at large economics loomed large too. Of course, the treatment of horses impacted on all aspects of their life, including housing, fodder, training, care and maintenance, as well as the way those responsible for their management handled them when working. Of vital importance were actions taken in the early years, for a good start improved an animal's health and prolonged its active life.

Evidence for actual practice is varied, though inevitably weighted towards the upper classes, with their estate and household accounts, their diaries, commonplace books and bundles of correspondence. Documentation for the population at large is more fragmentary and requires diligent searching among such sources as manor court rolls, probate material and depositions heard at quarter sessions, the assizes and the equity courts. Indirectly, horse toll books provide a means of assessing the issue in a quantifiable way. By looking at the ages at which nomenclature changed from young to adult horses, it is possible to find out if horses had gained a good start to their life, as well as the speed with which the pressure of work wore them out. Books on the management of horses also offer insights into the treatment of horses or at least indicate an ideal to which owners and keepers should aspire. Beginning with Thomas Blundeville's *The Arte of Rydynge* (c. 1560), the number of manuals produced increased steadily during the course of the late sixteenth and seventeenth century.

These manuals on horsemanship provide a different category of information from the other sources and ones which have to be treated with caution. Reviewing the literature from the vantage point of the mid seventeenth century, William Cavendish was scathing in his criticism of the writers of these works. He thought that Blundeville was 'a Better Schollar than a Horseman' and damned others, including de Gray and Markham, as mere copyists of Blundeville, with a few additional jottings. There is an element of truth in Cavendish's assertion: writers regularly drew on classical and contemporary Italian or French sources, plagiarized each other's work and recycled their own material in later publications. Blundeville's first book, in essence, was a translation of Frederico Grisone's work of the same name, though he did make a number of changes.[3] Nonetheless, even if they did copy material from elsewhere, native writers performed a service by bringing to the attention of an English readership contemporary continental practices. Cavendish was hardly a neutral observer either, for he had his own theories to publicize and sought to establish his own creditability by belittling his predecessors. Besides, his aristocratic view of the world and exalted approach to horsemanship coloured his judgement, which appears unduly harsh. Blundeville's second book, *The Fower Chiefyst Offices Belonging to Horsemanship* (1565), contained more original material, or at least drew on a number of other sources as well as on his own experience. Like Blundeville, many of the authors possessed some practical experience and, in the case of Gervase Markham, knowledge of both the aristocratic and plebeian worlds. Markham, born into a genteel but impoverished Nottinghamshire family in about 1568, had served as a soldier in the Low Countries before entering the earl of Essex's circle. Essex's execution for treason in 1601 blocked that path to advancement and, starting with his marriage that year, he spent the next nine years as a working farmer. His chequered career certainly helps to explain his emphasis on the importance of experience and 'his knowledgeable passion for horses and horsemanship'.[4]

THE CARE OF HORSES

The conditions, in which horses were kept, varied according to the resources of their owners. At the margin horses fended for themselves on open commons and survived the winter on a modicum of hay or whatever they could forage. They were not properly housed either. Horses belonging to yeomen fared better. Large farmers often possessed valuable rights of common, so they, too, put their horses on the wastes, along with their other animals. Because they had to feed their draught horses well, if they were to work effectively, they also supplied them with lush grass in pasture closes, as well as with oats and pulses. Stabling was functional rather than elaborate, where it existed. In post Restoration Winteringham only three of the sixty-eight inventories which list rooms refer to stables. Many of the horses, if not in the fields, were kept in the yard perhaps in an outbuilding. Significantly, Edward Boteler, the rector of Winteringham and a member of a gentry family, kept his saddle horses in the gelding stable and his draught horses in the plough stable.[5] Roxwell and Writtle inventories indicate that in mid-Essex, at least, stables, as dedicated buildings for horses, became more commonplace over the course of the seventeenth century (table 2).[6]

TABLE 2: Stables in Roxwell and Writtle (Essex) 1638–1750

Date	No. with stables	Total inventories	Percentage
1638–1659	3	26	11.5
1660–1714	50	176	28.4
1715–1750	25	38	65.8

Source: F.W. Steer, Farm and cottage inventories of Mid Essex (Chichester, 1969)

In comparison to the bulk of the horses owned by the population at large, the ones belonging to the upper classes were well looked after. Their owners tended to keep them in home closes or in a park, though they might send some horses elsewhere. At Lady Day 1666 some of the Earl of Westmorland's horses were in the stables at Apethorpe in Northamptonshire or in the park there, but the breeding herd was grazing in the woodland pastures of Morhay and Sewlhay. At the same time Lord Brooke of Warwick Castle was driving cattle and a few horses to Pulver Fen in Suffolk, where he had built a stable. In August 1701, as a result of the hot summer, Lord Fitzwilliam of Milton ordered his steward to reserve the park for the deer and put the horses into the woods or fens.[7] Even these horses stayed out most of the year. Nicholas Blundell of Little Crosby Hall in Lancashire only housed his horses between November and April or May, depending on climatic conditions. In 1719 his coach horses were not turned out at night until 16 May because of the cold weather.[8] Horses on the Earl of Oxford's Welbeck estate in Nottinghamshire in the 1720s followed the same regime. On 26 March 1729 Isaac Hobart, the estate steward, reported that he intended to put the chestnut mare to grass when the weather improved, remarking that 'it is as cold here as it was at Christmas'.[9]

Many people were employed to look after these horses. On a small farm a member of the family usually carried out the work, but on a large holding the yeoman delegated the care of the horses to his ploughman and carter and their lads. The upper classes hired servants to tend their animals, some of whom might have special responsibility for the horses. The stable accounts of Lord Paget of Beaudesert for the years 1579–81 include payments to seven members of staff for looking after their horses. Among the household servants Henry Percy, Earl of Northumberland, employed between 1585 and 1632, at least fifty-seven of them were working in the stables, while a further twenty dealt with hunting and hawking and ten more with the coaches. The crown maintained the largest complement of people. At the time of Henry VIII's death, for instance, Sir Anthony Browne was his Master of the Horse with a staff of 104 persons and a wage bill of £1132 10s. 2½d. a year. Personnel included officers to keep accounts and to look after different types of horses and vehicles. Others were responsible for tack and equipment. Aveners (for fodder), farriers and grooms catered for the horses' welfare. At the beginning of William and Mary's joint reign in 1688 the Master of the Horse, Henry de Nassau, Comte d'Auverquerque, had a similarly sized staff, 105 strong, costing £9067 a year.[10] Owners also supplied horses to their staff and paid for their maintenance. In 1512, for instance, the Earl of Northumberland maintained seven horses ridden by men employed at Wressle and Leconfield Castles alone. In 1590, Elizabeth I allocated 127 horses to the Master of the Horse's staff.[11] Maintenance costs might individually be small but over the year the sum total could be considerable. Outlay on the 119 horses and mules in Henry VIII's stables in 1526 came to £301 12s. 6d. and in 1547 the 109 horses and mules cost £769 12s. 4¾d. In 1688–9 liveries for the 102 horses added £5355 15s. 7½d. to the bill, that is about £1 a week per horse. On other estates, bills were obviously not as high but still significant; in 1614 expenditure in the Warwick Castle stables amounted to £48 10s. 3d. and in 1648 to £62 10s. 4d.[12]

TRAINING AND TREATMENT OF YOUNG HORSES

Writers on the management of horses stressed the importance of providing young horses with a good start in life, claiming that proper handling then affected the health and strength of the animals later on. They therefore discussed at considerable length such matters as the time to wean a foal, to cover a filly and to break in young horses. As they also gave advice on the means to accomplish these tasks, historians can assess the level of progress being made in the treatment of horses during the course of the early modern period. Inevitably, the authors disagreed with each other in detail but displayed a degree of uniformity in their general approach. In particular, they rejected the brutal methods of the early sixteenth century, advocating care and consideration and the use of coercion only as a means of last resort. Even Cavendish, who criticized all earlier writers, was basically in accord with this view. The influence of Xenophon can be seen in this change of attitude, with writers adopting his 'humane and commonsense' approach, one that recognized the horse as an intelligent creature and sought to work in harmony with its nature rather than against it.[13]

Most writers agreed that prolonged suckling enhanced the strength and wellbeing of foals. Early weaned foals lacked the essential nourishment that promoted good bone growth and in the long term this also reduced the foal's life span. Unfortunately, as economics rather than welfare often determined the time of weaning, foals did not necessarily suckle for the requisite length of time. As Blundeville observed, 'Here in England they will scant suffer them to sucke six moneths ... which trulie I cannot recommend'. He advised breeders to allow their young horses, especially colts, to run with their dam for a minimum of one year if they wanted them to be 'strong and healthfull'.[14] Ideally, he thought that breeders should not wean their foals before their third year. Cavendish criticized this view, pointing out that it reduced a mare's breeding capacity and produced 'heavy, flabby jades'. Markham, too, felt it sufficient for the foal to suck for only a year even on upper-class estates. Recognizing reality, he added that the husbandman, who needed his mares for the draught, could stop weaning his foals after six months. For Worlidge, too, October was the month to wean foals because it enabled the dams to help with preparing the ground for the following year's crop. At Henry VIII's studs foals were weaned at one year old.[15]

Concern for output also affected the time when fillies were first put to the horses and the rate at which mares produced foals. Whereas fillies could conceive at the age of two (and perhaps even younger), writers tended to advise a delay. Accordingly, the initial covering should normally take place in the third year, though gentlemen might wait a further twelve months.[16] With regard to covering, mares could produce a foal annually but as the gestation period amounted to about eleven months that was cutting it fine. For this reason, writers urged breeders to put the mare to the horse in alternative years. Conrad Heresbach was of this opinion, especially if one wanted good colts. Markham made a similar distinction, recommending that fine mares be covered every other year and ordinary ones every year. Even so, Heresbach acknowledged that breeders customarily horsed their mares every year, a decision which he asserted was due to covetousness.[17] If Heresbach based his comments on German experience, they

TABLE 3: Interval between foaling and covering in the 17th century: the Massingberd of Mumby estate

Name	Foaling	Covering	Name	Foaling	Covering
Black snipt mare		10.05.53	Fleabitten mare		10.05.53
	01.07.54	31.07.54		–	25/6.07.54
	12.06.55			12.07.55	22.07.55
		24.05.56		20.06.56	04.07.56
	24.04.57	04.05.57		–	04/5.05.57
	13.04.58	1658			–
	02.06.59				25.04.59
Bald coach mare		12/4.06.54		–	09.06.60
	12.05.55	23.05.55			–
	16.05.56	27.07.56	Great Flanders coach mare		06.06.53
	08.09.57			00.05.54	16/7.06.54
				28.08.55	
					17/8.05.56
		03.05.59		04.05.57	28.05.57
	29.06.60			17.04.58	
Dark coach mare		1653			1659
	19.05.54	19/20.06.54		–	1660
	22.05.55	31.05.55		–	
	12.0.5.56	28.05.56			

Source: Massingberd of Mumby MSS, Lincolnshire Archives Office, MM 6/1/1–5

reflected English practice too. Most gentlemen put their mares to the stallion every year. To prepare the mare, one writer recommended separating her from the herd a fortnight before foaling and putting her into a close of rank pasture with a gentle mare or gelding. This would not only make her 'lust' and accept the stallion but would also give her plenty of milk.[18] Owners often allowed a very short interval between foaling and covering, essential in a system of annual pregnancies. At Little Crosby, Nicholas Blundell had his mare, Bonny Buttocks, horsed on 24 May 1705, eleven days after it had foaled. The short gap allowed for initial failure, as it gave time for further attempts by the same (or a different) stallion. In 1676, a mare on the Bagot estate at Blithfield received the horse on 24 June and on 4 and 9 July. A decade later, the Foley family's steward at Stoke Edith wrote that the Yorkshire horse had covered the black mare twice; but, if she were not 'sped', he would put her to the other horse. Table 3 shows that stallions covered the mares on the Massingberd of Mumby estate in Lincolnshire every year.

The situation on the estates of the Massingberds of Gunby and the Penningtons of Muncaster Castle was very similar.[19] Some gentlemen, however, did follow the writers' precepts. In 1675, for instance, Roger Pratt of Ryston Hall noted in his commonplace book that, 'yt its best to haue ye Mares horsed … but once in two yeares, if theire colts bee intended to bee bred up for fine ones'. He also separated his heavily pregnant mares from the herd, having learnt that other horses kicked them and caused them to miscarry.[20]

Some fillies and mares were spayed: on 4 April 1616, for instance, Richard Cholmeley of Brandsby paid Francis Sanderson for gelding his waif mare, Stagg.[21] According to Heresbach, the procedure was not undertaken very often because of the risks involved and, indeed, it features rarely in estate records.[22] In practice, therefore, the process of neutering largely affected colts. Blundeville advised waiting until a colt was two years old, arguing that, if gelding were undertaken earlier, the process would stunt its growth and, if delayed any longer, it promoted thickening of the neck and hardening of the testicles. Gervase Markham thought it a good time too because by then the testicles had dropped and the colt was strong and able to 'indure both the griefe and torment'. Nonetheless, he counselled early gelding: specifically at nine days old or as soon as the testicles had dropped.[23] Estate evidence is thin but suggests that gentry waited a year, and often longer, before gelding their colts. In April 1597 Edward Leves gelded two of Lord Middleton's colts, the nomenclature indicating that the horses were virtual yearlings at least. Sandy, a newly gelded colt foal that Richard Cholmeley bought in May 1617, certainly was: he noted in his commonplace book that it had been born in the previous summer. In spring 1715, Nicholas Blundell paid James Addison for gelding his two colts, Diamond and Jewell, adding that they were 'something above one year old'.[24] Both Cholmeley and Blundell had more mature horses castrated, two belonging to the former gentleman being described as 'ould'.[25] Gelding might occur on a change of ownership. A list of horses stabled on the Garsington estate in September 1630 includes a black roan five-year-old horse acquired at Banbury Fair the previous May. Added to the entry as a superscript are the words 'now gelt'.[26] Fillies or mares might be spayed at that time, as in the case of Richard Cholmeley's waif mare, Stagg.[27]

Before breaking in young horses, progressive horsemen such as Blundeville and Markham recommended that breeders should gradually accustom their young horses to humans.[28] This did not happen at Elizabethan Tutbury with the consequence that the colts went wild and were difficult to train. To bring them under control, the staff had to employ harsh methods which, Blundeville believed, led to long term damage. As he asserted, 'For lack thereof [of careful handling] many a good colt at his first taking up, through his owne stryving is utterly marred, and maimed for ever'.[29] Markham thought that the process should begin in the first winter after foaling and continue right up to the point of breaking in. For this, he allowed two weeks of acclimatization, thereafter gradually introducing the saddle and by degrees mounting the horse. Cavendish advocated a similar regime. At the onset of cold weather around Martinmas (11 November) stablemen should take new foals from their dam and house them. There, they were to lie on fresh litter and feed on good, sweet hay, wheat bran and oats. The following summer the colts and fillies grazed outside but separately from each other. In the winter the colts stayed in the stables once more and, as far as possible, received the same treatment as the older horses. This cycle continued until they were over three years old, by which time they had grown accustomed to humans and had learnt from the other horses how to respond to them.[30] Cavendish believed that at that point they were ready for training. When schooling a young horse, Blundeville and Markham stressed the need to 'cherish' it, treating it kindly and rewarding it when it responded positively. This was done through the tone of voice and by patting, stroking or tickling the animal.[31] On no account, Blundeville wrote, should a rider use a rod on an unbroken colt and later he should only apply it gently.[32]

When deciding on the right age at which to break in their horses, people had to weigh up the benefits of delay against the economic costs of waiting. According to Polydore Vergil, writing in 1511, good horses were scarce in England because of poor treatment when young, being trained under age and worked too hard.[33] In a literary allusion to the practice, the adolescent Adonis compares himself to an immature colt in order to fob off Venus's sexual advances:

> The colt that's back'd and burden'd being young
> Loseth his pride and never waxeth strong.[34]

The problem lay in the length of time it took young horses to mature: fillies were not fully grown until five years old, while colts needed an extra year. Before then, as Blundeville pointed out, their joints had not yet knitted properly and the process could injure the animal. A century on, John Halfpenny was putting forward the same argument, contrasting late trained colts, which had strong, well-knit joints and sinews, tough hooves and good eyesight, with those broken in at the age of two or three, with their poor eyesight, brittle hooves and weak backs. Morgan agreed, for he also advised waiting until the colt was five years old.[35]

In practice, the writers observed, riders trained fillies at the age of two and colts at the age of two or three.[36] For Cavendish the third year was the right time to break in fillies for, if covered a year later, they would not spoil themselves or their foals. As this was not an issue with colts, he recommended a delay of a year before breaking them in. Markham agreed with him, pointing out that beyond that age they became less tractable and their 'wildness' made the process much more difficult. Baret also advised against further delay, maintaining that the practice had led to 'so many dogged and restiffe Iades'.[37] Halfpenny naturally disagreed; he claimed that 'there was never so sturdy, nor so wilfull a horse, which would not be tame and easie to handle, with watch and hunger, within one month at the furthest, if his keeper will use diligence'. Topsell adopted an intermediary stance; riders could break in colts at the age of three, but they should not do any work for an extra year.[38]

A trawl through the estate papers reveals no examples of gentlemen who waited until their colts and fillies had fully matured before schooling them. On the other hand, they did follow the writers' advice to delay the process until the colts were at least three years old. This was the age at which Sir John Newdigate, squire of Arbury in the early seventeenth century, began. A century later, the keeper on the Duke of Newcastle's estate at Haughton postponed the task until the young horses were approaching four years old: on 9 March 1710/11 Dobin asked permission to 'ride' the colts, 'it being now about the time to get them mought [mouthed] and turned out at mayday'. Several accounts refer to moving the colts to the stables or house, implying that they prefaced the business of training with a period of acclimatization. In a letter written in about 1620 to thank his cousin Fitzwilliam Coningsby for a colt, Sir Thomas Lyttelton told him that he would 'take him [the colt] into the house' at Michaelmas as he would then be three and a half years old. James I's agents moved the colts to his stables in their fourth year too. Even after training, it helped if the horses only did light work. On 28 January [1642?] one Tovey wrote a letter to George Warner, a London merchant, in connexion with his promise to find a horse for him. He was about to view his uncle's three-year-old colt, which the latter was shortly going to break in. If he liked the horse 'uppon his backing', he added, he would make an offer for him on Warner's behalf. He warned him not to overtax the horse, however, pointing out that, 'He will not be for any service this twelvemonteth yet, for he is about 3 yeares old now. You may play with him for a jorney of halfe a score miles, or such a trifle, but he will not be for any substantiall use yet.' On 2 August 1662 Walter, a servant of the Earl of Clare, passed on a similar message from the keeper to the effect that his master should not to travel to London on a particular colt, he 'being but now 4 yeares old'. The horse was ready for him to use, presumably for short trips, though even here there was a difference of opinion. Walter also reported the comment of one Abraham, who thought 'it will be no meddling with him, he is so tender a horse'.[39] As a sign that contemporaries were aware of the process of maturation, the racecourse, an area in which owners indisputably wanted the best for their charges, provides a significant example. For most of the period horses started racing at the age of six. Although a few younger colts and fillies ran in matches, racegoers viewed this as premature. Restrictions eased in the early eighteenth century and in 1719 Bonny Black, a four year old carrying equal weight, won the King's Gold Cup for five-year-old mares at Hambleton. The first designated race for four year olds took place in 1727.[40]

One or two gentlemen-breeders schooled their own horses. John Astley presumably was thinking about such men when he wrote of the pleasure to be gained from training a horse in such a way that 'he and you be one bodie, of one mind, and of one will'.[41] Even so, most gentlemen hired a horse rider as and when required. Normally, the rider came to the estate but on occasion they took a horse away to train at home, the practice being specifically noted in records of the Paget estate in Leicestershire in 1551, of the Foleys in Herefordshire in 1679, and of the Hares in Norfolk in 1690 and 1693.[42] In December 1693, for instance, George Freeman received £1 14s. from the Hares for breaking one of their mares and for her keep for seven weeks. Riders may have been local farmers, perhaps on the estate. Tim Burbro, who broke horses for the Cartwrights of Aynho, certainly was. In October 1691 he received a deduction of 10s. from his rent for pacing a bay nag.[43] The crown employed full-time riders. When, in 1519, Baldwin Heath became surveyor of the king's studs in Warwickshire and Worcester, three others were appointed to look after the horses and break in their foals. Some of the staff came from abroad, especially from France and Italy, the centres of horsemanship in the sixteenth and seventeenth centuries. One such man was Hercules Trinchetta, whom Thomas Barnaby recommended to the Earl of Leicester, the Queen's Master of the Horse, in 1564. Trinchetta, Barnaby claimed, had no peer in breaking young and rough horses.[44]

Prosperous farmers must often have employed trainers to break in their horses, but those of more modest means tended to do the job themselves. Unfortunately, few farmers have left records of their actions, so it is difficult to assess the extent to which their practices followed (or rather ran parallel to) the advice contained in the management manuals. They may have read one or more of Gervase Markham's books since he wrote for them as well as for their social superiors. Conventionally, he dedicated *Cavelarice* to Prince Henry as a promoter of horsemanship and then, politically aware, addressed the elite, who possessed the land and the finances to forward horse breeding. Thereafter, he moved on to deal with the problems facing yeomen and husbandmen with their more limited resources, thereby aligning himself with a group of agricultural writers and improvers who reached out beyond the landowners to influence the people who actually worked the land. In the last few years of his life he produced a collection of essays in a book entitled, *A Way to Get Wealth* (1631–8), a clear indication of

TABLE 4: Nomenclature of young horses 1627–1788

Age	Period	Horses	Colts	Stags	Nag colts	Gelt colts	Geldings	Nags	Fillies	Mares
1	1627–59	0	30	8	0	1	0	0	69	5
	1660–1724	0	30	0	3	4	1	2	17	4
	1750–88	1	4	0	0	0	1	0	6	1
2	1627–59	3	80	18	1	4	1	26	261	62
	1660–1724	6	151	0	23	22	24	61	181	99
	1750–88	8	11	0	0	1	19	1	23	26
3	1627–59	3	63	22	0	1	10	95	212	209
	1660–1724	32	136	0	35	13	53	210	85	290
	1750–88	14	3	0	0	0	16	0	4	37
4	1627–59	1	23	6	0	1	15	118	75	251
	1660–1724	37	25	0	5	1	72	279	11	384
	1750–88	16	0	0	0	0	17	0	1	58
5	1627–59	6	4	2	0	0	16	11	15	266
	1660–1724	29	3	0	0	0	74	273	1	351
	1750–88	16	0	0	0	0	19	0	0	41

Source: toll books

the audience he was aiming at. In this respect, his view of society, with his support for the middling orders, was at odds with Cavendish's aristocratic vision.[45]

To gain an impression of the methods of farmers it is possible to use the data on ages contained in some toll books (table 4). The point of reference is the statement made by Nicholas Morgan in 1609 that all horses were deemed to be colts (or fillies) until five years old but never thereafter.[46] If true, this implies that younger horses with an adult label had been broken in or, in the case of fillies classed as mares, covered. Self-evidently, this is not a perfect source, for it relies on the chance survival of toll books of individual fairs in various parts of the country and the degree to which sellers consistently used the correct nomenclature to distinguish between immature, incompletely broken-in horses and trained adult animals. Some of the horses, mares, nags and geldings must surely have been colts and fillies, but this was not necessarily so. If yearlings, listed as mares, had not received the horse by design, accidents did happen. Markham recognized the fact that yearling fillies might get pregnant and so offered advice on what the breeder should do in this situation.[47] In practice, such mares were almost two years old: thus, on 3 March 1691 the toll keeper at Eccleshall noted that the bay mare that Hugh Watson of Holderstone sold was coming two years old.[48]

Because few very young horses changed hands at fairs, toll books do no more than suggest that weaning generally took place in the first year of life. Toll book keepers tended not to note the ages of foals sold with their dam, perhaps implying that they had been born that year. Typically, at Carlisle in 1653–4 weaned foals offered individually were yearlings. Nonetheless, a handful of joint entries indicate that a few yearlings were still suckling. Occasional references in other toll books to the sale of mares with a colt or filly seem to confirm that some breeders waited until the second year before weaning their foals. At the Simon and Jude Fair (28 October) at Warwick in 1653, two Warwickshire men sold mares with sucking colts. Unfortunately, interpretation is affected by inconsistency in terminology: Markham, for instance, called all immature horses foals, adding 'colt' or 'filly' merely to denote gender.[49] At Carlisle the toll keeper recorded a five-year-old mare foal in 1632 and a four-year-old filly foal in 1654. On the other hand, rare but unambiguous entries to sales of sucking colts or yearling mares separate from each other imply an abrupt end to the weaning process. Francis Walker of Combrook, for instance, sold a dark grey sucking colt to Henry Middlemore, a gentleman from King's Norton for 17s. at Warwick Fair on 28 October 1653. The price indicates a young animal.

Gelding, the timing of which divided the writers, in reality seems to have posed less of a problem for the population at large. According to the toll books, most horses approached maturity as entire animals. The evidence, as revealed in graph 1, indicates that, whereas the proportion of gelded colts did increase over time, it remained at a low level until the mid eighteenth century. Numbers, however, varied considerably from place to place. In general, east midlands fairs had the highest proportions, presumably reflecting their specialization in draught horses. Conversely, the large numbers sold at Penkridge in the second half of the sixteenth century was due to its reputation as a centre for good quality saddle mounts. At Shrewsbury, the geldings that filled the market place in the 1620s mainly consisted of small work horses, particularly useful for pack carriage but not very expensive. After the Civil Wars, few geldings appeared in the toll books and those that did were far more valuable and resembled those on offer at Penkridge. This suggests a change in terminology and that horses that once had been called geldings were now being classed as nags. The absence of age data from fairs such as Penkridge and Shrewsbury also means that the figures, on which the graph is based, should be treated with greater caution than usual. Similarly, many toll books do not provide information on the sexual status of the colts. Even where given, as at Market Bosworth in the 1620s, it is not always tied to age. Indirectly, the evidence from this fair seems to indicate that colts were gelded at the age of two. As the youngest recorded 'geldings' were three years old, surely the gelt colts had been born at least a year later. A correction made to an entry at the St Peter's Day Fair on 29 June 1618 hints at this. When Christopher Hooke of Rugby tolled for his three-year-old colt, the keeper first of all noted the word 'colt' but then changed it to 'gelding'. Evidence from Stratford-on-Avon in 1646,

Graph 1

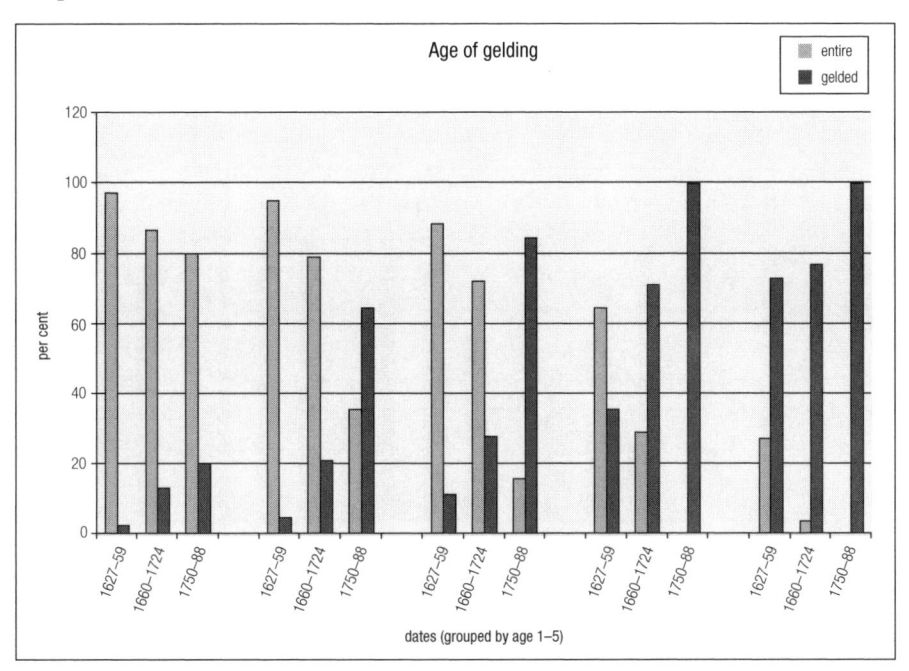

though slight, supports this interpretation. Apart from one yearling, most of the gelt colts were twinters.

The toll books provide more accurate information on the time when owners broke in their colts and fillies. While some of them did hasten the process, graph 2 indicates that most of them waited a reasonable length of time. Training for the vast majority of colts sold at fairs during the course of the seventeenth and early eighteenth centuries did not begin until the third year and, even then, numbers increased the following year. In the late eighteenth century, however, the third year became the norm. On average, fillies were trained a year earlier than colts, that is, if the process occurred a year before their first covering, as Cavendish suggested. Early seventeenth-century toll books reveal that breeders, in general, put fillies to the stallion when they were three years old, changing their nomenclature to mare when they gave birth the following spring. A couple of mares at Carlisle in 1653–4 had been covered in their second year, but most of the mares with foals were at least three years old. Toll books occasionally refer to young mares, thereby offering an insight into popular opinion concerning the best age for covering fillies. Naturally, the toll keepers who termed a mare 'young' did not normally bother to give its age as well. Fortunately, one did. At Market Bosworth in 1632 George Jones of Risley sold a black bay 'yonge mare age 4 yeres'

Graph 2

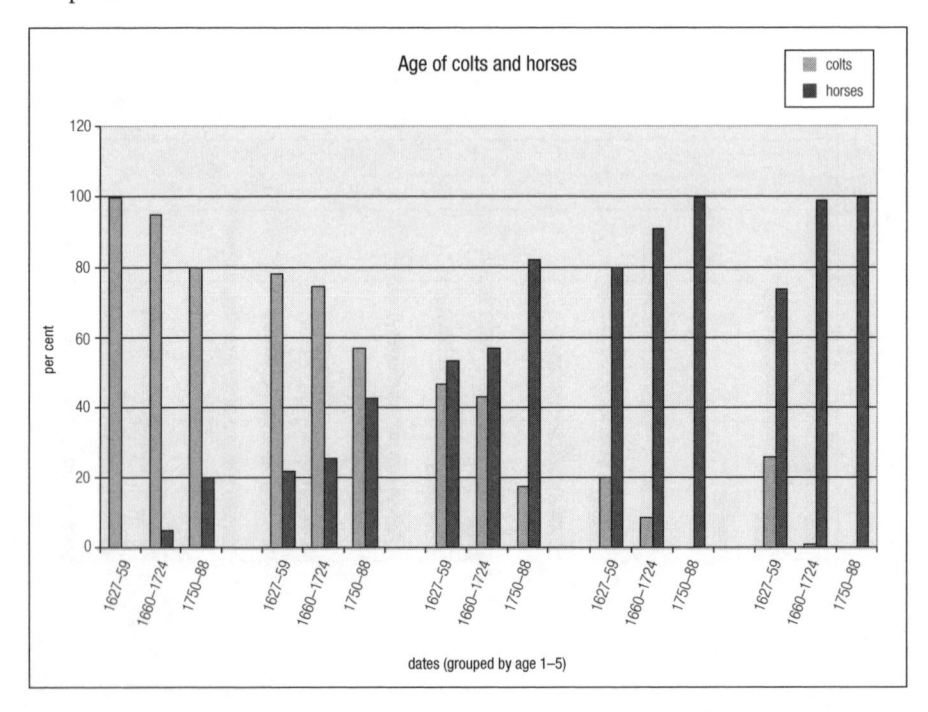

to Robert Childs of Harborough Magna for £6. This fits in with evidence from the royal stud at Malmesbury in 1620 where the accountant described four-year-old mares as 'young'.[50] Again, the process of training and covering speeded up over the course of the seventeenth and eighteenth centuries, as shown in graph 3.

Taken overall, it is clear that very few breeders and rearers acted on the writers' advice to delay the whole process until their horses reached or even approached full maturity. Indeed, the number of horses listed as colts and fillies in toll books drops sharply after the age of three. On the other hand, owners seem to have possessed some awareness of the physiology of their charges and tended not to break them in at the earliest possible opportunity. Even so, schooling did occur at a progressively earlier age over the course of the seventeenth and eighteenth centuries. Horses may have matured earlier but equally the trend could reflect growing economic pressure to put horses to work. Data on old horses suggests that horses did not survive for as long as they might have done, if provided with the best possible start to life (table 5). Naturally, one can understand their owners' need to procure a return on a valuable but costly asset and, in any case, their action was hardly more precipitate than that of their social superiors.

Riders did not merely break in young horses, they also improved their gait or changed their action. All horses walked, trotted, cantered and galloped, if

Graph 3

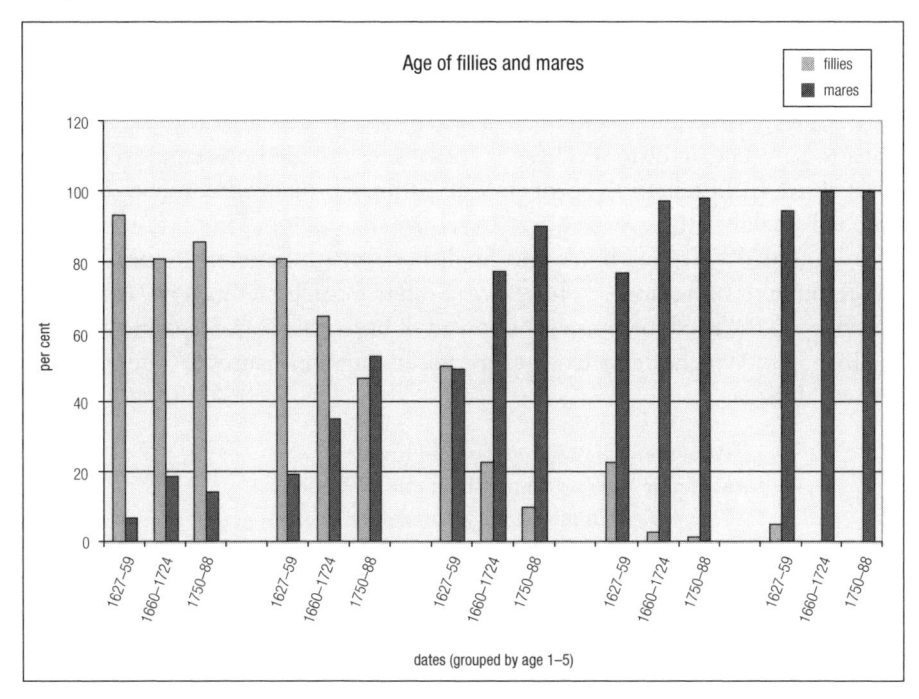

with unequal efficiency. Many were taught to amble, pace or rack. Ambling and racking are four-beat gaits with an identical sequence of beats: near hind, near fore, off hind and off fore. Trotting and pacing are two-beat gaits; in the former the horse moves diagonal legs together and in the latter a lateral pair. To get a horse to pace the trainer fitted trammels on each pair of legs.[51] To do the job well required considerable skill and, wherever possible, the gentry employed a person known to them or recommended by a friend. They did not want their valuable horses ruined. In 1626 Edward Gorges sent an ambler to Sir Hugh Smyth with the recommendation that the man was 'the best I have yet mett with in these partes. He is very carefull and diligent, and (as farr as I can perceive) no gadder abroad or haunter of ale houses.' The procedure was relatively straightforward if the horse had a natural tendency to move in the manner desired; if not, the outcome was less certain. In 1662 one Reynolds of Minton, hired to break two colts and pace three other horses on the Massingberd estate at Mumby, failed to teach a young bay chestnut to pace.[52]

At the beginning of the period, when the guiding principle in the training of horses was to instil fear in the animal, cruel methods were the norm. Riders sought to beat horses into submission and control them by the use of fierce bits. Horses being trained for the *manège*, a system of exercises developed in Italy in the early sixteenth century, suffered as much as an ordinary nag. Grisone, whose riding school at Naples attracted gentlemen from all over Europe, achieved his ends by subjecting his horses to a brutal regime. One of his pupils, Robert Alexander, became Henry VIII's riding master at Hampton Court. According to Sir Thomas Elyot, his results were exquisite but the means by which he achieved them severe. He used whips and cudgels to break a horse's spirit and curbs with fifteen-inch arms to jam its chin onto its chest.[53] These were the methods employed in the royal studs. In Elizabeth I's reign staff at Tutbury broke young horses by force and tied recalcitrant mares to a post to receive the stallion. Thomas Blundeville, who translated Grisone's book into English, damned these techniques as 'both dangerous and unnaturall'.[54] Shakespeare refers to such methods in *Henry VIII*. Referring to the need to counter the spread of heretical ideas, Stephen Gardiner, the Bishop of Winchester, advocates the use of harsh measures to 'reform' those who hold them:

> Which reformation must be sudden too,
> My noble lords; for those that tame wild horses
> Pace 'em not in their hands to make 'em gentle,
> But stop their mouths with stubborn bits, and spur 'em.
> Till they obey the manège.[55]

Unfortunately, estate and household records are silent on this issue, though a document occasionally provides a valuable insight. In 1621 Richard Cholmeley of Brandsby employed George Gascoigne to break his colts at 3s. 4d. a horse and then to cure their sore mouths. Gascoigne denied causing the injury which, he claimed, occurred because Cholmeley's servants had pulled too hard on the reins.[56]

The bits used provide a touchstone of attitudes towards horses. They were of two basic sorts: the snaffle and the curb. Snaffle bits acted directly on the lips, bars and tongue of a horse and, although generally milder than the curb bit, could injure a horse's mouth if used sharply. Curb bits operated indirectly, exerting pressure on the chin groove through the curb strap or chain, on the palate through the port and on the lips through the poll.[57] Blundeville condemned the common practice of starting off with a severe bit when breaking in a young horse. John Astley not only made the same complaint but, as noted earlier, also criticized the misuse of cavessans and musrolls, items that were supposed to save a horse's mouth rather than harm its nose and muzzle. These measures were often counter-productive, for some horses reacted to pain by becoming uncontrollable. Blundeville declared that they were the reason why the country possessed so many 'headstrong jades'.[58] Other horses became dull and unresponsive. To elicit a reaction, unfeeling riders increased the pressure, causing more pain and suffering, leaving Astley to declare 'by those meanes hath so dulled and deaded the senses and feeling, as he feeleth little of paine, of pleasure nothing at all, and of a sensible creature is made a sensles blocke'.[59]

It is perhaps no coincidence that the treatment of children improved in this period, since contemporaries compared the educative process with breaking in unruly colts.[60] Roger North, recalling his childhood in the mid seventeenth century, wrote about the beatings that he and his siblings had received at the hands of their mother. He remembered her saying that she had used the rod 'to break our spirits', which it did effectively.[61] At schools, too, many masters taught their pupils with a book in one hand and the rod or ferula in the other. The beatings similarly helped to repress the will and independence of the pupils, making them less likely to react against the tedium of the curriculum and the rigours of rote learning.[62] These were the principles that guided the training of a colt. Progressive schoolmasters like Roger Ascham, John Brinsley and Charles Hoole did argue against excessive use of corporal punishment, wishing to retain it merely as an instrument of last resort or in cases of really bad behaviour. Brinsley only referred to the rod at the end of an incremental list of punishments. Making a direct analogy to the treatment of young horses, he instructed that when administering the punishment the 'stubborne or unbroken boy' should be held fast as those 'who are to shoo or to tame an unbroken colt' do. Similarly on 3 December 1612 John Chamberlain, writing on behalf of Sir Rowland Lytton, asked Sir Dudley Carleton if he would take in Lytton's son, 'that you wold a little traine him, and fashion him to business'. Chamberlain advised him to think carefully before replying; if he could do it without inconveniencing himself, he would do Lytton a favour but, he continued, 'I know what a business yt is to have the breaking of such colts'.[63] A review of the Ariès-Pollock debate over parental attitudes towards children suggests that change occurred in the home earlier than in the school.[64]

ADVICE ON THE TREATMENT OF RECALCITRANT ADULT HORSES

After being broken in, horses spent a number of years in the service of their human masters. How did they fare as adult horses? Unfortunately the evidence is inconclusive, though it seems that over time the gentry did treat their horses better. Whether this was due to a more theriophilic climate of opinion or merely down to a question of utility is debatable. Thomas believes that a growing awareness of animal feelings and attributes did have an effect, as did the argument that as part of God's creation, animals deserved respect. Even if man enjoyed stewardship over other creatures, he should not commit wanton cruelty. Mascall, giving specific advice to carters, told them to exercise patience and moderation when dealing with their horses and to cherish ('love') them so that they [their horses] will love them in return.[65] For those unmoved by reason, practical considerations might be more persuasive. Harsh measures were counter-productive: horses became dull and unresponsive and would only react to stimuli of increasing intensity. Although most of the criticism was directed at riders who broke in young horses by force, it also related to the treatment of adult horses. Cruel owners could ruin an economic asset or a valuable status symbol, a matter of growing importance as the economic, social and cultural roles played by horses increased during the course of the period. After all, owners tried to protect their investment by enacting laws to prevent the theft of their horses. Incidentally to make identification of their horses easier owners mutilated their charges by branding them and taking chunks out of their ears.

All writers wrote about the need to correct an uncooperative horse and the means to achieve it. Blundeville listed seven ways: voice, tongue, rod, bridle, calves, stirrups and spurs. Markham also emphasized the use of the voice, spur, rod and bridle, indicating that the 'gentle' school did not discard the use of such coercive measures entirely, though its members might differ in one or two particulars.[66] Mascall might have preferred verbal exhortations to the whip but he still advocated its use from time to time. Similarly Blundeville disagreed with those who would outlaw the rod or cudgel, claiming that one sharp blow between the ears at the first sign of resistance prevented greater violence later. Markham rejected this practice, declaring that it 'doe distemper and incertaine the head'.

To reform a badly trained horse, he advocated gentleness and patience but, if it rebelled, shouts, application of the rod and 'other terror' would show it who was master.[67] On many occasions sharp use of the tongue sufficed. Yet in exceptional circumstances a rider might have to fit a harsh bit as a temporary expedient. This is what Walter Burdett of Foremark had to do in 1698. Discussing a fine horse of his to Thomas Coke, he wrote, "Tis pity he should ever be bitted, he has so fine a mouth, and carries himself so well in a snaffle'. As the horse proved so obstinate at the beginning of the hunting season, Burdett admitted that he, 'clammed him till I stirred his grease'. Only when he took the horse out again would he know how successful his action had been.[68] What they all emphasized was the need to employ these methods moderately or as a means of last resort. Referring to punitive bridling, Markham claimed that it corrected many faults but had to be done 'seldome and with great discretion'.[69]

These writers advocated even sharper measures for a particularly recalcitrant horse: Blundeville recommended continually pricking its rump with a nail, poking its genitals with a 'shrewed cat' attached to a stick, or tying a hedgehog or a whelp under its tail. He nevertheless stressed that the rider should only rarely employ extreme measures like these or his action would drive the horse to despair. Gervase Markham, on the other hand, thought that jabbing a horse with a nail made even the mildest horse 'leap, plunge and disorder'. He also felt that the other devices merely compounded the problem: 'they are all of that crueltie, either in outwardly tormenting ... or inwardly appalling the minde ... that they doe not so much good in redressing that one fault as hurt in breeding many faults of much more worse nature'.[70] Yet Markham was not averse to taking drastic action himself. When a horse that continually plunged fell down, he advised the rider to remain in the saddle and ask a bystander to lay dry straw around the horse's nose and face and then light it. If the rider could find a willing bystander with the necessary materials, the ploy would make the horse stand up. When it had done so, the rider should reward it immediately.[71]

As ever, Cavendish disparaged the views of other writers, openly stating that coercion was necessary. A horse, he said, had to know that the rider was the master. This could only be achieved by instilling fear in the animal and, through fear, love. Even so, his comment suggests that what he really wanted to inculcate in the animal was respect rather than fear. While he seldom beat his horses or punished them with a rod or spur, any resistance led to the use of force, 'which they obey willingly, for the most part'. Moreover, he did not let the horse's disposition dictate his actions but rather made it follow his design. He summed up his approach by declaring that when his horses did well he cherished them and when they did ill he punished them. In this respect, his approach was similar to that of the other writers, all of whom drew their inspiration from Xenophon. They, too, accepted the need to bend a horse to the rider's will and to punish a recalcitrant animal. Like them, Cavendish rewarded his mounts when they obeyed him.[72] In effect, Cavendish's bluntness and honesty made him stand apart. This, in itself, is an indication that the climate of opinion had changed over the preceding century, at least in the literature. In Henry VIII's days brutality was the norm. If in the mid seventeenth century people still had to coerce their horses to induce obedience, writers chose to focus on the more progressive and caring aspect of horse management.

THE TREATMENT OF ADULT HORSES BY THE UPPER CLASSES

Most of the authors aimed their advice at the elite and this probably had some effect. If the latter chastized their horses, they may have heeded advice only to do so sparingly. Then again, some had never heard of it. Edmund Verney (1636–88), described as 'good-humoured and incorrigible' by Lady Verney and as 'feckless' and 'undisciplined' by Dr Whyman, was one such person. In 1661 his father, Sir Ralph, blamed him for killing his black nag, a charge which Edmund denied, claiming that the horse had been in a poor condition when he had set out.[73] In spite of Edmund's excuse, his father maintained a low opinion of his son's attitude towards horses, later contrasting his treatment of them with that of his kinsman, Will Stewkeley. In a letter to Edmund, Sir Ralph wrote approvingly of Stewkeley, who had made 'soe much advantage of my gelding'. Pointedly, Sir Ralph declared that he would rather sell a fine horse to Will for £50 than to Edmund for £80 because 'he [Stewkeley] delights in a good Horse, & takes pleasure to improve him'. Edmund, on the other hand, would spoil the horse through lack of care and consideration 'by marketing, dungcarting, carrying double, and & which is worst of all, by sending him on idle errands, with idle, ignorant fellowes, that have neither care, nor skill to ride him'.[74] Even those who had read the manuals might still mistreat their mounts when wrapped up in their own concerns. Typically, they had embarked on a journey and, anxious to make good progress, either to get home or to reach their lodging for the night, overtaxed and coerced their mount. In February 1620/1, for instance, Mr Henry Vavasour's horse broke down while at Hoggesdon, and Vavasour himself was 'daylye so tiered and dirtied with beating his horse on'. Riders still acted in the same inconsiderate way a century later. In 1720 the Earl of Oxford rode a mount from his home at Brampton Bryan Castle in Herefordshire to London at such a pace that the horse foundered. Individual gentlemen and noblemen similarly mistreated their coach horses. In 1653 Dr William Denton, once Charles I's physician, left one of his team dead at Aylesbury. Three years later, hurrying to a confinement in Cheshire, he lamed three of his four coach horses.[75]

Members of the upper classes were particularly inconsiderate of their horses when engaged in a sporting or recreational activity and focused solely on their own pleasure. Most commonly this occurred while out hunting, the most popular pastime of the upper classes. Distracted by the thrill of the chase, they tended to spur their mount on unsparingly. In doing so, Thomas de Gray wrote, they overstrained their horses, which, although strong and able, are 'so toyled out therewith, as that when they come home at night, they would pitty the heart of him who loveth a Horse, to see them so be mired, blouded, spurred, lamentably spent, and tyerd out'.[76] In 1683, it was said of Charles II that he was an indefatigable rider, when hunting, 'loveing to ride soe hard that he usually lost his company'.[77] Racehorses, although cosseted, suffered too, especially during the course of a tight race. Gambling lay at the root of the problem and in upper-class racing circles huge sums were wagered. According to Thomas Tryon, horses, by their very nature, were susceptible to exploitation. As heat was the predominant humour, it produced animals that were brisk, free and proud, but also ones that were 'more easily apt to be forced by their Riders and Drivers'.[78]

Of course, many horses recovered if rested and treated with consideration. In his memoirs Oliver Heywood, a northern clergyman, provides a good illustration of the point, in an account of a horse deal that began with bad faith and ill-treatment but ended happily. In 1688 he made an exchange with Henry Burkhead, a carrier from Lightcliffe, swapping his horse plus £5 5s. 0d. for a good-looking mare that had cost Burkhead £11. Unfortunately, although the mare seemed fine and was an excellent mount, it was moon blind and likely to become completely blind.[79] 'Thus,' Heywood recalled, 'I was cheated, much perplexed, prayed to god about it.' The following year, he managed to exchange the mare for a worn-out horse of John Hey's, which had been overridden, was in a poor condition and had a sore back. As Hey intended to breed from the mare, he did not mind its blindness. Heywood's horse recovered and did him good service. Heywood, very pleased with the deal, was content to give Hey eight crowns to boot. As he noted, 'I have rid many miles on him, he fits me exceeding well, blessed be god, is free, sure footed, strong paceth'.[80]

Gentlemen may have accepted the writers' advice but they did not have the daily care of their horses. They employed servants to do this job and the latter had not read the manuals. They merely wanted to get the job done. Anecdotal evidence seems to indicate that servants regularly mistreated the horses in their care. It was probably John Beale who highlighted this problem in a letter written to Samuel Hartlib in March 1657/8. Extolling the hardiness of asses, he noted that 'our servants are very cruel but asses bear the injuries which would kill a horse'.[81] Even if they did not actually abuse their charges, servants tended to neglect them. When Sir Ralph Verney criticized his son for his lack of consideration for his horses, he implied that, unless carefully supervised, servants tended to act in an irresponsible fashion. Sir Ralph acknowledged that Edmund did provide the necessary resources but, as he added, it only mattered 'if your men doe not forget to feed him, as they always doe, to shoe, wash, or dresse him, all this being true (and a greate deale more)'.[82] Servants also treated their masters' horses as their own, using them for their own purposes but without the restraint of personal loss if they spoiled a valuable possession (the threat of dismissal notwithstanding). In August 1617 Richard Cholmeley of Brandsby wrote down in his commonplace book that two of his men 'by ryding and chasing' killed one of his mares and seriously injured two other horses. He immediately dismissed John Sampson, one of the two men.[83] In 1691 Amos, a groom on Peter Legh's estate at Lyme Park, took one of his master's horses from the stable without permission. Amos, a 'brisk, vain-glorious spirit', rode the horse to the wakes at Chapel-en-le-Frith, a village about five miles away. Intent on enjoying himself, he did not rub the horse down or do anything to help it recover from the gallop. Hours later, after his return, Amos was found in a drunken stupor and the horse in a 'wofull pickle'. At about the same time, one of the colts suddenly went lame, caused, it was said, by the 'rash and foolish leaping which Amos is too apt to glory in'.[84]

Even on well-run estates problems occurred. Few land stewards were more conscientious than Isaac Hobart, who served the Earl of Oxford in the early eighteenth century. Yet in September 1722 he was grumbling about the behaviour of the two servants in the stables at Welbeck, complaining to his master that they disappeared for days on end and neglected their charges. Dismissing the men, he nonetheless had difficulty finding someone suitable to replace them. A year later he wrote, 'We have much want of a sober careful groom on the spot here, who will stick close to business. Such a one is not to be had in this country.'[85] This was the dilemma which many estate stewards found themselves in. They could not supervise their subordinates the whole time, but if they could not find a trustworthy person abuses were likely to occur. This, in essence, was Daniel Eaton's predicament three years later when one of his master's horses suffered an injury.[86]

> As to Thomas Hutchinson [the groom], it is very natural for people to lay blame upon any body rather than themselves; therefore to avoid this as much as may be, I can only say that if my own mare had been taken so good care of when I rid her, as she ought to have been, I should not have sold her. And I declare that I have been always as careful of your Lordships horses as I have been of your business. I always ride them gently & feed them well while they are with me; but when they come home, whither they are taken care of or not, is not in my power to say.

Coachmen were in a particularly responsible position, but they did not always repay the trust. In 1685 it was reported that Lord Manchester's coachman had killed some horses that his master had bought at Northampton, presumably by driving them too hard.[87] Coachmen, it seems, had a reputation for drunkenness, perhaps because they frequently had to wait for hours for their master or mistress to reappear while on a visit. This not only affected the way they handled their horses but also put the lives of passengers in danger. On 19 July 1654 Evelyn recounted that, returning with Sir Edward Baynton after a game of bowls, they were lucky not to be injured on account of the recklessness of their coach driver, who had got very drunk while waiting for them. As he wryly observed, "Tis, it seemes by order of the knight, that all gentlemens servants be so treated: but the custome is barbarous, and much unbecoming a knight, still less a *Christian*.' In March 1669 it happened again. As Evelyn was dining with Sir William Ducie, the servants plied the coachmen with so much drink that they later fell off their boxes on the journey to London. In 1671 Robert Semple informed the Duchess of Somerset that he had received reports that her coachman frequented disorderly alehouses in the town in company with Joan Best, a whore. The coachman did not neglect the horses but the two of them had begun the practice of taking them to Chertsey Market, ostensibly to buy provisions at a cheap rate. However, Semple alleged, they spent four or five times as much and sometimes came home at night 'in no good condition'.[88] Stage coachmen, often employees of a coachmaster, similarly abused their charges, as William Schellink, a Dutchman, found out in 1661 on his trip from Harwich to Gravesend. He described the four horses that drew the coach as 'miserable nags', which, in spite of their 'miserably putrid and ulcerated legs', showed 'astonishing courage and strength'. They travelled along the road, with the coachmaster in front, while his servant, Thomas, 'drove the four poor creatures, caressing them mercilessly with a whip'. The horses, in consequence, overturned the coach, provoking a heated argument between the coachmaster and his servant, who denied that he was responsible for the accident.[89]

TREATMENT OF ADULT HORSES BY THE POPULATION AT LARGE

For most people the information on ages given in the toll books provides an insight into the way they treated their working horses. According to the manuals, horses, if handled carefully in the first few years, might be able to work until they reached the age of twenty-four or twenty-five.[90] Over the years they gradually lost their strength, but the rate of deterioration was determined not only by the process of breaking in but also by their subsequent treatment. Reliance on an ageing horse was likely to cause problems: it was slow, could not cope with great loads and was likely to break down. If ridden, it might stumble. Such animals often had to be 'coaxed' into greater activity with a whip or a spur. When these methods ceased to have an effect, owners sold the horses to the knackers, where they were slaughtered, flayed, butchered and boiled down for glue. But at what age did this happen? Morgan thought that horses started to decline at the age of ten and became old at fifteen. This even happened on gentry estates, as the values given to horses on the Blomfield family estate, at Stonham in Suffolk indicate. The link between age and condition clearly concerned John Pilkington when, in 1615, Roger Mawkin, a Warwickshire man, asked him to exchange his cow for a horse. Mawkin swore that the horse was 'under thage of x yeares and to be save and sounde of Wynde and Lymme and everye other degree'. Still dubious, Pilkington agreed to the swap only on condition that he could verify the age of the animal. He therefore took it to Coventry, where 'in the presence of dyverse persons, and by men of understandinge yt was founde there that the saide Horse was xiiii yeres olde and more, And also broken wynded and Unsounde of his Lymes'. The implication is that a nine-year-old horse still had its strength and would give good service, whereas a fourteen-year-old one was decrepit.[91]

Toll books confirm this view, for few horses aged over ten appear in them, presumably because fairs focused on selling active horses for specific functions (table 5).

That is not to deny that there was a market for veteran horses, perhaps operating in the same way as the trade in old bangers today. The majority probably changed hands privately and without a written record, but evidently one or two of them turned up at markets and fairs. Indeed, Kidderminster served as a centre for superannuated stock; between 1694 and 1711 almost one in seven of the horses with ages attached come into this category (8.3 per cent). The number tails off from the age of thirteen, though one mare was thirty years old, and what were the ages of the horses described as 'full age', 'old' and '99'? In general, Kidderminster stands out as an anomaly, for older horses were generally put on public display at markets rather than at fairs. The reason for this distinction lay in the character of the weekly market, where the sale of horses was a far more casual affair. As their disposal was normally incidental to the presence of the seller in town, entries in market toll books reflect the general ebb and flow of economic activity rather than the specific pattern that characterized the horse trade. At Chester and Oxford, markets dealt with nearly twice as many veteran horses as on average passed through the toll bars of contemporary fairs.

Kidderminster aside, one might infer that many of the horses owned by the general public had, indeed, passed their prime after the age of ten and that a significant number of them died or were put down over the course of the next few years. Horses aged over fifteen are very rarely recorded in the books. Clearly, therefore, many horses expired before they had reached the end of their natural span and in this respect horse users wasted a valuable resource. Where did the fault lie? Among the population at large few horses were allowed to mature naturally: training normally occurred long before the age of five or six. This undoubtedly had an effect, even if the process did not always begin as early as some writers said it did. Much depended upon the level of work expected of young horses: writers stressed the need to increase it gradually. This may not have occurred and, when coupled with the unremitting toil to which handlers subjected mature animals, it is not surprising to note that numerous horses suffered a shortening of their useful life.

TABLE 5: Ages of horses at fairs and markets

	Fairs 1626–59	Fairs 1661–1724	Fairs 1750–87	Markets 1658–99
followers	16	23	6	0
under 1/foals	97	4	1	0
1	151	58	13	0
2	462	590	88	1
3	634	838	76	6
per cent	44.9	31.6	32.2	1.5
4	496	833	94	34
5	425	760	76	61
6	356	764	81	86
7	145	406	51	83
8	147	198	15	77
9	41	105	6	50
10	30	50	33	37
per cent	54.1	65.0	62.2	92.0
11 to 15	30	50	2	25
16 plus	1	9	0	1
aged	1	107	30	4
per cent	1.1	3.5	5.6	6.5
Totals	3032	4795	572	465

Source: toll books

To what extent do other sources corroborate the toll books with their evidence of overwork? Tryon, for one, thought that the country was full of unscrupulous riders and drivers who worked their horses beyond their strength and capacity and who presumably beat them if 'restie'. Over a century later, Lawrence could strengthen his plea for better treatment of animals by including a catalogue of abuses committed on horses employed variously in posting, pulling carts and coaches and on the racecourse.[92] While it paid to look after an economic asset, by the same token economic necessity invariably meant the horse had to keep going, regardless. Users whipped stubborn horses, savagely bridled headstrong horses and allowed no rest to injured horses. Finally, when the brutal treatment had taken its toll and they had collapsed, they unceremoniously cast them aside. The records of the equity courts are full of references to horses carrying injuries incurred by a lack of care and attention.[93] In an early sixteenth-century case in Chancery, Thomas Howell, a Bristol beer brewer, complained that after he had bought a horse off Thomas Jones in Swansea, the animal 'did halte downe right and ... was not hole and sownne of lymmes'.[94] Writing in Elizabeth's reign, Harrison noted that the English, especially northern men, overstretched their mounts, riding them from dawn to dusk 'without drawing bit'.[95] Other horses that suffered were those employed in industrial concerns: at mines they not only operated gins but in some cases worked underground. In 1739, the agent at the Lowther pits at Whitehaven in Cumbria noted that the gin horses went, 'at full trot every 8 hours, and 3 changes are employed in a day and a night'. Some horses at the pits clearly died in harness: John Spedding, the agent, specifically noted that one of them, a grey horse, had been 'wrought to death underground'.[96]

Carriers were among those who habitually overburdened their horses. Because horse costs, mainly in fodder, formed such a high proportion of total expenditure (over 80 per cent) they had to squeeze as much work out of them as possible. After all, the animals continued to eat even when they were not working.[97] So they piled excessive loads on their back, pushed them too hard on the journey, and allowed them insufficient rest and sustenance. In a case heard in the Court of Requests, Richard Snelling, employed by John Ridley, a London poulterer, to buy poultry ware at country markets, caused the death of two horses and seriously injured another by his neglect. On one occasion, he killed a horse by overloading it on the outward journey. On another trip, returning late (and drunk) from buying goods at Potton in Bedfordshire, he drove two heavily-laden horses the thirty-seven or more miles back to London without rest or provender. One died and the other one never recovered its former strength, in spite of spending half a year recuperating in Ridley's stable.[98] When in 1581 Sir Thomas Wroth counted 2,100 packhorses on the road between Enfield and Shoreditch, another observer wryly declared that within seven years 2,000 of them would die through overwork.[99] The growth in theriophilic opinion did not end the abuse because commentators were still reporting on it a century later. In 1669 John Flavell, a Devon minister, wrote about pack horses 'fainting under their loads ... groaning under unreasonable burdens and beaten on by merciless drivers, till at last by such cruel usage they have been destroyed, and then cast into a ditch for dogs meat'.[100] Before this outburst, however, Flavell had written about the care and consideration which some men showed towards horses and other animals. In fact, he was less interested in man's treatment of animals than in his irreligious behaviour, illustrated, paradoxically, by his cruelty towards his fellow-creatures and by his scrupulous attention to their needs, with the consequent neglect of his children's spiritual welfare. John Evelyn, by common repute a man of integrity and virtue, was a more reliable, if mildly theriophilic, observer. In *Acetaria*, written in 1699 near the end of his life, he specifically linked the treatment of horses with the life-span they achieved. He pointed out that the reason why so many horses were prone to disease was because of the way their owners mistreated and overworked them. As a result, they wore them out before their time. With better handling, he stressed, these 'useful and generous Creatures' would have lived a good deal longer.[101]

If people ill-treated their own horses, they were even more likely to abuse those belonging to others. In 1575 a purveyor, Thomas Comptons of Margaretting, took a horse without warrant and 'worked it so hard and so unreasonably for three days ... that it became worth nothing and was completely spoilt'. Another purveyor, Matthew Potter of Danbury, seized a horse at the same time. After he had finished with it, he sold it for 12d., that is, for the value of its carcass.[102] Persons riding post, delivering official packets or letters, moreover, were more concerned with reaching their destination and the rate of progress than with the welfare of their mount. They had to maintain an average speed of seven miles an hour in the summer and five in winter. If, in practice, they rarely kept up this pace, many horses suffered in the attempt. In the early sixteenth century Horman declared that poursuivants '[de]stroye many horses'.[103] Private travellers, who hired post horses, were no better. Englishmen, it seems, had a reputation for hard riding. According to James Howell, they 'ride commonly with that speed, as if they rid for a Midwife, or a Physitian, or to get a pardon to save one's life, as he goeth to execution'.[104] In the late sixteenth century the postmasters on the north road to Berwick complained that their horses were being 'evilly used' because of the amount of traffic on that highway.[105] In October 1563, perhaps in response to an accusation of ill-treatment of a hired horse that had died, Simon Pede, a Cambridge notary, asked John Johnson, a horse leech, to be present when the carcass was examined. Johnson deposed that 'half his lungs was black and rotten and grown to his side', and that this was the cause of the animal's death and not any 'nuisance, negligence or fault of the said Thomas Pede'.[106] Of course, the presence of so many students at Cambridge and Oxford meant that hackney horses were in constant demand. According to Thomas Harley, writing in 1648, they did not treat them well. In a classical allusion to his cousin's cultural philistinism but love of riding, he remarked that 'he would be willing to try a journey to Parnassus, especially seeing it may be on horseback, did he not believe Pegasus to be but a tired Jade, having beene a hackney among scholars so long'.[107]

People were also wantonly cruel to horses in the name of sport. Mules and horses, like bears, might be baited, though probably not to the same extent.[108] In one incident, staged in the Bear Garden in Southwark in 1562, the horse played a supporting role in the show, which focused on the response of the monkey on his back to an attack by dogs. On one level, the audience, witnessing a humanoid monkey on horseback being tormented, were experiencing a more vicarious thrill than if they had merely been observing animals suffer. It was if they were spectators in the Coliseum in ancient Rome, watching Christians being torn to pieces by lions. On another level, they were also aware of the essential difference between the appearance and reality of humanness and this made the screams and antics of the monkey all the more comical. The desperate attempts of the horse to defend himself only added to the fun, especially if he put up a good fight.[109] A century later horses were still being baited. On 17 August 1667 John Evelyn noted that he had heard of an event in which a horse was to be baited to death. He refused to watch it, calling the sport 'wiccked and barbarous'.[110]

The justification offered, that the horse to be baited had killed a man, is significant, because it imbued the creature with rationality and intent. In doing so, it blurred the distinction between mankind and beasts. Although the continental practice of putting on trial animals that had harmed a human was rare in England, informal acts of revenge were not unknown. In 1682 a savage horse was baited to death.[111] By then, it had probably become a largely lower-class activity, genteel society having put aside such an irrational custom, along with the belief in witches. In this respect, Evelyn's reaction is illuminating, as is the excuse given, revealing that attitudes were changing by the second half of the seventeenth century and that horses, because of their special relationship to man, were among the first to benefit.[112] Scattered evidence in estate records suggests that the solution to a troublesome horse was to sell it rather than kill it, 'judiciously' or otherwise. At some point in 1644–5 Lord Brooke of Warwick Castle earned £12 from the sale of a 'biting' coach horse. Landowners similarly palmed off 'mad' horses which constituted a potential if not actual threat to life and limb. In June 1660 Sir John Wittewronge of Rothamstead sold Mad Jack, the coach horse, for £8 10s., whilst twenty years later Sir Roger Pratt of Ryston Hall received £1 5s. for the old grey mad mare. George Russell Esq. of Aston Abbots, on the other hand, still had the 'Rogue Nagg' in his stables when he died in 1684.[113]

The labouring classes might also abuse horses for what they represented; malcontents, angry at the iniquities of a hierarchical society, took their revenge on their 'oppressors' by maiming their animals.[114] All domesticated animals suffered but horses were obvious targets, given their emblematic status. In particular, they were associated with authority, as an ever-present adjunct of the process whereby the elite kept the lower orders under control. This might take the form of an admonishment by a mounted land steward on the local estate, a procession of gentlemen riding to the quarter sessions, the ceremonial arrival of the assize judges or the action of the mounted militia in putting down a food riot. Labourers also resented the emparking of commons and agricultural land. The imposition of savage game laws in the post-Restoration period further inflamed the situation, as did the abolition of a number of customary practices. In many parts of the country traditional usages such as gleaning, catching wild creatures on manorial wastes or taking timber and minerals from them were redefined as theft or, if already illegal, became more tightly controlled. As these resources were crucial to a large proportion of the population, such actions provoked widespread resentment.[115]

VETERINARY TREATMENT

In spite of a good deal of casual abuse, even by the upper classes, much time, effort and money were spent on the treatment of sick or injured horses. This may reflect a gradual shift in the intellectual climate towards the suffering of animals but, at the same time, owners wanted their charges fit and healthy. An ailing horse could not carry out its functions effectively, whether utilitarian, recreational or iconographic. In 1662, for instance, a nag belonging to Maurice Wynn of Wynnstay Hall suffered a galled back because of an ill-fitting saddle and could not be used for over three months.[116] The problem was a common one, for horses were particularly prone to illness and injury. In the letter written in March 1657/8, probably by John Beale, the writer asked the rhetorical question, 'which creature is more liable to diseases than a horse?'[117] Shakespeare in *The Taming of the Shrew* reveals the range of ailments which a horse might contract, when he describes Petruchio's horse as,

> possessed with the glanders and like to mose in the chine, troubled with the lampass, infected with the fashions, full of windgalls, sped with spavins, rayed with the yellows, past cure of the fives, stark spoiled with the staggers, begnawn with the bots, swayed [weighed] in the back, and shoulder-shotten, near-legged before.[118]

Gentlemen, wanting to know about horse ailments and the means of treating them, were well provided for: books on horsemanship invariably dealt with the subject, often at great length. Marginal notes that they made show that readers digested this advice and, by adding their own comments, indicate that they acted on it and evaluated the results. The elite also read the section on animal health care which formed a staple item in early modern almanacs.[119] As with human medicine, 'horse doctors' based their treatment upon the theory of the four humours and the need to balance them in order to maintain a good state of health. Hence the regularity with which sick humans and horses alike were purged or bled in order to remove the excess of one humour or another.[120] Nicholas Blundell of Crosby Hall was one of those who were proficient in horse medicine, making a number of references to purges, drinks, salves and powders in his diary. In 1708–9 Snowball received his attention. In March 1707/8 he ground up some calcined bay salt in an attempt to remove a film from the horse's eye, unfortunately without success. Thirteen months later Snowball went lame with the farcy and Blundell had to help apply a dressing. In June 1709 he gave the horse medicine for the disease.[121]

Even if they (or their stable keeper) were competent in treating their sick horses, members of the landed elite regularly employed specialists to tend to them. Of these men, farriers were the most skilled. Strictly speaking, they had to belong to the Company of Farriers, but as it was an elite institution with only forty members in 1674, in practice most of those operating in the provinces were not affiliates. Far more numerous were the horse leeches, whose expertise rested on practical experience rather than on formal qualifications.[122] Many blacksmiths treated horses too. Once they had found a competent farrier or leech, gentlemen tended to hire them on a regular basis. In Elizabeth I's reign the Pagets of Beaudesert frequently used George Middleton and the Petres of Ingatestone Hall gave much work to Henry Pickering.[123] The records indicate that such men treated horses for a wide range of ailments and that they were often successful. Unfortunately, the business contained its share of rogues and charlatans. The Company of Farriers, for instance, warned that a large number of 'unskillful persons inhabiting within the Liberties of the said cities [London and Westminster] have of late taken upon them the said Art and Mistery, who have thereby for want of due knowledge and skill in the right way of preserving of horses destroyed many horses in or near the same cities'. Gentlemen hired a person like this at their peril. In 1639 Henry Oxinden of Barham lost a horse to such a man, leading his cousin, Henry Oxinden of Deane, to conclude that, 'This may bee a warning to you hereafter not to preferre a pretended farrier before an experienced one'.[124]

If no real horse suffered from the exaggerated list of ailments contracted by Petruchio's horse, inflicted for dramatic effect, owners nonetheless had to spend money on remedies such as drenching, bleeding and poultices, as well as on the wages of a person to administer them. Treating horses took a good deal of time and effort. The cost of treating a colt impaled with a stake on the Misterton estate of the Paget family in 1551 came to 7s. 2d., involving six visits from William

Newton spread out over more than six weeks. Shortly afterwards he also received 9s. for curing fistulas on both flanks of a bay colt. Naturally, expenses were higher on crown estates. In September 1562 Martin Almayne, a servant of Elizabeth I, put in a bill for £8 6s. 6d. for tending to the Queen's coursers over the previous fifteen months.[125] Although, as in Newton's case, most farriers and leeches came to the estate to treat a sick horse, they might also nurse a horse at home. By doing this, an owner ensured that the horse was closely watched and given more regular treatment. In 1616 Richard Cholmeley paid Thomas Balrigg for curing his black mare, the cost including 'kepeing her in the howse almost a monthe and at good grasse 5 or 6 weeks'. When, on 16 July 1712, Nicholas Blundell sent his young foal, Ginson, to the farrier it clearly did require special attention because it was very ill with the strangles.[126]

Horses belonging to the bulk of the population were more vulnerable to an infection because they came into more regular contact with other animals, often at an inn or livery stable or on a common. Manor courts throughout the country tried to prevent the spread of disease by fining owners who put infected horses on the commons, but with only partial success. The rolls contain many presentments for the offence. On 21 October 1695, for instance, the homage found Richard Brookes guilty of putting a riffey horse onto the aftermath of the town fields at Wellington. The court fined him a punitive 10s., an indication of the seriousness with which it viewed the charge. Three years later, the court punished John Archer and James Taylor respectively for grazing a riffey horse on the common and turning a horse, sick of the pocky fashions, into the lanes and common fields of the manor. At a meeting of the manor court of Griff and Coton in Warwickshire, on 15 October 1700, the homage confirmed a number of pains, including one to prevent people washing 'surfeited or scabby' horses in the common horse pool or putting such animals onto the common or face a fine of 6s. 8d.[127]

Most horse keepers in the countryside seem to have tended to their animals themselves. Even those who could afford to hire a common farrier or a horse-leech often chose not to do so, put off by their inflated charges or a lack of faith in their ability. To help them they could make use of a corpus of specialized knowledge acquired in a variety of ways: oral testimony and a mixture of manuscript and printed sources. Writers of manuals on farriery helped supply the need for veterinary knowledge among the animal owning population, including them in their sales pitch. In 1636 the author of *The English Farrier or Countrymans Treasure* wrote that it described approved remedies for all 'Diseases, hurts, maymes, maladies and griefes in Horses' and would therefore prove a benefit for 'Gentlemen, Farmers, Inholders, Husbandmen, and generally for all'. William Poole emphasized the value of such knowledge in the preface to the 1648 edition of *The Countrey Farrier*. A boon to the poorer sort of people, who could not afford to pay for the services of a farrier or horse leech, it also provided a source of useful information for others who could. While acknowledging that they could look for a leech, he pointed out that this took time and in the meanwhile their cattle might die. In turn purchasers glossed the text and added their own remedies, or kept a record of ones that worked on convenient pieces of paper. In 1697, for instance, Benjamin Browne, a yeoman from Troutbeck, included in his accounts the ingredients of a poultice to cure fistulas, comprising calcanth, spirit of wine and oil of turpentine.[128] Cost and illiteracy ensured that cottagers, small-scale carriers and the like had less access to published material but, even so, they would have been aware of range of customary remedies, tested by experience as efficacious.

Given the conditions in which many horses were kept, it is not surprising that horse disease periodically swept the country. The second half of the seventeenth century was a particularly bad time, with outbreaks in 1658–9, 1661–3, 1666, 1668, 1671, 1683 and 1699. The plague of 1658–9, which attacked the central nervous system, was extremely virulent. There was no cure and mortality was therefore high. In 1659 tenants on the Earl of Clare's estate in Nottinghamshire lost 319 horses and the Earl a further forty. Hundreds of horses died in the Penrith area of Cumberland, disrupting agriculture and forcing farmers to use oxen.[129] In 1699 an exceptionally contagious bout of distemper swept the British Isles; few horses escaped the infection, though fortuitously among those that did were the racehorses at Newmarket. Even if few horses died from the disease, a contemporary claimed that it left survivors with a residual weakness. On the other hand, Lord Fitzwilliam of Milton thought that the horses may even have benefited in the long run. Only one or two 'old decayed jades' had died and of the rest, he observed, 'when they are recovered, it does them a good deale of good; for they purge very much at the nose'.[130] Nonetheless, because of these symptoms, correct diagnosis and treatment was vital: to add to the purgative effect could prove fatal. Instead, as Robert Harley of Brampton Bryan Castle declared, horses should be bled, fed scalded bran and boiled carrots, and a poultice, comprising a diapente of aniseed, elecampane, flour of brimstone and liquorice powder, mixed with treacle, applied to them.[131] Blundell records a similar outbreak in 1727.[132]

Because of their contacts and greater wealth, the upper classes were able to give better treatment to their horses at times of crises like these. In February 1662/3, for instance, Sir John Gell gave his son, John, a recipe and a 'water' for the plague, together with some advice on how best to treat his horses.[133] The gentry could also more readily obtain the services of a specialist when such men were at a premium. On 20 August 1662 Sir Thomas Pelham of Halland paid John Carpenter of Leigh for coming to tend to the horses 'yt was taken with ye desease'. They might even bring in someone from a distance. In 1671 Daniel Fleming of Rydal Hall in Westmorland sent a member of staff over to Yorkshire to fetch a man to cure his horses of the plague. He also obtained the services of Adam Allison of Barnard Castle, who administered potions to ten horses at 2s. 1d. a drink.[134]

Few people in early modern England did not believe that Man, as God's supreme creation, should not have dominion over animals. Even theriophilic writers argued for better treatment for animals from an anthropocentric stance. This is not to say that during the course of the early modern period attitudes towards and treatment of horses did not improve. They did, at least on paper. In published works, theriophilic views became increasingly common, especially in the years after the Restoration. Practical guides to horse management helped shape this shift of opinion and were themselves influenced by more progressive views. The first generation of English writers on horsemanship, reacting against the cruel methods of early sixteenth-century trainers, emphasized the need for gentle methods, while acknowledging that they might, on occasion, have to use coercion. These books were influential because gentlemen did study them and presumably learned how to 'cherish' their horses. In practice, there was a time-lag, since many of the people who actually trained the horses did not read them and continued as before. Besides, servants did not always appreciate the benefits that could accrue from treating their charges with respect. As far as they were concerned, a stubborn horse made their task that much more difficult. Without the time, patience or inclination to coax the animal, they tended to beat it into submission. For the same reason, horses employed by the population at large were often ill-treated. Even gentlemen were guilty of abusing their horses, especially when hurrying home, out hunting or gambling on the outcome of a race. Toll book evidence paradoxically acts as a slight corrective to such a dismal view, while also supporting it in part. Young horses did not receive the best treatment, as advocated by the writers: certainly not by non-genteel breeders and only by few gentlemen. Nonetheless, many people were aware of the maturation process and did not act precipitously. On the other hand, only a small number of horses worked as long as they were genetically capable of doing because few veteran animals turn up in toll books. Of course, they may have enjoyed years of happy retirement, but this is doubtful. Rather, the treatment they received during their working life seems to have worn them out by the age of ten to twelve. No longer of any use to their owners, they were sent to the knacker.

4

Horse Riding and Status

When, according to Shakespeare, Richard III pleaded for 'a horse! a horse! my kingdom for a horse!' he clearly had a practical use for it.[1] Moreover, faced with such pressing danger, he might have accepted any nag that could put one foot in front of the other. If so, Richard probably would not have effected his escape anyway because no ordinary horse was capable of bearing the weight of the plate-armoured king, even if it managed to avoid injury or death itself. Conversely, Shakespeare may have been writing metaphorically, symbolically portraying Richard's loss of kingship rather than an illustration of his actual defeat in battle. An unhorsed king was not a king at all. In one line Shakespeare not only encapsulates the variety of saddle horses required by the upper classes but also the iconic significance of the creatures. As noted earlier, gentlemen and nobles were able to earmark their mounts for certain tasks such as hunting, racing, the *manège*, cavalry and travel, as well as deploying them iconographically for display. The number and quality of the horses kept by the elite not only reflected their wealth but also their interest in horsemanship and equine pursuits. Of course, humbler people, when riding, had to make do with general, all-purpose horses, as they did not have the resources to keep a specific saddle mount. *A fortiori*, the bulk of the population did not possess a horse at all but at least had the opportunity of hiring one for a journey.

To ride a horse required considerable skill, especially when travelling at speed. Apart from the need to control and direct a powerful animal, the rider had to display dexterity and balance to avoid falling off over rough terrain and on the unmetalled and winding roads of the time. Hunting across country taxed a person's horsemanship to the limit. Horses stumbled and accidents could be serious. King William III was not the only person who died after a fall from his horse. On 20 August 1710 Lord Scudamore was fatally injured after being flung from the saddle.[2] Nicholas Blundell records two occasions on which he fell from his horse, each reflecting a common cause of accidents. The first occurred on 12 July 1707 as he was coming home after drinking in the Woolpack. He hurt his head and side. The second tumble happened on 4 March 1620/1 when his horse staggered and threw him.[3] His relatives, friends and servants suffered similar mishaps. On 23 April 1714 his wife's horse threw her when riding pillion on a trip to Liverpool. Presumably she was not hurt, for she walked home while her husband continued his journey.[4] Accidents occurred among the population at large and presumably in greater number too, although they are less likely to appear in the documentation. In the 1720s, for instance, we know of accidents that servants of the Earl of Oxford suffered because Isaac Hobart, the land steward at Welbeck, wrote about them in his letters. In May 1724 the head groom broke his leg when his horse fell on his way back from Worksop. In April 1728 the housekeeper, returning to Welbeck from Mansfield, got entangled in the harness of cart horse which she met in a narrow lane. Falling with her horse, she lay helpless 'till the carriage came up and by rushing her against the bank broke her left leg and bruised the other very much'. Although in no danger, Hobart thought that she would not be able to resume her duties for a long time.[5]

HORSES' GAITS

The gait of a horse affected its ability to perform certain functions and, indeed, the safety and comfort of the rider on its back. Owners, therefore, had to consider action when choosing an animal. Surveying the relationship between function and gait, Thomas Blundeville, writing in 1565, commented:

> For some perchaunce woulde haue a brede of greate trotting horses mete for the war, and to serve in the field. Some other againe would have a brede of ambling horses of a meane stature for the Journey and to travayle by the way. Some againe would have perhaps a race of swift runners to runne for wagers, or to galloppe the bucke, or to serve for such lyke excercises of pleasure.[6]

Lists of horses in gentlemen's stables reveal that they were aware of the link and kept horses with various actions to perform different jobs. The saddle horses belonging to Sir Richard Newdigate of Arbury had a variety of paces.[7] His four troop horses trotted, as they had to by law; his eight hunters might be rackers or pacers rather than trotters; and his five pads ambled or paced. His black tit was a horse of medium size, probably a trotter and with a turn of speed.[8]

Occasionally, toll books record the gait or gaits of the horses sold, reflecting the paces of animals purchased by the population at large. Unfortunately, the coverage is patchy both in time and place, and in the amount of detail that individual toll keepers chose to record. The Act of 1555 only required them to note 'the colour, with one speciall marke at the least' of each horse.[9] Table 6 indicates that most of the horses trotted and only a minority ambled.[10] It is perhaps no coincidence that the one fair where amblers did predominate was Penkridge, a centre for high-class saddle mounts. Riders could obtain a reasonable choice of ambling horses at Welsh Border fairs such as Chester and Shrewsbury and at a cheaper rate. They could obtain pacers at north midlands and north-western fairs but would have had trouble finding rackers anywhere, presumably as they were classed as amblers. A number of horses were multipaced, but perhaps not equally adept at all of them. A bay mare sold at Chester market in 1664 paced and trotted, but the seller admitted that it 'trotts most'. Many of the trotters, especially at Derby and Nottingham, were draught horses but might also serve as saddle mounts. All of the horses sold with saddle and bridle at Chester market trotted. The relative scarcity of amblers in toll books suggests that ordinary people could not afford to buy a good, well-trained specimen and had to use whatever came to hand.

The four beat gaits provided a more comfortable ride, so for this reason a person embarking on a long journey preferred to travel on a horse which ambled or racked. One rider in the 1590s said of a grey gelding that 'hee amled soe esely that you could not redd of him for slepping'. The hobbies of Ireland ambled naturally and, as Blundeville noted, they were 'verie meete for the saddle, and to trauell by the way'.[11] As both gaits had exactly the same hoof beats, they are interchangeable as terms. Possibly 'racking' was used to denote a quicker ambling pace, perhaps in excess of six miles an hour, the speed of a 'fine Ambelinge mare' in 1631. If so, a racker made an ideal post horse.[12] Naturally, at speed the rider of a racking horse had to sacrifice a certain amount of comfort. As Moll told Laxton in *The Roaring Girl*,

> There's the gold
> With which you hired your hackney, here's her pace,
> She racks hard, and perhaps your bones will feel it.[13]

Trotters were far worse, as Richard Persehouse discovered when riding one on a 'tedious painfull journey' in 1649. Reliving the experience, his brother-in-law Edward Chester concluded that 'you and I must leave trotting horses and hard saddles for younger youths'.[14]

Because of their action and conformation, hobbies made ideal 'summer' nags for a gentleman's family. In January 1600/1 Sir Carew Reynal sent Sir Robert Cecil a hobby as a gift, commenting, 'His pace is easy and I hope he will prove fit for your saddle'.[15] In this capacity, they regularly feature in stable accounts. Among the upper class hobbies retained their popularity throughout the period, though in the royal stables the death of Elizabeth I seemed to mark a shift in emphasis towards Spanish and eastern horses.[16] According to Blundeville, the ginete neither trotted nor ambled but possessed 'a comely kind of going like a Turk'. Cavendish wondered what he meant by this term, sarcastically asking, 'What strange going is that, which is neither these two. No horse that has four legs can do anything but amble or trot for galloping and running is another thing.' Blundeville probably meant an Arabian, whose gait was 'neither amble, racke, nor trot, but a certain kind of easie traine'. Cavendish probably questioned that term too.[17] To obtain fine amblers Blundeville recommended that a breeder should use a ginete or

TABLE 6: Horses' gaits recorded at fairs and markets

	Chester fair	Chester markets	Shrewsbury c. 1609	Shrewsbury fairs 1624	Shrewsbury 1629	Carlisle fairs 1631/2	Carlisle 1653/4	Penkridge fair 1558	Derby fair 1646	Nottingham fairs 1645, 1647–8	Market Bosworth fair 1616
	1579	1660–99									
amble	24	4	25	20	13	833	496	60	17	2	13
per cent	47.1	1.8	29.1	32.8	24.5	84.9	83.1	65.2	2.2	1.8	12.9
rack								1		1	1
per cent								1.1		0.9	1.0
amble/ trot	1	17	8	8	10				43		11
per cent	2	7.6	9.3	13.1	18.9				5.5		10.9
amble/ pace		1							1		
per cent		0.4							0.1		
rack/trot					1					7	9
per cent					1.9					6.3	8.9
trot	26	99	53	33	29			31	601	88	67
per cent	51.0	44.2	61.6	54.1	54.7			33.7	77.2	78.6	66.3
pace						130	44		41	1	
per cent						13.3	7.4		5.3	0.9	

HORSE RIDING AND STATUS

	Chester		Shrewsbury			Carlisle		Penkridge	Derby	Nottingham	Market Bosworth
	fair	markets	fairs			fairs		fair	fair	fairs	fair
	1579	1660–99	c. 1609	1624	1629	1631/2	1653/4	1558	1646	1645, 1647–8	1616
trot/pace		26				18	57		76	9	
per cent		11.6				1.8	9.5		9.8	8.0	
trot/ gallop		50									
per cent		22.3									
pace/ gallop		2									
per cent		0.9									
trot/pace/ gallop		20									
per cent		8.9									
all gaits		4								4	
per cent		1.8								3.6	
through paced		1									
per cent		0.4									
Totals	51	224	86	61	53	981	597	92	779	112	101

ginete-cross stallion or, failing that, a 'fair Irish ambling hobbie'. The mare should be either a ginete cross bred in England or a native ambling mare.[18]

Among the upper classes the term pad came into vogue after the Restoration to denote a high-quality, easy-paced saddle horse. Pads were highly prized, and therefore expensive and hard to find. According to Richard Blome, writing in 1686, a pad ought to be 'strong, light and nimble', a rare combination of qualities in a horse. In 1680 the Earl of Halifax, writing about a couple of pads that he had promised to get for his brother, complained that 'it is almost as possible to get a horse that flyeth as a horse that paceth, I mean one that doth it well, so rare that kind of creature is grown amongst us'.[19] Interestingly, Halifax equated a pad with a pacing horse, though William Cavendish associated it with amblers.[20] A rider would have noticed the difference. An ambler was more comfortable, for a rider, mounted on a slow moving pacer, would roll from side to side. At speed the pacing action was much smoother.[21]

This evidence indicates that pacers, like rackers, were used when one wanted to travel reasonably quickly (about four miles an hour) but in relative comfort.[22] Writing to his cousin, Fitzwilliam Coningsby, in about 1620 Sir John Lyttelton complained, 'I am in extreme want of a pasing horse, since I kept horses I was never worse furnished then at this present being forsed to ride on trotters'.[23] Of the native breeds, Galloways were the most suited to this task. According to Defoe, they were the best light saddle horses in Europe, noted 'for being good pacers, strong easy goers, hardy, gentle, well broke, and above all, that they never tire'.[24] If the horses sold at Carlisle Fair were Galloways or a similar breed, most of them were natural trotters. This suggests that the gentry took the best, those that paced, or trained them to do so. About one in five of the horses sold at Carlisle in the middle of the seventeenth century paced. Where instructions are noted in estate accounts, owners mainly required the trainers to teach a horse to pace. On Nicholas Blundell's estate at Little Crosby apparently this was all that they did.[25] Moreover, in an admittedly small sample, there are fewer references to ambling, which seems to confirm the value that the gentry placed on natural amblers like hobbies or their crosses.[26]

INCIDENCE OF HORSE RIDING

By European standards horse riding was widespread in England. In 1558 the Venetian ambassador reported that English peasants were accustomed to ride on horseback and concluded that the country could be called the land of comforts.[27] We should interpret 'peasant' as a farmer of some means rather than a smallholder and therefore a person of standing in his community. At the top of this group were those who kept a horse specifically to ride on. Inventories occasionally record saddle horses among the non-gentry. In February 1590/1, for instance, Robert Holdsworth, a yeoman from Clee left a riding gelding, valued at £5 and evidently a good quality animal. At the end of the period, in 1743, Francis Ryle of Edingale left a hackney mare, as well as ten draught horses and mares.[28] More often, the saddle mount can be identified by the composite entry of horse and riding tack. Appraisers might add references to spurs and riding boots too. When they valued the personal estate of Richard Barry of Farnsfield in November 1567, they assessed a horse with saddle, bridle, boots and spurs at £1 10s.[29] Unlike the gentry, these owners rarely kept riding horses for non-functional activities. Many of them rode their horse in the course of their work: carriers and drovers accompanying pack horse trains or flocks and herds; manufacturers and middlemen taking wares to their customers; officials going about their business. Depositions taken in cases heard at the quarter sessions, the assizes or in the Equity courts often give a context to the events, showing people going about their daily business. While one should treat with scepticism the accounts of suspects, the stories had to offer a plausible account of events and therefore reflected reality. The comments of victims and witnesses provide a corrective. The evidence reveals a kaleidoscope of people on the roads of England such as, for example, a Shrewsbury baker in 1602 taking a consignment of shoes from Llanymynech to sell at Llangollen in 1602 or a Northumberland yeoman riding home from Morpeth market in 1667.[30]

Even if the records seem to corroborate the contemporary view that horse riding was comparatively common in England, evidence drawn from a number of manuscript and printed collections of probate inventories suggests that few of the horses listed there were dedicated saddle mounts.[31] Most owners used their horses as multi-purpose animals, changing the saddlery according to function: work or riding. In February 1678/9, for example, John Putto, a miller from Writtle, left a horse, saddle, bridle, pannell, cart saddle and collar (and three pigs), worth £6 7s. and a cart, valued at £3.[32] This was not an ideal situation for, as Gervase Markham pointed out, using a carthorse for riding altered its pace and adversely affected its performance in the draught. The rider suffered, too, a further indication of the luxury afforded by the possession of a specific saddle mount.[33] The ride was even bumpier if one had to make do with a pannell, a padded cloth that normally went under a saddle but which could also serve as a rough seat. Mid-Essex inventories provide a number of examples of this practice. In May 1690 the appraisers of the goods of John Webb, a Writtle yeoman, valued his five horses and a mare, cart harness and saddlery, and an old pannell, stirrups and bridle at £16. Did Webb use the mare as a riding horse?[34] According to the data, the ownership of saddle horses was lower in towns than in the countryside. This may be illusionary, reflecting shortcomings in the sources, but there is some logic in this finding. Grazing and fodder were harder to obtain in towns and, in any case, should anyone have to make a trip, he or she could hire one off a hackneyman or a postmaster.

In general, women were less likely to ride than men from the same socio-economic level. If they did, it was normally in the course of earning a living, for example, taking goods to market. One who did was the daughter of Tobias Sturt, a yeoman from Kirdford, who in 1726 left her 'The little bay horse she generally rides on to market'.[35] Upper-class ladies, on the other hand, rode for pleasure and sometimes even for preference over vehicles. In June 1557 Litolfi wrote to the duke of Mantua that 'miladis', presumably those at court, used neither cart nor coach but rather went on horseback. Ladies did ride in vehicles at the time, as will be seen, but Litolfi's observation is surely an indication of the discomforts experienced when travelling in contemporary conveyances. Naturally, when out riding their footmen accompanied them, with their maids of honour following behind either on foot or in the saddle.[36] Although the new sprung coaches improved the situation in the late sixteenth century, ladies still took the air or visited friends on horseback. In the early eighteenth century Frances, the wife of Nicholas Blundell of Little Crosby Hall, often travelled by coach but equally regularly rode on horseback. For her safety and convenience she had a manservant or two to accompany her. On 24 February 1704/5 her husband wrote in his diary that she had stayed the night at Gorsuch but had sent the men home. On 13 April 1713 Mrs Hesketh of Rufford asked her if she could borrow a man and a horse to go with her to Chester the following day.[37]

Some women rode astride their horses. William Cavendish rather scathingly wrote that he had seen women run and gallop their horses as well as any men.[38] Cavendish directed his scorn at the men but others criticized ladies who rode in such a masculine fashion and in male attire. On 12 June 1666 Pepys noted in his diary that:

> Walking here in the galleries, I find the Ladies of Honour dressed in their riding garbs, with coats and doublets with deep skirts, just for all the world like mine, and buttened their doublets up the breast, with perriwigs and with hats; so they, only for a long petticoat dragging under their Men's coats, nobody could take them for women in any point whatsoever which was an odd sight, and a sight did not please me.[39]

Addison and Steele publicly voiced their dislike of the practice in comments made in the *Spectator* in 1711 and 1712.[40] Contemporary opinion felt it more fitting for ladies to ride side-saddle. Joris Hoefnagel depicts a lady riding in this manner in his painting of a marriage feast at Bermondsey (1569). In reality, the subject would not have ridden the trotter portrayed there. If she had done, she would have experienced a very uncomfortable ride![41]

Also designed largely, though not exclusively, with women in mind was the practice of riding 'double': most passengers comprised women and children and the riders mainly men. Just as many men today associate driving a car with masculinity and insist on taking the wheel, so in early modern England men held the reins. The practice formed the point of a joke in Shakespeare's *The Taming of the Shrew*. Grumio, reporting a mishap on road, refers to his master Petruchio riding behind his wife, Katharina. Astonished that a man should ride pillion to his wife, Curtis exclaims, 'Both of one horse?'[42] As passengers, women sat sideways on a pillion tied to the saddle. Hoefnagel's painting illustrates this arrangement. Sidesaddles and pillions did not have stirrups but incorporated a footrest called a planchette into the design as a support for the legs.[43] Inventory examples include the pillion seat owned by William Moore, a Winteringham yeoman, in 1672 and the pannell, girths and footstool left by Richard Clary, a Writtle yeoman, in 1694.[44] Riding 'double' was quite commonplace among all classes who travelled by horseback. The benefits to the population at large included a reduction in stabling costs, and companionship and protection on the road, as well as help if engaged on business. Well-bred ladies also rode double. Indeed, in 1655 Sir Ralph Verney declared that ''Tis now the new fashion for Maydens in town to ride a Pick Pack'.[45] Among the upper classes, the rider was normally a relative or servant. In the early eighteenth century Nicholas Blundell of Little Crosby Hall regularly went on visits with his wife or children riding pillion behind him.[46] Horses employed to carry two people were known as double horses but, although they had to be strong enough to do the job, the description was only an informal one. When, on 22 March 1723/4, Nicholas and Frances Blundell rode to Mrs Sadler's house on Jewell, the diarist noted that ''tis the first time he carried double'.[47]

As a coach horse, Jewell possessed the strength to carry Blundell and his wife. Even so, owners who did not want to overstrain their horses did not make them carry double all the time. In October 1588 William Kirkham sent his horseman to collect his roan mare, then 'full of grass', rather than allow his wife to ride pillion on it for her journey home.[48] Confusingly, the elite did not necessarily restrict the term to a horse that carried two people. In 1512 the Earl of Northumberland owned two double horses, one for his son, Lord Percy, and the other for himself, the inference being that the horses were particularly strong mounts.[49] A set of five accounts for Elizabeth I's stables, taken between 1570 and 1591, broadly confirms this interpretation. The accountant divided the stock into two categories: double horses and hackneys. The first comprised saddle, carriage and sumpter horses, including coursers and coach horses, as well as hobbies and litter mules, whereas the second consisted of the servants' saddle horses. The double horses received twice the ration of the hackneys.[50]

HORSE HIRE

Persons wanting temporary use of a horse could obtain one in various ways. First, they could hire one from a hackneyman. Their number grew during the course of the sixteenth century as a rise in the population stimulated the domestic market and drew more people onto the roads. Anyone with a horse might take advantage of an economic opportunity by offering it for hire, especially if he or she lived in a town or along a main road. At Southampton the situation had got out of hand by 1582, 'the cause is that every man almost in this towne that hath a horse do use to hyer owt to such as they lyke'. In response, the authorities restricted the service to eight 'sufficient' men. Within a couple of years, however, the inhabitants were complaining about this arrangement.[51] Apart from its appeal to small-scale operators, the business also attracted larger entrepreneurs. Andrew More, a London hackneyman living in Coleman Street at the turn of the sixteenth century, for instance, reportedly kept many horses standing at livery there.[52] Carriers, who similarly profited from the growth of internal trade, also hired out surplus horses. In 1617 Fynes Morrison noted that they, 'Let horses from Citie to Citie, with caution that the passenger must lodge in their Inne, that they may looke to the feeding of their horse; and so they will for some five or six dayes journey let him a horse, and find the horse meate themselves for some twenty shillings'. The Oxford carrier kept a dozen horses for the use of students and at Cambridge Hobson had forty horses in his stables.[53]

For particular journeys, where speed was essential, a wealthy or powerful individual might lay out a private chain of horses. Often, the event was a matter of national importance. In 1586 Richard Hawkins brought the news of the sacking of Carthagena from St Michael's Mount to Exeter in fourteen hours, riding 110 miles over rough terrain at an average speed of eight miles an hour. Even more significant was Sir Robert Carey's ride north to inform James VI of Scotland of the death of Elizabeth I in 1603. Although he rode from Richmond through Westminster in the early hours of the morning on 24 March 1602/3, the real start of his dash began at an inn near Charing Cross at 10 a.m. He arrived at Holyrood Palace in Edinburgh at supper time two days later, having covered about 400 miles in less than sixty hours, including overnight rests and a delay to discuss the situation with the local Northumberland gentry on the evening of the 25th and the morning of the 26th.[54] James I's son, Prince Henry, was an excellent horseman and on one occasion posted the sixty miles between Richmond and Huntingdon in nine hours.[55]

Self-evidently, relays of horses were expensive to set up. Consequently, this course of action was beyond the means of all but a handful of people. Travellers who wanted to complete their journey quickly could make use of the royal postal system, though they paid at a higher rate than the post did. At the opening of the period the sole postal road, complete with regular hackney stages, ran between Gravesend and Dover. Then, early in Henry VIII's reign, the King appointed Brian Tuke as Master of the Posts and charged him with the task of creating a number of staging posts along which royal dispatches could be speedily transported from hand to hand.[56] By the end of the sixteenth century the country possessed several postal roads with a postmaster at each staging point *en route*. The roads, which radiated out from London, terminated at Dover, Falmouth, Milford Haven, Holyhead, Carlisle and Berwick. Over time, the system filled out as branch routes proliferated.[57] To help finance the post, the government, at least as early as Mary I's reign, encouraged private traffic and gave the postmasters a monopoly of the business. Only if the latter could not find a suitable horse were travellers allowed to deal with common hackneymen. In Kent, the well-entrenched hackneymen resisted subordination to the postmasters and openly flouted the regulations. The position of hackneymen throughout the system improved when an Act of 1660 declared that a postmaster had to supply a horse within half an hour.[58]

Because they had to provide lodging and food and drink to riders on the through post, postmasters tended to be innkeepers.[59] Innkeepers in thoroughfare towns were also active in schemes to maintain a supply of horses in reserve, a custom designed to protect their guests' horses from seizure by the post. At St Alban's in 1584 the authorities raised enough money by subscription to buy eight horses, 'So that strangers and others, not inhabitants within St. Alban's shall be discharged thereof and their geldings, mares, and horses not taken for service at any time'.[60] Judging from the list of horses and tack listed in his inventory in 1666, Richard Annion, a Chester innkeeper, acted as a postmaster. He possessed three nags, two mares and a colt, worth £18, and tack, scattered around the house, valued at £3 19s. The latter comprised five saddles (10s.), new bridles and reins, stirrups and leathers, croupers, male pillions, horse locks, two portmanteaux and other implements (£2), one pillion for a woman (5s.), a hamper with chains and old bridles (6s.), old saddles (10s.) and a pillion, two wounties, a sidesaddle and three baskets (8s.).[61]

The cost of hiring horses was considerable. During Elizabeth I's reign the rate per mile for royal couriers rose from 1d. to 2½d. and for private travellers from 2d. to 3d. On the Dover Road they respectively paid 1s. 8d. and 2s. 6d. a stage.[62] The money paid for the traveller's horse and that of his or her guide, needed not only to point out the way but also to lead the horse back. The second horse also carried up to 40 pounds of luggage. In addition, the traveller had to pay the guide 4d. per stage and, when they parted company, a tip. It was only in the seventeenth century, when postmasters began to keep more horses, that it was possible to arrange for posting without guides. In the Orders of 1635 the traveller who only hired a single horse could leave it at the place where he or she obtained a fresh animal, paying 2½d. for the service.[63] Hackneymen charged 1d. or 1½d. for posting traffic and, it seems, what they liked for ordinary customers. The Orders for Kent in 1584 stated that the dominant position of the postmaster in the rapid transport business was not intended 'to hinder the liberty of any Englishman or natural born subject of this Realm riding in journey, but that he or they may take choice, and at such prices as they can'.[64] In Southampton the inhabitants complained about the excessive prices they charged. In 1576, therefore, the authorities ordered them to take no more than 6s. 8d. for a journey of up to eight days to London or Bristol and 8d. for every subsequent day.[65]

The quality and condition of post and hackney horses were matters of constant debate, travellers complaining of poor standards and the owners accusing the riders of ill-treating the animals. The post-warrant issued by the Crown stipulated 'hable and sufficient horses' but this term was open to wide interpretation and the animals presented to travellers often varied according to the status of the person demanding them.[66] Complaints about the horses used do appear in the documentation but, as accounts of poor service and worn out jades are more likely to have survived, they give a somewhat jaundiced view of the proceedings. When in 1566 Arnold de la Rue hired four horses from one Nicholson, a London hackneyman, he must have found them acceptable because he was happy for his friends to use them for a journey to Norwich shortly afterwards. Nicholson, however, swapped one of them, a black horse, for a brown bay horse, 'very sore hurt in one of his fore legs, between the knee and shoulder'. As Nicholson promised to take nothing for the horse if it broke down, the party set off, with John Paul on the injured horse. Although, according to de la Rue, Paul treated the horse gently and gave it sufficient fodder, 'he [the horse] fainted by the way' and he had to abandon it at Newmarket. Inevitably, riders accused the Southampton men with keeping unsatisfactory horses. An entry in the court leet records of 1580 described them as 'tyery jades that are not able to serve the jornis for the which they are hieried to the great disturbance of such as hyereth the same'.[67] The gentry were the most critical of all; with their stock of good quality horses they naturally viewed hackneys as inferior animals. In 1659, Edmund Verney observed that 'Horses good & able enough to carry him with credit are hard to bee found among hackenees.'[68]

In July 1638 Richard Newdigate of Arbury avoided having to hire a horse 'from toune to toune' because his brother had loaned him a mare to travel on.[69] This was a common practice, especially among the gentry with a stable full of horses and a tradition of hospitality. In January 1597/8 Sir John Hollis, in desperate need of 'a fair ambling or racking gelding', asked Lord Sheffield if he could borrow one for a month. It was, Sir John declared, 'One thing I want which upon this sudden I can no where provide and yet I must as needfully have it as clothes to my back'. Nicholas Blundell and his friends regularly loaned or borrowed each other's horses. Among neighbours, riders returned the horse when they came home. If a person lived at a distance, a servant did the job, either accompanying the borrower on the journey or being sent back by him or her with the animal.[70] Naturally, the lender first had to consider the likely treatment of the horse *en route* and the possibility that it might be stolen and sold. Evidence of the practice among the general public mainly turns up in depositions taken in cases of theft. In one incident in 1681, Henry Cowell of Newcastle upon Tyne loaned a gelding to William Leek, a butcher, to collect some lambs eight miles away. Leek, however, headed for Ireland, leaving the horse with a Cockermouth man, to whom he sold it on his return. Borrowing a horse was one of the stock stories that thieves offered when challenged. It seemed plausible but not to everyone. In 1663 Isabel Lister of Hensingham was sceptical when a stranger, who had arrived at her alehouse, informed her that a friend living near Lamplugh (seven miles away) had lent him the horse he rode on. She replied sarcastically that 'he was a kind friend would lend him his horse soe farr'.[71]

Another method of obtaining a horse on a temporary basis was to buy one at the outset of a trip with the intention of selling it at the end of the journey. Toll books of markets and fairs at port towns provide the clearest evidence of the practice. At Chester one of the largest groups of sellers comprised Irishmen, presumably on their way back across the Irish Sea. At a market held there in December 1665 John Eaken, a Londonderry baker, sold a horse to Thomas Hignett, a local labourer. A marginal note records that Eaken had acquired the horse, together with saddle and bridle, from Mr Hunt, a merchant tailor living in Coventry. Mariners acted in the same way: sailors sold horses at markets at Bristol, Chester, Plymouth and Portsmouth. The traveller, of course, had to balance the possible loss of money on resale against the cost of hiring a horse. He would also have to feed the horse. In 1565, the rate, according to a reference to baiting a hackney horse in Surrey, amounted to 6d. a day.[72] In 1610 Sir George Radcliffe, then a student at Oxford, carefully weighed up his options before deciding to hire a horse:

> To buy one were the cheapest way, for by that means I needed to pay him nothing to bring him up or carry him down, selling him here when I came again; but unless a man be very circumspect he may well be cozened; and, besides, horses be ill to get now, and will be ill to sell towards winter for many be going away and want horses, who then will come again and have them to sell.[73]

Losses were certainly made. When William Oumbler, a gentleman from Hedon sold a horse at Chester market on 9 May 1665 he received £2 8s. 0d. for it, 13s. 0d. less than it had cost him at the fair at Beverley two days earlier. Even with hiring charges and fodder he would have saved himself several shillings had he hired a horse.

RIDING AND THE UPPER CLASSES

For the upper classes riding was a leisure pursuit as well as a mark of distinction. In 1647 Henry Peacham wrote, 'Of recreations, some are more expensive than others ... but the truth is, the most pleasant of all is riding with a good horse and a good companion ... into the country'. Many gentlemen would have shared Montaigne's view, as expressed in his essay *Of Vanity*, that he would rather die in the saddle away from home than in a bed.[74] In October 1600 Dudley Carleton wrote that the seventy-five-year-old Lord Norris, although in decline, 'Retains his old stirring spirits', daily going out on horseback early in the morning. Sir Humphrey Mildmay was another person who liked to ride, travelling regularly on horseback between his homes in London and Danbury. On one occasion, in May 1638, he recorded his satisfaction at having come 'Well to this town [London] and house of mine in St John's, from Danbury, by a good hour before one'.[75]

Although members of the elite did not monopolize the activity of horse riding, what set them apart was the quality of the horses they rode and the skill they displayed while doing so. Undoubtedly, they gained pleasure from riding a mettlesome mount but, as noted earlier, their interest in horses and horsemanship had social and political connotations too. The practical application of horse riding as a symbol of aristocratic rule can be seen in the interest that the upper classes displayed in the *manège*. Gentlemen like Robert Alexander who had learned the art under Grisone at Naples introduced it into England during the reign of Henry VIII.[76] Elizabeth I's Master of the Horse, the Earl of Leicester, participated in the sport and encouraged a leading Italian riding master, Claudio Corte, to come to England.[77] During the course of her reign the *manège* became a fashionable pastime among the upper classes. In 1584 its popularity prompted Thomas Bedingfield to complain that 'The Gentlemen of this land have studied to make horsses more for pleasure than seruice.'[78] Bedingfield thought that horsemanship should be related to function: 'The principall use of horses is, to travell by the waie, & serve in the war: whatsoever your horse learneth more, is rather for pompe or pleasure than honor or yse.' Even so, he recognized the value to the elite of a public display of their horsemanship as a means of impressing onlookers, demonstrating their equestrian skills and showing off the capabilities of their mount.[79]

By 1600 Englishmen were looking to France rather than Italy for instruction. Edward Lord Herbert, for instance, did not merely learn to ride the great horse in France but also studied the *haute école* as the guest of the constable of France at Merlou. He later wrote that he had had the pick of fifty of the 'best and choicest' great horses in the country and the services of his squire, Monsieur de Discancour, as instructor. The constable, a devotee of the *manège*, esteemed de Discancour as the equal of de Pluvinel, who had introduced the sport in France from Italy, and La Broue.[80] About a decade later, in 1611, George Villiers and his brother, together with other young English and German gentlemen, received training in horsemanship and the *manège* at Angers. John Holles's father was therefore merely following a trend when he packed off his son to Paris in 1616.[81] The appointment of Monsieur St Antoine as riding master to Princes Henry and Charles gave the fashion royal approval. St Antoine had been the star pupil of de Pluvinel and came with Henry IV's recommendation.[82] Prince Henry became an enthusiast, building the first specially designated riding school in the country. The plan provided the model for others erected by fellow-students at Wolferton and later at Bolsover Castle. At the same time, the Earl of Northampton established a riding school in the grounds of Ludlow Castle,[83] with the avowed aim of improving the level of instruction available at home. Nothing could be better, he stated, than to provide the means whereby young gentlemen could acquire the skills of good horsemanship, 'a necessary part of every gentlemans breeding'. He hoped that others would follow his example, encouraging good horsemanship among the gentry and stimulating an interest in breeding and training horses 'fit for their own practices and service of their country'. Northampton employed an English riding master, who 'In the art of riding … is inferior to very few or none in this kingdom'. Northampton had to bring him to Ludlow from his estate in Warwickshire, an indication of the shortage of good teachers in the country. Among Englishmen, only William Cavendish later in the century acquired a European reputation.

The *manège* enjoyed a modest revival after the Restoration as returning cavaliers, who had observed foreign practices at first hand, promoted the sport and encouraged young men to interest themselves in horsemanship. Foremost among them was William Cavendish, whose influential book, *A New Method and Extraordinary Invention to Dress Horses*, appeared in 1667, a supplement to the one he had written in exile in the 1650s.[84] Cavendish built the existing riding school at Bolsover at this time. Other arenas were being erected too. In 1680 Monsieur Foubert, a Huguenot refugee from France, set up an academy, including an open *manège* near the Haymarket to teach riding, fencing, dancing, handling arms and mathematics. He attracted a high quality clientele, including Robert, the son of Sir Edward Harley.[85] John Evelyn and Lord Cornwallis visited this establishment four years later when they went to see the young gentlemen exercise their horses in the new centre in London. Lewis Maidwell opened a rival academy in King Street in 1687 where he taught a similar range of skills. However, he had gone out of business by 1699, the site being acquired by Foubert's son, Henry. Interest continued into the early eighteenth century, with Lord Stafford standing out as a particularly flashy performer. In a letter to Abigail Harley in 1717, her niece described meeting his lordship, who was riding a 'prancing' horse, 'A very beautiful one, set out as fine as his trappings could make him, the rider not falling short of anything that could dazzle the eye of the beholders'. In spite of its supporters and its iconic significance, the *manège* never attained the same popularity as it did on the Continent. In France Evelyn noticed the difference, commenting on the number of academies in Paris and pointing out that hardly any town of note lacked one or two of these establishments.[86]

In this respect, contemporary writers on horses seem to have judged gentlemen according to their degree of interest in the *manège*. According to this view, only those involved in the sport could class themselves as true horsemen. Naturally, gentlemen wanted to be competent riders, especially as most of them participated in hunting. They also recognized the value of being seen in public riding good quality horses and maintaining a stable full of horses, each with its specific function. Yet this was as far as most of them wanted to go. After all, it took time and effort to learn the skills associated with this discipline, and good riding masters were hard to find in England. Concern about this lack of interest seems to have developed at the turn of the sixteenth century, though in many ways it came from a biased source, from those who wanted to promote a greater awareness of and a more refined approach to horsemanship. In 1615 Markham condemned those gentry who aimed no higher than 'the riding of a ridden and perfect horse' rather than seeking to breed and train horses themselves. He tried to encourage them by pointing out the benefits of riding such a mount, claiming 'there can be no greater or better recreation either for health, profit, or renowning of their owne virtues, then the riding of great horses, which in the verie action is selfespeaketh gentlemen to all that are performers or doers of the same'. Thomas de Gray made the same point a generation later: 'it much troubleth me to see how little esteeme gentlemen now a dayes have thereof. Some horses they have, though not for the ménage (sic), yet for hunting.'[87] The consensus of opinion at the time was that the English lacked the refinement of their European counterparts. Henry Peacham, in *Coach and Sedan* (1636), has the surveyor assert, 'No Nation in Europe, is more backward and carelesse in breeding and managing horses, than we in England'.[88]

HORSE RIDING AS METAPHOR

The act of riding did not merely serve as a political signifier; it also provided, as hinted earlier, a metaphor for the gendering of social relationships and the locus of authority. In particular, it provided writers with a wealth of symbols they could deploy to describe aspects of a patriarchal society. Women and children did ride but horse-related activities were primarily run by and in the interest of adult males. The Duchess of Ormonde was surely acknowledging reality when she reported in a self-deprecating way on the quality of five colts she had seen at the stud on a visit there in June 1668. To convince her husband she wrote that others too had thought them very handsome, 'otherwise, perhaps, you would no more believe them to be so than you do the wine to be good that I commend, my skill in both being much alike'.[89] Riding manuals presumed a male readership. Besides, contemporaries made an analogy between breaking a colt and training it to obey its rider with the processes whereby women learned acceptable behaviour.[90] To early modern man, women by nature were closer to animals than were men and therefore had to learn how to conduct themselves properly. Thereafter (to pursue the riding analogy) men from time to time might have to rein in their women whenever they felt that their charges were 'slipping the bit'.[91] As Luciana tells her sister, Adriana, in Shakespeare's *The Comedy of Errors*, her husband 'is the bridle of your will'.[92]

The notion of male superiority enshrined classical and Christian traditions. Aristotle thought that warm-blooded animals were superior to cold-blooded ones and, as they were 'hotter' than women, that men were 'natural rulers'.[93] Christians based their belief on the conviction that if God had given man dominion over the rest of His creation, He literally meant man not woman. In Christian theology women, as personified in Eve, were responsible for the Fall. All women who followed her carried the stigma and paid for it by being put under male control. Men exercised authority and provided for their family, while women stayed at home and brought up the children.[94] When in *The Comedy of Errors* Adriana asks why men should have more freedom than women, Luciana replies, 'Because their business still lies out o'door'. Expanding on her theme, Luciana explains:

> There's nothing situate under heaven's eye
> But hath his bound, in earth, in sea, in sky:
> The beasts, the fishes, and the winged fowls,
> Are their males' subjects and at their controls:
> Men, more divine, the masters of all these,
> Lords of the wide world and wild watery seas,
> Indued with intellectual sense and souls,
> Of more pre-eminence than fish and fowls,
> Are masters of their females, and their lords:
> Then let your will attend on their accords.[95]

Society viewed women as 'the weaker vessel', a prey to their emotions and desires and lacking in reason. In this respect, they resembled headstrong jades and, as such, had to be curbed. Contemporaries defined the ideal woman as one who was submissive, discrete, charitable and virtuous. According to William Whateley in *A Bride Bush* (1617), they submitted 'with quietness, cheerfully, even as a well-broken horse turns at the least turning, stands at the least check of the rider's bridle, readily going and standing as he wishes that sits upon his back'.[96] When commenting on his fellow-parishioners at the end of the seventeenth century, Richard Gough of Myddle divided the women into two groups, those who exhibited such qualities and those who did not. He clearly favoured the former. William Watkins of Shotton Farm had a 'prudent, provident and discreet wife who is every way suitable for such an husband'. Similarly, Richard Hatchett had 'a loveing wife, a discreet woman, and an excellent housewife'. These women had been well-trained.[97]

To contemporaries, the smooth running of society depended upon men controlling the reins, for, if women were given their head, the country would soon descend into chaos. This was a real threat, part of a wider concern about a perceived breakdown in the social order in the critical years of the late sixteenth and early seventeenth centuries. In response, actions against scolds and termagents increased.[98] Communal censure of a disobedient wife or a hen-pecked husband often took the form of the shaming ritual of a riding, the 'mount' comprising a real horse or a pole known as a skimmington or stang.[99] To indicate the nature of the offence the man might be seated backwards, the couple set back to back or the male figure dressed in women's clothes. The punishment for scolds and shrews consisted of tying them in the cucking stool and ducking them or forcing them to wear the bridle or brank, which physically prevented them from speaking. Bridling, it seems, originated in the analogy between women and unruly horses and over time a metaphorical restraint became actual practice.[100]

The alarm felt at the perceived growth in the number of insubordinate women manifested itself in literary works as dramatists exploited an issue of popular concern. By inverting the normal relationship between the sexes and portraying it in a comic light, the audience could laugh at its own fears. Of course, at the end of the play the world had to be turned the right way up again, as in Shakespeare's *The Taming of the Shrew*. In it, Shakespeare contrasts the characters of the sisters, Katharina and Bianca,

> The one as famous for a scolding tongue
> As is the other for beauteous modesty.[101]

Petruchio's task is to tame Katharina, which he does in ways which, if they tend to mimic the training of a haggard falcon, also refer to the schooling of a young horse. In the final speech Katharina ostensibly executes a complete volte-face in her submission to her husband, though it is possible to read the passage in an ironic way. Conversely, Bianca has become assertive and independently-minded, displaying the faults of an ill-trained horse.[102]

Horse riding has an obvious sexual connotation. As Cleopatra exclaims in Shakespeare's *Anthony and Cleopatra*, 'O happy horse, to bear the weight of

Antony!' When in *Henry IV Part 1* Hotspur's wife asks him if he loves her, he replies,

> Come, wilt thou see me ride?
> And when I am a-horseback, I will swear
> I love thee infinitely.[103]

Likewise, the image of Hotspur, the male rider astride his horse, reflects the socially approved role of man as the dominant sexual partner. The link is strengthened by the long-established association between sexually active women and mares in season. Hence the relationship between horse and rider can be seen as a paradigm for the right ordering of a patriarchal society: rational man curbing his own base instincts and exercising control over irrational woman and her rampant libido.[104] Gough provides an example of the consequences that ensued when men did not give a moral lead in the case of the Tylers, the 'bad' family of Myddle. William Tyler's daughter, Elizabeth, 'was accounted a lewd woman, and had severall daughters who had noe better a repute ... Mary, the eldest ... was the comeliest of all the daughters, butt had no better a name than the rest. Her daughters are soe infamouse for their lewdnesse, that I even loathe to say more of them.'[105]

As expected, writers wrote about 'women on top', playing on male fears of cuckoldry and predatory women. Stories dealing with such themes were immensely popular. In his poem *Venus and Adonis*, Shakespeare uses the image of animal coupling as an overt sexual trope to illustrate Venus's aggressive carnality, thereby inverting conventional behaviour.[106] Venus's attempted seduction of Adonis, for example, is entwined with the sexual advances of his horse towards a 'breeding jennet, lusty, young and proud'. Venus uses the incident for her own purpose:

> Thus she replies: 'Thy palfrey, as he should
> Welcomes the warm approach of sweet desire
> ... And learn of him, I heartily beseech thee,
> To take advantage on presented joy.
> Though I were dumb, yet his proceedings teach thee.
> O learn to love!'

The image of the female cuckold was an even more common one.[107] Joseph Swetman's, *Arraignment of Lewd, Idle, Froward and Inconstant Women*, first published in 1615, had gone through nine further editions by 1634.[108] In Middleton's *A Chaste Maid in Cheapside* Allwit is a figure of fun because of his connivance in his wife's affair with Sir Walter Whorehound. Whereas he imagines that his status is enhanced by the liaison, it undermined his manhood for the other characters despise him for his inability to control his wife.[109]

In European terms a comparatively large sector of the English population rode horses, though those who owned one fluctuated according to economic circumstances and were always a minority group. Horses were expensive to maintain, even at a basic level. Besides, it was possible to hire a mount and during the course of the period the network of hackney services expanded along the postal roads and their branch lines. Few people below the level of the gentry possessed dedicated saddle horses and most of those who did used them in connexion with their work. The bulk of non-genteel riders therefore rode on all-purpose horses. When they had to mount a horse, farmers, for example, exchanged their cart saddle for a 'rode' saddle. Many made do with a padded cloth known as a pannell. There must have been an odd assortment of horses on the roads of early modern England. Moreover, as most of the animals had not been taught to move their legs in a way that was comfortable to the rider, travelling on horseback would have been painful.

On the other hand, virtually all the gentry rode and, if they did not, their status as a gentleman might be called into question. What is more, they did not merely possess general riding horses but maintained a variety of mounts, each with their own special function. Typically, they would keep hunters, pads, trotters and militia horses. A smaller group possessed 'great' or *manège* horses and racers. They spent large sums of money on their sport but felt the outlay justified as it projected an image of wealth and status. Riding a 'great horse' in public also made a political statement, showing the masses that their superiors were entitled, via their ability to maintain and control such a powerful and noble animal, to rule over them. They immortalized this image on canvas too. For a sophisticated horseman like William Cavendish, Duke of Newcastle, the dividing line in society was not so much the one between horse owners and non-horse owners or even between saddle horse owners and non saddle horse owners but between those who rode great horses and participated in the *manège* and those who did neither.

5

The Racecourse

Horse racing had been popular throughout the Roman world and the invaders brought it with them to Britain. It subsequently declined, though informal races did occur in the middle ages. It only became properly organized in early modern times.[1] The revival began in the early sixteenth century, mainly at the instigation of urban corporations, anxious to attract people to their towns and to encourage trade. The gentry, on the other hand, dominated the actual event. Interest in horse racing grew to such an extent that by the end of the seventeenth century racegoing had become firmly established in the social calendar. This was the period that witnessed the emergence of the modern racehorse, the thoroughbred, based on cross-breeding imported eastern and north African stallions with home-bred mares.[2] Horse racing was essentially an upper-class male pastime, but as the sport became fashionable the number of women at meetings increased. As for the crowds of ordinary people, they were bit players, an appreciative, if noisy and unruly, human backdrop against which the upper classes paraded their wealth and superior breeding.

In spite of gaps in the record the basic chronology of the development of horse racing in early modern England is reasonably clear. Initial references appear early in the sixteenth century. Reputedly, the first organized meeting took place at Chester in 1512 but the one held on Gatherley Moor near Richmond may have predated it. An entry in the registers of sanctuaries in Durham and Beverley records that, 'In June 1512, two men, probably on the race day, quarrelled on Gatherley Moor ... they were native of Richmond'.[3] Even so, progress was slow until the second half of the sixteenth century. By the time Elizabeth I came to the throne in 1558 the number of events amounted to about half a dozen. Thereafter, the pace picked up, further accelerating during the course of James I's reign. In 1625, the year that he died punters could choose from about three dozen venues. A few more were established under Charles I, that is in the period before the Civil Wars and Interregnum put a stop to new creations and, at times, even to racing itself. After the Restoration in 1660 the sport flourished once more under the patronage of Charles II, a keen racegoer and rider, and entered a period of rapid growth that lasted until the 1730s.[4] So dramatic was the rise in the number of meetings that in 1736 Francis Drake wrote that 'It is surprising to think to what a height this spirit of horse-racing is now arrived in this kingdom, when there is scarce a village so mean that has not a bit of plate raised once a year for this purpose'.[5]

In spite of Drake's hyperbole, he had a point: the market had become saturated by the end of the 1730s and this had a knock-on effect on the sport as a whole. Even a well-patronized, established meeting like Nottingham suffered. Looking back from 1751, Charles Deering observed that the gathering there 'could once have vyed with any course in the kingdom for a grand appearance of nobility … but since the great increase of horse-races it has rather dwindled'.[6] A shake-out was inevitable. This came in 1740 in the form of an Act 'to restrain and prevent the excessive increase in horse-races'.[7] Thereafter, with few exceptions, all prizes and matches had to be worth at least £50. As nine-tenths of the races in 1739 fell foul of the Act, this measure had serious consequences. By the end of the decade prize money had fallen by over one-third and the number of meetings by almost two-thirds. In Staffordshire Lichfield alone survived.[8] Recovery only occurred in the 1750s after the process of rationalization had begun to take effect and after money had started to flow back into the slimmed-down, healthier industry. At Nottingham, Deering credited the Act with helping the city to the extent that he thought that within a few years the race meeting there would 'recover its former lustre'.[9]

PATRONS AND VENUES

All horses galloped after a fashion, a facility which undoubtedly encouraged many riders to engage in impromptu but unrecorded races. Yet, as a sport, horse racing was almost entirely a genteel pastime and one that became more pronounced over time as participants required ever increasing sums of money to establish and maintain a racing stable. Horse racing, in fact, serves as a paradigm of the aristocratic lifestyle in early modern England, especially after the Restoration when the sport blossomed under the patronage of monarchs devoted to the sport. The turf provided a natural outlet for upper-class pretensions, for it was not only an expensive business but also demonstrably so. Oriental imports, brought in to improve the quality of the race horses, looked and were very expensive. They served as an obvious public manifestation of conspicuous consumption, as did the amount of money wagered on the outcome of a race. Moreover, as many of the elite competed in person, racing enabled them to display their horsemanship as well as their competitive edge. If they won a plate at a fashionable venue like Newmarket, they gained prestige and a prize to commemorate their achievement. On 5 April 1712 Lord Hervey, then at Newmarket, wrote to his wife to inform her of the exploits of one of his horses, which had won the Queen's Plate. With pride, he described how it had defeated all the horses of its age, thereby achieving 'immortal honour'.[10] The obsession with the bloodlines of racers must also have appealed to a class preoccupied with its own pedigree.[11]

The upper classes set up a number of races of their own. The Yorkshire gentry led the way, establishing a meeting at Kiplingcotes in the East Riding in 1555 and possibly even earlier. In 1619 their successors drew up the first formal set of rules, which served as the model for other racecourses.[12] By the early seventeenth century, they had begun to race at Hambleton, located on a plateau high in the Hambleton Hills in the North Riding. In his diary under 1613, Thomas Chaytor noted that Sir George Conyer's mare had beaten one belonging to Sir William Blakiston at Hambleton, the matter of fact tone indicating an established event.[13] As Yorkshire gentlemen bred the finest and fleetest horses in the country, the main purpose of these meetings was to try out their racers. They also enjoyed favourable natural conditions: a mild, moist climate that encouraged grass growth; calcium-rich terrain to enhance bone growth; and extensive tracts of open commons for training and racing. Of course, breeders elsewhere used races as a guide to form. In 1590, Edward Webbe commented that the local gentry came to Wallasey to try their horses, betting heavily on the outcome.[14] Webbe's observation also indicates that these events had wider appeal, providing a good day's sport, spiced up by the prospect of winning a prize and the opportunity to bet on the outcome. In his play *The English Traveller* (1633), Thomas Heywood has Dalavill, a young gentleman, describe Barnet, 'a place of great resort', on market day in the following words:

> Heere all the Countrey Gentlemen Appoint,
> A friendly meeting; some about affaires
> Of Consequence and Profit; Bargaine, Sale,
> And to conferre with Chap-men, some for pleasure,
> To match their Horses, Wager in their Dogs,
> Or trie their Hawkes; some to no other end,
> But onely meet good Company, discourse,
> Dine, drinke, and spend their Money.[15]

As horse racing became fashionable in the late seventeenth and early eighteenth centuries a few enthusiasts laid out courses on their own estates. Venues included Bramham in Yorkshire, Lynsted Park in Kent, Knowsley in Lancashire, Whittlebury in Northamptonshire and Worksop in Nottinghamshire.[16]

Meetings at spa towns also derived their inspiration from the gentry, since they grew out of their need for diversion as they whiled away the hours between taking the waters. Subsequently, they formed an essential feature of the entertainment package that developed as spa towns became leisure centres, catering for the fit rather than the sick. At Epsom the first recorded meeting took place in 1625, almost as soon as visitors started to arrive. By the time of the Restoration the venue had become a prominent feature of the racing calendar. Indeed, on 7 March 1660/1, it hosted the first meeting after the King's return from exile.[17] Because centres like Epsom and Tunbridge Wells presented a semi-rural aspect, especially in the early stages of growth, the authorities there emphasized the point as a means of enhancing their appeal. In this respect, the meetings were akin to the rural events referred to above. In terms of rank order within this particular hierarchy, Epsom's growing status put it on a par with leading venues like Hambleton and Wallasey. Ironically, as out of town spas centres such as Epsom and Tunbridge Wells developed the trappings of urbanity and prospered, Wallasey (and eventually even Hambleton) declined because of a lack of them.[18]

In the promotion of races, urban authorities were far more important than individual groups of gentlemen. Between 1500 and 1770 they put on 70 per cent of the events, a figure that increased as a result of the rationalization of the sport in the mid eighteenth century.[19] Their motives were primarily commercial, introducing a race meeting as a means of attracting crowds of people to the town and boosting the local economy. Significantly, races often coincided with the dates on which fairs took place. In June 1600 an examinant in a court case at Shrewsbury deposed that he had gone to the fair at Whitchurch on Whit Monday, staying overnight at Prees, a neighbouring parish, where the next day he watched the races on the heath.[20] At times, as in the cases of New Malton and Ripon, the connexion and the underlying motive is transparent. In 1692 New Malton held a fair on 6 September, the same day as the town sponsored a horse race. Horses competed for a second plate two days later. At Ripon the *London Gazette* in 1693 reported that two races would take place outside the town on 7 and 11 August, adding that the horse fair would follow directly afterwards. As the fairs at both towns enjoyed a national reputation for the sale of high-quality saddle horses, the authorities naturally wanted to encourage gentry, as potential buyers, to come along.[21]

The system of pre-registering by extending the lead-in period to a race added to the social and economic benefits of holding a meeting. At many venues owners had to enter and show their horses days or even weeks before an event. The horses might have to remain in the locality too. At Abingdon owners had to stable their horses in the town ten days in advance and display them in the market place a week before the race.[22] Introduced primarily as a means of preventing fraud or sharp practice, these measures also created interest in the meeting prior to the event itself. The build-up brought people into the town: grooms, accompanying their horses; owners sizing up the opposition, laying bets and arranging matches; and an assortment of racing enthusiasts and hangers-on. In November 1685 Sir John Newton travelled to Saltby in Lincolnshire several days before the race because he wanted to sell a valuable horse there.[23] Owners, racing their horses at leading venues like Newmarket and Epsom, established permanent stables and acquired houses in the towns, further increasing the impact of racing on the locality. Sir Robert Howard chose Ashtead Park as his training quarters because of the proximity of the house to Epsom Downs.[24]

Growing interest in horse racing should be seen as part of the so-called urban cultural renaissance of the seventeenth century. Throughout the country some towns developed as social centres, patronized by the gentry, drawn there by the increasing range of facilities and social and cultural activities on offer. In this respect, a race meeting formed part of a wider portfolio of activities designed to appeal to an affluent clientele: hence, the attraction of an urban venue to gentlemen of the turf. Towns also offered essential facilities such as stabling and accommodation, and eating and drinking establishments, at a level that non-urban centres could not possibly match. In addition, the involvement of urban officials in running the event and putting up money for prizes relieved the gentry of some of the chores of organization and the costs of financing a meeting.[25] In 1632, for instance, the corporation at Northampton agreed to fund annually a silver cup to be competed for at the newly inaugurated meeting at nearby Harlestone.[26]

Some gentlemen did involve themselves in a practical way. Wealthy individuals acted as patrons of their local racecourse, providing support by bestowing a prize, giving money or by associating themselves more intangibly with the event. In Elizabeth I's reign the Earl of Pembroke promoted racing at Salisbury and donated a golden bell worth £50 as a prize. The Earl of Essex provided a golden snaffle for another race. A century later the Earl of Derby, as well as holding meetings at Knowsley Park, supported the races at Ormskirk. In 1695 he funded a new race by giving a plate worth £20.[27] Groups of enthusiasts also contributed. In 1631 a number of Cheshire gentlemen subscribed £100 for a plate to be contested at Farndon near the Grosvenor estate at Eaton, the money collected being entrusted to Lord Cholmondeley. Later, the Blundells of Little Crosby Hall belonged to a similar group of genteel racegoers who helped run and finance the meetings at Great Crosby: they sat on race committees, occupied themselves with the administration and provided financial support in the form of annual subscriptions. In return, backers like these obtained one or two perks. When they entered a horse in a race at the meeting, for instance, they received preferential treatment.[28]

The success or failure of an enterprise depended upon the degree to which it attracted the upper classes to it. Not only did they provide money and know-how, and virtually all of the horses, they also spent the most and gave an event social distinction. In 1665, as a result of a dispute over the entry of horses at Chester, the gentry boycotted the meeting for a time. If they had not eventually relented, their action would have ended racing there.[29] The participation of the crown provided an additional fillip. In March 1611 the presence of the King and his court at

Croydon drew an 'immense' number of nobles, gentlemen and members of the general public to a great horse race there. In 1682 the corporation of Winchester, anxious to gain royal approval, promised Charles II that it would fund a new plate if he would grace the event with his presence. The race, they said, would attract many sporting nobles and gentlemen to attend him and to enjoy the leisure pursuits on the downs. The King not only accepted but also donated ten guineas to the plate, with the promise to do the same in subsequent years.[30]

However, upper-class racegoers were choosy and, as a result, a hierarchy of venues emerged. At the top Newmarket stood alone, its dominant position owing much to royal backing and, when that waned after 1714, to the continuing support of leading aristocratic racehorse owners. Racing at Newmarket dates from the reign of James I, who regularly went hunting in the area. The annual appearance of the court encouraged the pursuit of such activities as hunting, hawking and horse racing. Even so, it needed the patronage of Charles II to secure its ascendancy. He brought the court to Newmarket twice a year and helped formalize the racing season.[31] Although Charles II later thought about moving the centre of his activities to either Windsor or Winchester, nothing came of it. Similarly, while his successor, James II, favoured Winchester, he did not reign long enough for it seriously to challenge Newmarket's dominant position.[32] In the 1730s the value of races there accounted for about one-third of the total prize and match money contested. Newmarket also offered the most extensive racing programme in the country, based on spring and autumn meetings. Twice a year the cream of English society travelled to this small Cambridgeshire town where they could watch the pick of the nation's horses compete against each other.[33]

Below Newmarket, venues fell into distinct groups, with county meetings on the next rung down. Mostly, but not exclusively based in shire towns, they benefited from their position as the natural focuses of county society. The 'court list' of race meetings at these venues reads like a who's who of a county's resident elite, augmented by others coming in from outside. At Nottingham Defoe observed in the 1720s that 'here is such an assembly of gentlemen of quality, that not Bansted Down [Epsom], or New Market, produces better company … there we saw besides 11 or 12 noblemen, an infinite throng of gentlemen from all the countries around, nay even out of Scotland itself'.[34] Market town courses occupied the next layer. The county gentry did patronize them but in general they drew their clientele from a more confined area and from less exalted social levels. The distinction can be seen in the quality of the subscribers to prizes at the two sets of meetings.[35] The base of the pyramid comprised village meetings with purely local appeal and non-genteel patrons. Although numerous, they have left but a shadowy trace in the records. Several venues of this sort ringed London. These meetings were the ones targeted by the Act of 1740 and, as a consequence of this piece of legislation, their numbers fell dramatically.[36] In 1739 Cheny listed

357 races in England and Wales (and Edinburgh), though officials abandoned one or two of them due to a lack of entrants. In 1741 he recorded only 110 races in England and Wales with a further twenty-two in Ireland and two in Scotland.[37]

Ordinary people made up the bulk of the race-goers at most meetings and, given the openness of the courses, the elite could hardly keep them out. At first, the limited number of venues and the isolation of some of the sites made it difficult for the public at large to attend. As race meetings proliferated, especially in the late seventeenth and early eighteenth centuries, they became more accessible to a growing number of people. At Epsom, Pepys observed that on 25 November 1663 a great throng had gathered on the downs to watch the racing. Seven years later thousands of people witnessed a match at Newmarket, and in 1680 so many visitors came to the town that even those of the best quality had to share a chamber with strangers.[38] Ironically, while the act of 1740 reduced the number of small, plebeian events, it meant that the ordinary race-goer was more likely to frequent the fashionable courses. In response, the upper classes preserved their distance by erecting grandstands.[39]

The goods and services purchased by the punters at race meetings provided a boost to a town's economy, but this came at a price. While they welcomed the presence of the middling orders, urban authorities found the boisterous behaviour and uncouth manners of the masses embarrassing, especially if they were hoping to attract a high-class clientele. Thomas Heywood, writing of a forthcoming race at Halifax on 25 September 1678, reflected the tension between these two conflicting sentiments. He observed that 'it was given out that many races would be run, to gather the countrey to drink their ale, for it was hoped it would be a profitable to the town as a fair [and] the countrey came in freely'.[40] Evidently, Heywood thought that the emphasis on drink was bad. Besides, killjoys thought that the lower classes should be working rather than wasting their time at the races. The preamble to the 1740 Act emphasized this aspect of the measure, which aimed to curb 'the great number of races for small plates, prizes, or sums of money, [which] have contributed very much to the encouragement of idleness, to the impoverishment of many of the meaner sort'.[41]

HORSE RACING AND GENDER

Horse racing was essentially a masculine sport. It therefore reflected ideas, then current, about the relationship between man and horse and between men and women. *A fortiori*, racing did not merely demonstrate a man's control over a powerful animal, it also publicly displayed his success in channelling the horse's strength and energy towards a specific goal. Riding a race horse competitively provided a gentleman with the opportunity to show off his horsemanship, the acclaim he received being enhanced by the recognition that he was doing so under pressure. Racing was hazardous too, though this added to its appeal by boosting a rider's virile image. At a meeting at Harlestone in April 1672 Lord Sherard hurt himself in a fall in one race. A second rider lost consciousness and suffered extensive bruising, when unseated in another.[42] Many of the accidents occurred when driving hard for the line in a closely-fought race. At a race at Newmarket in October 1682 Colonel Aston and Sir Robert Gaer, locked together in the struggle, fell off their horses as they passed the finishing post. Both were seriously injured: Sir Robert broke his shoulder and Colonel Aston lay stunned on the ground, as if dead, for some time.[43] At the end of the period gentlemen were still riding in races, mainly in plates, but they were also sublimating their natural inclinations by employing jockeys to ride as extensions of themselves. Success lay in breeding a winner and in the receipt of money won in side stakes and bets. Gambling, itself an aspect of the male competitive urge, lay at the root of the change.

Men dominated all aspects of the business, from breeding and purchasing horses to racing them and betting on the outcome of a contest. Joined together by a common interest, *aficionados* consorted together not only at the racecourse but off it as well. Nowhere was this more apparent than at Newmarket, a town devoted almost entirely to horse racing. Defoe, who compared a race day there with the Circus Maximus in Ancient Rome, noted that the only ladies present were the wives of local gentlemen and that they went home directly afterwards.[44] Unaccompanied visiting gentry, on the other hand, headed for the coffee houses and gaming tables, and perhaps to dance with any available young lady. On 21 October 1671 John Evelyn, having just arrived at Newmarket, recorded in his diary that he had 'found the jolly blades, racing, dauncing, feasting & revelling, more resembling a luxurious & abandon'd rout, than a Christian Court'. He also noted in a censorious tone that the Duke of Buckingham was there with his mistress, 'the impudent woman, the Countesse of Shrewsbury'.[45] Lady Hervey, whose husband was a member of the racing set at court at the turn of the seventeenth century, was one of those who suffered from their spouse's addiction to the turf. Lord Hervey's absences occasionally pricked his conscience. On 5 April 1712 he wrote to his wife from Newmarket to say that he was almost indifferent to the result of the forthcoming race involving his horse, Ladythighs. If it lost, he promised, he would never make another match and then he would never have to part from her for such a trivial pursuit. It did lose, but in August he attended a meeting at Quainton Meadow near Aylesbury where Flanderkins beat all the horses of its age to win the 200 guineas stakes. In April 1713, moreover, he was back at Newmarket to see it win the Queen's Plate for the second time.[46]

The men-only environment, typical of early race meetings, is not surprising. Owners, involved in male oriented 'trials of strength', were preoccupied with testing their horses and making side-bets on the result. If they rode the horse themselves, this only narrowed their focus. The earls (later dukes) of Rutland bred racehorses at their Helmsley estate in Yorkshire in the late sixteenth and early seventeenth centuries and made use of local races to assess the capabilities of their mounts. Writing from Helmsley in May 1582, John Manners told his brother, the Earl of Rutland, that he was going to Gatherley to see which horses ran best.[47] He was doing it for recreational purposes, he wrote, but the impression gained is that he did not take his wife with him. A note in the corporation minutes of Salisbury indicates that four earls, three lords, five knights and a number of gentlemen attended a race there in March 1584 but makes no mention of ladies.[48] In Shakespeare's *Cymbeline* Innogen, the king's daughter, exclaims:

> I have heard of riding wagers
> Where horses have been nimbler than the sands
> That run i' the clock's behalf.[49]

This implies that, although she knew of their existence, she had not attended a race.

The type of ancillary sports put on at race meetings similarly reflects the predominantly male environment. Because racecourses required large open spaces their surroundings provided suitable facilities for hunting, hawking and coursing. James I hunted while at a race meeting at Lincoln in 1617 and mixed the two sports at Newmarket. Charles II hunted, hawked and coursed while at Newmarket for the racing. On 2 October 1668 he hunted the hare in the morning and in afternoon hawked and coursed with his greyhounds. Several meetings, as at Lilly Hoo, Ripon and Richmond (Yorkshire) in the 1690s, had races for hunters.[50] Cockfighting also featured prominently in the list of diversions. Charles II attended matches or 'mains', where, because of the mass appeal of the sport, he mingled with people from diverse backgrounds.[51] At social centres matches regularly took place throughout the season but at smaller venues they were put on especially for race-goers. Adverts for forthcoming races in the *London Gazette* often mentioned them, a clear sign of their popularity and their value as an additional draw. At Whitchurch in 1696 there was 'great cocking all week'. In 1699 visitors to Swaffham could enjoy three days of cockfighting, probably at the George Inn, the venue in 1737.[52] More than hunting, cockfighting came under attack from the theriophilic lobby and there were signs that the propaganda was beginning to have some effect by the middle of the eighteenth century. The authorities pulled down Beverley's cockpit in about 1730.[53]

Gradually the situation changed. As leisure facilities improved, and as race-going became part of the social round, women turned up in increasing numbers. Even if they had little interest in the sport, they could occupy themselves with other forms of entertainment in the daytime and rejoin the men at the evening functions. At the beginning of the eighteenth century, for instance, Lady Pye looked forward to the races at nearby Nottingham but mainly for the company she found there. Increasingly, the specific needs of women like her had to be catered for. Indeed, in July 1755 a member of the Wodehouse family of Kimberley, publicizing the race meeting at Swaffham, remarked to his correspondent that 'there is nothing will make Swaffham races florish so much as making 'em commodious for the Fair Sex'.[54] This is not to say that some women did not enjoy the sport. At Newmarket in 1669 ladies on horseback formed part of the cavalcade that tracked the racers as they neared the finish. More usually, they watched from a coach. Of Epsom in the 1720s, Defoe wrote that on race days Banstead Downs were 'covered with coaches and ladies, and an innumerable company of horsemen, as well gentlemen and citizens, attending the sport'.[55]

Naturally, race meetings held in towns that were developing as social centres were able to provide better facilities than others elsewhere. The focal point for off-course social activity was the building which served as a venue for the evening entertainments, which might include balls, concerts, recitals and drama productions. For most of the period the company had to make do with whatever was available, whether at the town or guild hall, or at an inn. The earliest custom-built assembly rooms seem to date from Charles II's reign, though they did not become numerous until the turn of the century. Epsom's assembly rooms were built in about 1692. At Bath Celia Fiennes noted in 1698 that, since her last visit, the authorities had erected 'a very fine Hall which is set on stone pillars which they use for balls and dancing'.[56] Additional social events were put on in race week. At Shrewsbury in 1729 the authorities sponsored a concert in the Guildhall for the duration of the races. At Epsom the company could attend a ball in the assembly rooms every evening during the season.[57] The atmosphere of a town at race-time is admirably summed up by Simon Scrope, writing in 1730 in anticipation of going to a meeting at York.[58]

> Tomorrow we set out for York to see the new horse course lately made on Knavesmire, and to join in the great doings of the week, the like of which no town or city can compare with for gaiety, sport and companie all of one mind. Every year there be more noble lords, gentle dames, and commoners of high and low degree at York for the races, the cockings, assemblies, and meetings of horse-coursers and hunters, all of one mind, looking on York as the place above all others for sports and sportsmen.

The amenities at the market town meetings were less impressive but, as Wodehouse observed, it paid to upgrade them. In fact, Swaffham (and Bungay) introduced race assemblies in 1737.[59] Similarly, efforts were made to improve refreshment facilities, put under considerable strain when a throng of race-goers descended on a small town. Adverts in the *London Gazette* regularly made specific reference to the provision of ordinaries at race-time in order to allay punters' fears that they would not be able to find anything to eat or drink. At Lilly Hoo near Hitchen in the 1690s the organizers promised race-goers a good meal at the Running Horses.[60]

HORSE RACING AND POLITICS

Horse racing did have its critics. On a general level, Puritans, intent on the 'reform of manners', deemed recreational activities to be frivolous and a misuse of time that could be better spent in edifying work.[61] Horse racing was particularly suspect. In Northamptonshire, Richard Samwell viewed the establishment of a race meeting at Harlestone with foreboding, claiming that 'many inconsiderate young men' would be utterly ruined by the 'desperate expense'.[62] Puritans and the like were also prominent in condemning cruelty in the sport. In 1683 the quasi-Quaker Thomas Tryon condemned it for this reason, writing that, 'We can't justifie the over-straining (in such manner as is commonly practised) and over-forcing Creatures, otherwise so truly usefull, beyond their strength'.[63] In one race in Lancashire, held on 18 March 1671/2, Wagtail, belonging to Mr Egerton, won but in the process was 'bloodied from shoulder to flank'. This was a common experience.[64] For many, gambling, with its inducement to cheat, was the problem. In his memoirs, Edward Lord Herbert archly wrote that he disliked horse racing, 'being much Cheating in that kynde'.[65]

In the Interregnum (1649–60) the aims of the godly revolution coincided with the dictates of state. In particular, the government feared that Royalists meeting at horse races were plotting rebellion. On 24 February 1654/5 the Council of State, acting on intelligence of an imminent royalist rising, banned all horse races in the country for six months. The ordinance was renewed from time to time and, even if the authorities did not enforce it rigorously and admitted exceptions, the measure did have a considerable impact on the sport.[66] Occasionally, action was taken to suppress a meeting: in Lancashire in December 1655 Major-General Worsley arrested a number of racegoers and in July 1656 Major-General Barkstead broke up a gathering on Hackney Marsh. In September 1656 Cromwell declared that the major-generals had been 'more effectual towards the discountenancing of vice and settling of religion than anything done these fifty years', adding that that they had successfully put down 'horse races, cockfightings and the like'.[67]

Politics and horse racing continued to mix in the post-Restoration period, when it became an element in the struggle between the Whigs and Tories. In spring 1681 the Newmarket meeting fell foul of the Whig-induced Exclusion Crisis and the King's response to it. On 18 January Charles II dissolved Parliament and summoned a new one to meet in the Tory stronghold of Oxford. On his way there in March he made a detour to Burford to enjoy the racing.[68] Determined to overawe his Whig opponents, Charles II persuaded the leading racehorse owners to come to Burford with their horses and entourages and in doing so getting them to abandon the meeting at Newmarket. Eighteen months later, with the crisis still fresh in the memory, the Tory race-goers at Lichfield cold-shouldered the favoured Whig successor to the throne, the Duke of Monmouth, who was passing through on his way to a meeting at Wallasey. A large crowd of people had gathered at Wallasey, leading Tories to suspect a Whig conspiracy, especially as two of the Duke's leading supporters, Lords Delamere and Macclesfield, resided in the county. The Cheshire Tories responded by banding together to prevent any 'ill attempts' under cover of a rival race in the Forest of Delamere. Eighty gentlemen and two thousand others attended the meeting, described as 'a private and surreptitious mobilisation of the militia'. Blocked politically, the Whigs achieved a sporting success when a 'ringer' from Lord Wharton's celebrated stud easily won the race.[69]

If this sounds petty, the underlying tensions were real. News of Monmouth's victory in the plate at Wallasey led to rioting in Chester by Whig supporters. The mob lit bonfires, proclaimed their backing for Monmouth and vandalized the homes of local Tories. The mayor, viewed as Monmouth's creature, did nothing.[70] From time to time trouble flared up again, notably in the aftermath of the Jacobite rebellion of 1745. In the elections of spring 1747, for instance, the Whigs won a surprising victory at Lichfield in what was normally a solid Tory constituency and planned a celebration at the September races there. In the event, the gathering degenerated into a riot. During the course of the affray hotheads assaulted the Whig leader, the Duke of Bedford. A couple of weeks later, on 23 September, the Tories called an assembly in the city to discuss plans for a rival meeting. It turned into a Jacobite demonstration, in which mobs from Birmingham and Burton toasted the Pretender and sang treasonable songs. As a result, for the next six years the Tories held their own event, a week before the traditional, Whig-dominated one. Naturally, each side strove to outdo the other one in terms of clientele and spectacle.[71]

THE RACECOURSE

Topographically, there was little difference between town racecourses and other venues. Apart from those set in parkland, they were mostly located on stretches of unfenced common ground, perhaps several miles away from the town itself. Amesbury's course lay near Stonehenge and was often so designated.[72] The names often indicate the location and type of ground: riverside at Quainton Meadow (Aylesbury) and Chilton Mead (Abingdon); moorland at High Brasside Moor (Durham) and Monkton Moor (Ripon); downland at Banstead Downs

(Epsom) and Winchester Downs (Winchester), and wolds at Langton Wolds (New Malton).[73] The best locations were those with springy turf and light soils, hence the preference for chalk downland sites as at Epsom and Newmarket or on the wolds as at Hambleton and New Malton. Hambleton prospered because, although far from any town and at a thousand feet's elevation, it provided the owners of studs in the area with a flat three miles stretch of natural turf that rarely dried out even in summer.[74] Some venues changed their sites, either to bring them closer to the towns or to get round problems at the old location. In 1709 the corporation at York moved the racecourse from the Forest of Galtres to Clifton Ings, situated close to the city along the River Ouse. This proved unsatisfactory too because of the marshy nature of the ground and the threat of inundation. In 1729, therefore, the corporation, in response to a resolution of the assembly rooms committee, set in motion plans to move to the present Knavesmire site. The first race took place there on 16 August 1731.[75]

Most racecourses required little preparation for an event. All that was needed were posts or flags to mark out the course. In the early eighteenth century Nicholas Blundell regularly helped set out the track on Crosby Marsh before a meeting, basically telling the workmen where to put the posts. At Newmarket, the officials used tall wooden posts, painted white and placed at regular intervals, the last one having a flag on it to denote the finish. In 1690 the corporation at Beverley agreed to make available a piece of ground at Westwood and ordered surveyors to plan the course and mark it with posts.[76] Running costs were therefore low. When Queen Anne founded Ascot in 1711 she paid £558 19s. 5d. for the course itself but only £15 2s. 8d. to make and fix the posts and £2 15s. for painting them.[77] Some courses possessed rubbing houses, where grooms used scrapers to remove the sweat from horses running in a series of heats. At Newmarket they were set at the fifth to eighth mile posts. The only other essential piece of equipment was a weighing post. In 1725 the one at Doncaster lay in a clump of trees and, according to Lord Oxford, looked like a gallows.[78]

The layout of the Hambleton course, a long straight track, was typical of many early sites, an indication that they were designed with the participants rather than the spectators in mind. Epsom's course was called Banstead Downs after the parish where the race started, several miles from the finish on Epsom Downs. At Newmarket the original course began at Fleam Dyke, eight miles away from the winning post on the edge of the town. Chester's course on the Roodee was unusual in that it covered a compact area of ground just outside the city gate. Races consisted of five laps of the course and this enabled spectators fully to follow the fortunes of the horses – and their bets.[79] By the end of the period viewing conditions had improved at a number of venues, notably by shortening the length of races and increasing the number of circular courses at the expense of linear ones. Changes tended to occur after the Restoration and reflected increasing interest in horse racing as a fashionable spectator sport. At Newmarket in 1665 the authorities created the Round Course, three miles six furlongs long, in order to bring the starting and finishing lines of the heats closer together. A few years later they laid out the four mile Duke's Course, with a start conveniently sited nearer the town. The lay-out at Winchester in 1682 was similar, horses competing in the plates running three times around the Round Course. At Great Crosby in 1683 William Blundell, acting in an official capacity, altered the course so that the race would start and finish in the same place. As the horses ran twice round a course less than two miles in extent, they were in view for most of the race.[80]

For most of the period racegoers watched the proceedings on foot, astride a horse or from a carriage. A temporary stand might be erected if the monarch were attending a meeting, as at Croydon in the 1580s or at Lincoln in 1617. At the latter event the corporation ensured that James I had a completely uninterrupted view by railing off the last quarter mile of the course too. Evelyn described the stand he saw on Salisbury's course in 1654 as like a pergola, which suggests a temporary wooden edifice.[81] A picture showing Charles II watching a race at Datchet Ferry near Windsor reveals what these structures looked like. At Newmarket Charles II could view the races from a permanent stand, put up in 1678.[82] Most racecourses did not acquire one until well into the eighteenth century, as the elite sought to distance themselves from the masses: examples include those at Doncaster (1751), York (1755), Manchester (c. 1760), Newmarket (1760s), Stamford (1766) and Beverley (1767).[83] In this respect, grandstands provided a social space akin to that of the assembly rooms. They too formed part of the social round, a place to go to and be seen. There the elite met each other and mingled in an environment that resembled an exclusive club. Even those who had no interest in the racing had to attend. Racing enthusiasts, naturally, haunted the place. At Great Crosby the stand that Lord Molyneux of Sefton built at the beginning of the eighteenth century was a favourite meeting place for his circle of gentlemen race-goers, who gathered there to watch the horses training or racing or to engage in a spot of shooting practice. On 20 November Nicholas Blundell wrote that he went to the New Stand to meet Mr Molyneux to go 'a shooting'. When he and Sir James Poole arrived there at midday Molyneux treated them to wine and ale.[84]

RACES, PRIZES AND PATRONS

The centrepieces of the town meetings were the plates, in which riders competed for a prize, typically a silver bell but perhaps some other item in gold or silver. By the end of the seventeenth century gold cups had tended to replace bells as the prize at prestigious meetings.[85] Depending upon the number of horses running, the officials organized the plates on a knock-out basis or as a series of heats. Horses distanced in a race took no further part in the proceedings. Even at Newmarket entries might be thin, perhaps four or five, so horses had to run repeatedly against each other. Where known, fields there ranged between three and eight between 1680 and 1719.[86] Away from headquarters few races operated a knock-out system, though the *London Gazette* advertised one at Epsom in November 1691. At the same time Durham, Richmond in Yorkshire and Ripon awarded plates for victory in a single race.[87] The format meant that the basic attribute needed by horses entered in plates was stamina. Typically, horses raced over four-mile courses, although some extended to six or eight miles. Horses contesting Lady Grantham's Plate at Lincoln in the 1690s ran three heats over the long course.[88] As most horses had to run more than once a day, the mileage soon mounted up. Between races, horses were rubbed down and ridden back to the start, with scarcely enough time for them to recover. At Newmarket and Winchester the rules allowed a half an hour between heats.[89] Adverse conditions could add to the problems. In a race, probably at Nottingham on 31 July 1662, the Duke of Newcastle's horse beat one belonging to Sir Henry Evorett, having been behind for the first three miles. As Sir Henry's horse was only a little nag, it could not maintain its pace on the heavy, ploughed up ground.[90]

Many meetings began with a single plate which, for a group of local gentlemen-breeders interested in trying out their horses, ensured a full afternoon's sport. As the sport widened its appeal, organizers sought to capitalize on its popularity by putting on more races. This was a notable feature of the racing scene from the late seventeenth century onwards. To coincide with the move to a new venue, the corporation at York in 1708 agreed to donate £15 per annum towards a new plate, hoping this would encourage the gentry to top up the sum and to enter their horses in the new race. The following year it asked the citizens to contribute money for the purchase of five plates. Consequently, between 1710 and 1712 the number of race days in the city doubled from three to six.[91] Several towns put on a second event at a different time of the year: in the 1690s Durham's meetings took place in late spring and late summer, with four races spread over six days. At Lilly Hoo (near Hitchin) in 1699 the organizers provided two plates for a new meeting on 29 March, complementing the traditional September date.[92] Often the authorities aimed to provide variety in terms of the horses entered, imposing restrictions according to age, sex, height, type and race record. Galloway plates, limited to horses below a certain height (fourteen hands at the most), were common throughout the country. At the meeting at Ormskirk on 10–11 July 1688 the great horse plate and the town plate for Galloways provided the first day's sport. The following day owners competed for the customary second plate and for a new plate (worth £10) for young horses no older than six.[93] As the racing calendar filled out, problems of congestion occurred. In 1713, for instance, the organizers moved the Queen's plates at York to other days in order to avoid a clash with the meeting at Nottingham.[94] An overcrowded fixture list not only affected attendance but also spread the supply of horses too thinly.

Apart from the possibility of making money from side bets, owners earned comparatively little in prizes. Although amounts varied, even in the late seventeenth and early eighteenth centuries the average plate was only worth £20. Few were valued at £100 or more. Small prizes undoubtedly had a deterrent effect, reducing the number of owners willing to enter their horses in races. The commentator, reporting the race between Newcastle and Evorett referred to above, observed that 'many finer horses were there but the owners would not put them in for so small a thing as a cup of £5'. Unless winning owners melted down the plate, they received no direct financial reward from their victory. Indeed, as the rules of some races stipulated that they had to return the trophy the following year, they might not be able to keep it as an investment.[95] In strictly monetary terms, the second-placed owner did better. Traditionally, he collected the stake money, amounting to a few pounds, which hardly defrayed the costs incurred.[96] Acclaim among one's peers, achieved by winning a race and a coveted trophy, had to be the main motive, together with the opportunity to lay a bet on the outcome.

By the early eighteenth century some owners were becoming disenchanted with the then current system of plate racing. While they enjoyed the credit and esteem which success brought them, they started to count the cost. They felt, in essence, that they were subsidizing what had become a leisure pursuit for the masses, as well as providing economic benefits for the host town.[97] In short, they gained an insufficient return on their outlay. In terms of prize money, contribution races, an innovation of the early eighteenth century, improved the situation by offering the owners the prospect of a reasonable return. Subscribers contributed a certain sum of money for a fixed number of years and for this investment they were entitled to enter a horse in the annual race. The winner took the pool. Newmarket introduced one in October 1709, the sum varying in subsequent years between £200 and 220 guineas. At Richmond in Yorkshire in 1724 the subscription race, worth 125 guineas, attracted a number of the most prominent northern breeders.[98] A second type of race comprised head-to-head matches. These originated in informal contests that took place in the middle ages and continued into the early modern period. In London, Hyde Park was a popular venue.[99] As the number of organized race meetings grew during the course of the sixteenth and seventeenth centuries, gentlemen made use of them as a place where they could match one horse against another. After 1660, in a handful of places where the aristocratic connections were strong, such contests dominated the racing scene. At Newmarket matches comprised nine-tenths (89.9 per cent) of the 366 recorded races that took place between 1680 and 1719.[100] At most venues matches were fewer and fitted around the plates. Reporting the north-western racing scene in the early eighteenth century, Nicholas Blundell refers to fourteen matches and twenty-nine plates at six different venues: Aughton Moor, Great Crosby, Crosby Marsh, Childhall, Knowsley Park and Ormskirk.[101] Even so, a match between two fine racehorses with rich backers still attracted attention and drew in the crowds.

TABLE 7: Distances run and weights carried, Newmarket 1680–1719

	Distance (in miles)				Weight (in stones)				
	1680–99		1700–19			1680–99		1700–19	
miles	no.	per cent	no.	per cent	weight	no.	per cent	no.	per cent
1	3	6.7	6	3	Under 6	4	4.3	6	1.7
2	0	0	1	0.5	6	4	4.3	0	0
3	1	2.2	6	3	7	7	7.5	10	2.9
4	26	57.8	149	75.6	8	31	33.3	240	69.2
5	2	4.4	9	4.6	9	38	40.9	30	8.6
6	10	22.2	21	10.6	10	6	6.5	36	10.4
7	1	2.2	0	0	11	2	2.2	12	3.5
8	1	2.2	4	2	12	1	1.1	9	2.6
Over 8	1	2.2	1	0.5	13+	0	0	4	1.2
Totals	45	100	197	100	100	93	100	347	100

Source: J.B. Muir, *Ye Olde New=Markitt Calendar* (London, 1892)

Typically, horses in matches raced over four miles, the same as in plates (table 7).[102] The main distinction lay in the format of the event, normally a single race. Occasionally, the horses ran the best of three heats, though they might take place on separate days, as in the match between the Duke of Devonshire and Sir Roger Mostyn in October 1699.[103] Horses did compete over longer distances but at Newmarket at least the trend was in the opposite direction. Races of over six miles were a rarity (table 7). At the same time sprints over the Rowley Mile began, the name deriving from Charles II's nickname. Horses still required stamina, for they often ran repeatedly in races within a few days of each other. In 1705 Lord Hervey's horse, Wenn, ran five times within a month at Newmarket, winning four of its races. It suffered the only defeat of its career on 23 April when Lord

Kingston's mare, Piping Peg, triumphed, reversing the result of races run eight and fourteen days earlier.[104] On 19 September 1726 Nicholas Blundell wrote in his diary that Mr Maikings's bay mare had beaten Robert Rigby's black mare at Crosby, adding, "Tis the third Race I have seen her winn since the 28 of last Month".[105]

Victory in a match was far more profitable to the owner than winning a plate. At Newmarket, the median stake ventured in the years 1680–99 amounted to 300 guineas. In the next twenty years it averaged 200 guineas, reflecting intensification of the racing rather than a diminution of the money circulating in the sport (table 8). Indeed, on 19 May 1707 Mr Young's and Lord Granby's horses raced for a purse of 3,000 guineas, 1,000 guineas more than William III and the Duke of Somerset had staked on the outcome of a match on 9 April 1698.[106] While provincial meetings could not match such large amounts of money, owners at gentry-sponsored venues like Hambleton and Wallasey might put up considerable sums. On 2 August 1681, for instance, Sir George Grosvenor's and Lord Brandon's horses ran at Wallasey for a purse of £200. In 1699, presumably as a result of a private wager, horses raced the twelve miles between Norwich and Bungay for a purse of 200 guineas.[107]

TABLE 8: Value (in guineas) of matches run at Newmarket, 1680–1719

value	1680–99 no.	1680–99 per cent	1700–19 no.	1700–19 per cent
under 59	1	1.8	1	0.5
50 to 99	1	1.8	9	4.4
100 to 199	13	23.2	77	37.4
200 to 299	11	19.6	71	34.5
300 to 499	8	14.3	31	15.0
500–699	17	30.4	12	5.8
700–999	1	1.8	0	0
1000+	4	7.1	5	2.4
Total	56	100	206	100
median	£300		£200	
Other	100 qrs. oats			

Source: J.B. Muir, Ye Olde New=Markitt Calendar (London, 1892).

At the end of the period gentlemen were still riding regularly in races. Significantly, they were more likely to appear in plates, which were usually set at higher weights and which offered them the opportunity to enhance their reputation. Charles II rode and won plates at Newmarket, purely, it was stressed, on his horsemanship. Lord Hervey rode Danvers to victory in the Newmarket Gold Tumbler in April 1691 and the following year won Burford's Town Plate astride Bald Manners.[108] As the regulations often stipulated that only gentlemen could participate in an event, it also enabled them to avoid racing against lower-class 'professionals'. At Newmarket, only gentlemen could enter the King's Plate of 100 guineas, riding horses carrying twelve stones, the same weight as in the Town Plate. On the other hand, the Nobles' Contribution Plate, founded in 1709, was a race for six-year-old horses carrying ten stones. In 1717 it became a race for five-year-old horses at nine stones, indicating the use of hirelings.[109] In terms of weight alone ten stones probably marked the dividing line. In a ten-stone race held on Melksham Common in 1689 the rules specifically allowed servants to ride. Yet owners did race at this weight. In a match at Liverpool on 18 July 1617 the riders, Mr Nicholas Assheton's cousin and Sir Richard Molyneux, agreed to ride as light as they could, so Sir Richard weighed in at ten stones. Moreover, Hore's list includes a ten-stone plate at Hurley in 1689 which only gentlemen-riders could enter.[110]

Gentlemen might ride in matches too, though the trend towards lighter, non-gentlemen riders is apparent in table 7. Owners might set some of the races at ten stones so that they could ride, but the most significant aspect of the table is the tremendous increase in the number of races fixed at below that weight. Indeed, the proportion of riders weighing under nine stones rose dramatically in the opening years of the eighteenth century, implying the emergence of a class of specialist riders. Owners still made use of boys, called feathers, a practice that went back to Henry VIII's reign.[111] Sometimes, both riders were boys, as in a match between the Honourable Bernard Howard's bay nag and Mr Walter's gelding at Newmarket in May 1681. On other occasions one horse had a feather on board to give it a weight advantage against a horse of superior quality. To make matches for his stallion, Careless, the best horse of its generation, Lord Wharton often had to give away several stones in weight. On 11 April 1698, for instance, he matched him with William III's horse, Stiff Dick, at nine stones to a feather over five miles for a stake of 500 guineas. Stiff Dick started at seven to four against, such was Careless's reputation, and his backers therefore did extremely well when it defeated the favourite. Lord Hervey won £800.[112] Give and take matches, in which racers received extra weight according to age and size, offered another way of handicapping horses. The principle is explained in a match between Mr Hervey's Nonpareille and Mr Tregonwell Frampton's Hall at Newmarket on 1 May 1712. Frampton agreed that Hall should carry 8 stones 4 lbs and would allow weight for inches.[113] Muir's Newmarket list includes twelve give and take matches between 1708 and 1717.

In March 1675, Sir Robert Carr, Chancellor of the Duchy of Lancaster and racehorse owner, wrote a dispatch to Secretary Conway at Whitehall, reporting on the racing at Newmarket. His observation that 'We are here hot in our wagers but cold in our carcasses' reflects the hold that gambling was exerting on the sport by that date. He included himself in this statement, made as betting on the forthcoming match between Lusty and Nutmeg was in full swing. In his next letter, written on 18 March, the day after the race, he informed Conway of the result, laconically acknowledging that 'we were all undone yesterday, Lustie Lord Montacute's Horse being sadly beaten'.[114] Taken together, these letters sum up the appeal of horse racing to the upper classes and provide an insight into the way they responded to the vagaries of good and bad fortune inherent in the sport. Racing provided an ideal form of entertainment for the elite, bringing excitement to the lives of a group of people with the means to indulge their every whim, especially if they ventured money in amounts which even they found significant. They liked to win, as Lord Hervey reveals in his diary, but in public had to do so in a gracious manner.[115] Besides, losses, as Carr indicates, had to be borne stoically, as if they were of no account to a person of such wealth and breeding. Defoe noted the reaction of Sir Tregonwell Frampton, who reputedly lost 1,000 guineas one day and then won 2,000 guineas the next, 'and so alternatively he made as light of throwing away five hundred or one thousand pounds at a time, as other men do of their pocket-money, and as perfectly calm, cheerful, and unconcerned, when he had lost one thousand pounds, as when he had won it'.[116]

The small coterie of wealthy racehorse owners who surrounded monarchs like Charles II and William III, and who dominated the sport in the late seventeenth and early eighteenth centuries, wagered huge sums on the outcome of a race, in addition to the stake money they paid whenever one of their horses ran. Although possessed of a relatively small patrimony, Frampton, as William III's racing master, was a central figure in this group. A fine judge of form, he was the most successful 'plunger' of the time and pulled off some remarkable betting coups, including the one when Lusty beat Nutmeg in 1675. On another occasion (23 April 1698), Frampton backed the King's horse, Turk, at two to one against, when it beat Lord Carlisle's Spot. Turk won easily and 'the swells lost a lot of money'.[117] Considerable sums of money might change hands at lesser meetings too. In September 1673 Thomas Isham noted in his diary that a notable horse race had taken place at Rothwell and that, although only three horses had started, there had been heavy betting on the event. On the other hand, Nicholas Blundell's diary, recording his visits to north-western racecourses, reveals more modest outlays. On 13 October 1720, for instance, he records in his diary that he won some money, presumably a few pounds, from Jack Sefton at a match on Crosby Marsh.[118]

Unfortunately, the horse racing fraternity did not always display the nobility of spirit required of members of their class and in the eagerness to win some individuals stooped to deceit and trickery. In *Hide Park* (1632) James Shirley satirizes the double dealing and sharp practice of race-goers, while at the same time using the event to make a more general comment on the human condition.[119] Defoe, writing almost a century later, was more pointed. Race-goers at Newmarket, he observed:

> were all so intent, so eager, so busy upon the sharping part of the sport, their wagers and debts, that to me they seemed just as so many horse-coursers in Smithfield, descending (the greatest of them) from their high dignity and quality, to picking one another's pockets, and biting one another as much as possible, and that with such eagerness, as that it might be said they acted without respect to faith, honour, or good manners.[120]

Although cheating was as old as horse racing itself, the sheer volume of money staked in the post-Restoration period inevitably had an impact on the probity of the sport. Gambling had a definite corrupting influence. Races were fixed (crimped), providing those with insider knowledge with the chance of making a betting coup. Sir Robert Fagg, a leading figure in the racing scene at the opening of the eighteenth century, reputedly was adept in the art of deception. According to Defoe, 'he scarce ever produced a horse but he looked like what he was not … and just in this manner he bit some of the greatest gamesters in the field'.[121] Riders might pull a horse during a race in order to lengthen the odds on the next outing or deliberately lose a race by falling off. In a race at York on 13 August 1713 the rider of Crutches jumped off the horse near the distance post when in the lead. As bumping and boring appeared to be part of the cut and thrust of the contest, a skilled practitioner could make it appear accidental. If racing was not a physical contact sport, contests could, nonetheless, turn into running battles with jockeys lashing at each other with their whips. In a match between Mr Hervey's Lobcock and the Duke of Devonshire's Looby, Lobcock won a bruising eight mile encounter after 'great working, jostling and crossing'. Hervey declared that this victory pleased him more than any other match. In another race, held at Nottingham in 1714, Mr Holbeck's horse broke its shoulder, reputedly because another horse had deliberately crossed its path.[122] In a literary allusion, Jockey, a character in *Hide Park*, tells his associates, who are planning a wager, to bet on him in spite of the odds. He darkly hints at the means, 'if I get within his quarters let me alone'. Sure enough, his opponent, Venture, fell off his horse.[123] Gentlemen-riders were not immune from chicanery. At Newmarket in 1702 Sir John Parsons and Mr Thomas Pulleine had to rerun their race because Sir John had seized the other's bridle.[124] The growing number of hired jockeys in the sport at this time, however, was a contributory factor in this unfortunate development. Not only were they more susceptible to a bribe but, as paid employees, they were dependent upon their wages and had to follow their master's orders. They therefore had to adopt a win (or, alternatively, lose) at all costs attitude, often to the detriment of the horse. In 1698 Lobcock's jockey whipped and spurred the horse 'from cheek to flank' while Looby went lame from the effort.[125] At the end of the eighteenth century Lawrence wrote of a young jockey, engaged to ride a horse, which he knew from experience would not win the race. When he told the owner so, the latter replied, 'Make him win, or cut his bloody entrails out – Mark – if you don't give him his belly full of whip you never ride again for me – I'll find horse, if you'll find whip and spur'.[126]

THE INFUSION OF EASTERN AND NORTH AFRICAN BLOOD

Imported oriental horses provided an essential ingredient in the evolution of the thoroughbred in the late seventeenth and early eighteenth centuries. Contemporaries wrote fulsomely about these foreign breeds, though they might have their individual preference. Blundeville recommended using Barbary or Turcoman (including Arabian) stallions to cover mares of a similar stature. He praised Barbs for their speed and stamina, which enabled them to maintain 'a verie long cariere'. Betraying a degree of reliance on ancient authorities, he claimed that all writers commended Barbs for these qualities. Desert Barbs, lighter and faster than those bred between the Atlas Mountains and the coast, were the best.[127] Markham preferred Arabians.[128] Like Blundeville, Cavendish later extolled the virtues of the Barb, though he took a side-swipe at the former's book learning when doing so. For him, the Barb was 'as fine a horse as can be', eminently suitable as a running horse on account of its 'clean strength, wind and stamina'. While he also advocated the use of Turcomans, he was somewhat disdainful of Arabian horses, thinking them both overpriced and overrated. Even so, he acknowledged their soundness of wind, repeating the claim that riders could travel eighty miles a day on their back and never have to pull on the bridle.[129] Nathaniel Harley, writing at the beginning of the eighteen century, praised Arabians without reservation. A merchant at Aleppo, he exported a number of Arabian horses to his family in England, so he was aware of their qualities.[130] He thought them beyond compare, possessing more courage and speed than any other strain, and providing the tap roots of the best breeds in the world. His sole complaint was the difficulty of finding Arabians of a reasonable size.[131]

It was not easy, however to acquire horses from these breeds. The Arabs were particularly reluctant to part with their animals, especially mares, which they preferred to horses because they withstood heat better. They charged outrageous prices for them too.[132] Even when the horses reached the quayside, problems could occur. Muslim rulers, as a rule, were averse to allowing the export of a valuable commodity that would enrich other countries, possibly enemies, and which might be used against them. Even when trade with Morocco opened up in Elizabeth I's reign, it was difficult to obtain export licences for them.[133] Later, the English occupation of Tangier (1662–84) did not help relations between the two countries. It was also difficult getting horses out of the Ottoman Empire. In the mid seventeenth century Cavendish complained that the Turkish authorities did not allow any of their horses to leave the country.[134] The situation had not improved in the early eighteenth century. On 21 February 1716/7 Nathaniel Harley, writing from Aleppo, told his brother that he did not know if he would be able to send a horse he had just put on board a ship, 'the prohibition being very strict at present'. Even after a ship had set sail problems continued; apart from wind and tide, those on board faced danger from pirates or privateers.[135] Horses might perish. In 1684, one horse in a consignment of four taken at Vienna the previous year died in transit.[136] The susceptibility of horses to illness and injury ensured that transport costs for horses were particularly high. When, in 1699, nine Barbary stallions and five mares arrived in England, the total expenditure amounted to £1103 3s. 4d.: £476 8s. 6d. for the fourteen horses and £626 14s. 10d. in expenses for the seventeen months' trip.[137]

Fortunately, Englishmen, by one means or another, did acquire eastern stock. Several rulers obtained them as part of the diplomatic process: as gifts, licences to purchase or in trade agreements. Henry VIII received several consignments of eastern running horses from the Marquis of Mantua.[138] After a dip in activity in the second half of the sixteenth century, interest revived under Buckingham's energetic stewardship of the royal stables in the last few years of James I's reign. As Master of the Horse he bought an imported pure-bred Arabian in 1616 and over the next few years acquired more Arabians and Barbs either at source or via Spain and Italy. When the Moroccan ambassador presented Charles I with a gift of valuable Barbs and expensive saddles in 1637, William Laud, the Archbishop of Canterbury, observed that it attracted a good deal of attention.[139] During the Interregnum Oliver Cromwell tried to obtain Arabians through diplomatic channels, instructing his ambassadors at Constantinople and Paris to make representations to the Turkish authorities. When in 1657 he asked Mohammed IV for an Arabian horse from Aleppo, the Sultan sent him a cross-bred Turcoman-Arabian stallion instead. This was typical. Harassed by constant requests for pure Arabians which they did not want to export, the sultans bred a substitute, one with a good deal of Arabian blood in it and endowed with similar qualities of speed and endurance. The horse sent to Cromwell, almost certainly Place's White Turk, had considerable influence on the evolution of the thoroughbred.[140] Charles II bought horses abroad and received others as gifts. In the winter 1684–5, the king of Suz presented him with horses.[141]

Subjects made their own arrangements. Some bought horses off Italian or French merchants who traded with the Levant or North Africa. In 1601 John Banks, then at Dieppe, offered Sir Robert Cecil, Elizabeth I's chief minister, a Barb or a courser for use as a stallion. Other Barbs arrived in the country in the winter of 1609–10, having been purchased by Lord Cranbourne, Sir Thomas Howard and Sir John Sheffield at Marseilles.[142] At the turn of the seventeenth century the Darleys and Harleys benefited from the presence of a relative as an agent at Aleppo, the port which served as the main point of egress in the Levant. Among other horses, Thomas Darley exported the Darley Arabian and Nathaniel Harley the Dun Arabian and the Bloody Shouldered Arabian.[143]

Although these imports did enhance the quality of the country's running horses, the thoroughbred was not merely an oriental horse transplanted in England. Equally important were the genes of the native horses and hybrids with which they were crossed. When racing expanded in the country in the early seventeenth century, imported stallions covered native mares already selected on account of the success of their lineage in the racecourse test. Native mares often came from hobby stock, perhaps with some Arabian or Barb blood via Spain in them. They may have used Galloways too, for several horses with Galloway in their name feature in the General Stud Book. However references to horses at the Welbeck stud in the 1720s indicate that the term also denoted any horse of no more than fourteen hands high. Writing to his master, the Earl of Oxford, about a brood mare on 28 April 1729, Hobart, the land steward, commented that she was seven years old, got by Bloody Shoulder out of the Betty Mare'. He added, 'She is, I think, a galloway'.[144] These horses were certainly quick. In 1609 Markham stated that 'some English horses and geldings [were] swifter than eyther Iennet, Turke, or Barbarie', citing, among others, the case of a black hobby belonging to Mr Carlton that beat choice Barbs in a race at Salisbury. In turn, it lost a match to Valentine, a horse that retired undefeated yet was 'a plaine bredde English Horse both his Syre and Dame'.[145] This practice of covering home-bred mares with imported stallions persisted into the eighteenth century: Lord Hervey and the duke of Somerset were still using native mares in the opening years of the century and with considerable success.[146] In this respect, they were merely following traditional views on genetics. Writers like Cavendish emphasized the role of the stallion in providing inner traits such as strength and courage, and the mare in ensuring physical conformation. They also believed that horses only retained their specific qualities over generations if they remained in their natural habitat.[147] Cavendish warned against using home stallions because 'they are too far removed from the purity, and head, of the fountain'.[148]

In the post-Restoration period a group of breeders, mostly based in north-eastern England, began to challenge these assumptions. While they did have imported horses at their studs, they also sought to breed oriental-style animals at home, using stallions or their offspring already in the country. Their scheme relied on these stallions breeding true. Oriental horses became very fashionable in this period, interest in them being as much a social conceit as a part of a sporting plan, so they were not all destined for the track. Nonetheless, these breeders were interested in racing and did produce horses for the turf. Conveniently, the growing popularity of racing at the time increased the demand for horses and provided an incentive to breed them, while simultaneously offering additional opportunities to test them out in race conditions. Local breeders profited from the presence of two of the three reputed foundation sires in the region: Captain Robert Byerley, the owner of the Byerley Turk, lived at Middridge on the Tees, and Richard Darley kept the Darley Arabian at his stud at Aldby Park, north east of York. The Darley Arabian remained at Aldby his whole life and, although he served few racing standard mares, his progeny had a significant impact on the development of the thoroughbred. Among those who benefited was Edward Leedes, whose estate at North Milford lay less than twenty miles away from Aldby. The Darley Arabian covered Leedes's mare, Betty Leedes, producing Flying Childers, one of the finest racehorses ever, and Bartlett's Childers, of even greater importance as a sire of thoroughbreds.[149] Bartlett Childers's great grandson was Eclipse, reputedly the best of all time.

By the turn of the seventeenth century breeders and owners of racehorses were well aware of the genealogy of their horses. Records of the duke of Newcastle's stud at Haughton in Nottinghamshire list the sires and dams of all foals born. Cuthbert Routh, who bred race horses at Dinsdale (and subsequently at Snape) in the North Riding in the early eighteenth century, regularly gave the pedigree of his horses when noting the price he obtained when selling them.[150] When on a journey to York in 1706 Lord Hervey obtained three young horses from Edward Leedes's stud, he carefully noted their pedigrees: a three-year-old filly, by Careless out of a full sister to Leedes; a two-year-old colt by a Barb William III had given Leedes's father out of Bay Pegg, a grand-daughter of Old Spanker; and a yearling colt by Careless out of a daughter of the same Barb.[151] In the same year Thomas Pulleine of Carleton Hall, who had held the post of studmaster to William III, sent two fillies and mare, along with their pedigrees, for the duke of Newcastle to look at. The lame filly dam was out of a Fenwick mare by Place's White Turk and the sire his Chestnut Arabian; the other four-year-old filly's dam was out of Sir Matthew Peirson's running mare, 'the most famous mare in my time' by Mr Place's Turk and the sire his Chestnut Arabian; and the six-year-old mare was out of a mare, got by Brimmer out of Bustler Mare and the sire his White Turk. He also claimed that the two fillies were in foal by a son of the Byerley Turk. In his sales pitch, Pulleine portrayed the deal as an opportunity for the duke to upgrade his stud with 'as good blood as any in the kingdom'. The lineages are certainly impressive. A year later, when the duke of Newcastle was thinking about buying mares from James Darcy, he asked for details of height, age, colour, price and breeding.[152]

When Defoe visited Bedale in the 1720s the emergence of the thoroughbred was almost complete, reflected in the number of horse dealers and breeders in and around the town and the quality of the horses there. These 'English' horses, he claimed, 'will outdo for speed and strength the swiftest horse that was ever bred in Turkey, or Barbary, taken them all together'. He was right, but he was talking about a hybrid horse, the thoroughbred.[153] In effect, the country was producing its own breed, one that was adapted to local conditions and which performed better on the racecourse than imports. This development, however, did lead to the decline of Galloway racing. In 1739 Cheny recorded fifty-four Galloway races and thirty-three races for horses of fourteen hands and under out of a total of 357 races. In 1741 he listed none at all, though three Galloway races occurred in Ireland. Of course, they continued to race in low-key events, as at Albrighton in the early nineteenth century, but they had ceased to feature at the prestigious meetings.[154]

Ironically, as northern bloodstock was reaching its apogee, the focus of the racing year was shifting further south. Newmarket had steadily been growing in importance since the Restoration and by the middle of the eighteenth century had come to dominate the sport, a position emphasized by the establishment of the Jockey Club there in 1752.[155] The key to its rise to prominence was the generous patronage of Charles II, who, after his restoration in 1660 was intent on setting up a southern racing centre within easy reach of his palaces. Once monarchs had given Newmarket their seal of approval (Charles II's immediate successors were also avid race-goers), the pace quickened, for the court followed. This ensured that the elite came to the town, bringing their horses with them and raising the quality of the competition. The Duke of Devonshire, the Whig magnate, only raced his northern bred stallion, Flying Childers, at Newmarket, although he stabled it at his home at Chatsworth in Derbyshire. Significantly, he defeated the northern racer, Fox, in a trial at York in 1723.[156] At the same time studs proliferated in the south: no longer did a Lord Hervey have to go to Yorkshire to find suitable horses. Breeders in the region, moreover, received a boost in the early 1730s when the Godolphin Arab, the third member of the so-called triumvirate of foundation stallions, began covering mares near Newmarket at Lord Godolphin's stud in the Gogmagog Hills in Cambridgeshire. By the time that Richard Wall wrote *A Dissertation on the Breeding of Horses* in 1758 the south had caught up with the north, as the results of races at Newmarket indicate.[157] The fashion for shorter races for younger horses, which began around the middle of the eighteenth century, further disadvantaged northern breeders, whose reputation had been based on producing horses with speed and stamina.

Horse racing had a profound effect on early modern English society, its influence being felt on the social and economic life of the country, its cultural heritage and on political affairs both at home and abroad. From humble beginnings (and a prize of a silver bell worth 6s. 8d.) at Chester in the early sixteenth century, by 1750 horse racing had grown into an extremely sophisticated enterprise worth many thousands of pounds per annum. By then horse racing was firmly established in the nation's sporting calendar, with a network of centres throughout the whole country and a comprehensive set of rules and regulations. All sections of the community attended meetings but the active participants were members of the upper classes. So popular had horse racing become that in the 1730s the number of venues had reached saturation point. The Act of 1740 culled many of the smaller gatherings and enabled the survivors, the high-class, socially exclusive events, to flourish. The industry entered the modern world in a sound condition and with a quality product, the English thoroughbred.

Towns sponsored most of the meetings. To establish a race cost comparatively little money: a few pounds to mark out the course and pay the officials and generally £20–£30 for the plate – and the commercial gains could be considerable. The upper classes, for their part, paid the entrance fees, often contributed to the cost of a plate and supplied the horses. For them, horse racing was an expensive business. Leading breeders and owners had large sums of money tied up in their strings of horses. In the mid seventeenth century Mr John Fenwick, Charles I's studmaster, reputedly kept horses worth at least £15,000 at his stud at Bywell in Northumberland.[158] To maintain a racing stable and stud like this was hugely expensive in terms of horse care and management, fodder, accommodation and staff, though, to take a wider view, it did offer employment to a range of people. Every care had to be given to the racehorses at stud and on the racetrack because of the capital invested in them, as well as a recognition of their potential earnings. A good specimen, which might have cost up to £20 at the beginning of the seventeenth century would fetch £100 or more a hundred years later. Breeders could defray some of the expenses through stud fees and the sale of the progeny, the value of which rose incrementally according their fortunes on the track or on the quality of their genes. Side stakes and betting greatly increased the amount of money circulating in the sport.

Horse racing created commercial links within the country and with foreign states. In England most racehorses changed hands privately, often directly to a friend or acquaintance but occasionally through an agent or middleman.[159] Owners rarely used fairs, although Penkridge stands out as an exception. In the 1720s Defoe observed that 'an incredible number of gentlemen attended with their groom to buy gallopers, or race-horses, for their Newmarket sport'.[160] Externally, the demand for oriental stock encouraged the establishment of trading connections with the countries where they were bred. In 1539 an enterprising young man put forward a proposal to establish a bilateral trade with the Ottoman Empire, exporting kerseys for the horses.[161] All it lacked was the sultan's assent. This was a perennial problem. In the late seventeenth and early eighteenth century, for instance, scions of racing families, who belonged to the merchant community at Aleppo, seem to have spent a good deal of time locating suitable horses, prising them out the hands of the Arabs and avoiding the authorities.[162]

Undoubtedly, many of the meetings were low-key affairs, in which the local gentry raced rather ordinary horses. At the top venues, however, a small group of very wealthy gentlemen and aristocrats dominated proceedings. In this respect, horse racing was an archetypal aristocratic pastime, for it allowed them to spend money on a frivolous pursuit in a highly conspicuous fashion. Of course, men like Lord Hervey were enthusiasts and passionately involved in the sport, but they were not unaware of the social benefits to be derived from owning a string of fine racehorses and from belonging to an exclusive club that included the monarch. This involved a good deal of male bonding, watching horses training and racing, and often competing against one another. After the race, they continued to socialize, drinking and gambling together. It is not surprising that women felt excluded and discouraged from participating, that is if they wanted to join in. Newmarket seems to have remained predominantly a male preserve for most of the period. Elsewhere, venues increasingly catered for ladies, putting on a range of social events to appeal to them. Change occurred when racing grew out of its male-oriented origins and became an integral part of the fashionable social scene. Ordinary people also turned up at race meetings in droves. Urban authorities had an ambivalent attitude towards them, welcoming the income their presence generated but objecting to their boisterous behaviour and lack of decorum. The elite tried to ignore them, viewing the races on horseback or from a coach. Towards the end of the period they further segregated themselves by constructing grandstands exclusively for their own use.

Culturally, horse racing was emblematic of the aristocratic lifestyle, fitting in well with upper-class interest in riding and horsemanship. Gentlemen, challenging each other in head-to-head contests, were prominent from the outset and members of their class continued to compete throughout the whole period. If owners were increasingly employing professional jockeys in matches at the turn of the seventeenth century, they still rode in plates, which enabled them to feel the thrill of racing and to demonstrate their equestrian skills. A trophy or two on the sideboard confirmed to the world their manly qualities and their mastery of their steed. As oriental horses arrived in growing numbers in the late seventeenth and early eighteenth century the relationship between rider and horse underwent a subtle change. It seemed wrong, indeed unnecessary, for riders to force such noble and intelligent creatures to obey their riders and, therefore, more natural to guide them with a light touch. The impact they created, moreover, may have influenced cultural norms. They prompted a new genre of equine portraits, in which the horses are represented in an idealized way, providing a metaphor for the image that the racing enthusiasts who commissioned them wished to promote of themselves. The paintings depict their subjects as gods, beautifully proportioned, serene and majestic, surveying their surroundings with an intelligent eye and in perfect control. It was as if the horses were setting the cultural agenda. Moreover, their demeanour seemed to prove the theriophilic case, refuting the Cartesian notion of horses as beast-machines and helping to change society's attitudes towards and treatment of animals in general.

The value placed on race-standard horses ensured their role as bargaining counters in diplomacy. They made ideal gifts, especially where it was important to create a good impression or to cement a political alliance. Rulers granted or withheld permission to export horses according to political or strategic calculations. At home, too, horse racing had a political dimension. At race meetings sporting monarchs like Charles II and William III could gain political capital by inviting individuals into their racing circle. In the same way, leading politicians used the racing milieu to strengthen their hold over their clients. A breeder of high-quality race horses like Lord Wharton, a leading Whig, could show favour by allowing his stallions to cover the mares of his allies. Racing was also associated with political unrest. In troubled times race meetings provided the cloak for gatherings of the disaffected – or so the governments of the day thought. In the last quarter of the seventeenth century one of the elements in the growing rivalry between Whig and Tory was the politicization of racing, leading to occasional outbursts of violence. The problem persisted well into the eighteenth century.

6

Preparation for War

Apart from specific training in the use of arms, members of the gentry and aristocracy prepared themselves for war by engaging in sporting activities which, contemporaries claimed, exercised a range of appropriate skills and exposure to a number of quasi-combat experiences. Field sports, jousting and the *manège* furnished them with opportunities to improve their proficiency in horsemanship in challenging situations, thereby rehearsing the circumstances they would face when serving as a cavalryman in battle. Hunting and jousting, moreover, added a psychological edge; participants risked life and limb and acquired a measure of the mental toughness so essential on the battlefield. They also provided occasions for male bonding which to an extent replicated the comradeship of war. In addition, hawking and hunting served a utilitarian purpose because, depending on the quarry, they provided meat for the table and helped to rid the countryside of vermin. In this respect, they also represented a human response to animal agency, that is, a means of protecting growing crops and domesticated stock from wild beasts. In truth, the upper classes probably valued these pursuits as much for social reasons as for functional ones because they enabled them publicly to demonstrate their wealth, privilege and horsemanship.

EQUESTRIAN SPORTS

Competitors at a tournament practised a range of martial exercises, either on horseback or on foot. The joust royal was the most prestigious event; in it mounted combatants, armed with a lance, rode against each other either side of the tilt. In the tourney, they clashed without a barrier in between them. Riders also competed at running at the ring, the winner being the one who managed to thrust his spear through the target the greatest number of times. In foot matches at the beginning of the period, contestants carried a spear or occasionally an axe or a sword, though over time the sword became the principal weapon.[1] At a projected match at Greenwich in May 1510 the two challengers required opponents to come armed with a casting spear with a blunted head and targe (shield), together with a rebated sword.[2] As an indication of the competitive nature of these tournaments, contestants could take part in various events and amass points awarded by heralds acting as umpires. In jousting, according to the rules formulated by John Tiptoft, Earl of Worcester, in 1466, a person scored by striking his adversary's helmet or coronel with his lance, unseating him or breaking his lance on the permissible part of the body. He lost points if he hit his opponent while his back was turned or if he was unarmed, or if he struck his horse or saddle.[3]

Hunting had its own equestrian and pedestrian forms and here too mounted activities took precedence. *Par force* hunting topped the list, that is hunting with dogs, with weapons only being used at the culmination of the chase. In James I's words, 'Hunting … with running hounds … is the most honourable and noblest sorte thereof …'[4] It also had a hierarchy of prey, organized into two categories: game (protected creatures) and vermin. The former included deer, hares, rabbits, pheasants, partridges and woodcocks, and the latter foxes, badgers and otters, together with other wild creatures such as polecats and martens and a range of birds.[5] Deer, especially the hart, were deemed the noblest quarry on account of their perceived warriorlike qualities.[6] Boars, though even fiercer, came a distant second. They lacked the deer's stature and air of majesty and survived from the middle ages only in semi-captivity in parks. These were the beasts that the aristocracy liked to hunt, though they also appreciated the qualities of the hare as game. Gascoigne wrote that 'I might well mainteine that of all chases, the Hare maketh greatest pastime and pleasure and sheweth more cunning in hunting, and it is meetest for gentlemen of all other huntings …'[7] In a sense, the hare recommended itself as an object for sport. Apart from its speed and sinuous running, it tended to double back, circling the same ground, and in doing so giving the riders foreknowledge of the obstacles the second time round. This trait ensured that the hunting party would almost always be able to hear, if not see, the hounds chasing their quarry.[8] As an added point in its favour, hares, like foxes, did not have the respite of a close season, so hunters could pursue them throughout the year.[9] For a long time aristocrats viewed fox hunting as a crude sport: nothing more than riding and running. Country squires, on the other hand, chased anything that moved.[10]

Coursing differed from hunting in that the hounds, normally greyhounds, hunted by sight rather than scent. Participants generally watched on foot because the usual quarry, the hare, remained in sight.[11] For Elyot, hare coursing was not an adequate preparation for war, though it provided pleasant sport for persons of a studious or timid disposition. Even so, it was very popular among gentlemen; hares were plentiful and sportsmen could pursue them comparatively cheaply and without fuss. Nicholas Blundell's diary indicates that, while he regularly hunted deer in the Liverpool area in the years 1702–26, most of all he coursed hares. Between 1702 and 1719 the diaries contain 164 entries referring to the sport. He even went out when his wife was in labour. On only two occasions did he note that the hunters rode with the hounds.[12] Hunting parties also coursed emparked deer and sometimes those in the wild. In 1591 Elizabeth I, then at Cowdray, watched while greyhounds coursed sixteen bucks.[13]

In falconry the birds rather than the prey defined the status, with individual species being allocated to a specific social stratum. According to the author of the *Boke of St Alban's* (1486), the list ranged from the eagles, vultures and merlins appropriate to emperors and the gerfalcons and their tercels belonging to kings down to the sparrowhawks of priests and the muskets of holy water clerks.[14] Naturally, the catalogue puts the noble long-winged falcons above the short-winged hawks since they hunted larger game and provided nobler sport. It is doubtful whether this order ever possessed the force of a sumptuary law but it did reflect late medieval concern for the niceties of the social hierarchy. In early modern England members of the elite chose their birds according to preference. In September 1533, for instance, Sir William Kingston wrote that the King hunted every day with goshawks and other hawks, namely lanners, sparrowhawks and merlins.[15] Unlike humans, male birds were smaller and less aggressive than females and therefore not so highly prized. Lesser hawks like a goshawk caught partridges, pheasant, bustards, rabbits and hares, while the larger falcon attacked deer and bigger birds such as cranes, herons and swans.[16] In a letter to his nephew, Robert, from Aleppo in about 1716 Nathaniel Harley described a mounted expedition in which his party hunted antelope with hawks and greyhounds. The hawks, when cast off, flew at the quarry, buffeting them to slow them down for the dogs. On the first day the hounds killed two antelope which the hawks had set up. The following morning the first cast proved indecisive, 'making the chase long and the riding very hard'. When they found a second herd, the party experienced another long ride because of the wariness of the antelope and the unfavourable terrain. Eventually, a hawk brought down a young antelope in spite of its mother's attempts to protect it. At this point, members of the party rode up and delivered the *coup de grâce*.[17]

All the pursuits featured here experienced considerable change (and mixed fortunes) during the course of the early modern period. Jousting disappeared, apart from occasional Gothic revivalist events such as the Eglinton Tournament of 1839. As noted above, the *manège* was never more than a minority interest, although it briefly raised its profile when royalist aficionados returned at the Restoration. The growing popularity of horse racing among the upper classes, however, quickly overshadowed it. Hawking declined too, if more slowly. Only hunting retained its popularity, though it had to adjust to changing circumstances. In particular, fox hunting, excoriated by the aristocracy for most of the period, achieved social acceptability by 1750. No doubt, aristocrats would have preferred to hunt the noble hart but their numbers were dwindling throughout the country. Stag hunting enthusiasts even went to the farcical length of carting deer from one venue to another.[18] Increasingly, those that did survive were kept in parks. Outside the park pale agricultural changes progressively destroyed their habitat. In particular, the need to increase the food supply to cope with the demands of a rising human population in the late sixteenth and early seventeenth centuries accelerated the process of enclosing commons and wastes. In the Shropshire parish of Myddle alone over 1,000 acres of land were brought into regular cultivation between the late fifteenth and early seventeenth centuries.[19]

Conversely, the clearance of woodlands encouraged fox hunting since it forced the quarry into the open. Foxes could less easily move from covert to covert in the manner that Gascoyne complained about in 1575: 'he [the fox] never fleeth before the houndes, but holdeth the strongest coverts, and fleeth from the fielde, as a beast which trusteth not in his legges, nor yet in his strength'.[20] In the open foxes ran straight and hard and when chasing them huntsmen came to realize that this particular quarry provided them with a good day's sport. Charles II and James II were among members of the hunting fraternity who enjoyed the exhilaration of the pursuit.[21] Enthusiasts, with their own packs, included Lord Grey of Uppark (Sussex) and the 2nd Duke of Buckingham initially at Cliveden and, after he fell out of favour at court, at Helmsley. Other aristocratic packs were established in the early eighteenth century, notably the Duke of Richmond's at Charlton and the Duke of Rutland's at Belvoir.[22]

Topographical change increased the attractiveness of fox hunting at precisely the time that the elite needed a substitute for their favourite quarry and helped overcome the deep-seated antipathy they felt towards pursuing a creature classed as vermin. While the hunted stag symbolically endowed its pursuers with its own noble qualities, few huntsmen wanted to identify themselves with the fox, an animal popularly perceived as clever and shrewd but also as wily, dishonest and cunning. Even worse, it used its talents to steal game and domesticated livestock, the property of humans. The fox's behaviour was therefore immoral; as a wild animal, its allotted prey consisted of other wild animals but it wilfully chose not to restrict itself to this fare. This was poaching not hunting. Hence countryfolk viewed the fox as a thief, a predator coming out of the 'world of the wild' to intrude into the human world and its concerns.[23] To make fox hunting acceptable these characteristics had to be recast culturally and a favourable gloss put on them. Contemporaries did this by presenting the hunt as a contest in which the huntsmen and the hounds pitted their wits and skills against a clever opponent.[24]

As the terrain opened up, forcing foxes to display their natural pace, hounds had to be able to follow a scent at speed to remain in touch. Existing hounds tended to lack one or other of these two qualities. In the north, the hound or beagle was fast enough (perhaps too fast) but hunted by sight rather than scent.

The southern hound, on the other hand, had a good nose but was too slow to catch a fox on the run.[25] In March 1622/3, when the southerner, Edward Ball, described the kind of horse he wanted John Fleming to obtain for him in Cumberland, he asked for one that would 'gallop finely after slowe houndes'.[26] In the sixteenth and seventeenth centuries, moreover, many gentlemen hunters selected their hounds for the timbre of their cry rather than for their pace. Markham wrote in 1615 that hunt masters who chose their hounds by this criterion had to assemble a mixed pack: a number of hounds with 'deepe solempe mouthes', twice as many with 'roaring and loud ringing mouthes' and some with 'hollow plaine sweete mouthes'.[27] Shakespeare reflected this order of priorities when, in *A Midsummer Night's Dream*, Theseus declares that his hounds were 'Slow in pursuit, but matched in mouth like bells'.[28] In *The Hunting of the Hare*, Margaret Cavendish evokes the sound of the hunt:

> Then *Hornes* blew loud, for th'rest to follow on.
> The *great slow-Hounds*, their throats did set a *Base*,
> The *Fleet swift Hounds*, as *Tenours* next in place;
> The little *Beagles* they a Trebble sing,
> And through the *Aire* their *Voice* a round did ring.
> Which made a *Consort*, as they ran along;
> If they but *words* could speak, might sing a *Song*,
> The *Hornes* kept time, the Hunters shout for *Joy*,
> And valiant seeme, *poore Wat* for to destroy.[29]

By the opening of the eighteenth century, however, the situation was changing, with the result that in the following half century crosses which combined the best qualities of both breeds were beginning to emerge.[30]

Similarly, riders could only keep up if their horses improved their speed-endurance capability. Cross-breeding with racehorses provided the answer. As racehorses were expensive animals, owners sought to maximize the return on their investment by offering stud facilities to all who could pay for the service. Many subscribed, perhaps to improve the quality of their saddle mounts in general but also specifically to obtain speedy hunters. The half or three-quarter thoroughbred proved ideal.[31] Even the so-called three foundation stallions sired far more hunters than they did racehorses.[32] Horse racing itself helped meet the need by putting on races for hunters. In 1739 Cheny recorded twenty-three designated races, half of them at twelve or thirteen stone, and scattered among at least thirteen counties.[33] As a result, the number of pacey but strong hunters increased in the hundred years after the Restoration. In August 1719 the Reverend George Plaxton informed his master, Lord Gower, that the horse he had just bought in Yorkshire for Ashley would win Newcastle Plate and carry him out hunting: 'England never saw a stouter and not a very slow one'. Twenty years later, a sale notice, advertising the disposal of the entire stud belonging to William Metcalf Esq. of Clifton described the colts as 'likely to be twelve stone horses, thorough bred and very promising either for gallopers or hunters'.[34] It appears, therefore, that Worsley's view that the breeding of such horses only began in the late eighteenth century is unduly conservative.[35]

This development would have been worthless had not improvements been made in saddlery. The archetypal seventeenth-century saddle had a high pommel and riders sat on it in an upright position with straight legs. As illustrated by William Cavendish in his original book, *La Methode et Invention Nouvelle de Dresser les Chevaux* (1658), it shows the rider in complete control of his horse. Unfortunately, such a pommel acted as a brake on the speed of the chase, especially when clearing barriers. To take a hedge at a canter, the rider risked castration. Moreover, the tight control of the horse's head, through the application of the bit, restricted the horse's ability to judge and clear obstacles in the field independently.[36] Such considerations account for the preference for open downland as hunting country during the course of the sixteenth and seventeenth centuries. As Celia Fiennes noted of Newton Toney on Salisbury Plain, it 'is all on the downs a fine Champion Country pleasant for all sports – Rideing, Hunting, Courseing, Setting and Shooteing'.[37] As enclosure altered the landscape during the course of the late seventeenth and eighteenth centuries, riders had to change their seat to meet the requirements of jumping hedges and ditches at speed. Taking their cue from jockeys, they began to ride in a forward position on flat saddles, with short stirrups and snaffle bridles on a loose rein.[38] Sir Thomas Myddelton of Chirk Castle, who kept his own pack of hounds, rode with one. On 27 October 1682 he paid William Glegg, a Wrexham saddler, £3 12s. for six hunting saddles and a further 6s. for two saddle cloths.[39]

If improved hunters benefited sportsmen, the country gained from a larger stock of strong, fast cavalry mounts (and from the development of saddles that enabled troopers to charge over rough terrain at pace). Indeed, military requirements lay behind the establishment of valuable plate races, which stipulated weights of twelve stones or above. As Richard Blome commented in 1686, 'By having plates run for at several times and in several counties, we come to know exactly the speed, wind, force and heart of every horse that runs which directs us unfallibly in our choice when we want to furnish ourselves for war, hunting, breeding, the road etc.'[40] A new fourteen stone plate (worth £100), introduced at Newmarket in October 1699, made the connection clear, the stated objective being 'to encourage the breeding of strong and useful horses'. Horses that had won prizes worth more than £20 could not enter.[41] This was a typical format, one designed to augment the number of suitable horses by promoting interest in the events. As the season progressed, successful horses found themselves increasingly barred from events, opening up opportunities for those coming behind them. The system therefore moved some horses up the ladder and allowed others to fill the gaps vacated. It therefore ensured a constant turnover of entrants and a growing pool of serviceable horses which the country could draw upon. Apart from selling plates, where the founder had first refusal, contributors had the chance of buying the winning horse, often on the throw of a dice. These events therefore contributed to spreading the blood of winning horses more widely and in doing so helped to improve the breeding stock.

ELITE PASTIMES

Hawking and hunting were hugely popular pursuits among the upper classes. Like horsemanship, an interest in hunting was a defining mark of a gentleman. Writing in 1575, Gascoigne pointed out the class distinction when he commented that hunting was:

> A sport for Noble peeres, a sport for gentle bloods,
> The Paine I leave for servants such as beate the bushee woods,
> To make their masters sport. Then let the Lords reioyce,
> Let gentlemen beholde the glee and take thereof the choice.
> For my part (being one) I must needes say my minde:
> That Hunting was ordeyned first, for Men of Noble kinde
> And unto them therefore, I recommend the same,
> As exercise that best becomes their worthy noble name.[42]

Robert Burton, later, made the same assertion, declaring that hawking and hunting were 'honest recreations and fit disports for some great men, but not for every base inferiour person'. He also emphasized the hold that these pastimes had over their genteel patrons: ''Tis all their study, all their exercise, ordinary businesse, all their talke, and indeed some dote too much after it, they can doe nothing els, discourse of nought els.'[43] Ben Jonson satirized this obsession. In 1657 Thomas Burroughs, the puritanical parson of Cottesbrook posed the following question at a funeral sermon: 'How many Gentlemen be there, of whom when they die, all that can be said is this, They were born, they did eat, and drink, and play, and hunt, and hawk, and lived like so many wild Ass-colts, never minding any thing that concern'd God's glory, or their own salvation … and so died, and dropt into hell.' Edward Lord Herbert, unusually for a member of his class, probably felt the same way. In his memoirs he declared his dislike of hunting because it wasted time that could be better spent studying. Even so, he recognized that, because of its popularity among his peers, he had to acquaint himself with the sport. Not surprisingly, he preferred hawking to hunting since 'lesse tyme is spent in it'.[44]

Monarchs were among the most avid supporters of field sports. One of the reasons why Henry VIII chose Cuddington as the site of Nonsuch Palace was the teeming wildlife on the nearby downs.[45] He was an avid hunter and hawker.[46] In 1519 he reputedly tired out eight horses in a day's hunting and, if he slowed down as he aged, he did not stop. In December 1540 the French ambassador reported that the King was out hawking at Woking with a party of sixty to eighty horsemen. When in the following February English emissaries told the French king that Henry VIII was fitter than ever, being always out 'hawking or hunting, were it never so cold, when divers of your servants had liever be at home', they were probably not exaggerating.[47] James I was even more addicted to the chase, a passion he had begun to indulge in as a young King of Scotland. In 1584 de Fontenay, a French envoy at the court, thought him 'too idle and too little concerned about business, too addicted to his pleasure, principally that of the chase'. Within months of becoming King of England in 1603 his obsession had become a talking point in courtly circles. On 22 June 1603 Thomas Wilson complained to Sir Thomas Parry that the King 'Sometymes ... comes to Counsell but most tyme he spends in fieldes and parkes and chaces, chasing away idleness by violent exercise and early risinge, wherin the Sune seldom prevents him'. Less than three months later (3 September) the Venetian ambassador reported to the doge that 'for the next twenty days he [James I] will be without his council, away upon a hunting party, and everything is at a standstill'. At the end of the following year the Archbishop of York, writing to Robert Cecil, criticized the King, *inter alia*, for neglecting his duties, citing his over-indulgence in hunting which distracted him from affairs of state.[48] If modern historians have reassessed James's overall reputation, emphasizing the soundness of many of his policies, they concede his fondness for hunting. It was therefore pure humbug for James to lecture his son on the need to limit the time he spent hunting or hawking: 'Observe that moderation, that ye slip not therewith the houres appointed to your affaires, which ye ought ever precisely to keepe, remembering that these games are byt ordained for you, in enabling you for your offices, for the which ye are ordained.'[49]

Jousting, similarly, had its adherents, especially at the beginning of the period, that is for most of the sixteenth century. Knights served as men-at-arms, so the exercise had a utilitarian function and this enhanced its popularity among the upper classes. All round the country, gentlemen with the means and the inclination created their own tiltyards, complete with wooden grandstands for the spectators.[50] The subsequent decline in the use of the lance as a weapon undoubtedly reduced its appeal. The sport, increasingly focused on the court, became highly exclusive and symbolic. Henry VIII, who saw himself as the embodiment of the courtly warrior-prince, participated enthusiastically. In the early years of his reign he surrounded himself with a number of like-minded companions, known as his minions, and regularly entered the lists. At a tournament held at Greenwich on 24 May 1516 the King, together with Lords Suffolk and Essex and Sir George Carew, challenged Sir William Kingston, Sir Giles Capell, John Sedley and others.[51] Edward VI, Henry VIII's son and heir, was only nine years old when he succeeded in 1547 but during his short reign he received instruction in tilting and the *manège*. He appeared in tournaments in 1551 and 1552, although, because of his age, he only tilted at the ring. Had he survived, he would undoubtedly have graduated to tilting against human opponents. James I's son, Henry, who shared many of his great-great-great-uncle's interests, was an enthusiastic jouster, making his first appearance at the age of twelve.[52]

The employment of archaic language and ceremonial further distanced the few who participated in these pursuits from the masses. A tournament, with its pomp and colour and its archaic rituals, spiced with an element of danger, perfectly encapsulated the aristocratic approach to life.[53] Hawking and hunting, similarly, had their lore and mystique. The etiquette that huntsmen had to observe at the death of a hart, for instance, was finely delineated and rigidly hierarchical. Gascoigne wrote minutely on the procedure to be followed and emphasized the differences between French and English practices. Pride of place went to the person occupying the highest social rank, whether monarch, aristocrat or gentleman, a feature that not only reflected the realities of human society but also respect for a noble beast.[54] Burkert argues that such rituals harked back to hunter-gatherer times. In his view the ritual dismemberment of the quarry and the preservation of trophies such as a stag's head and antlers were acts of atonement and symbolic restoration, necessitated by the shock of killing a large living creature imbued with mythical associations, and the accompanying feeling of guilt.[55] The *manège*, with its French and Italian terms and artificial movements, was similarly exotic.

To enter the lists, the *manège* ring or the hunting field was a costly business. This suited the upper classes, since it enabled them to flaunt their wealth and to maintain the exclusivity of these activities. Jousting, because of its association with state occasions, was particularly expensive. In Henry VIII's reign the king subsidized the events but Elizabeth, ever keen on making economies, tried to persuade individual courtiers to sponsor a tournament.[56] They also paid for the honour, spending heavily on their horses, weapons, clothing and armour, entourage and other items. In the 1590s the Queen's favourite, the Earl of Essex, dispensed huge sums on the sport and in 1616 the Earl of Rutland laid out £155 10s. 4d. on incidentals alone.[57] By far the largest costs involved the horses and armour. The chargers, typically great horses and similar to those employed in parades and the *manège*, were expensive to buy and maintain. A suit of armour could cost even more; apart from being tailor-made and fabricated from the finest and strongest metals, it had to be stylish and richly embellished. In 1518 Henry VIII spent £50 on three suits of armour, together with horse armour, and a century later Prince Henry paid £340 for a suit.[58]

Hawking and hunting did not necessarily involve the same level of expense, that is, for individuals who were satisfied with riding an all-purpose nag and, in the case of hawking, owning a single bird. Nonetheless, for those who wished to engage fully in the sports the costs were considerable. Only the wealthy could maintain a well-stocked park, a string of hunters, a kennel of hounds and a mews of hawks, together with the retainers needed to look after them. The annual bill for Charles II's hart- and buckhounds amounted to £2341 and an economy drive only shaved £183 off the bill.[59] Burton warned that those who attempted to ape their betters faced possible ruin. 'Whilst they will maintaine their faukoners and dogs, & hunting nagges, their wealth ... runnes away with dogs, & their fortunes fly away with haukes ... they devour themselves and patrimonies in such idle and unnecessary disports, neglecting necessary business and follow their vocation.'[60] Even gentlemen fell victim. In 1710 Charlwood Lawton petitioned the leading minister, Robert Harley, for a post in the revenue for his brother, Ralph, who had spent his fortune on hunting horses and sports but who 'had been a reclaimed, sober, sedulous man these many years'.[61] A hunter might cost £10 in Restoration England but a rider could spend a good deal more for a better quality mount. In 1686 Francis Forester, a Shropshire squire, bought two hunting geldings for £60.[62] These two horses were probably cross-bred thoroughbreds. Hounds added to the expense. In September 1699 Thomas Cartwright of Aynho bought a pack of beagles at Newbury for £51 1s. 6d. In the following year the dogs cost him almost £40 in expenses, mainly for horse meat.[63] Not surprisingly, therefore, suggestions put forward for economies on the Thorndon estate of the Petre family in Essex in 1707 included the sale of 'useless' horses, the disposal of the hounds and the dismissal of superfluous servants such as huntsmen. These measures, it was asserted, would effect major savings.[64]

Not content with pricing others out, the elite raised other barriers too. Encroachment by non-gentlemen was not an issue in the tiltyard since aristocrats controlled the whole event and the mass of the population merely participated as spectators, if they attended at all. At a tournament heralds vetted the combatants and received their coats of arms, which they certified and displayed on the tree of heraldry.[65] Hunting was different because many of the people who lived in the countryside possessed a horse, enjoyed riding and would have liked to chase game. Indeed, for them the sport had utilitarian appeal for, had they been able to participate, it would have provided them with meat for the table. To keep them out, landed society used legislative means, blatantly exploiting its dominant position in Parliament in its own interests. From the middle ages onwards individuals who wanted to hunt required a property qualification to chase deer and rabbits legally, adjusted to £40 per annum from land or £200 in goods by an act of 1605. The Game Act of 1671 raised the qualifications to £100 per annum in freehold land or £150 in leases for ninety-nine years. The son and heir of an esquire or the owner of a park, warren, chase or free fishery also qualified to hunt.[66] The Act did not include deer nor, from 1692, rabbits since their habitat, mostly parks or warrens, meant that the legislators viewed them as private property. Henceforward, poaching deer and rabbits laid the perpetrators open to charges of grand larceny and therefore liable to more severe punishment.[67]

The Act of 1671 in all its essentials remained in force until 1831. By determining who could hunt, net and shoot (and what) it was clearly divisive. In particular, it reaffirmed the superiority of land over other forms of wealth by removing qualifications based on trade, stocks and offices, and thereby sought to bar bankers, lawyers, merchants, farmers and the like from the sport.[68] The act did not directly affect people of more humble means since they did not lose a right they had never possessed. What concerned them was the taking in of commons into parks and warrens, which transferred areas subject to common rights into land in private ownership. Poaching, as noted above, incurred heavier penalties. Even more galling was the prospect that others were making money out of their misfortune. Manorial lords, who for centuries had paid little attention to sterile heathland, became increasingly aware of their potential as rabbit warrens, for game or commercial exploitation. Richard Cholmeley of Brandsby sold most of his rabbits; on 4 March 1613/4 Thomas Fentyman, his warrener, reported that he had killed 642½ couples of rabbits in the previous year, including 516½ couples which he had sold for £19 14s. 9d.[69] Some warrens were leased out. When Ezekial Archer died in 1693 his lease of the Box Hill warren was worth £10 and the 2,500 rabbits there £75. In 1685 William Boorne, a Weybridge husbandman, left rabbits worth £200 in his warren, together with nets and ferrets, valued at £3 7s. 0d.[70]

Of course, people still poached and risked the consequences. Among those indicted at the Kent assizes in March 1668 were a Leigh carpenter and a Riverhead labourer who had used greyhounds and 'setting dogs' to course deer or hares and nets and guns to kill partridges and pheasants at Sevenoaks a year earlier. Four years later the grand jury indicted Thomas Yeomans, a Rolvenden husbandman, for keeping a couple of greyhounds to course deer or hare. Then, in 1675, it considered the case of a labourer and a carpenter of Hothfield accused of catching twenty partridges with nets, snares, gins and other devices in the parish.[71] Penalties rose steeply in 1723 on the passage of the Waltham Black Act which meted out capital punishment to offenders, armed with weapons and with their faces blackened, who poached deer, hares, rabbits or fish in forests, chases, parks or enclosed grounds.[72] Farmers, barred from hunting game on their own land, might further object when the local pack of hounds led by a qualified master followed a quarry over their growing corn.

PREPARATION FOR WAR

In origin, tournaments really did mimic the brutality of warfare, being as far removed from the concepts of chivalry and honour, as embodied in medieval Arthurian romances, as it was possible to get. Jousters carried pointed lances and tried to run their opponents down and trample on them. Gradually, however, the authorities brought tournaments under control, subjecting the action to more stringent codes of conduct. The introduction of rebated weapons and tilt barriers, and the development of plate armour, further improved safety.[73] This was the situation by the time that Henry VIII was making his appearance in the lists. When he fought on the Field of the Cloth of Gold the rules of combat included an article that banned the use of sharp steel, 'in consequence of the numerous accidents to noblemen ... in times past'.[74] Unfortunately, such measures did not eliminate all danger. Injuries, even fatalities, continued to occur. On 22 November 1514 the Marquis of Dorset reported the death of a Frenchman at a tournament at Calais. In 1559 the French King, Henry II, died when a lance shattered in his face and shards penetrated his visor grille.[75]

Alan Young, the authority on Tudor and Jacobean tournaments, minimizes the value of these comparatively sanitized events as preparation for war but, in doing so, tends to overlook the importance of the transferable skills that they did inculcate.[76] Specifically, jousting helped to keep a man-at-arms in 'fighting trim' in peacetime, accustoming him to the use of the lance and to the problems of maintaining control of his horse under duress. Although the introduction of the rest, known as the *arrêt de cuirasse*, in the first half of the fourteenth century made it easier for a horseman to wield his lance in battle, it still required a high level of horsemanship to guide the point home while riding towards the enemy under fire.[77] The early Tudors certainly recognized its value as training for men-at-arms. At the tournament held to celebrate the marriage of Prince Arthur in 1501 the challenge spoke of the 'exercise and faictes of the Necessary discipline of armes'.[78] Nowhere was readiness for war more necessary than at Calais, the last English outpost in France, in the years before its capture in January 1557/8. In 1540 the town's chronicler praised its governor, Henry, Lord Maltravers, for his energy in furnishing its defenders with weapons and horses and for encouraging them to practise feats of arms.[79] While jousters were not under fire, they did expose themselves to danger and undoubtedly felt the same frisson of excitement and tension that they experienced in battle. In terms of the perceived value of jousting as preparation for war or, at least the possession of martial talents which prowess at the sport demonstrated, it is important to note that Charles II did not arrange for his (illegitimate) sons to receive instruction in the art. By then, the lance had ceased to be even a symbolic weapon of war.

The early modern rationale for hunting as preparation for war smacks of an excuse for a jolly good day out. Indeed, it is easy to see why the upper classes enjoyed it for precisely that reason. Burton wrote that hunting refreshed both body and mind, 'the gift of gods, a princely sport, which they have ever used ... as well for health as pleasure'.[80] Hunting provided them with an exhilarating chase, often lasting for several hours and spread out over miles of countryside. On one remarkable occasion (26 January 1738) the Charlton hunt started a fox at 7.45 a.m. and, having followed it in several circles around Sussex, finally killed it at 5.50 p.m.[81] As in this case, a hunt promised a dramatic finale. Even so, for many the kill only possessed a significance in the context of the chase, in which the pursuers, identifying themselves with their hounds, pitted their wits against a worthy quarry. Huntsmen therefore had to follow certain conventions, designed to balance the odds and to make the sport more challenging.[82] As an experience, the cry of the hounds, the sound of the horn and the hallooing of the riders all added to the excitement. In short, hunting offered them a good day's sport and exercise, encompassed within a series of colourful tableaux, which appealed to their sense of ritual and display.

Even so, contemporaries did view hunting as a suitable training for war, making numerous links between the two. Sir Thomas Elyot, in his handbook for governors, encouraged his audience to hunt, explaining, 'for therin is a very imitation of batayle'. He particularly praised forms of hunting that approximated most closely to war, drawing on the ancient author Xenophon for his inspiration.[83] Hunting, he declared, tested the courage of both horse and rider, especially when confronting dangerous beasts such as boars and stags. The fiercest animal was the wild boar. Lacking speed, a boar could not outstrip hounds and readily turned to face its adversaries, trusting to its tusks and strength. It could kill a hound with a single blow and inflict serious wounds on a huntsman.[84] In his memoirs Edward, Lord Herbert, recalled a confrontation with a boar while hunting in France. Cornered, the boar severely gored three or four hounds and then turned on Herbert when he tried to kill it with his sword. Herbert dismounted and, sword in hand, approached the boar, which in the meantime had injured more hounds. Although he succeeded in wounding the quarry, the beast continued to attack him, forcing him to sidestep in order to avoid its tusks. Then, when the surviving dogs had distracted the boar, Herbert attempted once more to administer the *coup de grâce*. This made the boar turn on him but, as it charged, the dogs drew it away again. Eventually, as Herbert recalled, 'soe relieving one another by Turns wee killed the Bore'.[85] The fleet-footed hart, on the other hand, invariably took to its heels and only defended itself when forced to do so. At bay, however, its antlers and strength made it a formidable opponent. In *The Master of the Game*, Edward of Norwich, Duke of York, reported an old saying, 'after the boar the leech and after the hart the bier'.[86] When delivering the final blow, the huntsman clearly had to take great care.[87] Peake's painting of Prince Henry, standing beside a slain deer and sheathing his sword, is a piece of propaganda, designed to emphasize the young man's bravery and hence his fitness to rule.[88]

Hunting, which entailed riding cross-country, also had a military application. Participants had to be skilled horsemen; depending on terrain, they had to learn how to cope with long hours in the saddle, often over rough ground, taking obstacles in their stride. As John Aubrey observed, referring to the outbreak of the Civil War, 'That advantage that King Charles I had: gentlemen tho [then] kept good horses, and many horses for a man-at-arms, and men that could ride them; hunting horses'.[89] At Edgehill on 23 October 1642 the Royalist cavalry, charging uphill and clearing hedges and ditches, routed the horse on the left flank of the Parliamentarian army.[90] According to Elyot, the rigours of hunting up hill and down dale developed such qualities as fortitude and resilience, attributes that enabled them, as soldiers, to 'sustayne travaile in warres hunger and thurst colde and heate'. He also pointed out the associated benefits of being able to read the landscape and to apply the knowledge strategically. As he wrote, 'it increaseth in them both agilities and quicknesse also sleight and policie to fynde suche passages & straytes where they may prevent or intrappe their enemies'.[91] William Higford of Dixton made similar points in 1658 when he declared in a memorandum to his grandson that, 'Hunting is usefull, to know the situation and distance of places; & to endure your body to labour'.[92]

Like jousting, hunting provided opportunities for participants to practise the use of weapons. When hunting in forested areas, Elyot wanted to use hounds merely to rouse the game, the pursuit being performed by the riders armed with javelins and other weapons 'in maner of warre'.[93] As Elyot was writing in Henry VIII's reign, his comments had some validity. Javelins were used by light horsemen, an important element in Henry's army. Although crossbows were becoming obsolete in battle during the course of the sixteenth century, huntsmen also discharged bolts on horseback, a feat which required considerable skill. In July 1572 the Earl of Leicester informed Lord Burghley that all the people on a progress he was about to join were 'hunters, and do nothing but ride about from bush to bush with a crossbow in their necks'.[94] In hunting, however, most of the people who fired weapons did so on foot and in a context that 'true' huntsmen deemed second rate. Elyot contemptuously remarked that killing deer with bows and arrows 'serveth well for the potte ... But it contayneth therin no commendable solace or exercise in comparison to the other forme of hunting if it be diligently perceived'.[95] As James I later told his son, Henry, in 1603: 'it is a thievish forme of hunting to shoote with gunnes and bowes; and grey hound hunting is not so martial a game'. To engage in the sport for utilitarian purposes, or to stack the odds so heavily against the quarry, seemed unsporting and undermined the nobility of the activity.[96] Yet the practice was commonplace. In parks, deer might be driven into 'toils' (nets or screens) and shot at with crossbows or firearms. In

July 1554 Sir William Petre, Mary I's Secretary, ordered 'a great toil of four or five miles long' for use in a hunt in Windsor Forest to celebrate Philip of Spain's arrival. At a similar event there in 1584 the Earl of Leicester put sixty to eighty harts inside toils so that Elizabeth and her courtiers could shoot at them. At times the carnage caused by this form of hunting exceeded even this number. In August 1541 the King's party, while hunting on Hatfield Chase on a progress, killed two hundred stags and does with bow and arrow and scarcely any fewer the following day.[97]

Advocates of the *manège* emphasized its value as training for war and promoted it as a means of strengthening the country's military capabilities. Elyot thought that riders schooled in riding the great horse benefited both in attack and defence: 'in pursuete of enemies and confounding them as in escapyng imminent daunger'. He also pointed out the offensive capabilities of the horse itself: 'a stronge and hardy horse dothe some tyme more damage under his maister than be with al his waipon: and also setteth forwarde the stroke and causeth it to lighte with more violence'.[98] Almost a century later, the Earl of Northampton set up his riding school with the express intention of training a cadre of skilled horsemen, who would serve with distinction in the cavalry in wartime.[99] William Cavendish also emphasized the practical value of the discipline, rebutting the view that the *manège* merely taught horses to perform tricks. He believed that it provided an excellent grounding for a cavalryman and his horse, claiming that a competent rider on such a mount had a clear advantage in single combat or in battle over someone whose horse had not received any training in the art.[100] There was some truth in this: undoubtedly, a cavalryman who had full control over his mount, especially a highly responsive managed horse, had a distinct, if theoretical, advantage over a less well-prepared enemy. Edward, Lord Herbert, who learned to ride the great horse at about the same time that William Cavendish was doing so, recalled in his memoirs one manoeuvre that was helpful when fighting a duel on horseback. To avoid being turned, the rider should make his mount move sideways until his opponent had ridden past him. In this way, he, rather than his adversary, would gain the advantage of attacking his opponent's left side.[101] This ploy, which might work in a duel when adversaries had no external distractions, was less easy to pull off in the midst of the stress and confusion of a pitched battle. After all, battles were not fought in the *manège* ring and the skills taught there were artificial and possibly inhibitory: far better to drill into the horse the manoeuvres required when engaged in actual fighting. Moreover, for war, horses required courage, composure and steadfastness if they were to cope effectively with the turmoil and terror of battle. While it was difficult to alter a horse's character, it was to a certain degree possible to replicate the experience of battle on the parade ground. In fact, there is some evidence that training did take place. In January 1598/9, for instance, Henry Farr accounted for 4s. 2d.

paid for match and gunpowder to train the earl of Rutland's great horses.[102] On 6 March 1627/8 the Council of War discussed Monsieur La Broue's method for accustoming a horse to battle. This consisted of dressing the groom attending it in armour; providing its provender on a drumhead; discharging a musket while it is eating its feed; and riding it against a suit of armour which it could knock over and trample on. Edward, Lord Herbert, had evidently read this advice because he discussed it in detail in his memoirs.[103]

These sports provided less tangible links to warfare in other ways as well. As men predominated among those taking part (even if some women hunted and hawked), hunting and tilting offered opportunities for male bonding and camaraderie. If the *manège* remained an individualistic pursuit, jousting was only partly so. Tilters met each other in single combat but often fought as members of a team, especially when challenging all-comers to fight them. At the tournament held on 12–13 February 1510/11 to celebrate the birth of Prince Henry, the King, with three other knights, issued the call to arms. Eight knights signed up on the first day and thirteen others on the second day. In the evening the parties socialized at the banquets and doubtlessly boasted about or made excuses for their performance at the day's events. In the May tournament of 1540 the six challengers kept open house at Durham Place from 30 April to 7 May, the guests at the evening suppers and banquets including the King, Queen and various nobles.[104] In Mary I's reign her husband, the Spanish king, Philip II, sponsored a series of tournaments, naively hoping that the experience of fighting alongside each other would engender a spirit of comradeship between the English and the unpopular Spaniards.[105]

Hunting, from the time that adolescent boys were initiated into the sport, similarly bound individuals together and reinforced friendships and alliances. In the early eighteenth century Nicholas Blundell of Little Crosby regularly hunted the Liverpool area in company with his friends, who included Lord Molineux, Messrs Syer, Clifton, Pigeon, Trafford, and his cousins Richard Butler and James Poole.[106] Some squires, seeking to improve relations with their tenantry, permitted them to join the hunt. In October 1667, for instance, Sir Thomas Myddelton of Chirk Castle allowed his agent, Thomas Edwards, 5s. for the 'Countrey people' accompanying him when he hunted the fox with Hugh ap Owen. In the absence of such an invitation, a number of local farmers and tradesmen established their own packs of foxhounds.[107] In the evening huntsmen enjoyed the conviviality of a post-hunt supper. On 8 August 1687 Sir John Reresby hunted with thirty others in the duke of Newcastle's park at Clipston and afterwards entertained most of them at dinner. When the duke of Newcastle dashed off a letter to the duke of Richmond on 28 November 1738, he had just come back from an exhilarating fox hunt of over ten miles of 'the best part of our Countrey'. 'You must not expect a long letter,' he wrote, 'being much wanted by a great number of friends, to go to dinner.'[108] In short, the shared experience, whether the anticipation of the exertions and dangers to come, the stress and thrill of the occasion itself, or the release of tension in the subsequent post-mortem, heightened the sense of group solidarity. Even those tenants, who hunted alongside their squires, were being drawn into a common appreciation of the benefits of paternalism within an hierarchical society.

EQUINE PURSUITS AND THE SYMBOLISM OF WAR

Collectively, these pastimes provided a range of symbols analogous to warfare. When Henry VIII and his companions met Francis I and his associates on the Field of the Cloth of Gold, both sides were fighting for the honour of their country, even if the action had been sublimated into the mock combat of the tiltyard.[109] Hunting, too, presented a semblance of war, in which the master as commander marshalled his forces – the huntsmen (staff officers), the mounted field (cavalry) and hounds (scouts and foot soldiers) – towards the goal of locating and overcoming the quarry (the enemy). Under the direction of the master and his officials, the hounds, having sought out the prey, advanced to engage it, followed by rest of the party. In the process they had to respond to the quarry's stratagems, utilizing their knowledge of their adversary and the terrain over which it was moving. As in real battles against able and noble foes, the huntsmen did not always achieve a kill and the enemy escaped. James Thompson, in 'Autumn' in his *The Seasons* (1730; revised in 1744), satirized the machismo of fox huntsmen, depicting them as show-offs, mainly concerned with displaying their riding skills and ability to outwit the fox.[110]

Analogies to warfare naturally led to tropes illustrating warlike concepts such as violence and domination. As noted earlier, the very act of riding in these equestrian pursuits served as a metaphor for man's command of the natural world. Hawking emphasized this control because it displayed man's authority over a wild creature possessing the freedom of the skies, even after training. The whole point of the process was not to break the bird's spirit but to school it to follow its natural predatory instincts when commanded to by its master.[111] Inevitably, some asserted their autonomy by flying off. Richard Cholmeley of Brandsby bought a goshawk for £3 10s. on 4 December 1613 but noted in his memorandum book that it (together with a tercel) failed to return when cast on 21 February 1613/4. Nine years later he lost one of the two merlins Richard Pullein had obtained for him in Ireland. Cholmeley relied on others to provide him with many of his hawks but, as he did not employ a falconer, seems to have trained his birds himself. Even so, three losses in the twenty-one years covered in the book indicates that the training process worked.[112] When out hawking and hunting on their estates, landowners like Cholmeley were not merely engaged in a sporting event but were also affirming their right to exploit all the fauna found there, domesticated and untamed, as they wished. Gascoigne asserted that, because He had given man dominion over all animals, God had created beasts of venery for man's recreation.[113] Horses, hounds and hawks were complicit in this arrangement, facilitating the pursuit and killing of their fellow creatures. If these subject animals had lost their ability to exercise their own agency through training and domestication, wild animals lost theirs at the hands of the huntsmen, their hawks or hounds or, at best, by imprisonment in parks and warrens.

Animal metaphors suggest strong analogies to occasions when human beings were being pursued and offer valuable insights into the mind of the huntsmen and the hunted. In *Henry VI Part III* Shakespeare likens Edward IV and Gloucester's pursuit of the defeated Lancastrians after the Battle of Hexham in May 1461 to

> a brace of greyhounds
> Having the fearful flying hare in sight.[114]

If this analogy conjures up a picture of vengeful victors hounding their terrified, fleeing opponents, Talbot's speech in *Henry IV Part I* evokes an heroic image of a noble stag at bay. Their plight,

> parked and bounded in a pale!
> A little herd of England's timorous deer
> Mazed with a yelping kennel of French curs,

was hopeless and, as the adjective 'timorous' momentarily suggests, likely to lead to abject surrender. Immediately, Talbot changes the tone, bellowing defiance; his band did not resemble cowed immature deer, 'rascal-like to fall down with a pinch' but 'moody-mad and desperate stags' who would

> Turn on the bloody hounds with heads of steel
> And make the cowards stand aloof at bay.[115]

Antony portrays the assassination of Julius Caesar in the same way, counterpointing the nobility of the victim with the bestiality of the killers, who like hounds, tore their quarry to pieces.

> Here wast thou bayed, brave hart;
> Here didst thou fall, and here the hunters stand
> Signed in thy spoil and crimsoned in thy lethe.[116]

The themes of pursuit and conquest, inherent in hunting, extended to the relationship between the sexes. Analogies were particularly apt because of the congruence between society and the sport, in both of which males played the dominant role. The concept of the 'love-hunt', linked etymologically in the double meaning of the word *venery*, reflected social realities because it normally portrayed men as the pursuers and women as the prey.[117] Women like Elizabeth I did hunt but contemporaries distinguished between those aspects of the sport which were suitable for them and those which were not. *Par force* hunting, for example, was essentially a male preserve. When, in the winter of 1614–15, John Chamberlain reported the manoeuvres of the suitors for the hand of Master Watson's 'fayre' daughter, he did so in hunting (and gaming) terms. Sir Lewis Watson, he wrote, 'hath her in chase, and pretends to have sure cardes to shew'. He also noted that Watson's rival, Sir Robert Sidney, was losing interest in spite of the urgings of his mother, Lady Barbara Sidney, for he 'growes wearie of hunting in a foyled s[c]ent, that hath ben haunted by so many suitors'.[118] Literature tended to follow social conventions, emphasizing male domination. Even when the wooing was jocular and good-natured, the metaphor implied a darker side. In *Titus Andronicus*, Shakespeare portrays the hunt at its most savage, as physical assault. While Titus prepares to chase the deer, others utilize the event to target a different quarry. Demetrius tells his brother:

> Chiron, we hunt not, we, with horse nor hound,
> But hope to pluck a dainty doe to ground.

That day, Lavinia, Titus's daughter, is raped and mutilated in a grotesque parody of the ritual of the dismembering of a dead hart.[119]

In the rutting season stags fight for the right to mate with the does, ensuring that the offspring descend from the strongest males. Arguments between young hot-heads over a particular lady notwithstanding, early modern society no longer insisted on such a test of virility to propagate the species. Even so, an echo of this primitive approach survived in the tournament, in which contestants competed against each other, wearing the 'badge' of their lady and fighting on her behalf. William Higford, in his advice to his grandson, recalled the exploits of his great-grandfather, Sir James Scudamore, a valiant soldier and a skilled performer in the tiltyard. In his account, William emphasized the element of display and the jouster's urge to demonstrate his prowess in front of the fairer sex. Sir James, he wrote, entered the arena, dressed in fine armour and mounted on a mettlesome horse. In the joust he broke as many lances as anyone else and all before the approving gaze of the Queen, her ladies in waiting and the whole court.[120] Dekker, in *The Shoemaker's Holiday*, made the same point when Hammon, describing ways to win a lady, exclaims,

> Or shall I undertake some martial spoil,
> Wearing your glove at tourney and at tilt,

> And tell how many gallants I unhorsed –
> Sweet, will this pleasure you?[121]

Even if they wished to impress a lady, men dominated the arena. The chivalric code prized chastity but it did so as a means of controlling women: men imposed it and they took it away. The double standards concerning sexuality commodified women by setting a value on their sexual state but not on men's, thereby making them 'tokens of exchange'. Moreover, in Freudian terms the lance represents the erect male phallus; in an amphitheatre bristling with lances, wielded by testosterone-fuelled competitors astride powerful horses, intent on demonstrating their prowess to watching females, the atmosphere must have crackled with an erotic charge. In the early days of the tournament the victor occasionally did obtain a sexual reward, but normally his conquest took a symbolic form, either a kiss or a token.[122] Of course, the lance as penis is but one trope for the analogy between weapons and aggressive male sexuality, which expands the metaphor to encompass the concept of 'the battle between the sexes'. In *Romeo and Juliet*, the Capulet retainers discuss the forthcoming skirmish with the Montagues in terms replete with sexual imagery.

Gregory	The quarrel is between our masters and us their men.
Samson	'Tis all one. I will show myself a tyrant: when I have fought with the men I will be civil with the maids – I will cut off their heads.
Gregory	The heads of the maids?
Samson	Ay, the heads of the maids, or their maidenheads, take it in what sense thou wilt.
Gregory	They must take it in sense that feel it.
Samson	Me they shall feel while I am able to stand, and 'tis known I am a pretty piece of flesh.
Gregory	'Tis well thou art not fish. If thou hadst, thou hadst been poor-john. Draw thy tool. Here comes the house of Montagues.
Samson	My naked weapon is out. Quarrel, I will back thee.[123]

Elizabeth I, on the other hand, was neither a passive nor a temporary virgin, resigned to fulfil a woman's allotted role of marriage and motherhood, in which a man would dominate her actions, influence her thoughts and penetrate her body. She therefore rearranged the iconographic elements of the tournament for her own ends. In particular, she manipulated its chivalric associations to underpin the cult of the virgin queen that she fostered, partly as a means of deflecting calls for her to marry. It also enabled her, as a woman operating in a man's world, to convert her weakness as a female into a source of strength by binding powerful courtiers (and possible intriguers) to her with personal ties of allegiance. She therefore made the Accession Day Tilt, instigated in the 1570s by Sir Henry Lee, the Queen's Champion, and held on 17 November, the high point of the court year. There, led by her champion, the flower of the country's young bloods did homage to Elizabeth in ritual combat.[124] In effect, she transformed her courtiers into knights errant, ready to serve her even to the death. Many did fight and die for her and, like Sir Philip Sidney at Zutphen, did so according to the promises they made at the tournaments over which she had presided. No doubt they acted out of patriotic motives but there were psychological undercurrents too. Subconsciously, Elizabeth I's continued virgin status must have had an unsettling effect on her courtiers because it reversed the conventional attitude that men were the ones who controlled women's sexuality. In this situation a natural response would be for them to prove their manhood on the field of battle.

Under Elizabeth I men had to come to terms with the fact that a woman was ruling the country. More worryingly, they came to realize that she was no one's possession, politically, matrimonially or metaphorically. If the queen had to work hard to convince her sceptical male courtiers and ministers that she could do the job by herself, for many the lack of a husband to guide her threatened to turn the world upside down. In one of her iconographic representations Elizabeth I was depicted as Diana, the virgin huntress, whose arrows denoted chastity and independence.[125] Dramatists regularly deployed the image of the hunt to play on male anxieties about the female sex. Shakespeare, for example, gives us the characters of Tamora in *Titus Andronicus*, Hippolyta in *A Midsummer Night's Dream* and Venus in *Venus and Adonis*. In *Venus and Adonis* he reverses the 'natural' order of the love-hunt: while the adolescent Adonis focuses on killing the boar as a means of becoming a man, Venus offers an alternative route by attempting to seduce him.[126] Moreover, hunting imagery in the shape of the cuckold's horns illustrate the plight of the husband whose wife seeks sexual gratification elsewhere. Emasculation and loss of authority were issues which greatly troubled Renaissance men. As Boehrer notes, 'No animal image is more commonplace to English Renaissance culture' than the horns of the cuckolded husband. Indeed, in *All's Well that Ends Well*, Shakespeare reveals the extent that it had permeated society's consciousness. When the Countess asks the clown, 'Will your answer serve fit to all questions', he replies, *inter alia*, as 'the cuckold to his horn'.[127] Faithful women did not cuckold their husbands or as Orlando claimed in *As You Like It*, 'Virtue is no horn-maker, and my Rosalind is virtuous.'[128]

Uncertainty even attends Katherina's submission at the end of *The Taming of the Shrew*, reflecting the mode of the training, comparable to that of schooling a hawk. So, Petruchio keeps her half-starved and deprived of sleep:

> And till she stoop, she must not be full-gorg'd,
> For then she never looks upon her lure …
> Last night she slept not, nor today she shall not …[129]

Skilfully, Shakespeare sets up the dramatic dénouement at the end of the final scene by incorporating elements of coursing, falconry and hunting in it. First, Petruchio taunts Tranio, who had wooed Bianca in the guise of his master, Lucentio, for having missed his aim. Tranio reveals the subterfuge in his reply:

> O, sir, Lucentio slipped me like his greyhound,
> Which runs himself and catches for his master.

He then aims a jibe at Petruchio in return:

> Tis well, sir, that you hunted for yourself
> Tis thought your deer does hold you at a bay.[130]

Irritated when the others laugh at Tranio's riposte, Petruchio lays a bet with Hortensio and Lucentio to see whose wife is the most obedient. Petruchio has reformed Katherina, having trained her as his 'haggard', but, presumably, she, like the hawk, has only sublimated her natural instincts: hence, the ambiguity of Katherina's last speech. Although submissive in tone, it contains the possibility that she will relapse into independence and 'shrewishness'.[131]

DIPLOMACY

If diplomacy represents war by another name, all the pursuits discussed here played their part in the process. Tournaments featured strongly in state occasions, whether a coronation, a royal birth or a meeting with foreign rulers or ambassadors. Their inclusion offered the visiting dignitaries a spectacular show, designed to impress them (and native onlookers) with the magnificence and power of the crown. In an age of personal kingship, in which the amount of effective power a monarch could wield depended upon his or her own special qualities, real or perceived, public image mattered. He or she had to act in a certain style, and an ostentatious display of wealth, especially when linked with a symbolic show of martial arts, produced the desired effect. As a usurper, Henry VII recognized the political and diplomatic value of the tournament as a means of enhancing his authority at home and his prestige abroad. In spite of a reputation for parsimony, he readily lavished money on them. If, like Henry VIII, the monarch himself took part in the joust, he had to look regal and this sent costs soaring.[132] Within the country itself, courtiers organized tournaments to entertain visiting monarchs on progress with the intention of ingratiating themselves with him or her. Because she used the tournament figuratively as a means of self-promotion Elizabeth I's ministers and favourites knew that by putting on a suitably lavish event they would please the Queen. But it had to have an acceptable subject. When the Queen's favourite, the Earl of Leicester, entertained her at Kenilworth in 1575, the motif of the accompanying masque, which extolled the benefits of marriage over virginity, did not go down very well and was not performed. At Woodstock, later in the progress, Sir Henry Lee was on far safer ground when he adopted the theme of subordinating personal desire to the greater goal of service to the state.[133]

Hunting, by its very nature, provided the astute politician with a useful diplomatic tool. An invitation to join a hunting party indicated favour, while freedom from the court encouraged greater informality and an opportunity to discuss affairs of state in a relaxed atmosphere. On 17 August 1545 van der Delft, the imperial ambassador, wrote to Charles V, informing him that Henry VIII had done him every honour, taking him out hunting and 'constantly holding kind and familiar conversation with him'.[134] At that moment England faced an invasion from France, provoked by the Anglo-Imperial campaigns in that country in 1544. In spite of Henry's anger at Charles V's withdrawal from the war and concerns over the peace terms, he neither wanted to reject the emperor's role as mediator nor to drive him into the French camp. In the same manner, the lavish welcome given to the special emissary from France at Christmastide 1620 should be seen in the context of the difficulties confronting James I's son-in-law, Frederick, the Elector Palatine, in the face of a Habsburg invasion of his ancestral lands.[135] According to Richard Cholmeley, the ambassador and his company stayed at Somerset House, dined at Westminster with the King, and daily went hunting and hawking in the royal parks with Prince Charles and parties of English nobles.[136] Conversely, the lack of an invitation represented a diplomatic snub or at least the diplomatic equivalent of a cold. When, on 20 July 1546, de Selve, the French ambassador, requested an audience with the King, he could not obtain one, being informed that the Henry VIII was going out hunting. As noted above, hunting might also distract the monarch and affect the running of the country. On 17 September 1540 the French ambassador, Marillac, wrote to Montmorency that he had no news worth writing, for the King, with a small party, had gone out hunting about twenty miles away.[137]

Monarchs also exploited the exclusive social cachet of hunting to strengthen their ties with influential subjects. Apart from inviting individuals to hawk and hunt with them, they gained political capital by giving or receiving deer, venison, hawks, hounds and hunting horses, and used posts in their parks, stables, kennels and mews for patronage purposes. Subjects sought these positions as marks of favour and as a source of local influence, especially if appointed to a prestigious position like a warden- or keepership of a park or forest. In 1537, for instance, Raphe Sadler asked Thomas Cromwell if he could have the keepership of a park near London so that he could exercise his geldings in winter and for 'other commodities'.[138] A gift eased the path to preferment. On 26 September 1585

Raphe Bowes urged Secretary Walsingham to accept the partridges he had caught, while hawking the previous day, an indication of his skill as a falconer and the prowess of his hawk. He then added that if old Mitchell's position were shortly to become vacant, he hoped to be appointed to it. In December 1624 the Earl of Rutland invited Robert Terrett, a royal equerry, to come to his stables to choose his best hare or buck hunter for the King, with the intention, it seems, to make the King favourably disposed towards a request from Lord Savidge for a post.[139] The upper classes made similar political calculations. They allowed their friends and associates to hunt in their parks and gave and received gifts too. Sir John Reresby of Thrybergh Hall was a member of Henry Cavendish, 2nd Duke of Newcastle's, circle and regularly dined, stayed and hunted with him.[140] As a valued ally, he received favours from the Duke: on one occasion two pied deer and a wild tup for his park and on another the use of the Duke's park at Clipston.

Hunting parties often took on a distinct political hue. The Whiggish Charlton Hunt, under the joint mastership of the Duke of Richmond and the Earl of Tankerville, provided an opportunity for their friends and political associates to socialize, discuss politics and, by issuing invitations, to show favour to actual or potential supporters.[141] As the Whigs held office, their gatherings did not raise governmental concerns about their thoughts and actions. In contrast, the authorities viewed meetings of its political opponents with suspicion. At times of crisis therefore they readily imagined that their rivals were using hunts, like race meetings, as a cover to plot mischief. For years after the deposition of James II in 1688 the authorities, worried about the threat of a Jacobite uprising, regularly searched the houses of suspects for horses valued at £5 or more and, if found, seized them.[142] In March 1707/8, for instance, Sir Gervase Clifton of Clifton had to give up four coach mares and two hunters. Nicholas Blundell, a Roman Catholic, living in a strongly Catholic county and with family links to known sympathizers, received several visits between 22 February 1704/5 and 18 August 1715.[143] The authorities made similar searches in 1744–5 at the time of the rising in support of the Young Pretender. They might also incarcerate Jacobite sympathizers. In general, members of the lieutenancy, charged with the duty of carrying out these measures, treated these potential traitors, mostly fellow gentry, with courtesy and consideration. Indeed, those involved often seemed embarrassed at having to proceed against their peers. In 1745, for instance, agents acting on behalf of the Duke of Newcastle, lord lieutenant of Sussex, exhibited 'the greatest distaste' when impounding the horses and arms of John Caryll. One of them, John Page, declared that he would return them to him 'with a thousand times the satisfaction [with which] I received them'. Sending their compliments to Caryll, Page and two fellow magistrates added that, 'they have not gone thro' a more disagreeable task [in] a long while ... You behaved with great propriety and politeness.' They hoped that he felt that they had acted in the same spirit.[144]

Contemporaries constantly emphasized the merits of the featured sports, hawking and hunting, jousting and the *manège*, as preparation for war and their comments suggest that they really did believe that these activities had some value. They were right. First, all four pursuits required participants to be skilled horsemen, often under pressure, and this benefited them when in wartime they enlisted in the cavalry. In the opening engagements of the Civil War the Royalist horsemen seem to have had the edge because their gentlemen officers and retainers had had greater experience in the hunting field. Furthermore, jousting (and the tournament in general) offered soldiers practice in the use of weapons that for much of the sixteenth century at least they might wield on the battlefield. Huntsmen too had to be dextrous with the sword and dagger, if they were to dispatch the formidable hart or boar. They might also shoot at their prey with a crossbow, a difficult feat on horseback. Over time, the transferability of these specific skills declined as lances and crossbows became obsolete. Jousting did survive into the seventeenth century, mainly as a spectacle and for its symbolism. Thus Princes Henry and Charles, the sons of James I, learned to joust because as a demonstration of their mastery of the martial arts, it confirmed their suitability as prospective monarchs.

These pursuits were predominantly male activities, although some women did hawk and hunt. The appeal of these sports to the upper classes is readily understood, for they pandered to their sense of manhood and showmanship In particular, they enabled participants publicly to display their riding skills, to demonstrate their bravery and fortitude, and to socialize and bond with each other. The tension and the excitement before the event and the social camaraderie after it were essential parts of the occasion. In general, women's presence was peripheral, though welcome, for men needed an audience and the opportunity to show their superiority over the opposite sex. So, even where the latter participated, as in hawking and hunting, men led the way, attempted the most difficult jumps and featured more prominently at the kill. Metaphorically, too, these sports, through riding and hunting tropes, reinforced the dominance of women by men. The lance's symbolism is even more pronounced. More grandly, these activities emphasized man's governance of the whole of God's creation, that is, by hunting creatures for pleasure as well as for food.

Of course, the sports featured here were not the exclusive preserve of military men or misogynists. People enjoyed them for their own sake, though each sport had its own discipline. Harshness and privation certainly played a part in training horses to perform the artificial steps of the *manège* or getting a hawk to take the lure. Even so, the sense of achievement in gaining mastery and exercising control over such independent creatures (and showing off one's success to an audience) was itself a worthwhile goal. Similarly, hawking and hunting provided an exhilarating day out, in which physical barriers had to be cleared and the quarry outwitted: man, horse and hound working in unison. Landed society also valued these pursuits because of their exclusivity. Contemporaries emphasized the point that they were only suitable for the elite, who alone had the funds, the time and the essential upbringing and quality of mind to appreciate them. Participation, in a real sense, defined a gentleman. If costs acted as an insufficient deterrent, as in hunting, the upper classes imposed social and legal barriers too. To add further mystique and accentuate the distinction between members of the club and the masses outside, the hunting and sporting elite created and sustained its own special terminology, lore and customs.

The Cavalry and Early Modern Warfare

Ever since Michael Roberts published his seminal work, *The Military Revolution, 1560–1660*, in 1956, military historians have hotly debated the subject, arguing about the pace, timing and nature of the change as well as the validity of the concept itself. Such is the level of disagreement on all these issues, which has widened over time, that it is difficult to continue to use the term 'revolution' in any meaningful way to describe advances made in between the Renaissance and the mid eighteenth century. As an example of this lack of agreement one might point to the diversity of opinion contained in the papers edited by Clifford J. Rogers and and published under the title, *The Military Revolution Debate* (1995).[1] This is not to say that the period did not see profound developments in the art of warfare, both offensively and defensively. Key elements of change included a rise in the proportion of infantry at the expense of the cavalry; the growing importance of gunpowder weapons (handguns and artillery); changes in cavalry tactics; greater sophistication in urban defences; a marked expansion in size and cost of armies; and the greater involvement of the state in the provision of men, arms and equipment. This period was a time of mixed fortunes for the cavalry. In particular, the heavy cavalry, the cutting edge of the medieval army, suffered from changes in tactics and developments in technology which gave priority to the infantry. Throughout the sixteenth century the shift became more pronounced as pike-shot tactics developed. As a result, the cavalry were often reduced to the status of mounted pistoleers. Even when the cavalry made a come back in the early seventeenth century, there was no return to the medieval heavy horse formations. Nonetheless, heavier horses of a different kind were still needed. The emphasis on firepower, for instance, enhanced the role of the artillery and with it a growing demand for draught horses. Similarly, as armies grew in size, so did their baggage trains and the number of teams needed to pull the wagons. England, largely isolated from the European conflicts, had less reason to change and the degree to which its commanders incorporated military innovations into their tactical and strategic planning is a matter of debate.

A MILITARY REVOLUTION?

The outcome of a number of late medieval battles revealed that on favourable terrain infantry could defeat heavily armoured knights. At Bannockburn (1314) the English cavalry foundered on the spears of the Scottish shildrons. The longer pikes were even more effective, as they outreached the lances held by the men-at-arms. Missile weaponry proved its worth as well; English archers destroyed the French cavalry at Crecy (1346), Poitiers (1356) and Agincourt (1415). Those who made it to the English lines died at the hands of infantrymen or dismounted knights, wielding their lances like foot soldiers. Infantry armed with pole weapons might win, even on open ground. At Laupen (1339), for example, Swiss halberdiers and pikemen, operating without cavalry cover, defeated a larger Burgundian army, complete with infantry and cavalry.[2] On terrain suitable for horsemen, however, cavalry still won battles, as the French did at Mons-en-Pévèl (1304) and Cassel (1328).[3] The adoption of the lance rest in the first half of the fourteenth century and developments in body armour in the second half gave the heavy cavalry a renewed, if brief, lease of life. Clad from head to toe in plate armour, rounded and polished to deflect missiles, men-at-arms were almost invulnerable to arrows except for direct hits at close range.[4] The revival did not last long, however, because armour proved ineffective against the firearms then emerging as a battlefield weapon. The battle of Pavia in 1525 marked a turning point, for it witnessed the humiliating defeat of Francois I and his mounted knights by a detachment of imperial harquebusiers.[5] Thereafter, the proportion of cavalrymen in armies steadily declined.[6]

At first pikes led the way, interest in deploying them strengthened by the success of the Swiss phalanx over the Burgundian cavalry in the 1470s. It influenced the thinking of the military leaders of the day, notably those who fought in the Italian Wars, and directly led to changes in army formations. All self-respecting commanders had to include a substantial contingent of pikemen in their forces. They also had to enlist detachments of harquebusiers, who protected the pikemen from attack.[7] Without them, their position was very exposed, as reflected in defeats at Cerignola (1503), Ravenna (1512), Marignano (1515) and Bicocca (1522).[8] As firearm technology developed during the course of the sixteenth century, leading to the replacement of the cumbersome harquebus by the lighter caliver or the more proficient and deadly (if heavier) musket, the relative importance of the two weapons changed. Even so, it required the reforms of the Nassau family in the 1590s fully to realize the potential of fire power.[9] They achieved this by arranging the musketeers in linear formations and improving their firing rate by thorough drilling. Through the countermarch, an infantry line comprising ten lines could now maintain a constant barrage. Gustavus Adolphus, the Swedish king who took his country into the Thirty Years' War in 1630, further refined this system. He speeded up the reloading process by using the recently introduced powder cartridge which enabled him to deploy his musketeers only six lines deep. He also trained them to 'double their files', a manoeuvre which entailed the even numbered ranks moving into the gaps in the odd numbered ones when they fired. Such a formation could even deliver a devasting single salvo. In this set-up, in which firepower dictated infantry tactics, pikemen found themselves relegated to a secondary role, that of protecting the musketeers. Nonetheless they still retained an offensive capability when the infantry advanced, engaging their counterparts in the enemy lines in 'push of pike'.[10] By the turn of the seventeenth century the use of the socket bayonet had made the pike redundant, since it enabled the musketeer to become his own pikeman. By then the widespread adoption of the flintlock musket, coupled with the pre-packaged charge, meant that three rows of musketeers could maintain a continuous barrage of fire.[11]

Even at the height of the fashion for infantry, no one contemplated dispensing with cavalry altogether. Mounted troops performed a number of vital functions that made them invaluable to a commander: to turn an enemy's flank, to probe at the fringes of the opposing army, to protect their infantry against skirmishers and even to make the traditional frontal assault on the enemy. Although ineffective against disciplined and well-protected infantry formations, they could decimate the enemy once openings started to appear, either through irresolution, bombardment or a prolonged mêlée. At Ravenna (1512), the French cavalry discovering a gap at one end of the Spanish line, were able to attack it from the flank and rear. Assailed from the front by the French infantry at the same time, the Spanish line broke. In a rout like this one cavalry were lethal.[12] Troopers also provided valuable service as scouts and foragers, and on lightning raids their mobility enabled them to travel further and more quickly than soldiers on foot. Based in garrisons, they could dominate a wide hinterland.[13] Such tasks were often undertaken by the light horse, an arm that grew in number and importance in the late fifteenth and sixteenth centuries. One section, the stradiots (in Spain, genitors) carried a spear or javelin and a sword and acted as 'prickers', harassing enemy formations. They tried to break up the opposing ranks by hurling their javelins and picking off stragglers with their swords.[14] The other section fired arrows and, subsequently, shot from horseback. Mounted harquebusiers first appeared in the late fifteenth century, toting the cumbersome harquebus. While many detachments dismounted for battle, becoming the dragoons of the seventeenth century, they did fight on horseback as well. According to Williams, a veteran of numerous continental campaigns, commanders made use of the speed and mobility of light horsemen to launch surprise attacks on the quarters of a distant enemy; to intercept convoys; to scout out the land and search for the enemy; to forage; and to spare the heavy horse from non-battlefield duties.[15]

Some units of lancers did survive through the sixteenth century. Henri IV of France, for example, made good use of heavy cavalry, winning battles at Coutras (1587) and Ivry (1590).[16] These troops mostly comprised what in England were known as demi-lances, because they wore lighter armour and rode unbarded horses. Increasingly, they carried firearms as a second weapon. Indeed, with the introduction of the compact and technically advanced wheel-lock pistol in the mid sixteenth century, many cavalry units primarily functioned as mounted pistoleers, performing the manoeuvre known as the *caracole*. This entailed the synchronization of individual cavalry detachments, which trotted forward in turn to discharge their pistols before making way for the next wave. Performed properly, it gave the cavalry the means of subjecting the opposite ranks to continuous volleys of fire. Riders, however, required a degree of dexterity and a good deal of courage, because, due to its low muzzle velocity, pistols were effective only at extreme short range. At Roundway Down on 13 July 1643 the Royalist Captain Atkyns, having failed to wound the cuirassier-clad Sir Arthur Hesilrige, observed that he was 'too well armed all over for a pistol bullet to do him any hurt, having a coat of mail over his arms and a headpiece (I am confident) musket proof'. Further shots from Atkyns and from two of his officers similarly failed to penetrate Hesilrige's armour.[17] Besides, the enemy's musketeers outgunned the troopers and the latter faced a far heavier barrage of shot to boot. For these reasons, the tactic was rarely successful by itself. To have any chance of achieving their goal the riders relied on gaps being opened up by their own infantry and artillery.[18]

In the seventeenth century the cavalry regained some of its former glory, the fortunes of the respective horse formations generally determining the outcome of the contest. Victory usually went to the side that, having defeated its counterparts, reformed to take the foot from the flank and rear and, if necessary, to squeeze the cavalry on the opposite wing in a pincer movement. The greater prominence accorded to the mounted arm is reflected in the greater numbers of horsemen serving in the armies that fought in the Thirty Years' War. At Lützen, one-half of Wallenstein's imperial army and one-third of the Gustavus Adolphus's forces comprised horse.[19] The reforms of Gustavus Adolphus provided the stimulus. He revolutionized cavalry tactics, curtailing the use of the *caracole* and reintroducing the element of shock. Unlike the Dutch his troopers took the initiative, charging in close order, a ploy that turned each squadron into a solid phalanx and maximized the force of the impact. They also formed up in three lines rather than the six ranks of the Dutch system. At the same time, aware of the problems outlined above, Gustavus Adolphus added detachments of musketeers and mobile artillery pieces to his mounted units. An artillery barrage, followed by a musket salvo, preceded the cavalry charge. Once the musketeers, who had advanced with the horse, had fired their volley, the troopers spurred their horses forward, exploiting the gaps which the weight of shot had (with any luck) opened up in front of them. The King instructed the first line of troopers to fire one of their pistols at close range before pressing home the attack with their sabres. The second and third rows followed them, sabres drawn, keeping their pistols for the ensuing mêlée. Meanwhile, the musketeers had reloaded and were ready to cover their cavalry's retreat or to join them in their next task.[20] Military historians have questioned the effectiveness of this arrangement, which reduced the speed of the cavalry and drew the musketeers out into the open, covered only by mobile artillery. Roberts, Gustavus Adophus's biographer, agrees that this was a compromise solution but it was novel and it worked. Others imitated his methods.[21]

The firepower revolution of the fifteenth century incorporated developments in artillery, enabling gunfounders to make cannon that were cheaper and quicker to reload, were more accurate and had greater penetrative power. When coupled with the introduction of stronger, more reliable 'corned' gunpowder, artillery became a much more powerful branch of an army. Medieval fortifications could no longer withstand a determined bombardment and, consequently, the balance of advantage shifted from the besieged to the besieger.[22] Engineers responded by creating the *trace italienne*, a defensive system designed to resist any attack. This entailed the construction of lower but thicker walls and the setting up of gun platforms. To provide flanking fire, projecting angled bastions punctuated the walls at intervals. Refinements included the digging of a wide and deep moat; the construction of casements or ravelins to defend it; and the further elaboration of projections in structures known as crown- or hornworks. Outlying star-shaped redoubts completed the plan.[23] In turn, the defenders now had the upper hand and besiegers generally only defeated them by conducting a prolonged siege and creating a double circumvallation, one line of trenches tightening the noose and the other one protecting the attackers from a relieving force. Apart from their use in sieges, armies also deployed ordnance in the field. While the larger pieces remained fixed, once put in position, the introduction of lighter, mobile guns, pulled by a couple of horses, added a greater degree of flexibility and a new dynamic on the battlefield.

Transporting cannon caused problems. Siege guns were immensely heavy and were moved by water wherever possible. If carried overland, they required large numbers of draught animals to pull them. When Henry VIII invaded France in 1513 he possessed six bombards, each firing a 260 lbs cannonball and requiring an 80 lbs charge of gunpowder. When on the march, it took teams of twenty-four powerful Flanders mares to move them. Two horses pulled the 1¼ lb. falconets.[24] Other animals transported gunpowder and shot and a wide range of tools and implements. All this impedimenta slowed down to a crawl the speed at which an army could move, and wet weather on clayey roads further reduced its progress.[25] Armies used oxen as well as horses for draught, though horses were usually preferred on account of their speed and versatility and, more debatably at the beginning of the period, their strength. In the late middle ages oxen on average may have been as strong, if not stronger, than horses. The most powerful animals of all, however, were horses, notably ones from Flanders. In England horses from the fen edge parishes in East Anglia also outperformed oxen. In 1544 estimates of the number of victualling wagons calculated the draught at seven horses or ten oxen. On the other hand, horses were more expensive than oxen: in 1544 the rate for the horses was £1 13s. 4d. and for oxen £1 3s. 0d.[26]

By the time of the Civil Wars the proportion of horses to oxen for the draught had grown, though, where convenient, armies still used the latter. In England, the Royalists were more likely to deploy them because of their territorial strength in the north and west, the regions where oxen were most numerous. Prince Maurice employed oxen in the Lostwithiel campaign in the south-west in autumn 1644.[27] Nonetheless, wherever possible the Royalist Council of War used horses. Earlier in the year, in March 1643/4, it had concluded that the fifty-three oxen in the artillery train were 'not to bee so fitt and usefull … as horses are' and had told the Wagon-Master-General and the Commissary General of the Draught Horses to sell them and buy horses with the proceeds.[28] In Ireland, the perennial shortage of suitable horses ensured that oxen performed a larger proportion of draught services. Oxen provided the Irish confederates with the bulk of their traction requirements. The Royalists employed them too: oxen pulled the ordnance at the Battle of Ross in March 1643 and they were still carrying out similar tasks in mid 1649. The Parliamentarians tried to a greater extent to make up for the deficiency by transporting draught horses from England.[29]

MILITARY SERVICE AND THE LANDED ELITE

When in 1495 Henry VII put the force of the law behind his subjects' obligation to fight for king and country, he particularly emphasized the duty owed by the landed elite. In an echo of their old feudal responsibilities, he expected nobles to answer his personal request by raising soldiers, arms and equipment. In doing so, the king was formalizing existing practice. In 1492, as he set about overawing France with a show of force, his nobles contracted to furnish a specific number of men, arms and equipment, the terms of the agreement being set out in detailed indentures.[30] Earlier in the century leading magnates had utilized a similar device, known as retinue and indenture, to gather around them bodies of professional soldiers, a system that could have supplied the royal army with an effective fighting force. Of course, it relied on a strong king to exert control; unfortunately, under the unworldly Henry VI the nobles were able to use their retainers for their own advancement and the country sank into civil war. As part of the Tudor pacification, monarchs passed measures against the practice, but they also adapted it to their ends. Henry VIII followed his father's example and in 1511–12 sent letters to his leading subjects, asking them to inform him of the number of able men they could recruit on their estates and through their offices. Although aristocrats did not thereafter indent to supply troops, they continued to make their own contributions. In 1522–3 the Earl of Shrewsbury recruited troops from his estates in Derbyshire, Shropshire and Staffordshire, while sixty-four of the Earl of Northumberland's contingent of 732 men comprised household servants.[31]

Because of their specific form of military aid the nobility were exempt from providing men, arms and equipment for the county militia. At times of crisis, as in the Northern Rising of 1569 or in the Armada year of 1588, their contribution was particularly valuable, since their local power and influence enabled them to raise men quickly. In 1588 the government asked the nobility, court officials and bishops to provide 16,000 men for the queen's bodyguard.[32] In a civil war, their support was crucial and the lack of it extremely damaging. Undoubtedly, the reluctance of a number of peers to support Charles I in the winter of 1638–9 was a serious blow to the King, hampering his attempts to raise forces against the Scottish covenanters.[33] On 14 February 1638/9, for instance, the Earl of Peterborough told Secretary Windebank that because of the short notice he was ill-provided with horses and arms. The following day the Earl of Thanet wrote in the same vein. Undoubtedly, some individuals did experience problems, but the excuses seem spurious. Supporters like the Earl of Huntingdon and Lord Fauconberg managed to deliver their quota. Fauconberg told Windebank that he would attend the muster with at least ten horse and twenty foot arms, adding that the King had no subject more ready to fight and die for him than he.[34] Besides, estate records of the time reveal well-stocked stables. In Yorkshire Lord Bayning possessed at least sixty-five horses in 1637 and in Westmorland Sir John Lowther's stud produced several foals a year. The Earl of Cumberland managed to acquire ninety-eight horses, mainly from the stables of northern gentlemen, including mounts from the celebrated Fenwick stud.[35] This region, it should be remembered, produced the best saddle horses in the country.

It was not long before Royalists and Parliamentarians employed the horses in genteel and noble stables for military use. On 10 June 1642 Parliament issued the Propositions, asking people to send in money, plate, horses and arms. The authorities promised to reimburse subscribers with 8 per cent interest, at least for the money and plate. Royalists responded with the Engagement, in which forty-five noblemen and government ministers swore to protect the King and agreed to provide over 1,935 horses, along with their arms and equipment.[36] Others followed their lead. As Sir Edmund Verney instructed his steward on 19 June 1642, 'When my mare Lea hath foaled, let the foale be knockt on the head, and the mare taken to Howse, for I cannot spare her this summer ... There will be a press shortly in the country'. On 20 July the Lincolnshire gentry offered 168 horses to the King and on 14 August their counterparts in Worcestershire donated more than seventy-three.[37] Overall, some noblemen disbursed considerable sums of money in raising and maintaining detachments of troops and arms for the King; the marquises of Newcastle and Worcester each reputedly spent about £1,000,000 in the royalist cause.[38] Among those who contributed to Parliament was Sir Gerrard Napper, who donated a great sum of money and furnished the army with many serviceable horses and arms. In Staffordshire Henry Jackson sent in eighty horses, plus arms and equipment, on the Propositions.[39]

Although the elite provided all manner of troops and *matériel*, they were disproportionately responsible for supplying the cavalry, the most expensive branch of an army. This was a long-standing association. In the middle ages only nobles could afford the cost of a *lance garnie*, the term given to the knight, together with accoutrements, horses (destriers and other horses) and servants. In the period 1250–1350 they spent between £50 and £100 (and perhaps even more) on a good destrier.[40] While horses belonging to most men-at-arms were less expensive, ranging from £5 to £10, they still had to pay for a suit of armour, which cost £10 to £15 in the late fourteenth century and a good deal more a century later.[41] In the early sixteenth century income tended to divide men-at-arms from the light cavalry. According to the Venetian ambassador, writing of musters in 1551, the heavy cavalry consisted 'for the most part of gentlemen rather than others as they are better able to bear the expense and to provide themselves with good horses'.[42] At the time, many gentlemen men-at-arms rode expensive Neapolitan coursers, their value reflecting their strength as well as the dictates of fashion and the standing of the studs which produced them, mostly located abroad.

Interest in horsemanship meant that the upper classes naturally gravitated towards the cavalry in wartime, as befitted their upbringing, status and training. In 1581 Sir Philip Sidney reported that Pugliano, his riding master, had said that 'soldiers were the noblest estate of mankind, and horsemen the noblest of soldiers. He said that they were the masters of war and ornaments of peace, speedy goers and strong abiders, triumphers both in camps and courts.'[43] Commensurate with their noble blood, aristocratic riders like Sidney rode valuable horses, but, in general, early modern developments brought about a certain levelling down in the status of mounted troops. Costs had fallen from their medieval peak. Cavalrymen performing the *caracole* did not need really expensive horses or costly plate armour. In the late sixteenth century they could obtain a troop horse for well under £5 and arms and equipment for £2 to £3.[44] In January 1597/8 the appraisers of the goods belonging to Arthur Lippincotte Esquire of Alverdiscott in Devon valued his light horse and furniture at £6 13s.

4d., an indication of the sums involved.[45] In the First Civil War the New Model Army bought troop horses for £7 10s., probably an excessive rate.[46] Of course, wealthy officers might ride expensive animals as an indicator of their social status but often because they had good quality horses in their stables. On 30 March 1645 Sir Samuel Luke, the Parliamentarian Scoutmaster-General, reported that he had heard that four cavaliers riding horses worth £50 each had been seen spying on the fortifications at Aylesbury.[47]

Advances in the art of warfare also economized on time. It took years to master the lance but not nearly as long to learn how to fire a pistol and to understand the basic principle of the *caracole*. For the same reason, it was easier to produce harquebusiers than archers.[48] The ranks of the cavalry therefore opened up 'to all who could sit a horse and fire a pistol'.[49] As the price differential between the costs of the horse and foot narrowed, the division between patrician cavalry and plebeian infantry became increasingly blurred. Sir James Turner objected to this development, complaining that 'the ancient distinction between the Cavalry and Infantry, as to their birth and breeding, is wholly taken away'.[50] For an enterprising young man, with the right attitude and martial qualities, the numerous wars of the age offered opportunities for social and economic advancement, provided he managed to stay alive and to enlist in successful armies. Younger sons of the gentry and nobility viewed military service as a means of advancement, but many others of more humble means prospered too. In this context, it is probably natural that the upper classes attempted to retain some marks of distinction. In the early seventeenth century, gentlemen tended to serve as cuirassiers or pistoleers, the successors to the demi-lances, while their servants and yeomen acted as shot-on-horseback or dragoons. If they joined the foot, gentlemen preferred to trail a pike rather than carry a musket.[51]

THE COUNTY MILITIA

The other source of soldiers and *matériel* in England was the county militia, controlled by a lord lieutenant as the monarch's representative in one or more shires. As a nobleman, with his own military obligations to the crown, he bridged the gap between the two systems. Originally the post was an informal one, based upon an individual magnate's local power and influence, which he put at the monarch's disposal in wartime.[52] Under the Tudors the office became institutionalized, first receiving statutory confirmation in 1549. In 1585, with war against Spain looming, the government filled the gaps in the lieutenancy and issued commissions for permanent appointments.[53] Although lords lieutenants performed a range of tasks, the military role defined the office: administering the collection of military rates, levying troops for service abroad, mustering the county forces and even leading them into battle.[54] Much of the actual work however, was, undertaken by the deputy lieutenants, usually three or four in number.[55] Although the origins of the militia went back to the Anglo-Saxon fyrd, the obligation of all able-bodied men aged between sixteen and sixty to defend their country in Tudor England rested on the medieval Assize of Arms (1181) and the Statute of Winchester (1285). These measures decreed what arms a man had to maintain according to his wealth.[56] Henry VIII, once he became king in 1509, prepared for war against the traditional enemy, France, and this accounts for the general muster he ordered in 1511. Others, held in 1522 and 1539, preceded later campaigns. Even so, he did not use the militia in his continental campaigns until the 1540s, reserving them for service within the country and against the Scots. Finally, in September 1544, pressure on manpower forced him to ship four thousand militiamen to France to supplement his forces there. Thereafter, the role that these local levies played both at home and abroad steadily increased.[57]

In 1558 Mary's government tinkered with the system by passing two Acts dealing with the supply of *matériel* and attendance at musters.[58] The first measure, 'for the having of horse, armour and weapon', set out each subject's liability according to his position on a sliding scale comprising ten wealth bands. At the bottom, those with goods worth £10 per annum, had to keep a long bow with a sheaf of arrows, a steel helmet and a black bill or halberd. At the top, those assessed at £1,000 or more a year contributed six demi-lances and ten light horse, together with their mounts and arms and accoutrements; forty pikes and pikemen's armour; thirty bows and arrows and steel helmets for archers; and weapons and armour for twenty harquebusiers and billmen or halberdiers. A sumptuary clause penalized men whose wives wore a velvet kirtle or a silk petticoat with the charge of keeping a light horse and accoutrements. An army equipped according to its provisions would have contained an excess of archers and billmen and few pike and shot. The ratio of demi-lances to light horse also suggests problems in finding sufficient heavy cavalry, while neither branch seems to have possessed firearms. The second measure, a virtual re-enactment of one passed in Edward VI's reign, sought to tighten up the regulations associated with musters in order to improve training and accounting procedure.[59]

Elizabeth came to the throne in 1558, shortly after the passing of these two Acts, at a time when the country faced the real threat of foreign invasion. What the Queen required above all was a structure that provided her with the means to defend the country with trained soldiers armed with up-to-date weapons. Unfortunately, the Marian Acts did nothing of the sort; on the contrary, they saddled her with an unworkable militia system, that hindered her attempts to create an effective, modern force, one that was capable of repelling an invader. Its emphasis on archaic weapons meant that the Queen received too few horses, firearms and pikes.[60] Furthermore, while the former measure did establish a comprehensive scheme that rated the laity according to wealth, it did not clarify the relationship between the 'feudal' contributions made by individual nobles and the militia assessments from which they were exempt. Then, it underassessed the capacity of people included in the returns; rating them according to the fossilized subsidy lists had the effect of putting them in a wealth band below their real ability to pay.[61] To make good these defects, the Privy Council had to try and persuade subjects to increase their contributions above the level the law obliged them to give.

Apart from the need for preparedness in the light of the threatening international situation, the gradual replacement of traditional weapons such as bills, lances and bows and arrows with pikes and firearms, during the course of Elizabeth's reign, further increased the importance of training. Troops also had to learn different drills, especially the art of manoeuvring in the new formations, whether operating as an infantry column or, if a trooper, performing the *caracole*. Soldiers who carried firearms had to practise firing and reloading. In 1572 three thousand selected pikemen and musketeers from the London militia demonstrated their prowess in front of the Queen at Greenwich, the success of the event prompting the government to extend the concept of the trained band to the whole country the following year.[62] When the government circulated the counties to find out the number of able-bodied men suitable for training, the proportion varied considerably. Initially the instruction given was hit or miss because of the shortage of skilled solders to undertake the job. As the number of Englishmen with experience of fighting abroad increased, however, the situation improved. During the 1580s professional soldiers serving as muster-masters or as captains of trained bands established themselves in the counties. Their introduction, initially at the government's expense and direction, did not proceed without comment, however, especially when the muster-masters argued that the existing trained band companies should be split up into smaller units for ease of training. Naturally, leading gentlemen in the shires resented the loss of power and prestige that the captaincy of a large company had given them, and often felt it demeaning to accept a lesser role. When the government shifted the cost of paying for the muster-masters onto the county and the task of appointing them onto the lord lieutenant, the gentry had further causes for concern. Typically, issues of finance and patronage worried them much more than the inevitable rise in the number of unqualified or corrupt muster-masters that the new system spawned. Indeed, the gentry preferred those who were incompetent since they were less likely to report shortcomings to the Council.[63]

On the northern border the lawlessness of the region led to the creation of a specific set of laws and practices designed to deal with the situation. In accordance with the custom known as 'Hot Trod', for instance, borderers, despoiled by reivers from the other side, could legally chase after the raiders with armed force.

Once across the border the pursuers had to observe certain conventions. An agreement made between England and Scotland in 1563 stipulated that pursuers engaged in a 'lawfull Trodd with Horn and Hound, with Hue and Cry and all other accustomed manner of fresh pursuit', had to pin a lighted turf on their lance-point, explain their purpose to the first person they encountered across the border and seek assistance. The existence of a quasi-military form of tenure known as border service made it easier for victims to deal effectively with their attackers. In return for occupying the land, tenants had to maintain 'a goode and a sufficiente horse suche ... as shalbe hable to do Service where any horsemanne ys to be charged'. The mount had to be capable of carrying a man for twenty to twenty-four hours without resting or at least able to take its rider twenty miles into Scotland and back. Riders wore a steel cap and a jack, carried a sword and dagger, and, as their main offensive weapon, brandished a spear. Later, firearms replaced the spear.[64] The will of Richard Blacklock of Long Park, drawn up on 8 June 1589, illustrates the practice. Richard bequeathed to his son, John, his farm held by tenant right in the lordship of Scaleby, together with a steel cap, jack and pair of boots. John also received a piece of meadow ground in return for discharging his mother from 'doing of any service owed to the Queen and the keepinge of a horse and do such things as a tenant ought to do'. Another son, Robert, received a little house, a sword and a leather doublet, and a third son, Michael, a steel cap and ordinary clothing.[65]

Unfortunately, by the time that Blacklock was making his will, the system of border service was in decay. Among the instructions issued in 1557, in an attempt to halt the decline in the number of northern horsemen, was one that emphasized the need to consider the ill-effect of the introduction of conventional leases. At Wark and Norham, captains who had obtained such leases had improved the lands, but their action had caused a fall in the number of inhabitants.[66] In 1571 the Bishop of Carlisle claimed that enclosure of the commons in the barony of Dalston had impoverished a large number of families, including two hundred able men who could no longer maintain a horse and armour for service. The country could not afford to do without these men, who 'for skill and courage ... were as serviceable ... as any on this Border'.[67] The situation was no better in 1583 when a commission, set up to examine agricultural conditions in the region, specifically looked into the question of the conversion of land to tillage. Illegal trafficking in horses across the border further exacerbated the problem, enhancing the quality of the Scottish cavalry while weakening that of the English. The commission insisted that more had to be done to punish offenders who seemed to be operating with impunity.[68]

In 1603 James VI of Scotland became King of England, uniting the two crowns and easing (though not ending) tensions caused by cross-border reiving. Within a year he had made peace with Spain and one of his first actions was to repeal

Mary's Militia Act of 1558. This did not absolve his subjects of their obligation to defend the country, but for a number of years it did lead to the end of formal musters and training sessions. Concern about a deterioration in the quality of the militia brought about their reintroduction in 1613.[69] The outbreak of the Thirty Years' War in 1618 stimulated further action and led to official attempts to tighten up the system both at the centre and in the localities. The authorities dealt with defaulters more harshly and the number of men entering the ranks of the trained bands rose. By 1623 a decade of mustering and training had improved the condition of the trained bands, though at the cost of an increase in military rates. Even so, in that year James told his lords lieutenant that antiquated methods of instruction had to cease forthwith: training, he declared, was not so exact as it should be.[70]

At the opening of Charles I's reign the Privy Council sent out new drill books. In January 1626 the King spoke of the trained bands as a source of strength but complained that they were still unfamiliar with the 'playne and exact rules' set out in the books. He therefore intended to bring sergeants over from the Low Countries, who, over a three-month period, would instruct the militia in correct procedure.[71] 1639 was the acid test, for in that year the King called out the militia to fight the Scottish covenanters.[72] In the event, most of the troops sent were untrained and ill-equipped, partly it seems because Charles I expected that the mere show of force would suffice.[73] On 10 May 1639 Sir Edmund Verney, the standard bearer, summed up the state of the English army in the following words: 'Our men are verry rawe, our armes of all sorts nawght, our vittle scarce, and provision for horses woarce.'[74] The government should have obtained better quality troops in the Second Bishops' War in 1640 since this time it actually intended to press men from the trained bands. As it turned out, the improvement was marginal because so many people sent in substitutes.[75]

In October 1641, a year after the signing of the treaty of Ripon with the Scottish Covenanters, Charles I found himself at war with the Irish confederates. In England the insurrection caused a political crisis. While the King and his parliamentary critics were united in their desire to suppress the rising, neither side trusted the other with the arms and soldiers needed to put it down. Over the winter of 1641–2 the struggle focused on control of the militia. Finally, on 5 March 1641/2, Parliament, lacking royal approval, passed a militia ordinance, enabling it to appoint its own supporters to the county lieutenancies. The King countered by issuing his Commissions of Array, a device based somewhat shakily on an unrepealed statute of Henry IV's reign.[76] As England descended into civil war during the course of 1642, rival sets of officials, armed with authorizations of dubious legality, toured the country in an unedifying struggle to win the support of county communities and to gain control of the trained bands and their weapons.[77] In spite of the desire of many to remain aloof, in a number of counties partisans were able to force the issue. In the struggle Parliament did better than the King. Both sides drew heavily on county forces during the course of the war, using them to control their locality or as a source of manpower for the field armies. Even so, localism hindered their plans and the relationship between the county levies and the regional Association armies was particularly tense.

Although some veterans were already training local militias, the approach of war in England prompted many more to return home to lend their support to one side or the other. Nearly all the commanders who served at brigade level in the Civil Wars had fought in continental campaigns. Largely as a result of the Thirty Years War, the proportion of peers with military experience rose from fifty-four per cent in 1620 to sixty-three per cent in 1630 and to sixty-nine per cent in 1640. Gentlemen similarly swelled the ranks of foreign armies but remarkably Oliver Cromwell was not one of them.[78] Many veterans enrolled as non-commissioned officers, in which capacity they played a vital role, drilling the raw recruits and keeping them in order on the battlefield. Others joined as ordinary soldiers and stiffened the ranks of the civilian forces.[79] Seasoned troops also brought a considerable degree of professionalism to the Scottish Covenanting forces. In 1638 the Swedes released one of their field marshals, Alexander Leslie, so that he could take command of the nascent covenanting army. In February 1638/9 Swedish ships, loaded with several units of soldiers and tons of arms and armaments, sailed for Scotland.[80] In Ireland, the Confederate cause received a similar boost when in July 1642 Owen Roe O'Neill, a commander in the Spanish army, slipped through the English blockade, bringing with him 200–300 veterans and a stock of arms and munitions. However, few other soldiers fighting abroad managed to return to Ireland. Soldiers from the disbanded army that Thomas Wentworth, the lord deputy, had assembled for an attack on the Scottish Covenanters, proved a bigger source of trained soldiers for the insurgents.[81]

In the spring of 1661 the government introduced a new Militia Bill into Parliament, a sensitive point, considering the consequences of the previous dispute in 1641–2. It again proved to be a divisive issue and, delayed by opposition in the lower house and then by disagreements between the Commons and Lords, it did not become law until 19 May 1662.[82] The Act confirmed the king's status as commander-in-chief of the militia and of all land and sea forces. A further Act the following year strengthened his position by the addition of a clause that emphasized his supreme authority by making it clear that Parliament could not abridge it.[83] Even so, the king seems to have gained little of substance; in return for inadequate revenues the measures restricted his power to exact money and services and hence his freedom of action.[84] Although individuals still provided men, arms and horses according to their means, the Act widened the circle of contributors by removing the minimum income required to furnish an infantryman. It only stipulated that proprietors of modest income should not be charged with finding horse. In terms of armour and weaponry the measure was conservative.[85] It took an Act of 1715 formally to modernize the militia's arms: pikes and armour disappeared and all infantrymen received a standardized musket five feet long, fitted with a bayonet, as well as a cartouche box and a sword. Cavalry acquired carbines and a sword and pistols of a different design.[86]

In 1663 an Act empowering the lieutenancies to keep a portion of the county militias permanently on call, if conditions warranted, ensured that troops were always available in an emergency, a particular worry at the start of the reign.[87] At the same time Charles II set about establishing a small standing army of foot and horse regiments in England (with smaller contingents in Scotland and Ireland).[88] When trouble threatened, and numbers had to increase, volunteer members of the trained bands provided suitable, if temporary, recruits for specially formed regiments.[89] They served in this capacity in 1666–7, 1672–4 and 1678–9. In England their value lay in the show of force they represented rather than their fighting qualities. Within limits, they enjoyed a modicum of success, whether inhibiting plotters at home, seeing off French and Dutch raiding parties or dealing with marauding privateers.[90] In Scotland, where the permanent establishment amounted to a regiment of foot and a troop of horse, plus some garrison units (altogether 1,200 men), the militia proved particularly valuable in the covenanter rising in 1678–9. To meet the threat, Charles II selected an elite force comprising one-quarter of its total strength of 20,000 foot and 2,000 horse. They performed so well that regular levies being raised in England were disbanded as not needed.[91]

DEFICIENCIES IN THE MILITIA HORSE

The history of the early modern militia was one of conflict. Occasionally its members took part in real battles but mostly they (and those who contributed arms and horses) fought the government over the level of financial, personal and material assistance, their attendance at musters and the legality of sending in a substitute. Expenditure increased in the late sixteenth and early seventeenth centuries as archaic weapons gave way to more modern ones. The creation of the trained bands added to the costs because they had to spend more days away from their job: the government suggested three training sessions, totalling ten days a year. Each militia man received 8d. a day and a further sum to cover his munitions. The total cost was considerable, if variable. Essex paid £320 per annum for three hundred men and Norfolk £350 13s. 4d. for five hundred.[92] Counties raised the money through military rates and when the lords lieutenant made additional demands, as in 1573, the inhabitants objected. In Derbyshire officials claimed that shortage of funds meant that they could only train five hundred of the four thousand suitable men in the county.[93] The expense of maintaining a horse and rider with his arms and equipment was far greater and this caused further problems.

The government was particularly anxious about the condition of the horse, the weakness of which was a matter of contemporary comment. In his report, written in August 1554, the Venetian ambassador noted that the country could raise 15,000 horse at musters but that English horses were not suitable for military service (or at least the ones he saw).[94] Blundeville endorsed this view. In about 1560 he specifically stated that he was writing his book, *The Arte of Rydynge*, to improve the quality of horse and rider, especially at musters.[95] There, he claimed,

> oftimes you shal see some that sit on their horses like winde shaken reedes handlinge their handes and legs like weavers. Or if the horsman be good, then the horse for hys parte shall be so broken, as when he is spurred to go forwarde, he will go backwarde. And when hys ryder wolde have him to turne on the right hand, he wil turne cleane contrary. And when he shoulde stoppe, he will arme him selfe, and runne away, or els stoppe sooner then his ryder would have hym, or use such like toyes.

In 1569, the year of the Northern Rising, the Privy Council told specially appointed county commissioners to tighten up on abuses and increase numbers brought in. In April the Council of the North gave the commissioners for musters in the northern counties a revised book of rates for the horse, explaining that the former one had under-assessed some individuals and had not rated others capable of maintaining horses.[96] The rebellion that broke out a few months later starkly revealed the depth of the problem, and the panic it caused helped the commissioners at the time and afterwards in their quest to increase rates and to exact contributions from defaulters. Yorkshire provided eighty-two rated horses, together with 172 donations and eighty-two for wives' apparel. In Leicestershire in 1573 fifty-four of the sixty horses were voluntary. Inevitably, the government's prodding also provoked a negative reaction, with commissioners objecting to the numbers that the Privy Council wanted their counties to provide. In Nottinghamshire, the Earl of Rutland, as lord lieutenant, received a round robin letter from the county's gentry in which they pointed out that, 'We doe not knowe that we are chargeable by anie lawe to so great a burthen as by your lordship hath bene geven us severally in note for to furnish, touching dimi-lances and light horsemen'. They protested that they could not afford to provide the numbers for which they were assessed, grumbling that 'it is farre more then we and oure livinges proporconally for eche one was able to perfourme'. Worryingly for the government, such complaints were coming from the wealthier inhabitants.[97]

It was in response to what it perceived as a lack of cooperation that the government in 1580 set up its high-powered Special Commission for the Increase and Breed of Horses. It justified drastic action by pointing out the worsening international situation, 'when all foreign princes being neighbours of this realm be in arms'. Although deputy commissioners did the actual work in each county, the 'principal' commissioners were expected to involve themselves personally in the process by advising and supervising the agents in the counties under their jurisdiction.[98] The clear intention was to tighten up the system, using the political muscle of the country's leading courtiers. As the preamble stated, 'Whereas finding upon view of the late musters and other information the number of horses both for demi-lance and light-horse be much less than we could anyway have imagined considering the wealth that our subjects be grown unto.'[99] The commissioners were therefore instructed to assess themselves and all other contributors 'according as their livings be indeed in value and not as they be rated in the subsidy book'. When they found examples of underrating they were to correct them. Other measures to increase the supply of horses of the right standard included ones which were already on the statute book: preventing serviceable horses being exported to Scotland and elsewhere; ensuring that individuals rated to provide demi-lances and light horse kept suitable mounts; and increasing the number of able horses in parks, pastures and commons. To improve the standard of breeding in counties allotted to them the instructions given to the principal commissioners suggested that they and their friends should make their stallions available to the local gentry.[100]

In spite of all this attention the horse bands remained stubbornly substandard. In Northamptonshire the national commissioners imposed a quota of forty-five demi-lances and 142 light horsemen on the county, upgrading the local commissioners' estimation by a further twenty-five and sixty-two respectively. They met considerable opposition. Sir Edmund Brudenell, for instance, sent in only one horseman to the muster of January 1580/1 rather than the listed two demi-lances and three light horseman. Edward Andrew, added to the list by the principal commissioners, pleaded poverty and made no return. The situation had not improved by 1583 in spite of the commissioners' exhortations. That year the commissioners found deficiencies in other counties too: in Surrey, Hampshire and Middlesex they described the cavalry as 'evil opoynted and badly furnished', while Leicestershire's was 'very mean'. The horsemen of Dorset were in a poor condition too. According to the county's deputy commissioners, this was due to the policy of the late Lord Howard, who, when captain, had enrolled his tenantry and others, men of modest means. When the commissioners had remonstrated with him, Howard had retorted that, as they would serve under him, he would supply them with forty horses from his own stables.[101]

Many contributors took a far more restricted view of their obligations than had Lord Howard. It was not that they could not provide more horses than their quota but rather that they were reluctant to commit themselves to extra expense and trouble. Commenting on the weakness of the horse bands at the York muster on 28 April 1588, the Earl of Huntingdon admitted that the number of 'good geldings' in the region had declined, but claimed that there were more available than those on display. It was a question of making the right approach; he felt that a number of gentlemen would respond positively if asked personally to supply as many horsemen as they could manage. As he observed, 'I find by proof that he who has six good horses is scarcely willing at a muster to show one, unless compelled by law; for all men here have no liking to be inrolled in a muster book, but if called in this sort, will willingly charge themselves to the uttermost.' The northern gentry, even in the year of the Spanish Armada, were also worried about having to contribute to defending the country from invasion from the south, 'a service to these countrymen, and never required of any here before'. On the other hand, Huntingdon did point out that the government's attempt to require justices of the peace to help equip the new units of petronels had caused difficulties: 'many in the commission of the peace are not able to furnish both a light horse and two petronels, and yet for the service of the country as justices of the peace, they are men not to be spared'.[102]

The situation remained essentially the same in the early seventeenth century. Although the responsibility for provisioning the horse lay with the gentry and other people of means (including, after 1608, the wealthier clergy), this merely ensured that delaying tactics were more sophisticated and effective. Before deputy lieutenants could contemplate training the horse, they first had to get the horses and riders to the muster.[103] The hiatus of 1603–12 particularly affected the cavalry units. In 1611 the Earl of Northampton told his deputy lieutenants in Warwickshire to take new musters and to remedy the defects in the horse by levying as many 'good and serviceable' mounts as the county had owed in 1591. A year later the light-horse in Essex were 'very much impaired and out of order', which the two deputy lieutenants blamed on 'the late discontinuance of musters and trayninge'. Often, counties reported that all was well with the militia, except the horse.[104] In 1618, the year that the Thirty Years' War broke out, the Privy Council wrote to the lords lieutenant and commissioners of musters to tell them that they had to act to improve the situation. The order explained, 'And whereas the numbers of horse have ben so long neglected, as they are for the most parte defective both in armes and serviceable horses, it is high tyme at length after so many admonicions that care be taken that the troupes of horse be filled upp and made complete with all provision and furniture appurtayning'. In Derbyshire the officials protested that losses through death or removal of a number of wealthy individuals rather than a want of endeavour had caused the deficiencies. In Norfolk in 1623, on the other hand, the deputy lieutenants reported that a number of contributors 'either obstinately refuse or undutifully neglect to show or serve with their horses and arms'.[105] Even so, some counties did show signs of improvement. In Leicestershire numbers had increased and in

Devon (1620) and Lincolnshire (1621), hitherto centres of opposition, the horse were complete.[106]

Under Charles I the sergeants brought over from the Low Countries achieved some success but if they improved the quality of the foot, this showed up the continuing deficiencies in the horse.[107] In 1625 the deputy lieutenants of Sussex reported that the horse bands were, 'as we have often signified ... very weak in number and many meane horses and ill furnished'. In May 1627 Essex's deputy lieutenants, having twice found the horse defective, told the Privy Council that that they saw little hope of progress unless the principal offenders were disciplined.[108] Added to the perennial problem of getting contributors to honour their obligations was the issue of equipping the horse with up-to-date weapons. To try to improve the condition of the horse the Privy Council planned a series of regional musters in 1628, which were ultimately shelved in the face of widespread opposition. Harking back to Henry VIII, the government also proposed the establishment of an elite corps of cavalry, with the further brief of encouraging good horsemanship throughout the country. At its core were the gentlemen pensioners, supported by other members of the royal household.[109] Most horse bands, however, did not reach the required standard and were in poor shape when mobilized in 1639 for action against the Covenanters. On 17 January 1638/9 Sir Thomas Morton told Secretary Windebank that the horses in one troop of horse were so small that most of them were not fit for cuirassiers and were being converted to carbine mounts, though completely unfurnished. Elsewhere, there were problems too. Norfolk, for example, experienced difficulties in supplying horses and armour.[110] Few counties found themselves in the position of Lancashire and Cheshire, where the militia horses were strong and of good quality, even if the riders and arms were faulty.[111]

During the English Civil Wars both sides had to share the country's resources and this put pressure on the supply of horses. Control of county militias provided one source and a mechanism with which to raise them. More came in via the Propositions and the Engagement of June 1642.[112] Although voluntary, the appeal of these measures was similar to that which underlined people's obligations to provide horses, arms and equipment to the militia. In this case, their duty was to provide material aid in the face of the threat from within. Both sides seem to have expected that these devices would raise enough horses, calculating that contributors would bring in more than their paltry militia quotas. They were soon disillusioned and in the new year both sides introduced an element of compulsion. On 10 May 1643 Parliament added clauses to the Propositions allowing it to impose county quotas. Before long the Royalists followed suit. Moreover, the authorities used requests for money, *matériel* and horses as a touchstone of loyalty to the cause and viewed non-contributors as enemies.[113] These were among the first to have their horses requisitioned.

Initially, the Propositions provided the bulk of the horses, arms and equipment raised to fit out Parliamentarian troopers. With the money collected, the authorities bought further supplies. On 5 July 1642, the House of Commons put aside £7,500 to buy horses. Two months later John Hampden received £1,000 of the money brought in on the Propositions in Buckinghamshire to procure horses and arms.[114] As this source dried up over time, commanders and commissary officers had to acquire horses through normal commercial channels. The problem was that the conditions created by Civil War were not normal ones. Owing to the insecurity of the times and the reluctance of merchants to take to the road, the traditional outlets, namely markets and fairs, declined during the years of conflict. Parliament's answer was to put out contracts to a group of Smithfield dealers who had already achieved prominence in the trade before the outbreak of hostilities. They supplied thousands of horses to the armies; in the seventeen months beginning on 1 April 1645 they delivered 7,801 horses, mostly for the cavalry, to the New Model Army.[115] The Royalists also bought horses: in October 1642, for instance, the Earl of Cumberland spent £7 10s. on a horse, probably for a trooper in his garrison at Skipton Castle.[116] Unfortunately, we know little of their sources of supply, though as pre-war horse toll books indicate that many dealers lived in Royalist-controlled areas, they must have done business with them.[117] Inevitably, soldiers engaged in plunder and if opponents were 'fair game', they did not always draw a distinction between supporters and adversaries. In June 1645 the Parliamentarian news-sheet, *Perfect Passages*, accused the Royalists of this failing, complaining that when they 'finde better horses then their own they take them, be it friend or foe: they stand not to expostulate the matter, and by this means the Kings horse are all well mounted'.[118] On occasion, a protest to the local military governor did lead to the restitution of the horse, especially if the complainant could prove that he or she was 'well-affected'. In addition, the authorities realized that in the long run it paid not to alienate the local population.

The peculiar nature of a civil war made it particularly difficult to find suitable cavalry horses. First, by dividing up the country into two parts, it restricted each side's choice of mounts. In this respect, the Royalists held the advantage, as they had ready access to the best saddle horses in the country, which were bred in north Yorkshire and the Tees Valley. Secondly, war wasted resources at an alarming rate and horses were particularly vulnerable. In autumn 1646 Humphrey Bulkeley of Cheadle, a Parliamentarian captain, calculated that his troop had lost 137 horses between 2 March 1642/3 and 16 October 1646: twenty-eight put out of action at two skirmishes; another sixty-eight captured with their riders; and a further forty-one through capture, theft, injury or disappearance.[119] Not surprisingly, shortages did occur from time to time: in autumn 1644 both sides lacked horses in the aftermath of the Lostwithiel campaign.[120] Even so, deficiencies were made good and, in general, shortages did not seriously hamper the war effort. Remarkably, virtually all of the horses were home bred; there are very few references to imports from the Continent and those that did come in amounted to a mere handful.[121] Either through donation, requisition or purchase both sides obtained sufficient horses to mount their troops and to find remounts as and when necessary. Moreover, these were animals available at the beginning of the conflict. As horses were not broken in until their third or fourth year, and preferably not ridden hard for a further year,[122] breeders, responding to a market opportunity after the war had begun, would only have had suitable stock ready near the end of the First Civil War.

DRAUGHT ANIMALS

The system for supplying draught horses and wagons for the artillery and baggage trains differed appreciably from the ways in which the army acquired its cavalry mounts. For his expeditions Henry VIII, as far as he could, made use of the royal privilege of purveyance. This enabled his officials to appropriate the horses he needed at fairs or parish by parish. In 1513 commissioners in sixteen counties, operating under William Jekyll, the commissioner general, bought at least 2,587 cart horses. In Northamptonshire the commissioner, George Browne, paid £327 12s. 8d. for 302 horses at prices that ranged from 13s. to a mean of £5 4s. 5d. for nine large horses. The median number of horses taken from each place was six. In Buckinghamshire it was three.[123] Commissioners also hired men to drive the army's carts, paying them 6d. a day and providing them with a coat worth 4s. Head carters earned 10d. a day. Wagoners, who brought their own vehicles, received 10d. a day for every horse in the team.[124] As the number of horses raised proved insufficient, the government had to buy others abroad. When in April 1514 the army was being restocked with *matériel*, it needed 796 Flemish mares and seventy-five wagons to transport it.[125]

In 1522 the government estimated the relative costs of obtaining teams at home and purchasing them abroad. Home supply, it transpired, was cheaper, even before adding in the capital value of the horses and carts that survived the campaign. In addition, carters could be used as pioneers or even as troops in an emergency.[126] The calculation, however, did not include the loss of production that occurred when commissioners took horses off the farm or the road at critical times of the year. A further comparison in 1544 similarly indicated that it was cheaper to obtain wagons and teams at home. This time, the authorities did consider the interests of the English farmer, for commissioners had to find horses or oxen 'as might be conveniently spared without disfurniture of necessary tillage and husbandry of any man'.[127] For draught horses, Henry VIII had to rely to a greater extent on his ally, Charles V. On 12 April 1544 Chapuys, the Emperor's ambassador to England, informed Mary of Hungary, imperial regent in the Low Countries, that Henry VIII was upset at the small number of horses she had offered him and that, if she could not give him any more, he would have to reduce the size of his army. Alluding to English practice, Henry argued that if each parish in Flanders, Brabant, Hainault and Artois supplied one wagon and team there would be four times as many horses as he needed. Mary did what she could. Indeed, stung by further English criticism in early July, she protested that she had provided almost all of the 2,500 draught horses (known as limoners) and 2,200 four-horse wagons asked for in the spring, even though the number was excessive and it meant that few remained for the Emperor's army.[128] The English were particularly keen to acquire Flemish limoners because they were much stronger than native draught horses. On 23 June 1544, for example, the Duke of Norfolk wrote about the lack of wagons and limoners and horses to draw the ovens 'for the horses sent from England are so evil that it takes 14 or 15 horses to draw one'.[129]

When fighting in Ireland, on the other hand, the English found the local stock inadequate, even though they hoped to draw on local supplies. Tenants, for example, often had to provide garrons as a condition of their tenure.[130] In O'Neill's rebellion at the end of the sixteenth century the authorities initially acquired horses on the spot, but during the winter of 1596–7 they had to supplement them with consignments from England. In spite of these imports shortages persisted and hampered operations. When Essex arrived in Ireland in April 1599 he lacked sufficient draught horses to mount an offensive. The country was hardly able to supply half the number required. In addition, an expected cargo of two hundred carriage horses had not arrived from England. Even with these horses he could do little and therefore asked the Privy Council for two hundred more. Without them, he claimed, he could not furnish enough horses for the present expedition into Leinster, let alone attack the rebel stronghold of Ulster.[131]

At the opening of the war against the Scottish Covenanters in 1639 the government, as far as possible, sent essential military supplies and provisions by boat.[132] Once unloaded, carts were needed to take the *matériel* to the front. Unfortunately, few horses capable of pulling heavy ordnance were available locally. As the Marquis of Hamilton reported, 'there are non to be had ther that will be abill to draw them ther'.[133] Counties further south therefore had to supply the animals, and lords lieutenant had quotas imposed on them, indicating the number of carts and teams they had to find within their county or counties. On 29 March 1639 the Council of War informed the lord lieutenant of Northamptonshire that he had to provide fifty strong and able horses and seventeen able carters, and ensure that they reached Newcastle-upon-Tyne by 20 April. Carters obtained 8d. a day and the owners of the horses 1s. a day each. Only when they had arrived at the rendezvous did they receive official pay.[134] The government also had 400 wagons specifically made, which, when loaded on board ship, were dismantled and the parts marked for ease of storage and reassembly.[135]

Both Parliamentarians and Royalists maintained a complement of carts and teams, mainly for use in the artillery train. Thomas Bateman, the Ordnance Office's wheelwright, made wagons for Parliament, while wheelwrights and wagon makers working in towns and villages near the Charles I's headquarters at Oxford performed the same task for the Royalists.[136] The two sides also hired carters and teams; Parliament paid carters 2s. 6d. a day per horse. Packhorses cost 1s. to 1s. 6d. a day. At first, armies hired carters and wagoners, as and when required, and laid them off once they had completed the task. Records of payments to carters hired by Essex, the Parliamentarian commander-in-chief, on the other hand, indicate that some men gained almost continuous employment in his army. Isaac Peare, for instance, started to work in the opening Edgehill campaign and served in the train until the army's disbandment in 1645. Both sides regularly requisitioned horses for the draught too. At the centre, the wagon-master-generals, Thomas Richardson and Henry Stevens, oversaw the task, respectively for Parliament and the King.[137] Because of the degree of decentralization, however, commanders tended to requisition horses and carts when they needed them. In July 1643 Lord Capel, preparing to attack Parliamentarian Nantwich, asked Denbighshire and Flintshire each to provide twenty carts and teams.[138]

The circumstances of a civil war meant that the authorities could back up their request with the threat of military force and this made it easier for them to obtain what they wanted. Soldiers might plunder carts and horses. Even so, as already noted, military authorities normally tried to pay for what they received, especially in their home areas. Anthony Johnson and Francis and Robert Twistleton, who worked as carriers for the Royalist garrison at Skipton Castle, received payment reasonably promptly. So too did the ten men who hired out their sixty-one horses, probably pack animals, to the New Model Army in 1645. For the fortnight's work they earned £89 5s. 8d., which they obtained shortly afterwards. Sergeant-Major-General Skippon, who signed the authorization, noted 'the owners of theis horses having be haved themselves and it being conceived for the benefit of the state to deschardg them al'.[139] Much depended on the availability of cash. If money were scarce, soldiers had to give a voucher to the owner, who could redeem it later. Many of the carters employed by the Earl of Essex had to wait months even years before being fully recompensed. George Greasley, one of Parliament's regular carriers, worked with his team of six horses in the artillery train for 201 days between 14 February and 2 September 1644. At 2s. 6d. a day per horse he earned a total of £150 15s. At the end of his term of employment, however, he had only received £44 10s. and had to wait until 6 March 1644/5 for the remaining £106 5s.[140] Even if the army did pay for the horses and carts it hired or impressed, the owners still suffered from the loss of their animals and vehicles. The situation was far worse than it had been in earlier conflicts because the fighting was taking place on home soil and soldiers were the ones organizing the collection. Armies wanted horses immediately and in large numbers and could not be denied. According to the time of year, farmers would have found it difficult to prepare the ground, harvest their crops or market their produce. As they hired or impressed horses along with the vehicles, officials did not have to look for them separately.[141] They did, however, have to obtain horses to pull the carts they kept in hand. Parliament, again, dealt with the Smithfield dealers, who sold them a recorded total of 1,200 draught horses between April 1645 and May 1646 at £6 or £7 a horse.[142]

By the end of the century armies had grown bigger, creating even greater demands for draught animals, especially horses. At the opening of the eighteenth century Marlborough's army required 470 horses to pull twenty-five siege guns and their equipment.[143] Baggage trains added to the numbers deployed. When Marlborough marched to the Danube in 1704 to relieve Prince Eugene he took with him 21,000 men and 1,700 supply carts drawn by 5,000 draught horses. The artillery train, even without heavy siege cannon, required the same number.[144] Although described as 'a masterly piece of logistics management', the train only averaged 12–14 miles a day. As the army expected to buy some of the provision on the march, the train could have been even bigger and slower moving. Unfortunately, it proved difficult to obtain supplies en route, so windfalls like the 2,000 sacks of meal, the large quantity of oats and other corn and all sorts of provision and ammunition captured at Donauwörth were particulary welcome.[145] To obtain the necessary animals, the army reverted to the policy of purchasing horses and wagons abroad. When campaigning in the Low Countries in the War of the Grand Alliance (1689–97), commissary officers could readily obtain strong local horses for the baggage train or to pull artillery pieces. In an agreement made on 1 March 1692/3, contractors promised to supply sturdy Brabant wagons, each with a carter and a team of four well-nourished horses at least four years old. They were also to supply reserve animals in order to rotate the horses in the team and avoid stopping to let them recover. Eight days later two dealers contracted to deliver two hundred wagons and six hundred horses for the artillery. The horses, the agreement stipulated, had to be well fed, between fourteen and fifteen hands, and to be at least four years old. The contract also allowed the two men sixty and eighty guilders respectively for each horse and wagon lost through no fault of their own. To prevent the enemy obtaining similar horses the terms specified the punishments that the dealers would suffer should they sell them any horses.[146]

THE ENGLISH 'ART OF WAR'

The unique character of the English 'art of war' was partly due to relative insulation from European conflict and partly due to its own military traditions. Between the late fifteenth and early eighteenth centuries the army royal fought few campaigns abroad and even more rarely without the support of continental allies. In general, therefore, home forces were slow to adopt contemporary continental practices and, when needed, employed foreign mercenaries to do the job. Even so, soldiers from England (and from Celtic parts of the British Isles) were not unaware of technological and tactical advances being made abroad, many of them learning about them at first hand. Throughout the course of the sixteenth and seventeenth centuries thousands of soldiers of fortune left these shores to fight in the army of one or other European power, their choice mainly but not exclusively dependent on religious or political convictions. As indicated above, in times of crisis at home, these men returned, forming the nucleus of an army and providing a set of instructors who could teach raw recruits the rudiments of musket and pike drill or cavalry manoeuvres of *caracole* or charge.[147]

Back at home they adapted their knowledge to local circumstances. This made sense, for when the English went to war it was commonly within the British archipelago, normally against the Scots or Irish, though occasionally against rebels in the country itself. Between 1639 and 1654 civil war consumed all parts of the British Isles. As a result, campaigns tended to display a domestic air, even if returning soldiers brought continental practices with them. The nature of England's army also made it difficult for it to react quickly to developments on the Continent. If the crown had possessed a large standing army, it would have found it easier to make the necessary changes. Opinion in the country was, however, against the very notion of one, a resolve strengthened by the experience of the power wielded by the army in the Interregnum (1649–60). Charles II faced opposition in Parliament when he created several guards regiments after the Restoration, but it was only when James II sought greatly to enlarge the army in the years 1685–8 that the threat became a real one.

By European standards the army that Henry VIII sent to France in 1513 'was an old-fashioned force, raised by quasi-feudal methods, fighting with out-of-date weapons for an anachronistic cause'. The bulk of his infantry comprised archers and billmen and contained no handgunners.[148] The lack of a sufficient number of large saddle mounts at home affected the size of heavy cavalry arm.[149] The King's Spears, a bodyguard of fifty well-born men-at-arms, each accompanied by an archer, light horseman and mounted attendant, formed the core of this branch of the army in the years 1510–15. Contingents of light cavalry of the stradiot type, on the other hand, were more numerous.[150] The army did possess an excellent artillery train: each battle had over sixty guns to it, the heavy siege cannons being drawn by Flemish limoners and the lighter ones by English horses.[151] Nine years later little had changed: the weapons and armour listed in the General Proscription were overwhelmingly medieval in character: bows and arrows and Almain rivets but few firearms. Even in the 1540s Henry's subjects were supplying him with the same sort of *matériel*.[152] A proclamation of 1544 encouraging able-bodied men to practise firing handguns might have improved the situation, but two years later the government rescinded the order.[153] Although still deficient in large horses, some progress was being made, especially in the royal studs, where imports from Italy and elsewhere augmented the breeding stock.[154] The establishment in 1539–40 of a fifty-strong body of gentlemen pensioners, charged with enhancing horsemanship and horse breeding, provided the basis for improvement in the ranks of the heavy cavalry. They added to the active military establishment which Henry VIII was fostering in the Privy Chamber. Like their forerunners, the King's Spears, they formed an elite cavalry corps and, along with other members of the household, led detachments of troops in battle. Hertford, who commanded the army royal between 1545 and 1549, was aware of developments on the Continent and, given time, would undoubtedly have modernized it. Unfortunately, he fell from power before he had the chance to do so.[155]

In spite of some progress, the home contingents in Henry VIII's armies abroad were archaic and increasingly out of step with their continental rivals.[156] In practice, however, the forces that the early Tudors put into the field were not as outdated as this implies. Allies furnished auxiliary troops and foreign mercenaries hired themselves out to the English crown. In 1513 these two categories accounted for over one-fifth of the strength of the army in France. In 1523 the figure had risen to one in three and their importance to the war effort was so great that, when Charles V's auxiliaries and most of the mercenaries left, Henry VIII's agents desperately combed Europe for replacements. By 1546 almost a half of the forces were foreigners. They served as men-at-arms, augmenting the small English core, and also supplemented the light cavalry. Among these men were those acting as mounted harquebusiers.[157] In 1513 skilled gunners recruited from the Low Countries manned the artillery pieces.[158] There were drawbacks: foreign mercenaries were expensive and the supply of auxiliaries depended on diplomatic circumstances. In the 1540s Henry VIII, allied to the Emperor and with monastic money at his disposal, could readily make good the deficiencies of his own forces. Such a combination of circumstances would not occur again and in this context the Marian legislation should be viewed as a lost opportunity.

At the same time, England also fought campaigns against its neighbours, notably against the Scots. In the Flodden campaign of 1514 its army, comprising mainly northern levies, contained some heavy cavalry, a larger body of light horsemen and contingents of archers and billmen.[159] It possessed a good artillery train too. Like the Scots, when the army drew up for the encounter it did not assemble into the traditional three battles but rather in a larger number of smaller units, in line with contemporary European practice. In the 1540s Henry VIII was deploying foreign troops in both theatres of war. Mercenaries appeared on the northern border for the first time in 1545, reflecting the influence of Hertford over the composition of the army. His forces were complete, self-contained armies, which 'bristled with pike and shot, effective field artillery and a powerful cavalry arm'.[160] The Scottish army in itself was more modern; while it had its archers and units of Highlanders wielding two-handed swords and axes, it also possessed columns of pikemen and an excellent artillery train. Ironically, the English gained the day with their traditional weapons, though the Scots should have won. The English archers decimated the ranks of the closely packed Scottish pikemen and in the mêlée bills were more effective than the longer pikes or the shorter Highland swords.[161]

In these campaigns both rulers drew on the light horsemen of the border, who had honed their military skills in the lawless environment of the region. At Flodden, the English border horse proved very effective. Indeed, Dacre's borderers, operating as a conventional cavalry unit, prevented the Scottish infantry column from outflanking the English right wing.[162] Nonetheless, armed like the stradiots with light lance or spear and sword, their customary role was to act as 'prickers and scourers', snapping at the heels of rival formations. At Solway Moss (1542) a detachment of 700 border horse under Sir William Musgrave was instrumental in the rout of a Scottish army of 18,000 men as the latter struggled across the boggy ground. Musgrave's men attacked from the flank; employing hit-and-run tactics, they probed at the edges of the packed infantry ranks, thrusting at likely targets with spear and sword and thoroughly disconcerting them. Wharton, the overall commander of the force, wrote of the engagment that 'our prekers ... gatt thym in a shake all the waye'.[163] In the Pinkie Clough campaign they were joined by a contingent of two hundred Italian mounted harquebusiers under Captain Pedro de Gamboa, 'mounted firearm troops of the most modern kind'. After the Scottish pikes had stopped the charge of the heavy cavalry, they proved more effective, wheeling in front of their formation, firing their handguns.[164] In the aftermath of Hertford's victory at Pinkie Clough, light horsemen formed an integral part of his design to control the country though a series of garrisons and mobile 'police' forces.

During Elizabeth I's reign the authorities gradually modernized the English army: infantrymen acquired pikes and muskets and the cavalry, pistols and carbines. Horsemen armed with firearms seem to have been uncommon in 1569, the year of the rising of the northern earls. In a letter written to the Queen on 26 November 1569 Sir Ralph Sadler thought the fact that the rebels included mounted pistoleers proved that the earls had been planning the uprising for some time. On the same day, Elizabeth's commander, the Earl of Sussex, reported that the northern levies were short of horse and that those they had were mainly archers, 'which is not so serviceable as other shot'.[165] Sussex was certainly aware of the value of firearms, as is indicated in a letter he wrote to Sir William Cecil four days later. In it he claimed that, although the earls' army was far larger, all he needed to defeat them were a thousand horse with lances and pistols and a thousand foot, half pikemen and half harquebusiers.[166] Yet in the north little had changed by 1584 when a muster of the militia on the Border recorded 827 horsemen with jack and spear and 1,547 with spear alone, as well as 2,500 archers and 2,500 billmen.[167] The situation was somewhat different in the south, where the Spanish threat was felt more acutely. There some units of light horsemen did possess firearms. According to the instructions sent to the Norwich officials in 1584, a light horseman should be armed with a pair of pistols, a staff, a sword and a dagger and wear a skull (steel cap) and a jack or a burgonet and corslet. He had to ride a serviceable horse or gelding, seated on a light saddle. The lighter petronels or shot on horseback firing petronels or carbines made their appearance at the same time, hence the government's attempt to oblige the justices of the peace to pay for their maintenance. Demi-lances had only fitfully embraced firearm technology; few units had become pistoleers and many still continued to carry axes as their second weapon. In the 1590s the Ordnance Office was still purchasing the parts for making lances, ordering staves and heads from separate suppliers for subsequent assembly.[168]

At the same time archers and billmen in county forces were being converted respectively to musketeers and pikemen, though bows and bills had not completely disappeared by the end of the sixteenth century.[169] Ships, in particular, possessed complements of archers. In the 1590s Richard Bolt and William Reynolds, respectively the Queen's bowyer and fletcher, delivered consignments of bows and arrows and repaired damaged stock. Reynolds also supplied arrows that were fired from muskets. In addition, the Ordnance Office continued to stockpile bills. In June 1596, for instance, Robert Goare, the Queen's purveyor of timber, sent 500 black bills to the stores.[170] Nonetheless, the bulk of the orders were for pikes and firearms, both calivers and muskets, though rather more of the older weapon. In 1596 the Privy Council ordered the county lieutenancies to abandon bows and bills for muskets and pikes.[171] The process of change was already under way at Lyme Regis in 1573 when seventy-six of the 178 able-bodied soldiers carried harquebuses (42.7 per cent) and forty-one trailed a pike (23 per cent). The town's twenty archers and twenty billmen still carried traditional weapons (22.5 per cent). By 1591 the proportion of firearms, now calivers, had grown: of the known weapons twenty-six were calivers (44.8 per cent) and six were pikes (10.3 per cent). There were still eight billmen (13.8 per cent) but only two archers (3.4 per cent). In 1599, presumably in response to the order of 1596, all the 168 soldiers had become musketeers.[172]

This process of modernization made it easier for the English to integrate the infantry into the ranks of their continental allies.[173] Many of them fought in the Low Countries where the nature of warfare put a premium on foot soldiers. English soldiers also proved their worth in siege operations. In France, Henry of Navarre possessed cavalry of his own and valued the English as reliable, pugnacious infantrymen.[174] Even so, detachments of English cavalrymen did sterling service abroad too. In the Low Countries, they operated as mounted pistoleers and even the demi-lances carried pistols and swords. At Zutphen in 1586 a detachment of about two hundred English heavy cavalrymen under Sir John Norreys rescued a group of fifty young noble lancers who had recklessly charged a much larger enemy force. Norreys' men attacked the Spanish force which comprised several thousand horse and foot with such ferocity that they cut swathes through their ranks and forced them to give ground. Unfortunately shortages of cavalrymen did hamper operations in which English troops participated. In 1591, for instance, Sir John Norreys could only take one squadron of cavalry with him to Brittany, Lord Burghley and the Queen assuming that the French would provide the bulk of the mounted troops. This restricted Sir John's capability for independent action. He therefore asked for additional horse, arguing that he was having difficulty in finding out about the enemy's movements. He even offered to swap two infantrymen in the Queen's pay for every cavalryman provided. Thirty were sent in July.[175]

In the late sixteenth century the English were also engaged in almost continuous fighting in Ireland, which periodically intensified into full-scale warfare. The rebellion of Hugh O'Neill, the earl of Tyrone (1594–1603) posed a particular danger to English hegemony on account of the scale of the rising and the skilled leadership of O'Neill himself. The English troops who faced him comprised diverse elements: units from the Irish military establishment, militia recruits from England and veterans sent over from the Low Countries.[176] They therefore consisted of infantrymen skilled in pike and shot tactics and troopers who had executed the *caracole* in foreign cavalry units, as well as raw recruits from the shires. The importance of supplying the troops with modern weapons is reflected in the warning given to the Caernarvonshire deputy lieutenants that, since the levy was 'to go against the Spaniards who use great store of muskets, their bows must be changed for musket or other shot, and their brown bills for halberds'.[177] County levies, although mostly foot, did include cavalry contingents. Kent sent heavy cavalry to Ireland in 1595, as did its clergy the following year. Altogether, the clergy, who traditionally raised horse, supplied 285 infantry and 300 horsemen in 1596. Between 1598 and 1601 English counties contributed 720 horsemen. Kent, the county most at risk from a Spanish invasion from the Low

Countries, remarkably sent the greatest numbers.[178] In 1596 virtually all of the infantrymen carried firearms and pikes, in roughly equal measure, that is except for a few halberdiers.[179] The nature of Irish warfare meant that the cavalry were proportionately fewer than the norm and the demi-lances and northern borderers still carried their traditional weapons, respectively lance and spear. Among the consignments delivered by the government's contractors were bundles of lance staves described as 'of the Irish fashion'.[180] One-third of the cavalry comprised shot on horseback.[181] On paper, the English horse outclassed that of O'Neill and in cavalry country it was a valuable asset. Unfortunately, O'Neill's tactics were to avoid pitched battle and to fight a guerrilla campaign. When, at Kinsale on 24 December 1601, the Irish finally lined up against the English on an open plain the Queen's forces annihilated them.[182]

The Irish had learned some of the lessons of continental warfare and under O'Neill put them to good use. It is to O'Neill's credit that he managed to create a modern, disciplined army, while retaining the best elements of traditional Gaelic practice. He increased the number of native mercenaries, maintaining them through a levy known as the bonnaght. O'Neill drilled them in the use of the pike, and after the end of the campaigning season, held them in reserve as a trained militia. The gallowglass, armoured axemen who had migrated from Scotland in the middle ages, became pikemen, as did his Scottish mercenaries, the redshanks. He created his shot out of the kern, irregular infantrymen, hitherto armed with a targe and a dagger and either a bow or darts. In spite of O'Neill's interest in pike-shot formations, he also retained units of soldiers using traditional weapons such as bows and arrows and swords and bucklers. His cavalry arm comprised light horsemen, who owed service to their lord.[183] They rode native horses without stirrups. According to Blundeville, the hobby was 'nimble, light, pleasaunt and apte to be taught ... Irish men both with dartes & with lyght speares, do use to skyrmishe with them in the fielde. And many of them do prove to that use verie well by meanes they be so lyght and swyfte.'[184] These horses were ideally suited to O'Neill's defensive tactics and his policy of keeping the English at a distance. In skirmishes his light horsemen operated as stradiots, employing hit-and-run tactics, while his shot, positioned in front of the main force, fired on the enemy as soon as they came into range.[185] In ambushes, the shot broke up the English ranks and, once disorganized, the horse and sword and buckler men moved in to finish them off.

Although James I made peace with Spain in 1604, Englishmen who wanted to practise their martial skills in a real war still crossed the Channel to the Low Countries. A twelve years' truce, agreed between Spain and the United Provinces in 1609, did little to reduce their employment opportunities, for there were other conflicts in which they could participate.[186] At home, modern arms continued to replace archaic weapons as they wore out: in 1618 the Privy Council prohibited calivers and insisted that the handgunners use muskets.[187] Modernization, in turn, led to calls for uniformity, for example, in the length and bore of firearms. In 1618 the international situation worsened as a direct result of the attempt of the King's son-in-law, Frederick, the Elector Palatine, to wrest the throne of Bohemia from the Habsburg candidate. The realization that England might have to intervene militarily to secure Frederick's patrimony led to renewed vigour at home. In 1621 James made preparations to send an army, comprising 25,000 foot and 5,000 horse, to Germany. The composition of the horse reveals that by then both arms of the cavalry had adopted firearms. The 3,500 cuirassiers, hitherto demi-lances, carried pistols and the 1,500 petronels, carbines.[188] In the event, the expeditionary force never set out, mainly because the native arms industries could not supply more than a fraction of the required weapons and munitions in the time available.[189] When Charles I came to the throne in 1625 he inherited the war from his father. In the Cadiz expedition of 1625 the only horses used were the fifty draught animals employed to pull the ordnance.[190] In 1627 Charles I opened a second front with an attack on France. The expedition, designed to relieve the Huguenots besieged in La Rochelle, included a cavalry arm as a supplement to the foot.

At the beginning of the British Civil Wars only the Scottish Covenanter forces continued to maintain units of lancers, for neither the Parliamentarians nor Royalists armed their cavalry with the weapon. Very few cuirassiers survived too; in England Sir Arthur Hesilrige commanded the only regiment so clad, known as the 'lobsters' because of their articulated armour. They achieved some initial success but few emulated them. Troopers disliked the weight of the armour, which restricted their mobility and made them vulnerable when unhorsed. At best, troopers wore a corslet and pot, though many merely donned a thick leather buff coat. Also, according to General Monck, horses capable of bearing the weight of a cuirassier were hard to find.[191] This is debatable but even if true it only illustrates contemporary opinion, which emphasized mobility rather than weight. Lighter, more agile horses of 14½ to 15 hands were therefore preferred.

Most of the cavalry were known as harquebusiers, though by the 1640s they had swapped their harquebus for a carbine, of similar length but with a larger bore.[192] They also carried a pair of pistols and a sword. Dragoons fought with carbines too, but as they normally dismounted before a battle, they should rather be regarded as infantrymen. Occasionally, a commander deployed them as cavalry but, as their mounts were smaller and less powerful, they were less effective than troopers.[193] The firearms mainly possessed flintlock mechanisms, which were cheaper and more reliable than wheel-locks, though the latter were easier to use on horseback. Troopers affixed the carbine to a swivel, attached to a belt worn over the shoulder. According to Firth, pistols gradually replaced carbines as the main weapon, adding that, if so, the term harquebusier became a misnomer.[194]

The evidence of the contracts made with London gunmakers supports this view: they supplied few carbines to either the Eastern Association or the New Model Army. Nonetheless, some units did use carbines. Captain Greathead's company, which served in Lord Fairfax's regiment from May 1644, were armed with carbines, pistols and swords. Retrospective company and regimental accounts, drawn up after the war and which contain a number of references to carbines, provide further evidence.[195]

Conventionally, the proportion of foot to horse lay between two and five to one. Parliamentarian forces normally adhered to this ratio but Royalist armies tended to contain a higher percentage of cavalrymen.[196] At times, the Royalists fielded more troopers than infantry. Even at Naseby, a key battle, they possessed almost as many horse as foot.[197] This imbalance partly reflected their inability to recruit and retain infantry and partly the social composition of their forces. The Royalists were overburdened with gentlemen-officers, a problem that grew worse over time as losses depleted numbers in troops, companies and regiments. Unfortunately, its Council of War was less ruthless than its Parliamentary equivalent in amalgamating the survivors into reformado units. When Rupert's northern cavalry joined the main field army in 1645, General Monck described it as so hopelessly top-heavy with officers that it seemed 'a rabble of gentility'. The high command from the king down were aware of the discrepancy and wished to rectify it but with little success.[198]

The shortage of serviceable horses affected the composition of the Scottish Covenanting and Irish Confederate forces. The Covenanter army had no separate cavalry regiments until 1640. In Ireland the confederates possessed few regular cavalry units. Even in its premier force, the Leinster army, only one in ten of the soldiers were troopers. Scottish Galloways and Irish hobbies made excellent skirmishing horses but lacked the size for pitched battle. To provide themselves with suitable troop horses the Scots secretly bought up stock at northern England fairs in 1638. Some of them may have served in their troops of lancers. As in England, the authorities imposed quotas on the counties but the horses netted were variable in quality. When the Scots invaded England many of the troopers were mounted on 'the verriest nags'.[199] In Ireland the insurgents had specifically sought serviceable horses, as well as arms and munitions, in the initial surge. They also asked for people to bring in horses, for which they promised to pay them a reasonable price. As time wore on, the situation worsened because, unlike in England, the pool of horses steadily diminished. Even the loyalists under Ormonde were affected.[200] The Confederate weakness in cavalry had serious military repercussions: in all set battles, except Benburb, they lost because enemy cavalry succeeded in breaking up their infantry formations. On the other hand, the Leinster cavalry did achieve some success in lesser engagements, leading one modern commentator to declare that the weakness was quantitative rather than qualitative.[201] Even so, when, in the wake of Parliament's victory in England, Cromwell was able to deploy the full might of the English war machine on the Scots and Irish, the Celts were 'outgunned' in every department.

Initially the cavalry tactics employed by the two sides in the English Civil Wars offered a distinct contrast. The Royalists, like the Swedish army, charged in close order, sword in hand, but differed from them in that they charged at greater speed and did not fire their pistols at all until the mêlée, possibly because of a shortage of weapons. Later in the war Rupert adopted the Swedish device of stationing detachments of musketeers among the cavalry. The Parliamentarians, on the other hand, subscribed to the more defensive Dutch model which relied on the firepower of musketeer and dragoon units to blunt the charge of the enemy cavalry before its own horse mounted a counter-attack. Over time their tactics moved towards those employed by the Royalists prompted it seems by Cromwell, who came to realize the value of taking the initiative. Wanklyn and Jones suggest that his conversion occurred at the battle of Grantham in May 1643, when the Parliamentarian cavalry defeated the Royalist horse, having virtually been forced to make the first move.[202] In southern England Parliamentarian commanders were reluctant to change, and it was not before the second battle of Newbury in October 1644 that both cavalry wings advanced on the enemy without waiting to receive an attack. Cromwell's insistence on keeping formation and retaining control meant that his troops did not charge as quickly as did the Royalists. It was not easy to rein in troops of cavalrymen in full flight but Royalist cavalry commanders, notably Rupert, have long been criticized for not reforming after a successful sally. This is unfair: it did happen at Edgehill but thereafter they learned their lesson. Even so, a major reason for Cromwell's success as a leader of cavalry was the discipline he instilled into his regiment of Ironcoats. At Marston Moor, on 2 July 1644, for instance, this turned potential defeat into overwhelming victory. Whereas Cromwell, operating on the western wing of the Parliamentarian army, had broken through the Royalist ranks, Goring had routed Fairfax's cavalry on the eastern flank. Cromwell, reforming his horse, attacked the victorious Royalists and trounced them. Then, working with Crawford's foot, he prevented the collapse of the infantry on the right.[203]

When the Irish Catholics gave their support to the deposed king, James II, in 1689, they had at their disposal an expanded army and one purged of its Protestant officers. In January 1689 Tyrconnell, the leader of the rebellion, issued warrants for the raising of 40,000 new troops, to be formed into forty regiments of foot, four of dragoons and two of horse. Unfortunately, the loss of so many officers hindered their training, while they also suffered from a shortage of arms, clothing and equipment.[204] If the infantry was poor even after Sarsfield had weeded out the worst recruits during the course of 1689, the cavalry was excellent, in marked contrast to the situation during Civil Wars of the mid seventeenth century.[205] This was partly due to the merit of the officers and troopers and partly due to an improvement in the size and quality of the horses bred in the country since the mid century.[206] The cavalry soon proved its worth, routing Lundy's inexperienced infantrymen at the passage of the fords near Lifford in April 1689. At the two major battles of the wars, the crossing of the Boyne in June 1690 and at Aughrim in July 1691, Irish cavalry units performed with distinction, even if they could not prevent overall defeat. At the Boyne they supported their outnumbered infantry units at the Oldbridge crossing and for a time threatened to change the course of the battle. Sheldon's horse acquitted itself particularly well. The outcome remained in doubt until William III led a cavalry contingent across the river, rallying his men and putting irresistible pressure on the Irish. Even so, when the Jacobite infantry broke, the cavalry heroically covered their retreat. Parker's regiment repeatedly charged William's troops until only thirty men remained. As a result, the Boyne was not the decisive battle that William III had wanted. At Aughrim, Sarsfield, although outnumbered, kept the enemy cavalry at bay for hours and thus prevented it from turning the right wing of the army. Unfortunately, the death of the Jacobite commander, Saint-Ruth, prevented Sheldon on the left wing from acting decisively. Attacked by English cavalry units, he withdrew from the field. Sarsfield, on the right, could do nothing and, in spite of repeated charges, could not prevent William's cavalry from slaughtering the Irish infantrymen.[207]

In the initial stages of the war Irish Protestants had to act alone, though they were strengthened by officers and recruits dismissed from the Irish army. At Derry eight regiments, totalling about seven thousand men, defended the city, all but one of which consisted of infantry units. The cavalry under Adam Murray, though mostly restricted to garrison duties, made several successful sorties against the besiegers.[208] The garrison at Enniskillen comprised three infantry battalions, two regiments of dragoons and one of cavalry. There the cavalry commander, Thomas Lloyd, effectively deployed his troops as skirmishers, dominating the surrounding countryside through lightning raids. They also routed the Jacobite cavalry at Belleck in May, having outflanked them by advancing through a bog. In July the Enniskilleners, luring Jacobite dragooners into a trap at Lisnaskea, decimated them with sword and pistol. Then, linking up with the infantry, they defeated the Jacobites under Mountcashel who were strongly entrenched on a hill overlooking a road which ran through a bog near Newtonbutler. In a combined operation, the infantry first cleared the artillery placed at the end of the causeway, allowing the cavalry to cut the disorganized infantrymen to pieces. Lack of coordination between the cavalry and infantry arms of the Jacobites contributed to this disaster because Sarsfield, the cavalry commander, did not know of the whereabouts of Mountcashel's forces and failed to turn up.[209] The arrival of William III's expeditionary army in the months from August 1689 transformed the situation. His forces were professional, better trained and included greater numbers of cavalrymen. While man for man they were not necessarily any better than the Irish cavalry, the weight of numbers, as noted, was an important factor in the victories at the Boyne and Aughrim.[210]

At the opening of the eighteenth century Marlborough perfected the coordination of horse and foot in his campaigns against Louis XIV's army. In essence, his cavalry squadrons were light horse, wearing a breastplate and armed with pistols and sword or, like the mid-century petronels, carrying a carbine.[211] Contrary to normal practice, Marlborough held most of his cavalry in reserve in the centre, making his initial thrust on the wings with a combination of infantry and small, supporting cavalry units. Once this tactic had drawn the enemy wide, he punched a hole through the middle with the weight of his horse. Emphasizing the element of shock, Marlborough used the sword as the main offensive weapon.[212] Marlborough's insistence on close infantry support proved its worth at Blenheim on 13 August 1704. Having made progress through the centre, the allied cavalry units found themselves checked by the desperate charge of the remaining French cavalry. Fortunately, Lord Orkney's twenty-seven battalions of foot, following up close behind, stemmed the French attack and allowed the allied cavalry to reform. Lord Orkney later noted, 'I really believe, had not ye foot been there, that the enemy would have driven our horse from the field'.[213] At Ramillies (23 May 1706), on the other hand, an advance by Lord Orkney's foot stalled because of the lack of close cavalry support on the marshy ground. At this battle, infantry fire, which relieved pressure on the cavalry facing a French counter-attack in the centre, decided the outcome. It held up the French until the arrival of Orkney's foot tipped the balance in the allies' favour. The Danish horse then delivered the *coup de grâce*, charging through gaps in the French flank.[214]

Between the opening of the Civil Wars and the conclusion of Marlborough's campaigns the British learned how to deploy field artillery effectively. The heavier pieces, demi-culverin (9 lbs) and the occasional culverin (16 lbs) were difficult to set up because of their weight and lack of manoeuvrability. Once in position, they were virtually impossible to reposition or realign, seriously reducing their ability to respond to the unfolding events on the battlefield.[215] So, commanders increasingly made use of lighter pieces, ranging from the five-pounder saker to the one-pounder leather guns and known as galloping guns because of their mobility. Gun crews moved these pieces around the battlefield, harnessed to between two and four horses, according to the weight of the cannon. Used in this way, the artillery arm added an extra dimension to the role that horses played in contemporary warfare.[216] Both Parliamentarians and Royalists adopted the Swedish practice of assigning two light cannon to each regiment of foot. The Scots, with their experience of fighting in Gustavus Adolphus's army, were the first to appreciate the value of light mobile guns on the battlefield. At Newburn on

28 August 1640 the Scottish superiority in ordnance contributed greatly to their victory.[217] In England, field artillery did not play a very great part in determining the outcome of the conflict, though the battle of First Newbury featured an artillery duel between the two sets of gunners.[218] Marlborough more successfully integrated his mobile field guns into his overall plan. Each battalion possessed two 1½ to 3 lbs cannon, firing grapeshot, which, because they provided close fire support, materially affected the course of events. Marlborough's gunners were also able to drag the heavier pieces from one position to another, according to circumstances, thereby enabling them to operate in a more dynamic way.[219]

When Henry VIII prepared to go to war against France at the beginning of his reign, the country was ill-equipped to support his enterprise. His infantry employed archaic weapons, his cavalry lacked suitable mounts and his artillery and baggage trains had to make do with weak draught animals. In terms of horseflesh the situation was little better at the end of the reign for Henry's wars had taken its toll on England's resources. Henry, along with some of his household officials, bred strong horses, suitable for men-at-arms and demi-lances, at his studs, but otherwise only Wales produced a significant number. Most of the men-at-arms who fought in Henry's army were foreign mercenaries or allied auxiliaries. Moreover, although horses for the light cavalry were numerous and spirited, they were weak and broken-winded.[220] The draught horses were so poor that the commissary officers were forced to buy Flemish horses, which did the job with half the number.

Paradoxically, Henry's wars provided the stimulus which ultimately led to a complete transformation in the quality of native stock in general and in the standard of horses required by the army in particular. Apart from his own personal involvement, Henry encouraged the landed classes to breed serviceable horses. To the carrot he added the stick, as the Acts of 1537 and 1541–2, stipulating the size of breeding stock and the number of suitable stallions that they had to keep, indicate. Elizabeth's commission of 1580 marked a further step in this process, since its avowed intention was to improve the quality of cavalry horses. Judging from the standard of horses that appeared at musters (or excuses from contributors who had not sent them), much still needed to be done. As the Earl of Huntingdon pointed out in 1588, however, it was not so much that gentlemen did not have a number of serviceable horses but rather they did not want to have their liability recorded in a list. By the end of the sixteenth century English horses were in demand abroad; many left legally under licence or as gifts to foreign dignitaries, while others travelled clandestinely. Still the horse remained substandard and Charles I had trouble recruiting cavalry to fight the Scottish Covenanters in the winter of 1638–9. The English Civil Wars revealed the true picture. If horses suitable for armoured cuirassiers were hard to find (and this

1. Detail from Hoefnagel's painting *A Fête at Bermondsey* (c. 1570); showing cart and pack horses, as well as a variety of saddle mounts. (*The Marquess of Salisbury, Hatfield House*)

2. Henry VIII rides with his retinue to meet Francis I of France on the Field of the Cloth of Gold near Calais in June 1520. (*The Royal Collection ©2006 Her Majesty Queen Elizabeth II*)

3. Wootton's portrait of the Bloody Shouldered Arabian exported from Aleppo by Nathaniel Harley. It initially stood at his nephew's stud at Welbeck and then at the duke of Somerset's stud at Petworth. It sired several noted racehorses. (*The Hoare Collection, Stourhead, The National Trust/The Paul Mellon Centre for Studies in British Art*)

4. and 5. Exterior and interior views of the Duke of Newcastle's riding school at Bolsover Castle in Derbyshire. (*English Heritage*)

6. A. Sijmond's painting *Five of the Dukes of Newcastle's Managed Horses*, commissioned by the duke of Newcastle while in exile at Antwerp. It shows from the top: A Neapolitan courser, a Turcoman, a Russian, a Spanish Ginete and a Barb. (*Private Collection*)

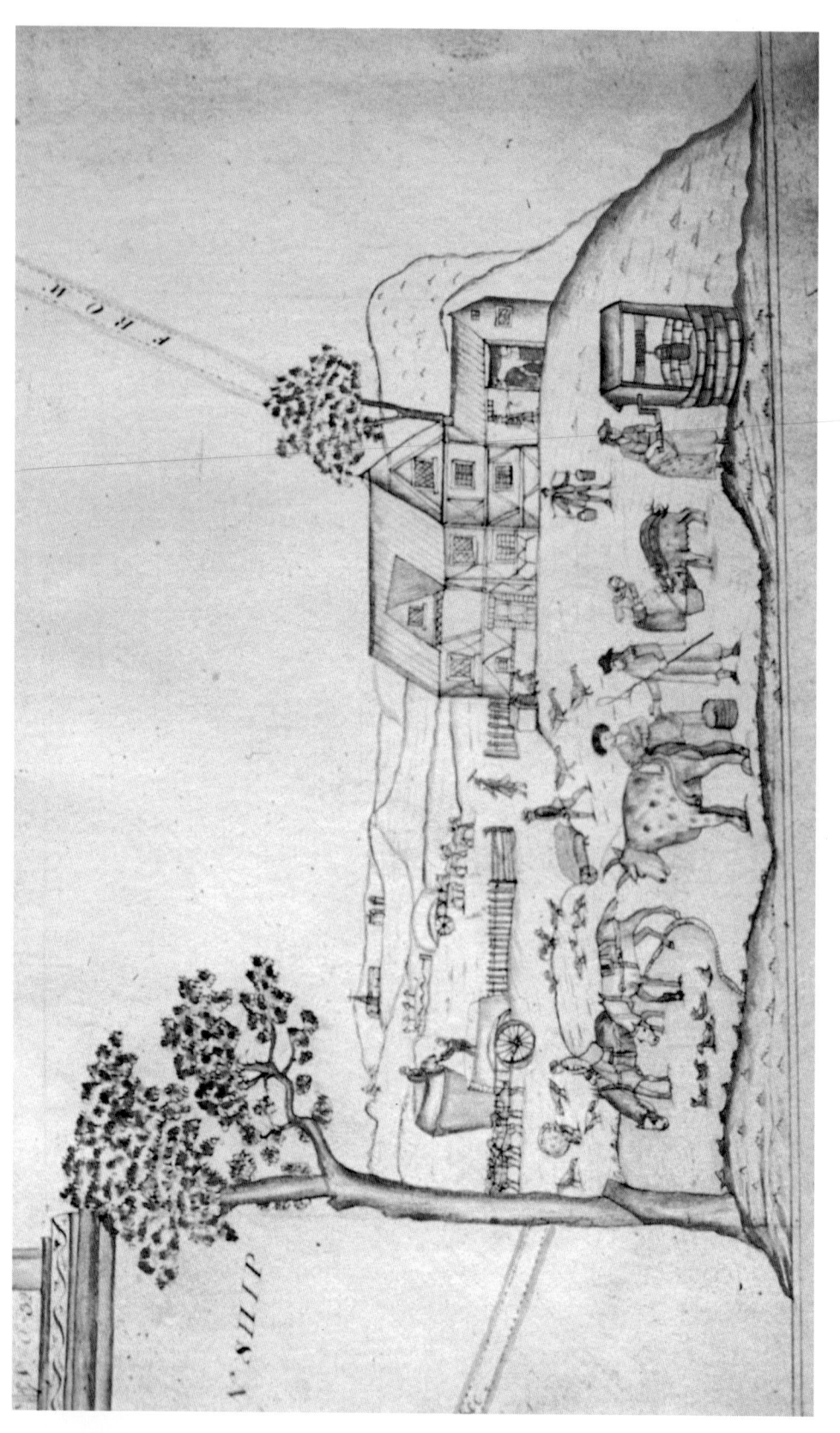

7. A farm scene at Twyford in Shropshire in the early eighteenth century. (*Shropshire County Council Record Office*)

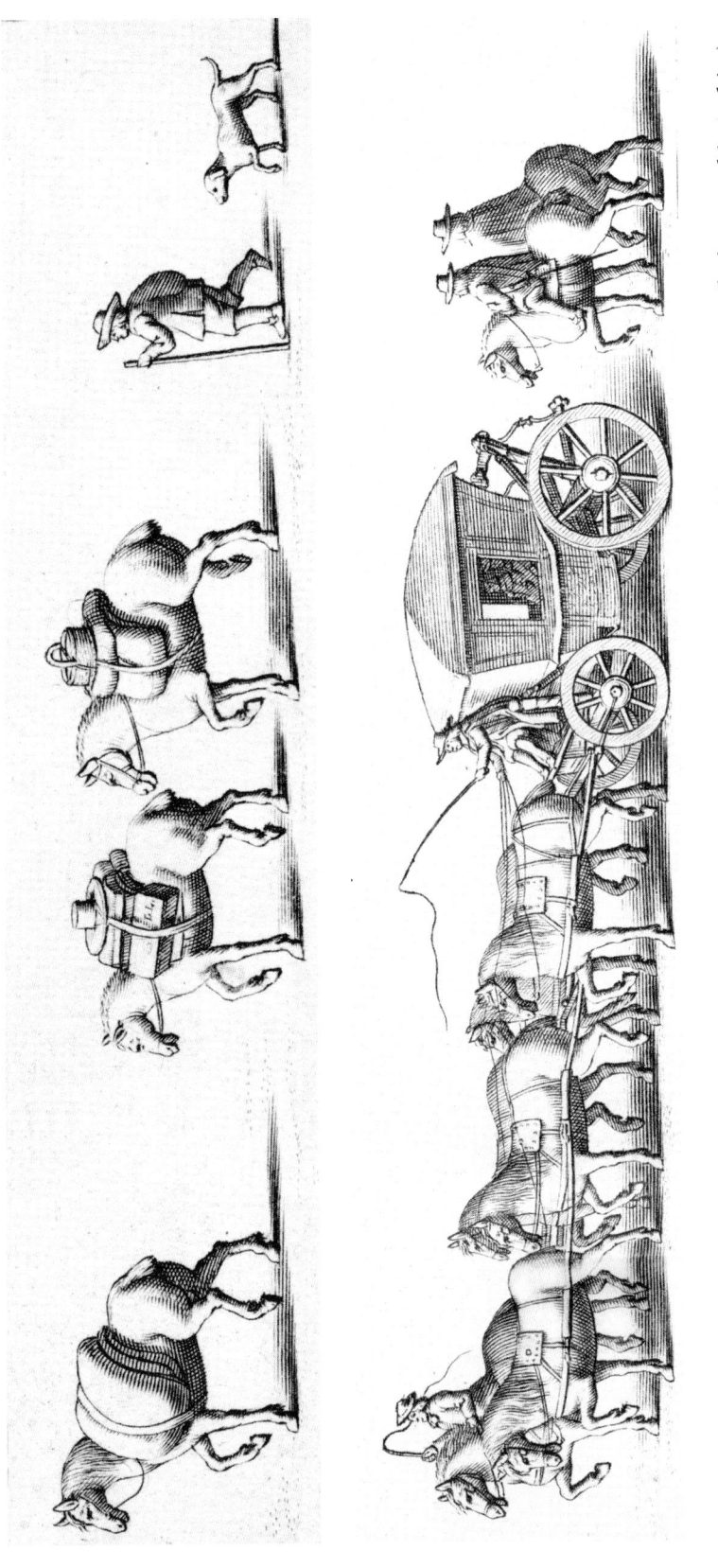

8. and 9. Loggan's engravings of a stage coach and packhorses at Oxford in c. 1675. (© Oxfordshire County Council Photographic Archive)

10. Charles II leaving Nonsuch Palace by coach. (©*Berkeley Castle*)

is debatable), there were sufficient mounts for the light horse. Unlike arms and armaments, neither side had to import war horses from abroad.[221] Officials and commissary officers, backed up by military muscle, effectively tapped the equine resources of the country. The conflict stimulated the breeding of serviceable horses but these animals mostly missed the conflict. They added to the nation's wealth, however, for within a few years they were being exported freely.[222]

England was slow to adopt the gunpowder revolution. Henry VIII's army possessed cannon cast at home but its detachments of harquebusiers and shot on horseback were foreigners. Most of its infantrymen still fought with bows and arrows, the weapon that began the shift towards firepower. The government, at least as early as the mid sixteenth century, was aware of the advantage of handguns but still encouraged archery practice, partly to keep young men out of mischief. During Elizabeth's reign harquebuses and calivers gradually replaced bows and arrows, and pistols became the primary weapon of the demi-lances and the light horse. Bills gave way to pikes. The armies that lined up on Edgehill on 23 October 1642 comprised pike and shot formations on foot; light horse carrying pistols and harquebusiers equipped with carbines; and artillery trains featuring a range of field guns. The Royalists even argued which infantry system to use: the Dutch or the Swedish. Marlborough, at the end of the period, successfully made use of Gustavus Adolphus's tactic of coordinating cavalry and foot units.

Although England did not possess a standing army, this did not mean that its inhabitants lacked skill in the exercise of arms. Thousands of them fought on the Continent and provided a pool of professional soldiers, whom lords lieutenant in the counties could employ to instruct the part-time troops in the militia, especially those in the trained bands. They also commanded the armies and stiffened the ranks in wartime. These people were aware of developments on the Continent and aided the process of modernization at home. In the Civil Wars of the mid seventeenth century the Scots and, to a lesser extent, the Irish benefited from the return of troops serving abroad, who also brought with them much needed arms and armaments. Some helped in other ways. When Swedish ships, carrying a consignment of war materials bound for Scotland, sailed through the Sound in late summer 1640 the Danish navy did not challenge it: an unprecedented occurrence. The Danish admiral, Axel Mowat, a Scot, adopted a Nelsonian approach and saw no ships.[223]

Work Horses

Many thousands of ordinary people working in early modern England used horses in a host of utilitarian tasks. They put loads on their horses' back or hitched them to a vehicle; the debate over which mode was preferable only being resolved at the end of the period. On farms, horses helped prepare the ground, pulling ploughs, harrows or rollers, and drew the wains, tumbrels, carts, wagons and even sledges that carried farm produce off the fields or to market. At the beginning of the sixteenth century horses shared the work with oxen so that farmers and, to a lesser extent, carriers had a real choice to make. Increasingly, people chose horses and over the course of the following two centuries horses gradually ousted oxen, first on the country's roads and then on its farms. For some people, albeit a minority, asses did the job. Naturally, some horses were more suited to some tasks than others. So, when the people who employed them became more specific in their requirements, breeders started to pay particular attention to the production of horses with the requisite qualities. General developments in agriculture, notably the enclosure of commons and open fields, growing regional specialization and the integration of the market at a national level, aided the process. The upper classes required horses to carry out similar jobs but, even if they used them for practical purposes, they still demanded the best.

HORSES ON THE FARM

On the farm, horses steadily took over from oxen at the plough, although the timing and pace of the change varied from place to place. As early as the thirteenth century horses were being widely used, especially on peasant holdings and, as in Norfolk, where sown rather than natural fodder crops were being developed. Arguments which Walter of Henley put forward at the time, moreover, were reiterated in the early modern period by writers such as Fitzherbert and continued to be aired as late as the nineteenth century. On the credit side, horses were more sure-footed on stony or hilly ground and worked more quickly on lighter soils. They were also more versatile than oxen, performing tasks that ranged from ploughing and harrowing, through carting and pack carriage, to riding. On the other hand, horses needed a more varied diet, were more expensive to maintain and less willing workers in heavy going. In addition, unlike oxen, they lost virtually all their value at the end of their working life. Fat oxen fetched considerable sums in the market. In the middle ages oxen on average pulled greater loads than horses and may still have done so in the 1520s, the time when Fitzherbert was writing.[1] During the course of the early modern period, however, the balance shifted the other way: as a result of developments in horse breeding, draught horses progressively outstripped oxen in terms of strength. For many farmers the availability of fodder was the decisive factor. Oxen needed lush grass to function effectively, hence the numbers kept in pastoral areas or in mixed farming districts where enclosed grasslands existed. Farmers, working in areas of intensive agriculture, on the other hand, were more likely to employ horses: they grew large amounts of fodder crops and, if they operated in a communal system, could tether their horses on leys or balks in the open fields.[2]

The change-over occurred earliest on the lighter soils, on land most suitable for horses. On chalklands oxen had largely disappeared from the plough by the early eighteenth century. In the Wiltshire chalk country in the years 1540–1640 most farmers preferred to use horses for all traction, especially for ploughing the lands that stretched up the slopes of the hills. Out of a hundred farmers with ploughs listed in their inventory, sixty-five possessed horse ploughs and fourteen mainly ox ploughs. The rest had ploughs with a mixed complement of horses and cattle. Sometimes farmers harnessed the horses in pairs but mainly they hitched them up in threes. Oxen as well as horses were working on Hampshire and Sussex farms at the turn of the sixteenth century, but the latter were gradually gaining the ascendancy, especially on the chalklands of the South Downs. On the North Downs the situation was very similar. In Kent the trend towards horses was already discernible in 1600 and by the end of the seventeenth century they had almost entirely replaced oxen in the plough. Horses had achieved a dominant position on Surrey's downlands too.[3] In northern England farmers on the wolds pursued the same form of sheep-corn husbandry as their counterparts on the chalk and were also moving over to horses. In Yorkshire, moreover, holdings on the wolds were on average larger than in any other part of the county, so local farmers needed a greater number of horses to service their enterprises. Their counterparts on the Lincolnshire wolds also kept comparatively large complements of horses; in Tudor times they maintained on average five horses for the plough and other work, while the richest farmers owned far more. By the 1690s the mean number had risen to nine. In the Cotswolds, sixteenth-century farmers used horses and oxen in equal numbers, but thereafter the proportion of horses increased so that by the eighteenth century they outnumbered oxen by two to one.[4] On the light soils of East Anglia the native punches, working in teams of two, ploughed up to two acres a day. In 1681 Thomas Baskerville, travelling between Bungay and Beccles, noticed a man ploughing with such a team, the first time he had seen it, though, as he wrote, 'they seldom do with more at any time in these parts'.[5]

In the open field parishes of the east midlands the soil was heavier but here too farmers kept horses.[6] In the sixteenth century cultivators in the Melton Mowbray and Lutterworth districts of Leicestershire, with little enclosed land available to feed oxen, were employing horses for all farm purposes. At the same time horses were taking over from oxen as plough animals in north Oxfordshire, another mixed farming, horse-rearing area. In a survey of inventories, appraised between 1550 and 1590, ninety-two mention ploughs and of them forty-four include references to draught horses and cattle. While only five farmers relied entirely on oxen or bullocks, thirty-seven others only deployed horses on the land.[7] In the early eighteenth century punches supplied all the draught in High Suffolk, working in teams of four or five at the most. In the woodland part of the county some oxen still cultivated the stiff clays but plough teams normally consisted of four to six punches. In Huntingdonshire too the switch to horses was virtually complete by the end of the seventeenth century.[8]

Oxen were more likely to persist in areas of heavy soil where pasture was plentiful and where the steadier pull that they exerted was often more effective. In the weald of south-eastern England inventories reveal this difference of emphasis between local farms and those on the chalk downs. At the end of the seventeenth century oxen remained the predominant working animal on the clays, though an occasional farmer had horses for the plough or cart. In the Sussex weald horses merely supplemented oxen in the early Stuart period, sometimes in mixed teams, and oxen were still in general use over a century later. At Kirdford most farms kept draught oxen into the eighteenth century, but thereafter only the more substantial holdings maintained them. In Surrey post-Restoration farmers in the Wealden parishes of Burstow and Charlwood normally used oxen as draught animals. John Humphrey, a Charlwood yeoman, for instance, left six working oxen at the time of his death in 1686.[9] In north Wiltshire in the mid-seventeenth century farmers were also keeping oxen as plough animals in contrast to their counterparts in the southern parts of the county.[10] In western England, where the Butter Country, incorporating the Vales of Blackmore, Glastonbury, Ilminster, Wardour, Glamorgan and Marshwood, formed one farming region, teams, maintained only by the larger farmers and jobbing ploughmen, usually consisted of oxen. In Devon too oxen continued to share the work with horses throughout the seventeenth century. Of the western part of the county, William Marshall later wrote that 'oxen have ever been the PLOW TEAM of the District', sometimes, as elsewhere, being led by horses but in general working alone.'[11] Although outside the period being studied, it is worth pointing out that between the late 1770s and about 1820 farmers around the country showed renewed interest in employing oxen for the draught. Apart from the peculiar circumstances of the

French wars, the reasons given were similar to those offered two hundred years earlier.[12]

In some areas where oxen pulled the plough, horses performed ancillary tasks such as harrowing and carting, a development which went as far back as the twelfth century at least. This was particularly noticeable in southern and eastern England, where by the second half of the thirteenth century horse-drawn vehicles had become the dominant mode of peasant vehicle transportation in East Anglia, the Home Counties and the East Midlands.[13] In the Southwell district of Nottinghamshire in the mid sixteenth century farmers normally ploughed with oxen but often employed horses to harrow their land and pull their carts. A century later inventories indicate that this distinction still persisted in the weald of Surrey. When Ann Martin, the widow of a Charlwood yeoman, died in September 1680 her agricultural stock included forty-nine acres of crops growing in the fields, £16 worth of hay, four working oxen and three working horses, two wagons, one cart, two ploughs, three harrows, tackling and other implements of husbandry. Not surprisingly, in areas like the Wiltshire downs and in Oxfordshire, where they had become more important as plough animals, horses were also being extensively employed for other jobs too. In Wiltshire, farmers with surpluses to sell used cart horses to pull their vehicles. Oxen did draw farm vehicles but tended to pull wains, whereas horses were associated with carts.[14]

WORK HORSES ON THE ROAD

On the road horses were far more dominant. In some parts of the country farmers and carriers might use oxen on the highway and, as noted above, the peculiar circumstances of the Civil Wars forced armies to deploy them in greater numbers, especially in northern and western England and in Ireland.[15] For professional long-distance carriers, the real choice was not between horses and oxen but rather between small pack ponies and larger draught horses. On the one hand, a horse harnessed to a vehicle pulled more than it could manage with a load on its back. A draught horse readily drew six hundredweight between the shafts, whereas a packhorse could only carry a little over two hundredweight.[16] Packhorses, however, possessed certain advantages: they were faster, could operate in hill country or on rough or muddy ground, and were especially effective over long hauls. They also cost less money to buy and feed and, because it was easier to add or subtract horses in the train, offered greater flexibility in terms of number. Chartres, referring to the London trade, thought that wagons were clearly superior over short and middle distances but were less effective as distance from London increased.[17] Gerhold questions this conclusion, though concedes that the benefits wrought by the greater speed of packhorse trains increased with distance.[18] Balancing costs against income, packhorses were thirty per cent more expensive than draught horses per ton mile.[19] At the end of the seventeenth century carrier services to London divided equally between those using packhorses and those employing wagons. The balance only tilted appreciably towards the latter during the course of the eighteenth century when, among other factors, the diffusion of turnpiking improved the quality of the roads.[20]

Land carriage was certainly more expensive than transport by water. Wherever possible, therefore, most cargoes, especially those of a bulky nature and low unit cost, floated along rivers or around the coast. Overland, the price of coal doubled every ten miles so the most fully exploited mines of the time were the ones, like the Northumberland and Durham field, which lay close to navigable rivers or to the coast.[21] Even so, consignments often had to travel overland to and from the wharf and this gave employment to carriers. On the Northumberland and Durham coalfield large numbers of vehicles took coal to the staithes in small two-wheeled carts with a capacity of about 8¾ hundredweight of coal, drawn by one horse, or in larger wains with twice the volume and pulled by a team of two horses and two oxen. In 1696 some 20,000 horses were working in the Newcastle coal trade.[22] In 1725, when Lord Oxford met packhorses near Darlington, he observed that the horses carried two sacks of coal, each containing more than a bushel (totally nearly two hundredweight). For many inland towns overland transport marked the final stage of the journey. In west Somerset, barges took coal from south Wales up the River Parrett as far as Bridgwater, where it was transferred to smaller craft which were able to push upstream as far as Ham Mills. A deponent, giving evidence in a case of 1672, declared that he had on occasion driven packhorses laden with coal from Ham Mills to Taunton, North Curry, Langport and Wellington. He had even taken loads to Stoke St Mary's, Yarcombe and Chard in Somerset and to Holcombe Rogus and Tiverton in Devon, that is up to thirty-five miles away.[23]

Carriers transported other commodities down to the riverside, as, for example, linenware from the Manchester area to the Severn at Shrewsbury; metalware from Sheffield and lead from Derbyshire to Bawtry on the Trent; and corn from the Thames Valley to transshipment centres on the Thames.[24] During the course of the seventeenth century Lechlade, at the head of the Thames navigation, became an important river port. Here cloth and cheese, brought overland from the Vales of Berkeley and Gloucester, continued their journey downstream to London. In 1719 a deponent calculated that between 140 and 200 wagons, laden with cheese, together with consignments brought on horseback, converged on the town for the cheese fairs on St John's bridge. He also stated that numerous stage wagons brought cloth to the town from the Stroud district.[25] Items travelling back up the country's rivers as back carriage included raw materials and luxury goods. Wine, which was awkward to move by land, normally went by water to the point closest to its destination, whence it continued its journey by cart.[26]

Horses were more efficient if they pulled vehicles floating in water or running along rails. Horses – and men – regularly hauled laden barges, especially when travelling against the current or wind. Both were employed on the Thames. The Glover map of 1635 depicts a team of halers at Richmond pulling a boat upstream, presumably as far as Ham Hawe where 'The Barges First Take Horse'. In 1662 William Schellink, a Dutch traveller, did not see any halers at Richmond, the point at which the tide ran out, noting that 'ships have to be towed up the river by horses'. Horses were also being used on the Great Ouse in the early seventeenth century. On the other hand, only men pulled the boats on the Severn.[27] For a regular service, horses were more cost-effective than men in spite of additional maintenance charges.[28] In 1723 a witness at the hearing of the Yorkshire Derwent Bill deposed that a single horse towed a barge along a four mile stretch of the river at a cost of 1s., whereas the charge for four halers amounted to 4s. plus 'drink'. On the Thames in 1730 a witness calculated that six horses could do the work then being performed by upwards of sixty men. When barges increased in size horses were essential. By the mid eighteenth century, therefore, horses were being used more widely on navigable rivers, even if landowners might charge higher wayleaves for them.[29]

Overland, wooden wagonways, first used on coalfields in the opening years of the seventeenth century, enabled horses to pull far greater loads, reputedly in excess of two tons.[30] Huntingdon Beaumont constructed the first wagonway in 1603–4 in order to transport coal from his Strelley pits in Nottinghamshire to Wollaton Lane End, where carriers dispatched it to Nottingham or took it to the Trent for transshipment by river. The two-mile track enabled him to move at least an extra 180 tons of coal a week.[31] Unfortunately, the pits remained unprofitable, so Beaumont moved to the north-east when his lease ran out. Here too he constructed wagonways, linking collieries at Cowpen and Bebside to the River Blyth. Again, he succeeded in raising output and speed of delivery but failed to compete with the larger established fields around Newcastle. By the middle of the seventeenth century wagonways were running down to the Tyne from nearby pits.[32] In the early seventeenth century wagonways for coal were also operational on the Shropshire coalfield at Broseley. In a case heard in Star Chamber in 1606 a witness stated that, 'The said engine would by all likelihode have conveyed unto the said River [Severn] with little help, more coales in a day than a wayne & 6 oxen were able to convey to any of the said places in 3 or 4 days'.[33]

The trend towards regional specialization in agriculture and the concentration of industry ensured that the roads carried a large and growing volume of goods around the country. In the early seventeenth century Dorset and Wiltshire farmers took as many as twenty cartloads of corn to Shaftesbury for sale each market day, besides other consignments carried on the back of their horses. Only the constricted site of the market prevented further expansion. Of Warminster, another busy corn market, Camden observed, 'it is scarce credible what quantities of corn are every week carried hither and presently sold'. Aubrey later calculated that sellers disposed of twelve or fourteen score loads of corn there each market day, primarily for consumption in Bristol.[34] Corn moved considerable distances in the north too. Richmond in the North Riding was an important centre, being well placed to sell corn in the lowlands to consumers living in the uplands to the west. William Brass of Richmond, who died in 1675, was one of those who participated in the trade, dealing both in corn grown in the Vale of York and in more distant supplies shipped up to the port of Stockton. In east Yorkshire Henry Best took his corn to a number of markets on the back of his horses. He always sent oats to Beverley; wheat and maslin normally to Malton; and barley to Beverley or Pocklington in winter and to Malton in summer. Occasionally, he contracted with shipmasters at Bridlington, who dispatched his wheat to Newcastle or Sunderland. Best seldom sent fewer than eight loads of grain at a time to the market and for such a trip he employed two men.[35]

Processed grain in the form of meal and malt similarly travelled overland. Early in Elizabeth's reign the transport of malt and grain from Enfield to London provided employment for hundreds of carriers. Some of the Enfield maltmen reputedly possessed a hundred hired horses apiece. One consequence of the implementation of the River Lea Act of 1571, which made the river navigable as far as Ware, was the complete disappearance of the overland trade. According to a carriers' and loaders' petition of 1581 (with allowance for special pleading), many thousands of people in the counties of Hertford, Middlesex, Cambridge, Bedford and Essex who earned a living taking corn and other grain to London by land were now 'utterlye decaied'.[36] Elsewhere, the carrying trade continued to expand; in 1718, for instance, 'great drifts of malthorses' were crossing the Pennines via Alport on their way to Manchester. In the Peak District malt provided carriers, who had taken lead and millstones to ports on the River Trent, with a valuable return cargo.[37] Dairy produce, similarly, had a wide distribution. In the late seventeenth century factors, resident in the Cheshire cheese country (which included the adjacent parts of Lancashire, Shropshire and Staffordshire), collected the cheese off the farms and then took it by road to Chester or Liverpool for shipment to London. Other consignments, brought to riparian ports such as Shrewsbury and Bridgnorth, went down the Severn. Middlemen also took London-bound cheese overland to the Trent or across the Pennines to the Don at Doncaster.[38]

Textile production employed the greatest number of non-agricultural workers, including many who carried raw materials, as well as textile products in various stages of manufacture, around the country.[39] One group of wool staplers, resident on the Welsh Border, collected the fine March wool of the region and distributed it over a wide area. In the late sixteenth century, one of their number, Richard Baynes of Newport, Shropshire, sold most of his wool to Essex clothiers, notably those at Coggeshall and Dedham, though he also dispatched some consignments to Somerset.[40] Carriers took the finished cloth long distances too. Between the late fifteen and mid sixteenth centuries, for instance, Kendalmen transported Kendal 'dozens' to Southampton for export abroad.[41] Thereafter the rise of the Blackwell Hall factors to a position of dominance in the export trade, and the decline of Southampton's port, forced a switch to London. In between, finishing centres like Shrewsbury or Exeter acted as local *foci*, receiving parcels of unfinished cloth, which packhorse trains in their droves brought in from the surrounding villages and towns. At Exeter in the late seventeenth century Celia Fiennes wrote of 'The carryers I met going with it [serge] as thick all entering into town, with their loaded horses'.[42]

Even coal, a commodity with a particularly high cost differential between land and water carriage, was largely an overland trade. Seaborne transport accounted for only a little over one-third of all coal mined at the end of the seventeenth century. To a large extent this was due to the absence of suitable water communications, typified by the north-east Warwickshire field which served customers living in Leicestershire, Northamptonshire, south Warwickshire and even Oxfordshire. The small scale of operations is also discernible in the development of pits on Kingswood Chase in the seventeenth century to provide coal for Bristol. In the post-Restoration period, when about seventy pits were producing coal, cottages to house the miners, coal drivers and ancillary workers covered the landscape. In 1675 coal drivers reputedly kept over 500 working horses.[43] On the northern part of the east Shropshire field coalmasters did not have the easy access to the Severn that enabled their colleagues at Broseley and Madeley to the south to sell their ware throughout the Severn Valley. Reliant on road transport, they sold much of their ware in the locality. In 1604, all those owing money for coal dug at the Wombridge mines of Gilbert Groom and Robert Cleaton lived within a ten mile radius of the pits.[44]

A good deal of traffic moved along the roads of early modern England. Of the long distance trade, a significant proportion of it was going to or coming out of London. Metropolitan carriers had already established links with the provinces at the opening of the period and by 1600 they were operating regular services to many parts of the country, including Chester, Manchester, Keswick and York in the north.[45] These links multiplied over the course of the following 150 years, though the rate of expansion is debatable. Chartres claims that services to and from London increased rapidly during the seventeenth century, growing appreciably between 1637 and 1681 and then accelerating between 1681 and 1715.[46] Gerhold disagrees, arguing that no real evidence exists either for an 'appreciable' growth in services between 1637 and 1681 or for the subsequent spurt to 1715. He calculates that the number of carrying services rose by less than one-third between 1681 and 1705, the date to which Chartres's 1715 figure really refers.[47] Gerhold's revisionism similarly affects the reliability of Chartres's conclusion that provincial linkages grew 'very substantially' during the course of the seventeenth century.[48]

CARRIER SERVICES

Common carriers supplying the London market were professionals and had some standing in their community. They generally owned land and often farmed. If so, they cultivated hay and fodder crops for their horses but might also grow crops for human consumption, whether bread corn or malting barley. When the appraisers listed the goods of William Claroe, a Worcester carrier, in September 1680, they valued his twenty-three horses with their gearing and packsaddles at £115; his four wagons and a tumbrel, with their irons, ploughs and a cart, at £22 10s.; and a beam, scales and weights at £1. They also found eighty bushels of wheat (£10) and malt (£2) in the house and ricks of barley (£10), pulses (£10) and hay (£16) outside. Silvester Keene, a carrier from Minety, left both working horses and oxen at his death in March 1684/5. He certainly farmed because he possessed a flock of 102 sheep, a cow and a heifer, a drag and plough gear. Presumably his six oxen pulled the plough and his ten draught horses his wagon. He probably accompanied the wagon on one of his 'running' horses. Men like Claroe and Keene normally hired others to do the driving but tended to shadow their vehicles in order to keep an eye on the driver and to make contact with customers and innkeepers.[49] They transported all manner of goods but, like the Kendal carriers, often specialized in the movement of a specific item produced locally. Their employees were less well off but also benefited from adding a secondary source of income. This was difficult, given the nature of their job, but James Nonneley of Derby found a way of combining two occupations. Described as a carrier by profession in a court case at Shrewsbury in December 1626, he had recently begun to earn money in the summer burning ground, presumably stubble (and possibly undergrowth on wastes, prior to enclosure). In winter he drove carriers' horses down to London.[50]

Short-distance carriers, operating within a thirty mile radius, were men of more modest means, and rather conservative in their practices. Many were private rather than common carriers, for whom carrying was often a part-time occupation. Small farmers, for instance, regularly undertook carrying work at slack times of the year, using their farm horses and carts.[51] The business attracted others of more slender resources, carriers who plied their trade with a single horse. One such man was John Jollett of Kingsbury, who at a quarter sessions meeting in 1620 deposed that he earned a living by carrying apples and kept one horse for that purpose. To people like Jollett, the loss of their animal spelt disaster. In the Shropshire parish of Myddle Richard Gough, writing at the end of the seventeenth century, recorded the case of Richard Maddocks, a carpenter turned carrier broken by the death of an old horse. In 1710 the justices of the peace in the North Riding of Yorkshire received a petition on behalf of Christopher Perkin of Boltby, a very poor man, whose horse, the source of his livelihood, had died by the side of the road.[52]

Also travelling on the highway were a host of middlemen, known as badgers and a variety of other names, who traded in the goods they moved. They also tended to deal in a particular commodity, often, in the case of manufactured items, having graduated from the process of making it. In Staffordshire in 1603 the local metalworkers complained about the activities of their former colleagues, men who 'brought up to these trades have now given over the said making of ware; and buying the wares of others that do make them, do sell to other countries [counties]'.[53] Badgers were particularly important in the provisioning of farm produce. They gained formal recognition in an Act of 1552 which allowed any badger, lader, kidder or carrier, licensed by three magistrates, to buy grain, cattle, fish, butter or cheese where he or she wished, provided he or she did not forestall the market and if the price of corn was not above a certain level. In 1563 a further Act tightened up control by insisting that these traders had to be married householders, at least thirty years old, and to have lived in the county for at least three years.[54] Their licences were valid for one year and might impose specific restrictions on the goods traded, the amounts dealt in, the area of business and the number of horses in the team or train. In January 1629/30, for instance, Edith Doddington, a widow from Bishop's Hull near Taunton, obtained a licence to buy butter and cheese in Somerset and dispose of it in Wiltshire, Hampshire, Dorset and Devon, returning with corn to sell at any market in Somerset. She could not employ more than three horses, 'mares or geldings for the most part'.[55]

Packmen differed greatly in the scale of their operation, ranging from the single horse owner to the 101 left by Joseph Naylor of Rothwell, a West Riding parish, in 1718.[56] Local carriers worked with a few horses at the most. Beyond a thirty-mile radius carriers had to keep more horses in order to maintain the regularity of their services. Jonathan Beadnall of Stokesley in the North Riding of Yorkshire, for instance, carried goods between Stokesley, Guisborough and York on the back of five or six horses at the turn of the seventeenth century.[57] An analysis of the twenty probate inventories of packmen mentioned in De Laune's 1681 list of carriers reveals that the five who journeyed between thirty and fifty-four miles to London owned on average five horses, while the seven who travelled between 105 and 146 miles left nine horses. Among those travelling over

152 miles, Naylor was still exceptional, for the seven on the list had on average seventeen horses.[58] Some of these businesses involved partnerships, increasing the number of horses members could deploy by pooling their resources.[59]

Carrying was a dangerous profession, for drivers risked being waylaid by highwaymen, intent on stealing their load. While this was a perennial problem, it was a particular issue during the period of the Civil Wars in the mid seventeenth century. One carrier who ran the gauntlet was Thomas Priestley of Soyland near Halifax. Thomas, according to his brother's account, took cloth down to London on the back of his eight or nine horses throughout the 1640s. He travelled with others, sometimes hiring convoys and sometimes not, but they were never stopped, neither 'he or his horses or goods, all that dangerous time'.[60] He was fortunate because his journey took him through Royalist territory, where soldiers stationed at garrisons such as Newark on the Trent were on the look out for consignments going to the capital. The carriers used by the Parliamentarian inclined Wiltshire clothiers were not so lucky. In June 1643 troops from Wallingford garrison intercepted their convoy and carried away enough cloth to 'make new clothes for all their soldiers'.[61] Many carriers worked for one side or the other; if at times they suffered impressment, they also gained contracts, which, if paid, recompensed them handsomely. Even if the authorities did try to pay for such services, especially in areas they controlled, the carriers had to compete with others for a share of limited funds.[62]

TABLE 9a: Size of horses at markets, 1658–1758

	Chester		Oxford				Bristol	
	1658–98		1673–99		1700–45		1705–58	
size	no.	per cent	no.	per cent	no.	per cent	no.	per cent
small: below 14 hands	22	47.8	66	31.4	23	32.4	14	23.0
medium: 14 hands	16	34.8	123	58.6	41	57.7	41	67.2
Large: 15 hands+	8	17.4	21	10.0	7	9.9	6	9.8
Totals	46	100	210	100	71	100	61	100

Source: toll books

Carriers doubtlessly employed an assortment of horses, but they particularly valued ones with the right qualities. According to Blundeville, packhorses had to be good travellers, that is to be tractable, hardy and possess stamina. They also had to have tough hooves to enable them to pick their way sure-footedly through rough and stony ground, as well as to economize on shoeing. Finally, they had to be moderate feeders to save on food bills. Accordingly, carriers preferred geldings to stallions, which were harder to handle and ate more. As Blundeville remarked, 'packemen here in England, do most commonly go with gueldings which lacking the fervent heat that stoned horses have, cannot consume so much meate as they do, but chiefly perhaps because the gueldings are more easy to rule by the waye then horses'.[63] Markham provided more detail on the ideal physique: 'chuse him that is exceeding strong of Body and Limbs, but not tall, with a broad back, out ribs, full shoulders and thick withers; for if he be thin in that part, you shall hardly keep his back from galling'. He also emphasized the value of choosing a horse with a good stride for, as it went at a mere foot pace, 'he which takes the longest strides goes at the most ease and rids his ground fastest'.[64]

TABLE 9b: Size of horses at fairs, 1684–1779

size	Warwick 1684–94 no.	per cent	Kidderminster 1694–1711 no.	per cent	Rothwell c.1684–1720 no.	per cent	Rugeley 1768–79 no.	per cent
small: below 14 hands	85	25.1	146	40.9	11	22.0	44	19.8
medium: 14 hands	215	63.6	188	52.7	21	42.0	116	52.3
Large: 15 hands+	38	11.2	23	6.3	18	36.0	62	27.9
Totals	338	100	357	100	50	100	222	100

Source: toll books

Most packhorses were small because lightness was an asset in difficult terrain. The data for the markets in table 9a is particularly relevant since to a greater extent than at fairs their presence was associated with the carriage of goods, whether in packs or vehicles. The continued buoyancy of the market in pony-sized horses in the post-Restoration period, as reflected in toll book entries, therefore reveals the continuing importance of packhorses in the carrying trade.[65] Since the horses were small, and performed a functional rather than a fashionable purpose, they were comparatively cheap. On the Welsh border hill ponies, many of which did become packhorses, cost on average about £1 to £1 10s. in the third quarter of the sixteenth century and between £2 and £3 in the post-Restoration period. At Kidderminster the median value of the sub-fourteen hands horses sold between 1694 and 1711 works out at £2 18s. Many cost less. On one market day at Ludlow in May 1691 John Bottfield, a collier from Cleobury North, bought a horse for £2 off James Sherwood, a collier from Ditton Priors. Sherwood sold a further five horses and mares there for £9 1s. In Lancashire in 1677–8 Sarah Fell of Swarthmoor Hall acquired four horses to carry ore, including a little Galloway for which she paid £1 3s. 3d.[66] When they neared the end of their working life, prices fell further. Among the possessions that Thomas Pringle, a collier from Pixley Hill, Auckland St Andrew (Durham), left in 1695 were seven old coal Galloways and an old blind Galloway worth £5 9s. 4d., together with eight old saddles, sixteen little coal pokes and some halters and girths valued at 10s.[67]

ROAD AND FARM VEHICLES

Carriers, who transported goods in vehicles, traditionally used the two-wheeled wain or cart. From Elizabeth's reign onwards, however, larger four-wheeled wagons introduced from the Low Countries complemented and, to a certain extent, replaced these vehicles,[68] Stow gives 1564 as the approximate date of their first appearance, after which they gradually spread throughout the country.[69] Progress was slow at first, even in the Home Counties. Norden, describing Essex in 1592–3, noted that Essex carriers, though active in supplying London with all manner of goods, dispatched them in carts and carriages. They had begun to employ wagons by 1605 when Stow stated that these vehicles were bringing goods (and people) from Canterbury, Norwich, Ipswich, Gloucester and elsewhere.[70] At first, wagons were largely confined to the roads of lowland England. According to Aubrey, they appeared in Wiltshire in the second quarter of the seventeenth century, initially driven by carriers on the London route. By 1700 they had spread to the north and west.[71]

Wagons appeared later on farms, though the pattern of diffusion from the south-east outwards remained the same.[72] References occur in inventories of southern farmers in early Stuart times but only turn up in significant numbers after 1660. It is possible, of course, that the paucity of probate inventory evidence in the period of the Civil Wars and Interregnum masks the precise timing of the change. In the 1630s mixed farmers at Roxwell and Writtle in mid-Essex employed load carts for carriage, though one of their number, John George, also possessed a wagon. In the 1660s appraisers regularly listed wagons in local inventories, which, with the in-built time-lag, suggests that farmers in these two parishes were using them in the 1650s. In general, these wagons did not replace existing vehicles, which seems to indicate a differentiation of function: load carts for farm work and the wagons for bulk transporters of grain to market.[73] Farmers in the Sevenoaks district of Kent acted in the same way. Of those whose goods were appraised in Charles II's reign, most of an admittedly small set of fourteen farmers owned carts and wagons. Three only left carts but no one solely possessed wagons.[74] Collections of inventories for St Albans and Buckinghamshire, on the other hand, indicate that long carts continued to function as road and field vehicles throughout the late Stuart period. In Buckinghamshire farmers either possessed all-purpose carts or dung- and long-carts.[75]

In the late seventeenth century wagons also appeared on farms in a wider arc, stretching from Wiltshire in the south to Lincolnshire in the north. In Huntingdonshire the first reference to wagons postdates the Restoration, but by the end of the century more than one in seven farmers' inventories refer to them. They were most common in the two northernmost farming districts, their adoption there perhaps influenced by the use of wagons by farmers in adjoining counties. By the middle of the eighteenth century wagons had spread much more widely through the county and more generally through farming society. The late seventeenth century was the crucial period on the Wiltshire downlands too. According to Aubrey, 'Wagons not used (commonly) in south Wiltshire till about 1655. Before that they altogether did use carts which are now grown quite out of fashion.'[76] Generally, ownership was restricted to gentlemen and prosperous yeomen. In the Lutterworth district of Leicestershire, where appraisers began to record them from the 1680s, all but two of the fourteen references occur in inventories with a valuation of over £120. These farmers grew considerable acreages of crops so, as they retained their carts, they clearly took the grain to market in their wagons.[77] Of Oxfordshire, Dr Plot remarked in 1677 that farmers at that time mainly used two-wheeled long carts, which, with shambles over the shafts, a cart ladder over the breech and hoops over the wheels, enabled them to carry large loads. Although overloading made them less secure or stable than wagons, the latter were little used except by carriers.[78] Here too sampled inventories reveal that the larger farmers were the first to obtain wagons. In the period 1670–90 slightly under one in ten farmers left wagons, a proportion that rose to almost four in ten over the course of the following forty years.[79] This pattern is repeated at Horbling, a fen edge parish in Lincolnshire, with the more prosperous farmers the first to purchase wagons. Between 1660 and 1699, of the eighteen inventories which record farm vehicles, five list wagons. Whereas the median value of the personal estate left by their owners amounts to £444 18d. 10d., that of the thirteen others works out at £68 3s. 8d. Conversely, at Winteringham, a clayland parish bordering the Humber estuary, wagons had come into more general use by the end of the seventeenth century. At the time local farmers used wains in the fields. In the early eighteenth century, however, they were utilizing wagons for their farm work too.[80]

Wagons made slower progress in western and northern England, though in the vales some large mixed farmers had acquired them by 1700. Of Staffordshire Plot reported in 1686 that 'For waynes, carts, and waggons, they use the very same for carriage of their corn, and other matters, that they doe in other counties'.[81] William Walker, a substantial mixed farmer in the Trent Valley just outside Lichfield, was the sort of person who first used them to transport his grain to market. When he died in 1679 he left 57½ acres of corn growing in his fields, two wagons, two carts and a tumbrel, and eight horses and mares.[82] In Shropshire the situation was the same, with wagons only appearing in any number in the early eighteenth century. By 1750 yeoman farmers in many parts of the county had obtained a wagon, primarily as a road vehicle as they also owned a variety of carts, wains and tumbrels.[83] In the Frampton Cotterell district of the Vale of Gloucester the first reference to a wagon, described as old, occurs in an inventory of 1691. There oxen continued to provide much of the draught on the farm, though a discernible shift from wains to carts over the years 1660–1741 implies a switch to horses to lift off crops.[84] Some large farmers in the northern vales had also acquired wagons by the end of the seventeenth century. In south Yorkshire they turn up in inventories from the 1690s, perhaps introduced into the area by Dutch settlers, who moved in after the draining of Hatfield Chase.[85] Nonetheless, even where conditions were suitable, farmers did not necessarily abandon their traditional vehicles. At Ashton and Bowden in Cheshire, for example, they moved loads in carts or on the back of a horse.[86] Upland farmers, like those in Wensleydale, used fewer vehicles (either carts or wains) deploying packhorses with pokes on their back for much of the work.[87]

DRAUGHT HORSES

When carriers introduced four-wheeled wagons onto the roads at the turn of the sixteenth century, they could draw on a stock of suitable horses to pull them. Blundeville, writing in 1565, claimed that England contained many good draught horses, even if he makes the point to complain about the decline in the standards of breeding strong saddle (cavalry) horses. He declared that countrymen seeking horses for draught or burden 'may easily fynde a number of strong Jades more mete for that purpose then for the saddle and all for lacke of good order of breeding'.[88] He was very specific about the qualities that a good cart (and plough) horse should possess. 'So that he be great of stature, depe, rybbed, side bellied, and have stronge legges and good hoves: & therewith wyll stoupe to his worke, and lay sure holde of the grounde with his feet, and stoutelye pull at a pinch, it maketh no matter how foule or evil favoured he be.'[89] This description admirably fits the Suffolk punch which, with its thickset body and short legs, made an ideal workhorse.[90] Apart from punches, horses in fen edge parishes in Lincolnshire, East Anglia and on the Somerset Levels had size and strength. Those, who could, acquired horses with Flemish, Dutch or north German blood in them.[91] The process of improvement was a slow one, however, and the average size of English draught horses did not increase significantly until the early eighteenth century.

At the end of Elizabeth I's reign, carriers could buy a draught horse for about £3, but to obtain particularly powerful specimens they had to pay in excess of £4 and go to a specialist fair to find it. In February 1595/6 Margaret Carter, a Mitcham widow, intent on setting up a coal-carrying business, gave her brother-in-law, Rowland Bates, £10 to go to Dunstable Fair to buy a horse and cart. Bates could not obtain anything suitable but on the way home met Richard Hogg, a Southwark innholder, and agreed to buy from him three horses for £14 16s. 8d. and a cart for £3 3s. 4d.[92] Bedfordshire fairs, like those in the east midlands, specialized in good quality draught horses, but one wonders why someone from Mitcham did not look in the Smithfield market, where he or she would have had the pick of the biggest draught horses on offer anywhere in the country. For those who did not live in such a convenient location there were several options: buy a suitable horse when in the capital; travel to a specialist centre; look for one on offer by a dealer at a local fair; or hope that they chanced on an owner disposing of a superfluous horse in the market. Boughton Green, near Northampton, provided one outlet for strong draught horses and, according to the toll book for 25 June 1627, London and Home Counties dealers mingled with carriers looking for carriage and wagon horses. Two-fifths of the buyers at the fair came from outside Northamptonshire, mostly from London and the intervening counties.[93] The median values of recorded sales of horses and colts amount to £5 and £4 11s./£4 12s. respectively, with a good choice of better animals above that figure. When John Haddock of Hollowell in Northamptonshire vouched for a colt sold to William Cann of Worton (possibly Wootton) in Warwickshire for £6, he stated that it was a 'good workaman'. London dealers, with a ready market among the capital's carriers, tended to buy the most expensive animals, including a brown bay horse that cost Richard Cannon of St Saviour's, Southwark, £13.

Prices naturally went up in the 1640s as the war pushed up demand, commissary officers having to pay £5 to £7 for those draught horses they bought rather than merely requisitioned or stole.[94] After the Restoration good draught horses still cost around £5 at a number of midlands fairs, prices that held for the rest of the century. Flat markets for agricultural produce helped keep prices low but it also shows that, outside specialist outlets, sellers had few really strong horses to dispose of. Table 9 reflects the slow pace of change with the bulk of the horses measuring 14 to 14:3 hands. On the other hand, some large, powerful horses were available at fairs serving the top end of the market. In *The Gentleman's Recreation* (1686) Richard Blome recommended the reader to buy English horses of 15½ hands high for travelling or for draught work in the countryside.[95] He presumably knew that it was possible to buy them at specialist fairs, such as the one at Rothwell.[96] Besides, if the toll keeper there had recorded the height of the sets of horses bought by the London dealers, the average size would have risen. In this respect, perceptions of the size, strength and quality of horses depend on the chance survival of the records of one fair over another. Evidence from probate inventories indicates that some wagoners and carriers at least were using large, powerful horses, those worth about £5 and more. In 1663, for instance, Robert Beechcroft, a Norwich carrier, left five wagons worth £45 10s. and twenty-eight horses, which, with harness, were valued at £163. In 1692 the appraisers of the goods of Robert Barnes, a Lincoln carrier, assessed his wagon and ten horses with tack at £100.[97]

The process accelerated after the Glorious Revolution of 1688 which, by putting the Dutchman, William of Orange, on the throne, facilitated the movement of horses from the Netherlands to England. The accounts of Henry de Nassau, William's Master of the Horse reveal that the King spent thousands of pounds on imports. Others undoubtedly followed his lead. Anne maintained this link after William's death.[98] The situation duly improved during the course of the early eighteenth century. Defoe's observations, made in the 1720s, indicate that by then the system was beginning to produce a considerable number of fine quality draught horses. Of Leicestershire, he wrote that[99]

> The horses produced here, or rather fed here, are the largest in England, being generally the great black coach horses and dray horses, of which so great a number are continually brought up to London, that one would think so little a spot as this of Leicestershire could not be able to support them.

Indeed! Most of them had come from breeding grounds elsewhere. When commenting on the Somerset Levels, Defoe remarked on the great number of colts bred on the moors, where drainage provided the rich pasture grounds needed to sustain heavy horses. Dealers from Staffordshire and Leicestershire bought many of these colts, which they sold on to mixed farmers in the midlands. Returned to local fairs, metropolitan dealers bought them as fully-trained cart and coach horses for work on London's streets, 'the breed being very large'.[100]

In general, farmers lagged behind professional long-distance carriers in obtaining really strong draught horses, though some substantial yeomen did own them. Several farmers, included in a set of Bedfordshire probate inventories for the years 1617–19, had acquired them by the time of their deaths. The appraisers of the goods of Peter Clarke of Marston Moretaine valued his six horses and colts at £30 and those of John Ensome of Hawnes fixed the price of his nine horses at £45.[101] Naturally, in rearing areas mixed farmers, who trained colts in the collar for a couple of years before passing them along the chain, had the use of them in the meantime.[102] The practice of training colts and the manner in which it was done is revealed in inventory entries which include a colt among a team of horses. When John George, a Writtle yeoman, died in 1638 he left four cart horses and a colt worth £30. These horses also pulled his plough and the harrow on the farm as well as carrying out transport duties in the field and on the road, in vehicles that comprised a wagon (£4), a load cart (£5) and two dung carts (£2 6s. 8d.).[103] As this example shows, the colt, harnessed to a team of mature horses, learned by emulation. After the Restoration horses worth about £5 or more turn up more regularly in the inventories of mixed farmers in areas such as mid-Essex. When William Pinney of Loughton died in 1664, he left eight horses and two colts, worth, with their harness, £50 and sixty-two acres of growing crops valued at £112. In the Lutterworth district of Leicestershire the same yeomen farmers who owned wagons were the ones who also possessed expensive horses. In the early eighteenth century strong horses also appeared on farms in western counties. In 1745, for instance, Thomas Sheinton of Chelmarsh, Shropshire, left three draught horses, which his appraisers valued at £5 each, together with two wagons (£12) and two tumbrels (£5).[104]

The emphasis on improving the size of draught horses may explain why so few asses were being employed in the country for draught (and pack) purposes. According to Holinshed there were no asses in the country in Elizabeth I's reign. Even if he overstated his case, they were not very numerous. In 1657 one of Samuel Hartlib's correspondents wondered why people did not fully recognize the benefits of working with asses. After all, he observed, they ate less food and thrived on thistles and weeds. They were also tough, worked well under duress and were less prone than horses to disease. What is more, he claimed, on dry, sandy, infertile ground an ass pulling a light plough was 'the fittest team', being both productive and economical. As pack animals, they were ideally suited to transport such items as grain to and from the mill, dung to gardens and 'reasonable' burdens to the field. They powered gins too. The writer acknowledged that some people were using asses, a point confirmed by John Worlidge at the time.[105] The earls of Clare, for example, were breeding asses (and some mules) at Haughton in Nottinghamshire throughout the course of the seventeenth century. In 1616 the list of horses there includes two he- and four she-asses and an ass foal and in 1642, seven he- and five she-asses and four followers. Of the four mules recorded, two were in use and two were not. In 1672 Thomas Isham of Lamport noted in his diary an experiment in which an ass was attached to a roller to see how well it would draw. Asses seem to have grown in popularity during course of the eighteenth century. In 1725, for instance, Lord Oxford saw a number of asses among the gangs of horses carrying coal, when he met them near Darlington. Beilby, writing at the end of the century, confirms this impression, noting that 'their utility becomes daily more universally experienced'.[106]

REGULATING WAGONS AND THEIR LOADS

The authorities viewed the four-wheeled wagons with considerable reserve, blaming them, rather unfairly, for destroying road surfaces. Long carts carried similar weights and, with only one axle, pressed down more heavily on the highway. Even so, carriers in Kent in 1604 and in Essex in 1614 had to appear before the magistrates to answer charges that they overloaded their wagons. The indictment of John Browne of Little Canfield, for instance, stated that he regularly carried loads of between 1½ and 2 tons from Dunmow to Epping and thence to London, whereby the highways were 'much impaired'.[107] In 1618 a royal proclamation sought to bar the wagons from the road as well as restricting the draught to teams of five horses. Another proclamation of 1620 limited vehicles to loads to one ton.[108] Carriers from Buckinghamshire, Hampshire, Northamptonshire, Oxfordshire and Wiltshire signed petitions against the measure, an indication of the area in which these wagons were operating at that time. Those subsequently charged at the quarter sessions with infringing this regulation, moreover, came from the same counties or adjoining ones.[109] After a temporary lull the carriers soon reverted to their former practices, the lead being taken by those provisioning the capital. The destination of all the ninety-one carriers prosecuted in Star Chamber in the years 1619, 1623 and 1624 was London.[110] Justices of the peace were the ones who brought the abuse to the attention of the government, having had to deal with it at their own sessions. In the first half of 1621 magistrates in Middlesex issued a number of recognizances to carriers to appear to answer charges of overloading their wagons and employing too many draught animals in their teams.[111] In Essex the magistrates wrote to the Privy Council in January 1622/3, complaining that carriers were once more driving heavily laden wagons, thereby ruining the surface of the highways. Within a month the case was being heard in the Star Chamber where the attorney general censored 'common carriers [who] for their singular and private profit have of late usuallye travelled with Cartes and wagons with fower wheeles drawne with eight, nyne or ten horses or more and have commonlie therein carryed sixtie or seaventie hundred Weight att one burden att one tyme'.[112] One ploy used was to augment a legal number of horses with oxen. In January 1622/3 the Middlesex magistrates highlighted the ruse: 'Carriers and wagonners ... have ... by subtiltie instead of horses drawen their said loades with oxen and horses above the said number, thinkinge thereby to avoyde the danger of the said proclamacion.' They therefore fixed a ratio of three oxen for two horses and four oxen for three horses and so proportionately.[113]

Among the arguments put forward by carriers was the greater stability of four-wheeled wagons. In Star Chamber the Essex carriers admitted that they had driven such vehicles but claimed that the two-wheeled version 'would oftentymes be overthrowne and mens goods & merchandizes in them much spoyled and marred'. They painted an apocalyptic picture of lost profits, large-scale redundancies, and death and injury to passengers and drivers. They even cited James I himself in their support. Allegedly, he had declared that 'he cared not if your peticoners did goe and travell with eight wheles (yf it were convenient) so as they did not carry thereuppon above xx^{tie} hundred weight'. With this endorsement, why shouldn't they start to use the larger vehicles again, especially as, they claimed, the roads were 'never a iott bettered nor amended' when they had restricted themselves to two-wheeled carts?[114] If the argument, linking wagons with greater stability, left the government unmoved, it did make concessions to petitioners who put forward a persuasive economic case. In 1623 the Privy Council allowed carriers to use four-wheeled wagons to move chalk from the downs to the weald where it was needed to ameliorate the cold, wet clays of the region. The carriers claimed that the smaller two-wheeled carts could not transport sufficient material to effect a real improvement, adding that in any case 'those waies being out of all usual roades no inconvenience can arise to travellers'. Carriers, transporting the King's ordnance, could also use four-wheeled wains.[115]

After the Restoration legislative control relaxed a little, that is, if it had ever had much effect. In 1662 carriers could legally use four-wheeled wagons and employ seven horses or eight oxen, though they could only cart loads of up to 1½ tons in summer and 1 ton in winter. In 1696 they could add an extra horse to the team but the horses had to be harnessed in pairs. A statute of 1707 reduced the number of horses to six, though it allowed justices of the peace to license a greater number of horses or beasts to pull vehicles uphill. Parliament repealed the measure in 1710 because of the loose interpretation of 'hill' adopted by carriers. In 1715 it further lowered the team to five horses and oxen and the width of wheels to at least three inches. In 1718, opponents, claiming that it was 'prejudiciall to trade and to tend to the lessening the rent and value of lands and to the great impoverishing of the farmers landholders and tennants of England', introduced a bill, allowing an additional horse in the team, but they did not succeed in pushing the measure through.[116]

If the authorities vainly tried to restrict the size of vehicles and the loads carried, they also promoted schemes to improve the condition of the roads on which they travelled. An Act of 1555 placed on the parish the responsibility of maintaining its roads, authorizing the vestry to appoint two surveyors of the highways to supervise the work. Male parishioners had to provide four days of labour on the roads, a chore lengthened to six days in 1563. The regularity with which parishes had to account to magistrates or assize judges for their failure adequately to fulfil their statutory obligations suggests that the job was often poorly done, though (less likely) it may indicate that the amateur surveyors of the highways rigorously enforced the process.[117] In spite of inadequate surfaces, the roads were not so bad that they prevented vehicles from using them. Even in such an inhospitable area as south Yorkshire and the Derbyshire Peak a considerable number of wheeled vehicles, mainly wains, were able to use the roads and had done so since the late middle ages. In this area, as elsewhere in the highland zone, wheeled traffic on the highway mainly operated in the summer months, but the fact that it functioned at all supports the view that the conditions were better than commentators have traditionally believed.[118]

In the long run, turnpiking proved to be the key improvement. In 1609 and again in 1621–2 promoters introduced bills to authorize the raising of money through tolls to repair a five-mile stretch of the Great North Road between Biggleswade and Baldock. The preamble to the later bill explained the need for action. Because of the continual passage of droves of cattle and the stream of wains, carts and carriages, 'the same is made soe fowle, full of holes, sloughes, gulles & gutters that yt in the winter tyme made impassable and soe dangerous that noe coach carte nor horse loaded cane almost passe that waie'.[119] The measures failed and the first successful Act only received royal assent in 1663. The second Act came thirty-two years later, but thereafter the pace speeded up so that by the middle of the eighteenth century turnpiking had improved most of the country's arterial roads.[120] In the 1720s Defoe remarked on the transformation brought about by the system, especially for towns near London. He also noted that travel on the roads through the midland clays was getting better. Rashly, he even predicted that as a result of the process of turnpiking the country's roads would in a few years be fully repaired, and restored to the same good condition (or perhaps a better, than) they were during the Roman government'.[121] The diffusion of turnpikes brought the greatest benefit to stage coach operators, allowing their vehicles to travel faster without greatly increasing costs. Turnpikes also contributed to the demise of packhorse services, but not the same extent; other factors which played a part in the eventual dominance of wagons included stronger horses pulling greater weights and the introduction of measures to speed up the vehicles.[122]

GIN HORSES

Industrial concerns needed horses to provide the motive force to work gins and other machines. Among the largest employers were coal works which used horses to wind up coal and to drain the pits. Their gins were of two types: the horizontal cog and rung gin, and the less common vertical whim-gin. Whim-gins were more suitable for deeper and more productive pits because coalmasters could increase the diameter of the drum, erected at a distance from the pit-head, without inconveniencing the operation. They could readily add horses and the number of the bars to which they were harnessed as well.[123] While travelling through Flintshire at the end of the seventeenth century, Celia Fiennes noted that 'there are great coal pitts of the Channell Coale thats cloven huge great pieces, they have great wheeles that are turned with horses that draw up the water and so draine the Mines which would else be overflowed so that they could not dig the coale'.[124] Before the end of the seventeenth century the Lowthers had installed whim-gins at their Whitehaven pits in which the horses turned a horizontal wheel, eighteen feet in diameter. At the time, gin horses worked eight hour shifts.[125] *The Compleat Collier*, published in 1708, recommended that coal masters, operating a sixty fathom deep pit, should use four shifts of horses plus two spares. In this way, they could maintain continuous production, the reserves covering for injured or sick animals.[126]

The number of horses involved in operating the machinery could be considerable. In January 1602/3, Lord Willoughby had sixty-five pump horses at work at Wollaton near Nottingham to drain his pits there.[127] At the same time many pump horses were toiling in the mines on the north-east Warwickshire coalfield. Pits belonging to John Gifford at Potters Coton and Temple 'Lay desolate and drowned with water', but with the help of a water mill and a horse gin they had become workable again by 1602. Flooding affected the mines at nearby Bedworth too, causing extreme hardship among the local population, many of whom, as miners or coal drivers, were dependent upon the mines for their livelihood. In about 1619, after a successful drainage operation, sixty horses were being employed to pump out the water.[128] The introduction of Newcomen engines, first used at a Staffordshire pit in 1712, reduced reliance on horse power for drainage. At Griff in the north-east Warwickshire coalfield the coalmaster installed a Newcomen engine in about 1713. When operational, it made fifty pump horses redundant.[129] Nonetheless, horses were still being used to drain the Lowthers' Whitehaven mines in the early eighteenth century, even though the family was investing in Newcomen engines too. When Scalegill pit flooded in late 1749 horses, working forty-four double and forty-one single shifts between October and December, laboured at the pumps.[130]

The Wollaton gin horses were ordinary animals apparently not chosen for their strength nor specifically for the work they had to do. In March 1601/2 five horses for the pumps cost £8 14s. 4d. or a mean of £1 14s. 10½d., the price of a packhorse.[131] The horses working at Whitehaven at the turn of the seventeenth century, on the other hand, came from superior stock, a change of approach probably based on accumulated experience and a greater emphasis on efficiency. John Gale, an agent of the Lowthers, wanted gin horses to perform that job alone. On 16 May 1693 he wrote, 'I am positive that such horses at worke at the water pitt must be intyrely set asyde for that use only and nothing else'.[132] Writing to Sir John Lowther on 28 February 1696/7, Gale maintained that the problems that Anthony Benn was experiencing in draining Sir John Lowther's pits were due to the inconvenient location of his stables and to his mistake in buying 'very ordinary and insufficient horses'. Accordingly, Benn struggled with these 'sorry' horses, 'ever keeping the water at the brink of danger, soe that it frequently masters him with his four setts and reverts into the worke, as at this very instant it doth'. Gale returned to the theme the following November in response to Benn's request for better pay to deal with heavier flooding of the pits. In essence, Gale blamed Benn for buying inadequate horses, scarcely of middling size. If only he had bought larger horses, which, though ponderous (dull), were 'by their weight most proper for this business'.[133] *The Compleat Collier*, in fact, emphasized the need to employ strong, healthy horses, ones costing at least £7. They were not only much better suited to the job, they survived longer too.[134] When the horses could no longer carry out the task effectively, the coalmasters sold them off, often at a large discount, a reflection of the debilitating nature of the work. At Wollaton the sale of two old pump horses brought in 12s. and 10s. in 1597 and 1603 respectively. At Whitehaven in 1733 seven horses that had cost £44 13s. were sold for a fifth of the price after intervals that varied from one to ten years.[135]

Gin horses were also used for the opposite purpose, namely to obtain water for human consumption. Many horses, like the one operating at Ashridge in 1682, drew water from a well.[136] They even powered machines designed to raise water from rivers. At Chester, on 11 July 1673, the authorities granted Thomas Evans, gent, a lease of a piece of waste ground near the water tower, on which he intended to erect a horse-drawn engine to lift up water to the water works in the summer time. At Worcester in Charles II's reign the River Severn helped drive the machine. According to Thomas Baskerville, the current drove the 'suckers and forcers' on the wheel, which lifted the water so high into a lead cistern that it could feed any part of the city with water. To improve the flow, horses provided additional power. He also noted that at Worcester, as at Ely, people sold water, which they brought into the city in leather bags slung across the backs of horses.[137] On a domestic level, numerous inventories record horse mills which carried out tasks such as grinding the corn. Several horse mills, perhaps in their own housing, were working at Horbling in the mid sixteenth to mid seventeenth centuries.[138] At St Alban's the appraisers gave more details. When Henry Kentish, yeoman, died in 1577, he left a horse mill and its appurtenances, with the tubs and troughs in the mill house worth 4s. 4d., a grindstone and spindle in the fore yard at 1s. 8d. and a beam, weight and scales at 6s. The appraisers of the goods of his eldest son, Thomas, described the equipment as an old horse mill with sifting troughs and all other necessaries belonging to them and valued the items at £2.[139]

WORK HORSES BELONGING THE UPPER CLASSES

In some respects horses belonging to the elite functioned in the same way as they did for the rest of the population. They increasingly took over from oxen for draught and carriage work, ploughing the demesne and transporting produce to market, as well as moving other goods, whether timber, bark, stone, minerals or even venison, off the estate. The upper classes were among the first to adopt innovations such as the four-wheeled wagon. In Northamptonshire a Naseby squire reputedly owned the first one in the early seventeenth century, while on the Wiltshire downs they arrived in 1632 when, according to Aubrey, Mr Canent of Woodyates obtained a wagon at Amesbury.[140] Likewise, their horses, were generally of superior quality and better bred and therefore more valuable than those of the population at large. Between 1646 and 1688 agents of Sir John Wittewronge of Rothamstead accounted for the purchase of five cart horses for £75 14s. and the sale of six more for £92 11s. 10d., including two blind horses which were of no further use to the estate. In 1658 Sir John sold a cart horse that he had acquired at Dunstable Fair, one of several fairs in the county attended by agents of the family on account of the quality of the horses on offer there.[141]

The gentry and members of the aristocracy also patronized local and long-distance carriers on a regular basis. Sir John Petre of Thorndon Hall in Essex often made use of those operating along the roads that radiated out of London. In 1576–7 he gave much business to John Exeter, who travelled from nearby Shenfield to Aldgate in the city. Exeter brought goods direct to Thorndon Hall and even collected items from the family's London house in Aldersgate Street. When Jones, the Romford carrier, did not take loads beyond his home base, Exeter picked them up and dropped them off at Thorndon.[142] Exeter and Jones reflect the two approaches that carriers could adopt towards their genteel clientele. While they all valued their custom, some clearly did not want to be totally subservient to them, if only because it upset their timetables. Land stewards, intent on serving their masters, might take a more 'feudal' view. In a letter that Daniel Eaton wrote to his master, the third Earl of Cardigan, on 20 January 1728/9, he informed him that he had ordered the Harringworth carrier to come to talk to him about the carriage of his lordship's goods. The present carrier, though honest, lived some distance away and this had proved very inconvenient. Chatteris, the Harrington carrier, on the other hand, could easily make a detour through Deen rather than going via Bulwick whenever occasion arose.[143] Carriers transported a range of items and if, like Chatteris, they did business with the elite, they included luxury items. In the deal which Eaton made with him, Chatteris agreed to carry venison from Oundle to London in a day; to deliver oysters from London to Deen every Saturday night; to send a man to Deen every Sunday; and to come through Deen with his cart whenever required.[144] Drink, as noted earlier, featured strongly among the items taken to country houses. In the 1730s and 1740s Roger Strickland, a Catholic gentlemen living in Richmond in Yorkshire, obtained regular consignments of wine, shipped into York and Stockton-on-Tees respectively up the rivers Ouse and Tees, before being loaded onto the carrier's wagon for the final stage of the journey. He similarly obtained cider from Newcastle, via the Tyne and overland carrier.[145]

Animals employed by the upper classes had additional tasks to perform, including the transportation of household goods and personal effects whenever the family progressed from one place to another. In his description of Elizabethan England William Harrison noted that the crown and nobility used large numbers of carts for carriage. Harrison concluded that the fashion for loading possessions in carts meant that 'the ancient use of somers and sumpter horses is in maner utterlie relinquished'.[146] While a shift towards wheeled vehicles did occur, there was no sudden demise in the use of packhorses. In 1603, according to the Venetian secretary in England, middling ranks of the elite, comprising junior members of the Privy Council, lesser peers and gentlemen, in public needed forty to fifty pack horses and at times between one and three hundred horses in teams.[147] Typically, within the overall category of draught and carriage, the elite earmarked specific horses to carry out particular jobs. Naturally, the crown took the refinement of function the furthest. When Henry VIII died he left three wagon horses, twenty-two carriage mulettes and a car. A car, like a carriage had a double meaning: some of these vehicles might have transported people rather than goods, though they probably did not do so in this case. Henry's 'close carre' with his robes in it evidently contained his wardrobe of clothes. Henry also possessed fifteen packhorses in 1547. Many of them carried a specific item, presumably because it made it easier to find things when the train reached its destination for the night. The six sumpter horses transported goods largely associated with washing and eating and drinking, while the besage horse carried goods for the scullery in its pair of saddle bags. To the stole horse Henry entrusted his commode. The male horse carried a travelling bag or trunk, in which servants stored various items. The bottle horse transported bundles or hay.[148]

Prices which the crown paid for these horses in the 1620s indicate that they resembled draught horses rather than pack ponies. Indeed, Richard Graham, Gentleman of the Horse, described a replacement male horse, bought for £12 off Alcock, a Smithfield dealer, as a large grey gelding. Graham's accounts record twelve sumpter horse and ten bottle or scullery horses with median values of

£11 and £10–£12 respectively. Five smaller horses, bought as mounts for the men who led the sumpters, cost on average £6. At the end of the seventeenth century William III's Master of the Horse paid £15 and £16 10s. for two bottle horses.[149] According to their price, members of the upper classes bought similar types of horses. In January 1616/7 Lord Clifford gave £7 for a sumpter and in April 1639 Lord Kilmorrey laid out £6 13s. 4d. for a nag to carry his trunk.[150] A reference in the Chirk Castle accounts indicates that sumpter horses did occasionally pull road vehicles, a practice that probably grew over time as wheeled traffic increased. On 13 August 1686 Sir Richard Myddelton paid Richard Jones of Shrewsbury £7 17s. for a grey gelding which he intended to team with his Flanders horse in the 'Sumpture Cart' heading for London.[151]

Ironically, the elite paid less for transporting goods than the extent of their operations warranted. The crown, when on progress, did not have to buy all the horses and vehicles it needed because its officials, armed with open warrants, impressed draught animals *en route*.[152] Harrison noted that, when she moved, Elizabeth I took up 400 cars, each with a team of four horses, in the neighbourhood through which she was passing.[153] Some gentlemen and nobles benefited by having carrying duties inserted in their tenants' leases, a relic of the feudal practice of providing land in return for services. In 1603 Richard Cholmeley of Brandsby noted in his memorandum book that all his tenants who had draught facilities, owed a day's ploughing and two further days getting in the hay and corn harvests or the equivalent, transporting stone, timber and the like between Brandsby and Brafferton. At Little Crosby in the opening years of the eighteenth century Nicholas Blundell used his right to exact boon works from his tenants to cart muck, turf and coal.[154]

By the middle of the eighteenth century far more horses were being employed on the farms and roads of England than had been the case two centuries earlier. Numbers would have increased anyway because the demands of an expanding population led to a growth in agricultural and industrial output. Enclosure brought extra land into cultivation and a larger workforce turned out more manufactured items. Improvements were qualitative as well as quantitative. Farmers increasingly specialized in the production of goods best suited to the area, while industry tended to concentrate and develop in a few favoured places. Naturally, this process had the effect of stimulating trade between the regions and a greater integration of the national market. More horses were therefore needed to move goods from one part of the country to another. Overland transport, however, was more expensive than waterborne traffic and the tonnage being moved by barge and coaster increased at a faster rate during the course of the period. Even so, merchants and producers sent some goods by road as a matter of course, either because of the value to weight ratio or because of the need to avoid contamination by water. Others took goods to and from staithes and moved consignments in areas lacking navigable waterways. Of course, the number of oxen could have increased in proportion. It did not happen and by 1750 horses had virtually taken over, even in areas where oxen had once predominated. Although some work was being carried out by asses, this did little to alter the overall balance.

Coach and Horses

The wealthy landed elite who dominated early modern English society displayed their riches in many ways, most notably in the construction of imposing mansions in the countryside. More money was spent in extending, modifying and even rebuilding these houses as fashion changed. Conspicuous consumption also characterized their daily lives, with large sums being spent on such items as food and drink, clothing, entertainment and travel. In all matters they insisted on the best and were willing to pay top rates for quality goods. Indeed, high prices were an attraction because they ensured exclusivity. This is what makes the growing interest in coaches shown by the English upper classes during the course of this period such an interesting phenomenon. Coaches were functional but they also provided a highly visible and mobile means of ostentatious display. A richly embellished coach, adorned with the family's coat of arms and drawn by a fine team of matching horses, was an impressive sight and proclaimed the wealth and standing of the owner. Others wanted to ride in coaches, too, though only a small number of people could afford the purchase and maintenance costs. For everyone else (and, at times, the gentry, too), there were coaches to hire, first the private hackney coaches and then public stage coaches, operating along fixed routes according to a set timetable.

COACHES AND OTHER VEHICLES

Until the mid sixteenth century personal conveyances, used largely by women, the old and the infirm, were rather basic in construction and very uncomfortable for passengers. Of all the modes of transport the litter, comprising a bed or couch supported on a frame and carried on the back of either two or four horses, inflicted the least amount of jolting. For upper-class women, litters also seem to have denoted status. When Margaret, the daughter of Henry VII, travelled north in 1503 to marry James IV of Scotland, she rode on a fine palfrey for much of the way. Whenever her train passed through a town, however, she mounted the accompanying litter, carried by two 'faire' coursers 'vary nobly drest'.[1] The countess of Rutland, on the other hand, rode all the way to Belvoir in Leicestershire on a litter when she journeyed from London in June 1539.[2]

The upper classes also travelled in 'wagons' drawn by teams of horses harnessed in echelon, like the later carriers' version. When the royal entourage came to Guisnes on 5 June 1520 a litter and four wagons, covered with cloth of gold and pulled by teams of coursers, followed the queen and her ladies.[3] Alternatively, the elite could go on progress sitting face forward in a two-seater chariot, a cumbersome vehicle with four wheels and built like a small wagon slung on chains.

The introduction of coaches in the mid sixteenth century did not spell the end for the traditional vehicles, but they had to adapt to changing circumstances. First, wagons went down market, offering a cheaper version of road transport, though occasionally gentlemen rode in them. Fashion, on the other hand, accentuated the exclusivity of the chariot, transforming it in the seventeenth century into a lightweight, elegant four-wheeled vehicle with seats for two passengers. A lighter, two-wheeled vehicle known as a calash also appeared at that time, comprising little more than a shell and a hood, fitted with two wheels and capable of carrying one or two persons.[4] Both forms of coach found favour among the upper classes in Restoration England, their owners valuing them as summer conveyances. With the top down, passers-by could see them and be suitably impressed.[5] When he rode in a chariot belonging to Sir William Penn on 25 June 1667, Samuel Pepys described it as 'plain, but pretty and more fashionable in shape than any coach he hath, and yet doth not cost him, harness and all, above £32'.[6] In spite of admiring Penn's stylish chariot, Pepys chose a more traditional (and costlier) model when he decided to obtain a coach in October 1668. His friend, Mr Povey, promptly condemned it as old-fashioned and cumbersome. The two of them therefore looked for something more modish and Pepys eventually plumped for a little chariot, with which he was 'mightily pleased'.[7] By the end of the seventeenth century chariots were becoming popular in the countryside too. In June 1686 Robert Hooke, the scientist and engineer, informed Thomas Mostyn of Gloddaeth that few people used a coach in town or country because a chariot was 'easier and lighter for the horses'.[8]

The coach seems to have originated in fifteenth-century Hungary and from there to have spread westwards over the course of the fifteenth and sixteenth centuries. Although the defining attribute of the early modern coach was its springing, it is not certain that the first ones incorporated this feature. Munby, following traditional opinion, claims that initially they did lack springing, though he also points out that sprung vehicles of one kind or another existed in classical Roman times and in the Middle Ages. On the other hand, Coczian-Szentpeteri argues that suspension was the feature that characterized the early coach.[9] She cites an example from 1457 when the Hungarian king, Ladislas V, seeking the hand of Charles VII of France's daughter, sent a number of gifts, including a vehicle with a suspended body. Coczian-Sentpeteri's evidence is persuasive and makes sense too. If they did not offer something better than other forms of conveyance, they would not have spread so widely. According to Coczian-Sentpeteri, the word 'coach' derives from the Hungarian town of Kocs, situated on the road between Budapest and Vienna and the place where this particular type of vehicle originated. The first description of a coach, she reveals, occurred in an account of a journey that the Austrian diplomat, Herberstein, made through Hungary in 1518. Distinguishing marks included the coach's speed and lightness, the virtual absence of iron parts and its team of three horses.[10]

Coaches first appeared in England in Mary Tudor's reign (1553–8). According to Stow, Walter Rippon built a coach for the earl of Rutland in 1555 and another for the Queen the following year. In 1556 Sir Philip Hoby owned a coach too, perhaps brought over from France where he had served as ambassador.[11] Elizabeth I made coach riding fashionable and by the mid-point of her reign in the 1580s many courtiers had acquired one of these chic accessories.[12] Coaches were technically superior to earlier conveyances and, with their leather braces, a little more comfortable, even if they still gave a bumpy ride. In spite of a possible reference to metal fitments on royal coaches in the 1620s, steel springs seem only to have been invented in the 1660s as a result of experiments by the Royal Society. Even so, they did not come into general use until well into the eighteenth century.[13] Other structural developments of the time included lighter vehicles and more compact shells. Convenience improved with the fitting of better designed doors and the insertion of glass windows.[14] The Duke of York introduced the first 'glass' coach into the country shortly after the Restoration, an invention that brought light to the erstwhile gloomy interior, hitherto protected by curtains or leather flaps.[15]

In Thomas Greene's play *Tu Quoque: or The Cittie Gallant* (c. 1611) the newly knighted Sir Lionel Rash tries to persuade his daughter, Gartred, to court a man who had recently come into a fortune with the argument that he would provide her with luxuries, including

> the keeping of a coach
> For country, and caroch for London.[16]

The distinction lay in the size and ornamentation of the two sorts of vehicle: the caroch was larger and more highly embellished and therefore considered by the elite of late sixteenth and early seventeenth century England to be more imposing and eye-catching. As expected, the crown possessed particularly fine examples. It was said of the two new caroches acquired by James I in 1624–5 that the like had never been made in England before. One was constructed in the German fashion, with a folding roof, and the other built in the Spanish manner.[17] His successor, Charles I, ordered several others as soon as he came to the throne in 1625. A set of warrants directed to the earl of Denbigh, Charles I's master of the wardrobe, between 1626 and 1630 provides details of the workmanship and materials and reveals how impressive these vehicles were. Three caroches built in the French fashion for Queen Henrietta Maria had painted, gilded and silvered bodies, covered with hide leather. The interiors were lined with velvet, garnished with buckles, pendants and bullions of copper gilt and silvered with gilt. The furnishings were decorated with fringes and laces of silver and gold; the beds, seats and chairs were adorned with laces and fringes of gold, silver and silk; and the damask curtains were embellished with laces, fringes, buttons and loops of gold and silver. Altogether, the Master of the Wardrobe paid out for fourteen new caroches and one new chariot; for repairs to ten old caroches and a crimson velvet litter; and for the refurbishment of a tawney coach and nine caroches used by the king, his queen and ambassadors.[18] Because of their size and opulence these vehicles perfectly conveyed the impression of grandeur that monarchs wanted to communicate to the onlookers on state occasions. They therefore tended to ossify stylistically, a trait that the cultural influences emanating out of France under Louis XIV did nothing to eliminate. The end of the regency in 1665 enabled the French king to impose, as standard, an ornate royal state coach solely reserved for state occasions, a concept which other European monarchs bought, as well as the actual vehicles. But, these caroches were conservative in design and did not readily incorporate technical developments that were changing coach construction in general.[19]

ATTITUDES TOWARDS RIDING IN COACHES

At first, traditionally minded gentlemen were reluctant to travel in a coach, many of them preferring to brave the elements astride a horse. The image of a rider on his horse had become so deeply engrained in their psyche that they felt it was 'unmanly' to ride in a conveyance. John Aubrey, recalling the words of Thomas Tyndale, an old gentlemen who remembered Elizabeth I's reign and court, wrote, 'In Sir Philip Sydney's time 'twas as much disgrace for a cavalier to be seen in London rideing in a coach in the street as now 'twould be to be seen in a petticoate and wastcoate'. In a fictional dialogue of 1633, the country gentleman declared that 'wee thought it a kinde of solaecisme, and to savour of effeminacie, for a young gentleman in the flourishing time of his age to creepe into a coach, and to shrowd himself there from winde and weather'. They even welcomed the chance to 'out-brave the blustering Boreas', as a means of displaying their hardiness.[20] It is possible to infer this reticence from accounts of high society that John Chamberlain gave to Dudley Carleton in James I's reign. When the City of London entertained Robert Carr, the royal favourite, and Frances Howard at the Merchant Taylors' Hall after their marriage in January 1613/14, Chamberlain wrote that 'The men were well mounted and richly arrayed making a goodly shew, the women all in coaches'.[21]

Gentlemen also complained that their underused coaches gave them little return for the considerable amount of money invested in them. They did not necessarily object to paying for something that allowed them to display their wealth and standing in public but, if wedded to the masculine image of riding astride a horse, they personally gained little benefit from the purchase. The wives of these diehards therefore had to persuade their husbands to buy a coach, pointing out the advantages and denying the costs involved. Sir Robert Harley of Brampton Bryan must have been one of the 'old school', for in 1641 his wife, Lady Brilliana, wrote to her son Edward at Oxford to enlist his support. In her briefing she emphasized the moderate expenditure and the positive effect it would have on her health.[22] Coach horses, when not needed, might do such mundane jobs as drawing the plough or pulling a farm cart. In 1663 Frances Russell told her husband that she could not possibly travel at that moment because 'the horses are at plough'. In a tithe dispute at Ellesmere in 1695 it was said of the defendant, Owen Barton, a gentleman, that his coach horses did all the draught work at Knolton Farm.[23]

Women predominated among the early passengers and it is easy to see why they were more readily convinced of the value of a coach: it kept them clean and dry and enabled them to converse with their fellow travellers. We know of Sir Philip Hoby's coach, for instance, because he offered to send it to pick up Sir William Cecil's wife, then pregnant. He thought that it would give her an easier ride, though with its basic suspension Mildred Cecil risked a miscarriage. Fortunately, nothing untoward happened and Mildred gave birth to a daughter, Anne, five months later.[24] In 1577 Lady Petre, stuck with no coach for the London season, had to make shift as best she could, hiring one or travelling on foot or by water, when she could not borrow Lady Alington's vehicle. She quickly acquired one of her own.[25] Evidently, a coach was one of those luxuries that a lady had to have. As Anne, Lady Frugal's daughter, tells Lord Lacie in Philip Messinger's play *The City Madam* (1632):

> When I am one
> (And you are honor'd to be styl'd my husband)
> To urge my having my Page, my Gentleman Usher,
> My Woman sworn to my secrets, my Caroch
> Drawn by six Flanders Mares, my Coachman, Grooms,
> Postilian, and Footmen.[26]

Coaches offered women a further advantage, for in one a wife, with her family, could accompany her husband to London whenever he went to the capital on business. Hitherto they had travelled separately in a passenger wagon, although occasionally they accompanied him on their own horse or on a pillion.[27] Once in the capital, coaches also influenced social convention, as they increasingly became the mode of transport to ferry individuals around when visiting other members of fashionable society. As Whyman observes, 'By the late seventeenth century, calling upon one's friends in a carriage became an important expression of London sociability'. Accordingly, John Verney, on his arrival in London, found that he had to have a coach in order to maintain his social contacts. Naturally, he, like his father (and, no doubt, many other gentlemen), turned to his female relatives for advice on coaches, since they were more likely to understand the rules concerning the polite use of such conveyances.[28]

While old attitudes did not die out completely, the upper classes did adopt a more accommodating attitude towards the possession of coaches as the seventeenth century progressed. The change, clearly dicernible in the post-Restoration period, was already underway during the Interregnum, in spite of puritan censure. Estate and household records for the period 1650–1750 are full of references to coaches, coach horses and coach staff. No doubt, a younger generation, brought up alongside coaches and without the same prejudices, was less opposed to them and more likely to value them for the prestige and status they conferred.

The impact created when the family of a great nobleman moved around the country was certainly considerable. On 4 February 1680/1 Sir John Reresby, who had accepted an invitation to go down to the country with the Duke of Newcastle, wrote that, with his three coaches and about forty servants, 'he [the duke] travelled indeed like a great prince'.[29] Members of the upper classes attending social events similarly showed themselves off by parading in a coach. When Celia Fiennes visited Epsom Spa in the 1690s she noted that the 'company' had created a ring like the one at Hyde Park on the racecourse on the downs, where 'they come and drive round'.[30] A special occasion like a wedding often prompted the purchase of a coach because of the importance of projecting an image of wealth and standing at the event. Among the preparations for his marriage on 7 January 1706/7 Sir Walter Calverley of Esholt spent £82 7s. on a new coach and a further £30 7s. in lining. He also bought new coach horses for the occasion at a cost of £50. For the same reason Sir Edmund Denton 'bought a fine equipage to make a figure' when elected as MP for Buckinghamshire in 1710.[31]

Gentlemen also tended to take to riding in a coach with advancing years. As they aged and became less active, the lure of a coach must have become almost irresistible. Dr William Denton, for example, had for years conducted his business on horseback, but in September 1657, aged forty-five and encouraged by his wife, he decided to obtain a coach. His friend, Sir Ralph Verney, warned him that 'a coach were more convenient than healthfull for you' but promised that he would 'exercise' him.[32] There is a hint of this in Montaigne's comment in his essay, 'Of Coaches'. He wrote that he did not like travelling by litter, coach or boat for very long, adding that 'I could endure them less easily in my youth'. Whereas he disliked going by boat because of the effect on his head and stomach, his aversion to going by litter or coach seems to be related to their association with women. Young men, no doubt, felt more keenly the inglorious image evoked by riding in such an unmanly way.[33]

According to Tyndale, as coach travel became more acceptable to the landed classes, the latter lost their intense interest in good horsemanship and with it a skill vital to the preservation of the state. Referring back to Charles I's reign (1625–49), he observed that gentlemen then kept good horses and could ride them. 'Now', he continued, 'We are come all to our coaches, forsooth! Now young men are so farre from managing good horses, they know not how to ride a hunting nag nor handle their weapons.'[34] Undoubtedly, coach travel did reduce the amount of time gentlemen spent on horseback and, by sheltering them from the elements, made them softer and less resilient. It also affected the number of saddle mounts they required. Even so, steady riding along roads did not really prepare a person for battle. Hunting, on the other hand, did and, in spite of Tyndale's assertion to the contrary, many gentlemen toughened up and gained appropriate martial skills there. Similarly, the emergence of swift, strong hunters with eastern blood in their veins helped to maintain the country's stock of suitable cavalry horses. In any case, individuals did not necessarily make a complete switch. For Sir Ralph Verney a present of a fine roan mare from his aunt Sherard in October 1655 led him to rediscover the joys of riding after months out of the saddle. Thanking her, he noted that 'I am soe in love with this maire, that I am now growne almost weary of my coach, and choose to ride on her to Hillesdon presently, perhaps she may put me into such a gadding humour, that you (and all the rest of my friends & acquaintances) may have just cause to repent your Bounty'.[35] Even when embarking on a journey by coach, gentlemen might take a spare mount with them. On 10 August 1657, for instance, Marmaduke Rawdon set out from London in the York stage coach with his servant, Tosta, riding alongside, leading a gelding 'for his master to ride uppon when he thought fitt'.[36] When in Spring 1725 Lord Oxford toured England and Scotland by coach with a couple of companions and several servants, he spent many days in the saddle.[37]

THE MANUFACTURE OF COACHES

Initially, private coaches had to be imported, the best coming from Hungary and Bohemia, though most were German.[38] In 1576 Sir Henry Sidney sent a servant to Pomerania to procure 'a strong cowche with all maner of furniture therto belonging and covered with leather'.[39] Highly priced coaches continued to enter the country during the course of the seventeenth century, their value being augmented by the tag of exclusivity. In February 1644 the Earl of Leicester owned a rich French coach that had never been used and which had cost him £400.[40] The crown bought abroad too. In October 1699, for instance, Mr van Hulst received £369 4s. 0d. for a coach made in Paris that the Duke of Albermarle had procured for the King's service.[41] Because of their value and social significance, rulers obtained coaches and horses as diplomatic gifts. The one that Frederick, the Elector Palatine, presented to James I's wife, Anne of Denmark, when he came to England to marry their daughter in February 1612/3, was particularly fine. Chamberlain described it as 'an exceeding fayre carosse made in Fraunce of pall [purple] coloured velvet richly embroidered with gold and silver both within and without, with six horses and two coachmen all in the same liverie, and the wheels with all the yron worke richly gilded and curiously wrought'. He estimated its value at £8,000 or £9,000 at least.[42]

A home-grown industry did develop in the country, with the first native coachmakers establishing themselves in London. Their business flourished on account of the scale of the market there, based on the demand for hackney coaches for hire as well as for private coaches for the elite. Others subsequently set up in the provinces in order to cater for the interest shown by the upper classes across the country in these fashionable conveyances. Sir Simonds D'Ewes of Stowlangcroft obtained a new coach at nearby Bury St Edmunds in 1641.[43] Even so, many provincial gentlemen bought coaches in the capital, which they could easily do when up in town. London offered the discerning buyer so much more than was available elsewhere: the chance to obtain the latest model; a greater selection of vehicles, both new and second-hand; and a concentration of coachmakers. Edward Harley bought a chariot for his father in London in 1699, which he dispatched to Brampton Bryan in Herefordshire. His brother, Robert, who rode in the chariot, told his father that the vehicle was 'very light and very easy'.[44] Even traditional coaches from London were likely to be superior. When, in the late seventeenth century, Sir Richard Temple's bailiff at Stowe told him he needed 'a working not a playing chariot', he found that the country coaches at Northampton were 'not so fine' as those in London.[45] According to Henry Peacham, Hosier Lane, the Smithfield and Cow Lane were the places where people went to look for new or refurbished coaches in the capital. When Samuel Pepys wanted to buy a fashionable chariot in November 1668, he and Mr Povey spent an afternoon visiting the yards of coachmakers in Cow Lane. He looked at several suitable ones before making his choice.[46]

Fashion-conscious gentlemen resident in the provinces might order a custom-built model designed to their own specifications and collect it when visiting the capital. Thus Robert Hooke wrote his letter to Thomas Mostyn of Gloddaeth in June 1686 to let him know that he had 'bespoke a handsome chariot which will be ready by the time you come to town'.[47] The capital's coachmakers were able to respond relatively quickly to such orders because they had stocks of basic parts available. They also had a selection of coaches on display. When James Masters, a coachmaker from St Sepulchres, died in 1685 he left three complete coaches, namely a coach with four horns to it, a mourning coach and a chariot, and a new body and carriage for a fourth. He also possessed numerous parts. Roger Brown, also of St Sepulchre's, worked on a grander scale. In 1662 his appraisers valued a new coach and chariot at £20 6s. and £20 2s. respectively and nineteen new bodies at £35. Altogether, they assessed his work stock at £443 11s. 1d., two-fifths (59.6 per cent) of his total personal estate or almost two-thirds of it (64.5 per cent), if debts are included.[48] Among his stock Masters had two old bodies and two old carriages, which suggests that coachmakers reused materials, perhaps from vehicles acquired in part exchange. As today, the practice of trading in an existing model for a newer one was common. When the earl of Bedford bought a new coach in 1642 it cost him £37 10s., but Prosser, the coachmaker, allowed him about £5 on his old coach. Six years later Lady Brooke swapped her old coach for a new one, paying a balance of £22.[49] Entries in Nicholas Blundell's diary indicate other ways in which the upper classes tried to keep abreast with fashion. On 26 November 1705 he began to fit his chariots to lighter carriages and the following day he affixed the wheels designed for them. On the other hand, when he suggested making modifications to his chariot on 28 November 1722, the coachmaker, Mr Archibald, did not think it worthwhile. Blundell also tried to sell Archibald his old stock, presumably to buy new models. Unfortunately, when the coachmaker came to Little Crosby on 3 March 1724/5 they could not agree on a price.[50]

As with a new house, the construction of the coach body was only the first task, and often not the most time-consuming one. To build a coach required a wide range of skills and entailed the services of a number of craftsmen. Obviously, much depended upon the quality of the workmanship and a degree of doubling up of jobs occurred. Yet accounts regularly record separate payments to various people. While the coachmaker might make the shell, others provided the furnishings and embellishments. Among those working on the exterior were wheelwrights, harness makers, fine leather and metal workers, painters, engravers, wood carvers and gilders. Inside, one might find in addition drapers, tailors, embroiderers, upholsterers and saddlers. The detailed lists of items given in the accounts reveal just how intricate the craftsmanship could be. The strapping of Lady Petre's coach, for instance, comprised 4,141 bits and pieces of metal, many of them garnished and embellished.[51] Materials included lace for the cloth; silver and gold leaf for the fringe and tassels; leather for the seats and to line the coach; damask and taffeta for the curtains; and silk, satin, lace and velvet for the cushions and coverings. It is therefore not surprising to note that the bill for the furnishings often exceeded the cost of the shell. In terms of ostentation it was the quality of the fittings which made the difference. In 1661 Lord Brooke gave Mr Saer, the coachmaker, £125 for constructing the shell, a further £82 to Mr Gerrard for lining it and £94 to Mr Beckett for fringe and for lace for the foot cloth.[52] Since a major reason for possessing a coach was to show off, it was important that they bore marks of identification. After all, the owner wanted it to be known who it was who could afford such an valuable object. Coats of arms on the side panel were therefore a customary embellishment. Owners also asked for other status symbols as, for example, the set of bosses with coronets on them which adorned the coach ordered by Lord Brooke in 1677–8.[53]

COACH HORSES

Just as the upper classes did not think of their coaches in purely functional terms, so they did not choose their coach horses according to strength alone. Even the number of horses in a team became a social statement. James Chamberlain, writing to Dudley Carleton on 28 May 1625, commented disparagingly on the equipages in which ladies of honour met the queen at Dover. They rode in coaches pulled by six horses, 'which comes altogether now in fashion, a vanitie of excessive charge and of little use'.[54] While the horses had to be able to do the job – and Nicholas Blundell's diary indicates that gentlemen carefully tested out new coach horses between the shafts – prospective owners also considered aesthetic criteria too: colour, action and conformation.[55] The ideal aimed at was a matching set of elegantly proportioned horses of the same height and with coats of a modish colour. In January 1658/9 Sir John Wittewronge paid his servant, Milward, £97 for a set of four young black brown coach horses he had bought for him. During the course of 1664 Milward put together a further team, this time comprising five black coach horses bought at a cost of £96 10s. When, on 13 October 1685, James Darcy wrote to Christopher Crofts, asking him if he could find Mr Harrison two coach geldings at Richmond, he told him to buy brown bay or blood bay ones. He also provided him with a list of further qualities he had to look for: 'well turn'd, good lofty foreheads, good limbs but not long-legged'. Mr Harrison, he noted, did not mind if the horses stood at no more than 14:2 hands so long as they were strong, for he intended to harness them to his summer chariot.[56] The inference here is that the horses were smaller than average, though Harrison insisted that they should be strong and matched for height and colour. Most coach horses were at least fifteen hands. In 1725 Daniel Eaton failed to sell a fine colt to his master's brother, James Brudenell, because the latter thought that, at 15:1¼ hands high, it was too small to fit in with the rest of his team.[57]

By the time that coaches had come into vogue there were horses of the requisite size and strength in the country to pull them. At fifteen hands and over, however, they were relatively few in number, especially those with the right qualities. When Richard Blome recommended 15½-hand English horses for draught and travel in 1686 he probably intended most of them to pull coaches.[58] Significantly, newspapers advertisements from the late seventeenth century onwards portray coach horses as if they were a distinct type. In a letter which Daniel Eaton wrote to his master, on 3 June 1725, he described a colt he had bought as 'of the coach breed'. It stood 15:1 hands high with a star and one white foot and was 'a very nimble, handsome and sound horse'.[59] Such horses therefore cost a good deal of money. Table 10, drawn from estate accounts from every part of the country, indicates the range of prices paid, revealing that they were far more valuable than similar-sized wagon horses. The horses that pulled the monarch's coaches cost even more. In the early 1620s the median value of the twenty-two purchases of Richard Graham, Buckingham's Gentleman of the Horse, came to £25. At the end of the century, William III's Master of the Horse paid on average £33 for the forty-seven coach horses recorded in his accounts.[60]

TABLE 10: price of coach horses 1620–1719

	No.	median	lowest	highest
1620–59	45	£14 10s.	£6 5s.	£31 5s.
1660–1719	193	£17 2s. 16d.	£3	£45

Source: estate accounts

Foreign horses, especially those from Flanders, were particularly valued for the coach. Flemish horses were eminently suited to the job, being strong and tractable by nature. Even if the link established by Henry VIII served mainly to bring in strong cart horses, imports included finer specimens designated for the coach. In 1608, significantly just after James I had made peace with Spain, the Earl of Huntingdon paid £47 for a pair of Flemish coach mares.[61] Apart from their strength, the dictates of fashion added to the interest in them. They were predominantly black, a colour which grew in popularity during the Stuart period, largely at the expense of bay. In 1700 one could still find horses in various shades of brown but black was by far the commonest coat colour for coach horses. Other coach horses came from Friesland, Denmark and north Germany. Lord Howard of Naworth obtained two grey Friesian geldings for £40 5s. in 1630.[62] In 1626 a set of five Dutch coach mares and geldings chosen by Sir Richard Graham for the crown cost £90. The Dutchman, who sold them, assured Sir Richard that they were the best he had ever brought over. Even if this were mere sales talk, the evidence indicates that he regularly trafficked in them. The trade expanded after the Dutchman, William III, acceded to the throne in 1688. On one occasion, Henry de Nassau paid £695 0s. 6d. for forty-four Dutch horses, many for the

TABLE 11: **William Kirmond's expenses from Gunby to Northampton and back**

Place	Item	1706	1707	Comments
River Witham	ferry	1d.	1d.	
Donington		8d.	1s. 2d.	
Stamford	meat & drink	1s. 4d.	2s. 10d.	
Stamford	accommodation	NK	NK	
Northampton	meat & drink	4s.	} 12s. 6d. (2)	
Northampton	accommodation	2s. 6d. (1)		(1) 2 nights (2) Fri. night to Tues. morning
Northampton	toll	1d.	8d.	
Northampton	halter (3)	4d.	3d.	(3) halter & hemp to tail mares with
Gainington	toll		1d.	
Stamford	meat & drink	1s. 6d.	2s. 10d.	
Stamford	accommodation	1s. 2d. (4)	5s. 10d. (5)	(4) 1 night (5) 1 night
Stamford	3 horses	4s.		
Stamford	toll		2d.	
Doninigton	his horse	3d.		
Boston	meat & drink	1s. 6d.		
Boston	accommodation	3s. 6d. (6)	5s. 10d. (7)	(6) 1 night (7) 1 night
Boston	toll	2d.	2d.	
	new shoes	1s.	4d.	
Totals		£1 2s. 2d.	£1 12s. 9d.	
no. of days		5	7	

Source: Massingberd of Cunby MSS, Lincolnshire Archives Office, MG 5/2/7

coach.[63] Family links similarly promoted the import of Danish horses throughout the course of the seventeenth century. When Anne's husband, Prince George of Denmark, died in 1709, his stable of horses included seven black Danish horses and one gelding. Even though one was blind and another had bad eyes, a third suffered with a spavin and a fourth was broken-winded and good for little, their total value amounted to £170; £26 9s. more than a set of English coach horses in his possession.[64]

The valuation of the Danish horses indicates an assessment based on an appreciation of the breed rather than on their current performance. This was the point that Nicholas Morgan had made in 1609 when he had satirized the uncritical approach taken by some horsemen to foreign imports.[65] Buyers, judging by breed alone, could make mistakes. On 8 April/29 March 1664 Denzil Holles, ambassador to France, complained to his son, Francis, that

> I must have a sett of coach horses, for my Flanders mares that I bought in England prove starke nought, three of them are dead, the foure left not fitt to be kept, I was cheated in them. So I would have seaven stone horses, bright bay, to be bought in Northamptonshire, as my black ones were, large and all trott not amble, which is the fault of one of these black ones; the money must come out of ye Sussex and Surrey rents.[66]

By then it was possible to obtain high-quality English coach horses. On 6 July 1685 Sir Stephen Fox, keeper of William III's stables, offered Lord Dartmouth a set of seven top-quality English geldings 'fit for the king's own coach' for £280.[67]

Coach owners obtained their animals from a number of sources. If they bred them at home, they saved themselves (or at least their agents) the time and the effort in going to look for them. On the other hand, they still incurred expenses and there was no certainty that the horses produced would be suitable. They therefore conducted a good deal of business among family and friends or with other members of the landed classes. In this way they could inspect the animals at leisure and have greater certainty about an animal's pedigree. In November 1641, for instance, the Earl of Bedford bought six coach horses off his neighbour, Lord Wharton. Besides, gentlemen might obtain easier terms off their friends and acquaintances. In April 1695 Sir John Chester of Chicheley bought a coach gelding for £15 from his cousin Fortescue; subsequently he noted in a memo in his accounts on 17 June 1695 that he had made several payments to him and had discharged his debt in full.[68] Some breeders gained a reputation for the quality of their horses and attracted a high-class clientele. In the 1690s Mr Russell sold several valuable coach horses to William III. The Villiers family, which provided two Masters of the Horse to the crown during the course of the seventeenth century, offered a similar service. In April 1685 Sir William Villiers received £142 from Nathaniel Cholmeley of Whitby for five coach horses and ten years later

Lord Villiers sold the King a set of black coach horses for £300.[69] An analysis of estate and household accounts confirms the importance of personal contacts in the purchase of good quality coach horses, especially if cheap superannuated stock sold privately to local farmers are excluded. Purchasers obtained many of their best horses privately; apart from those bought by the crown, the most valuable animals listed were the two coach horses which Sir Edward Mansell purchased from Sir John Wittewronge of Rothamstead for £80 in January 1661.[70]

There were clear advantages in obtaining horses privately, if only, as Samuel Pepys thought, to reduce (but not eliminate) the chance of being cheated.[71] In spite of this, it was possible to obtain suitable animals at fairs. Henry Peacham observed in *Coach and Sedan* that 'the breede of our best horses in England, are reserved, or rather bought up in Faires and Markets, onely for the use of the coach'. Richard Blome, in *The Gentleman's Recreation*, later included coach horses among those categories for which the highest standards were not required and which gentlemen could therefore obtain at fairs and from horse dealers.[72] This is a debatable point. While it is true that the upper classes paid the most extravagant prices for certain kinds of saddle mounts, with racehorses topping the list, they had exacting standards when they came to choosing horses for their coaches and were prepared to spend lavishly on them. Besides, they used fairs to palm off old, injured and broken down stock. Even so, they could obtain suitable horses at a number of select fairs.

Naturally, they were readily available at the Smithfield in London, largely due to the activities of dealers, based in and around the market place there, who travelled to buy stock at specialist fairs in the provinces.[73] The centre of the trade, nonetheless, lay in the east midlands.[74] If most of the colts trained in the collar on local farms ended up between the shafts of a cart, well-shaped specimens, with a fine action and the right coat colour, made suitable coach horses. In the post-Restoration period many upper-class families sent their agents to the region's fairs to acquire fine specimens. Among the fairs they visited were Hinckley, Leicester, Lutterworth and Market Harborough in Leicestershire; Fotheringhay, Oundle, Northampton and Rothwell in Northamptonshire; and Uppingham in Rutland.[75] Not surprisingly, the crown' servants joined them there. In 1695 Henry de Nassau twice visited Northamptonshire on his travels to look for horses for the King. He also dealt with leading metropolitan horse dealers, who visited east midlands fairs. Between 1684 and 1695 Edward Horton tolled for forty-nine horses on eight visits to Rothwell, many of which were destined for the coach. Henry de Nassau put all thirty-three of the horses he bought from Horton in one or other of the King's coach teams, whether Williams's, Kilby's, Stocks's or Serle's sets or the team of short tailed bays. The median value of these horses was £38 2s. 6d. George Arnold sold a further ten coach horses to the crown at an average price of between £28 and £30.[76] Of the leading fairs, Northampton was the best of all.[77] In 1683, at a time when good horses were hard to find, the Duke of Buccleuch noted that if his servant, Posso, could not obtain one locally 'he will [go] to Northampton wher the best are'. Defoe later endorsed this view, writing that Northampton 'is counted the centre of all the horse markets and horse fairs in England ... Here they buy horses of all sorts, as well for the saddle as for the coach and cart, but chiefly for the two latter'.[78] This is borne out in the choice which landed families made when they sent their agents out to buy coach horses. Northampton was by far the most popular destination, drawing in people from the south and west midlands, the west country, the south-east and eastern England, as well as from the east midlands. Bedfordshire fairs, located to the south of Northamptonshire, were also renowned for the sale of strong horses, with those at Biggleswade, Dunstable and probably Leighton Buzzard specializing in coach horses.[79] Thomas Cotton, writing on 30 March 1640, told his mother that as 'good horses are usually to be had' at the Easter Monday fair at Biggleswade, Edmund and Kellam were going to buy her coach horses there. Lord Brooke bought a coach horse at the fair in March 1645/6 for £15 8s. 4d.[80] At the end of the century Leighton Buzzard fair was reputed the greatest fair for geldings and the one at Biggleswade on Candlemas Day was noted for the sale of stallions.[81] It was also possible to buy valuable stock at a scattering of other fairs around the country as at Amesbury in Wiltshire, Ashbourne in Derbyshire and Banbury in Oxfordshire, for instance.[82] Such places may have acted as important local centres, drawing in good quality horses and attracting custom from a wide area.

Coach owners went to considerable pains to put together a fine set of horses and sent agents far and wide to find suitable animals at fairs and in private stables. The whole process might take months. Between February and May 1709, John Pruce, a servant of the Cartwright family of Aynho (Northants) had to make several trips around the midlands, visiting gentry families in Leicestershire, Northamptonshire, Oxfordshire and Warwickshire (and perhaps elsewhere too) before he managed to obtain six bay mares. The horses cost £87 12s. 0d. in total, ranging in price from £12 1s. 0d. to £16 2s. 6d. John's expenses amounted to £1 4s. 10d. and later in the year he received a gratuity of £6 9s. 0d. for his efforts.[83] The accounts do not break down Pruce's costs but there are others that do give the details. Those recording expenditure on the Massingberd of Gunby estate in Lincolnshire reveal that their agents regularly obtained coach horses at Northampton, about eighty miles away, at the beginning of the eighteenth century (table 11). In 1706 William Kermond bought two coach mares there for £31 13s. 6d., the five days' trip costing £1 2s. The following year, when he bought two more black coach mares (£31 12s.), the outlay for himself and an assistant amounted to £1 12s. 9d. Incidentally, when Briggs, the previous agent, had travelled to Northampton in 1704 he spent £2 7s. 6d. on an eight day trip to buy two coach mares in the town.[84]

COACHMEN

To complete the picture image-conscious coach owners dressed the coachman and postilions in matching liveries, as they did their other servants. They had to have other gear too. Because they were exposed to the elements it was customary to give them boots or shoes and protective outer garments, such as coats or capes and perhaps a hat. When Thomas Coate entered the service of the Massingberds of Gunby as a coachman in the 1660s he was allowed a 'Coat livery'. In 1676, the Earl of Northampton's coachman, postilion and grooms received boots, frocks and trousers.[85] At times the account records the type of cloth used, enabling us to assess the quality and warmth of the garment. In 1653 Lord Brooke's coachman was given a suit made of stuff and in 1669 the Duke of Bedford's man received a frieze coat.[86]

On the very largest estates the owner might retain coach staff solely for that purpose. Clearly, monarchs, with a position to maintain and a constant round of ceremonial events, required their services on a full-time basis. In 1668 Charles II and his queen between them employed ten coachmen and nine postilions, apart from nine littermen and a chariot driver.[87] On most estates, however, driving the coach was not a full-time job and coachmen had to carry out other tasks. Indentures drawn up at the time of their hiring often set out their duties. In 1665 John Wells, the coachman on the Massingberd estate at Mumby, had to look after the coach and saddle horses, brew beer, slaughter animals for the table, and work with the coach horses when carting or doing other tasks. A marginal note extended his duties to encompass anything that his master wanted him to do. In return he received £4 a year, a coachman's cloak at the end of the first year and others at two year intervals.[88] Being, in essence, a general 'dogsbody' rankled with some individuals. In 1695 the Verney's coachman handed in his notice so that he could set up as a hackneyman in London, in which job he did at least retain a certain independence. John Verney noted that, 'His wife is a proud woman and he hath a little of it himself, and they think it below 'em to be a servant.'[89]

COACHES FOR HIRE

Few people below the level of the elite could afford to own a coach and team, even if they had managed to overcome their diffidence in embracing an archetypical aristocratic mode of transport. However they proved enthusiastic customers for the coaches for hire, known as hackney cabs, which appeared on the streets of London early in the seventeenth century.[90] For their clients, hackney coaches replicated the privacy achieved by gentlemen travelling in their own conveyance. Even if they lacked the embellishment or refinement of private coaches, their passengers journeyed in some style too, for the coaches had their trimmings. One critic, John Taylor, complained of the vast wastage of cloth and the use of superfluous items such as lace, fringe and gilding. In 1617 a person could hire a coach and two horses for 10s. a day, fodder included, or for 8s. without.[91] Only the prosperous middle classes could afford to pay for such treats, but a larger sector of metropolitan society made an occasional journey in one. At first, hackneymen worked from their own yards and only came out on call, but in about 1625 a Captain Barley set up a stand with four coaches at the Maypole in the Strand. Other hackneymen soon joined him there.[92] This made it easier to hire a coach and, by increasing demand, added to the number of coaches on the streets of the capital. When Peacham published his *Coach and Sedan* in 1636 he had the surveyor claim that the area covered by London, its suburbs and four miles beyond contained six thousand coaches. They therefore clogged up the streets and in some places brought traffic to a standstill. The worst jams occurred whenever a big event, such as a masque at Whitehall, a lord mayor's feast or a new play, took place. Then, the surveyor ruefully noted, 'you would admire to see them, how close they stand together, like (Mutton pies in a Cookes-oven) that hardly you can thrust a pole between'.[93]

Peacham's remarks confirm that he formed part of the backlash against coaches, especially those out for hire. The upper classes naturally resented the debasement of this mark of status, one that had set them apart from the rest of the population. In 1633 Nash's country gentleman not only complained about city streets 'barrocaded with coaches' but also grumbled about the usurpation of this mode of travel by 'shop-keepers and artizans of all kindes'. Even so, the people who felt the greatest resentment were those whose livelihoods were threatened. The watermen of London were particularly aggrieved. John Taylor, the so-called Water Poet, wrote, 'This infernal swarm of coaches have overrun the land that we can get no living on the water'. He calculated that when the court was at Whitehall, watermen could lose up to 560 fares a day to the coaches.[94] Opponents mainly levelled their criticism at the hackney coaches rather than at the private ones owned by the upper classes. As John Taylor stated, 'I do not enveigh against any coaches that belong to persons of worth or quality, but only against the caterpillar swarm of hirelings'.[95] The government did make an effort to restrict the number of hackney coaches through a licensing system. In 1637, in what looks like a money-raising scheme, fifty persons, headed by the Master of the Horse, received licences to maintain twelve horses each. Inevitably, the licencees had trouble policing their monopoly and the number of hackney coaches continued to grow.[96] In 1662, when there may have been more than 1,200 of them in London and its environs, Parliament fixed the limit at 400 and required their owners to obtain a licence. By 1696 the number of licensed coaches in London had risen to 700, but many more were operating illegally.[97]

People could travel much more cheaply in stage wagons, the successors of the medieval personnel carriers. The new four-wheeled wagons and the development of carrier services in the later sixteenth century provided the stimulus: with their four wheels they were less likely to overturn than the two-wheeled carts and therefore more suitable for passengers. The practice of conveying passengers probably began in an informal way with carriers offering room to people heading in the same destination. Over time, a timetable evolved. In these 'coach wagons' people had to share the vehicle – and the discomfort – with strangers. Many of these vehicles had the minimal amount of modification, perhaps not even inserted seats, though possibly some of them possessed a separate compartment for passengers. They carried up to twenty-five people. Teams of horses, hitched up in echelon, supplied the power.[98] Gentlemen or their sons (especially those at Oxford or Cambridge) might occasionally travel in a coach wagon but the bulk of the passengers came from more modest backgrounds. Fynes Moryson wrote in 1617 that, because of the long hours on the road, they were used by 'none but women and people of inferior condition, or strangers (as Flemmings with their wives and servants)'.[99] They provided an ideal mode of transport for 'sick and Antient people' because they travelled at an easy pace, covering about twenty to twenty-five miles a day.[100]

A few coach wagons continued to operate into the early eighteenth century but the more elegant stage coach gradually replaced them in the hundred years after their introduction in the 1650s. Although services to Norwich and Exeter may have predated it, the first explicit reference to a stage coach appears in an advertisement for the York to London coach in 1653. The coach seated fourteen passengers in three compartments, suggesting its origin as a coach wagon.[101] Within a few years, however, six passengers became the norm, confirming that stage coaches in shape and construction resembled private and hackney coaches.[102] A network of routes developed rapidly, especially at local and provincial levels. In De Laune's lists of 1681 and 1690 only between twenty-five and twenty-eight of the 450–80 services a week extended further than 130 miles.[103] London hackneymen often took the initiative. It seems as though many of those who had not obtained a licence in the aftermath of the 1662 measure moved to towns and villages surrounding the capital and set up in business there. They also helped to develop longer distances routes too.[104]

Passengers in stage coaches travelled more quickly than they had in coach wagons and, comparatively speaking, in greater comfort. They achieved the extra mileage, as much as fifty-one miles a day (the London to York service), by changing their horses and carrying fewer passengers. The added expense had to be passed on to customers: in the second half of the seventeenth century coach-masters charged their stage coach passengers about 2.4 pence a mile, compared with 1.2 to 1.7 pence per mile for those in a coach wagon.[105] Flying coach services, starting early in the morning and arriving late at night, made longer journeys possible. By the end of seventeenth century travellers could even reach Cirencester, ninety-two miles from London, in a day.[106] Most services operated throughout the whole year, though costs were higher in the winter than in the summer, for coachmasters had to add a pair of horses to the normal team of four. Proprietors had to employ a postilion too because the driver could not control more than four horses harnessed two abreast.[107]

As in carrying services, horses incurred the greatest expenditure. In the accounting year 1688–9, 88 per cent of William Morris's running costs for his quarter share in the Exeter coach directly related to the horses: 77.5 per cent for provender and other direct costs and 10.5 per cent for new horses. Expenditure on coaches amounted to 7.4 per cent of the total and on staff 4.6 per cent.[108] The horses which coachmasters used, mostly between fifteen and sixteen hands high, were among the biggest in the country and were very similar in size and strength to those pulling the private coaches of the elite. Of course, size alone did not make them suitable for a gentleman's coach, since non-functional criteria also dictated choice. Ugly, badly proportioned horses in the wrong colour did not make the grade. In value stagecoach horses were probably a little more expensive than strong wagon horses, though the evidence is too fragmentary to construct a price series. Inventory valuations are particularly suspect because constant use led to considerable depreciation in value. Some of the twenty-nine horses belonging to Robert Toobey, a Reading coachman, at his death in 1694, had clearly passed their peak. His appraisers valued them at sums ranging from £1 10s. to £10 10s. with a median of £6.[109] £6 may well have been an average price for a horse in the late seventeenth century. In 1659 a London hackneyman bought a horse off the Massingberd estate at Mumby for £6 5s. and in 1694 John Chain, an Oxford coachman, sold a stallion and a gelding, respectively sixteen and fifteen hands high, for £11 2s. 6d.[110]

The rapid expansion of stage coach services in the post-Restoration period provoked the same reaction as had accompanied the success of the hackney coaches in the early part of the century. In 1672 it was the turn of innkeepers and postmasters to complain that other forms of conveyances were ruining their livelihood. A number of them petitioned the Privy Council and a lawyer, John Cressett, wrote pamphlets on their behalf. Cressett put forward a number of arguments, which, in effect, repeated what opponents of private and hackney coaches had said. He claimed, for instance, that stage coaches destroyed the breed of good horses in the country and reduced interest in horsemanship among the gentry. He also alleged that, as more people rode in the coaches, they required fewer saddle horses, while the number of coach horses did not sufficiently increase to compensate for the loss. Moreover, he contended, stage coaches had a deleterious effect on the economy as a whole: among those who suffered were watermen, excise men, innkeepers, provincial traders and manufacturers, land owners, farmers and graziers.[111] Cressett then listed every problem that could possibly occur on a coach journey, inferring that they happened all the time. These included getting stuck in muddy roads, up to the knees in mire; sitting around for hours in the cold, waiting for help; suffering further delay while the coach was being repaired; travelling with strangers and being subjected to abuse from surly coachmen; and putting up at inferior inns not fit for gentlemen. The rigidity of the coach timetable reduced its value too, hindering business and inconveniencing travellers: it left at a set time rather than when it suited the occupants; it did not detour from its route; it only stopped at fixed points to change horses; and it pressed on regardless of sick or injured passengers. In comparison, horse riding offered freedom, choice and flexibility, as well as better value for money.

Many of Cressett's arguments were ridiculous and helped to damage the case against the stage coaches, which for a time gained influential support. In the event, no action was taken and this mode of travel continued to grow in popularity.[112] As ever, vehicular transport proved a boon for women, the young and old, and the infirm and short-sighted. These people travelled comparatively cheaply because of savings on the cost of companions or servants and the expense of making special arrangements for them. An unaccompanied man on horseback might travel more economically, but in practice the differential was not that great, especially if the rider had to kit himself out properly. In a coach, he did not need special clothing and, like other passengers, arrived at his destination, 'dry, unmuddied and in his ordinary clothes'. Ironically, Cressett's calculations seem to bear this out for a rider posting to York only saved 4s. on the coach fare (and admittedly a good deal of time). For many, the joy of riding in a coach, in spite of the discomfort, the jolts and the boorish fellow-passengers, lay in the wonder of it and the freedom from having to pay attention to the road and to make the innumerable petty decisions essential for a safe journey.[113]

A letter written in June 1701 by Lady Peregrina Chaytor of Croft in the North Riding to her husband, Sir William, then incarcerated in the Fleet Prison in London for debt, provides an insight into the respective merits and disadvantages of travelling in a coach, on horseback or by sea. With little money, Lady Peregrina clearly had to think carefully about the expense, but there were other considerations to bear in mind too. In particular, she was worried about the dangers of a sea passage in a small boat from Stockton, for she did not know if she could reach Hull or Shields in time to board a larger vessel there. Even so, she asked someone to find out about a coach at Darnton, apparently to take her to either Hull or Shields. She also weighed up Mrs Hutchins's offer of her brother, who would ride double with her (Lady Pelegrina) while she (Mrs Hutchins) would ride alone on a Galloway. She did not immediately accept the proposal, aware that she would have to buy a double horse and pay the expenses of Mrs Hutchins and her brother. Lady Peregrina also had to decide whether to take her children with her or not, and to consider their preferred mode of travel. Harry, her eldest son (aged fourteen) was happy to go by sea, as were his two younger brothers, though the latter could only travel with her if she could afford to maintain them in London. Nancy (aged twenty-three), on the other hand, was unwilling to board ship. If she (Lady Peregrina) went on horseback, Harry could accompany her on their Galloway, if sound, while Nancy could travel by coach. She then computed the costs, coming to the initial conclusion that 'hors back is cheaper by much then a coache, even but not by much soe cheap as by sea'. At this point, Lady Peregrina's fear of going by boat outweighed the price advantage and inclined her to travel on horseback. Then she remembered the hidden costs of riding. Would the horse be able to cope with a double load on such a long journey, and what condition would it be in when they reached London? How much would she lose when trying to sell it, that is if it survived the trip? She therefore concluded that going on horseback might 'make my charges all moest as great of hors back as by coache'. Lady Peregrina hoped that her husband would be able to resolve the issue and thereby save her the great expense of journeying down on the York coach. If it came to that, she would have to travel alone.[114]

Even the upper classes, who had their own vehicles, made regular use of stage coaches. As Edward Chamberlain observed in 1672, 'there is of late such an admirable commodiousness both for Men and Women of better rank to travel from London to almost any great town of England, and to almost all the villages near this great city, that the like hath not been known in the world, and that is by stage coaches'.[115] Sometimes, like Marmaduke Rawdon, they hired the whole coach to ensure a congenial journey. In 1655, he and his party paid the full cost of £12 in order to have exclusive use of the Exeter coach bound for London. Nicholas Blundell had similarly booked the Chester coach for his own use when, on 27 May 1723, he set out for London, accompanied by his wife and maid, his cousin, Jane Gillibrond, and Lieutenants Barker and Sole. They arrived two days later.[116] For gentlemen, stage coaches also provided a convenient way to transport relatives or servants about and, in general, to avoid the trouble of getting the coach out. On 18 August 1704, for instance, Sir Richard Myddelton of Chirk Castle booked a seat for Mr John Morgan on the Shrewsbury to London coach.[117] All too often, however, gentlemen shared a coach with strangers and their comments reveal that they found contact with them distasteful. On one occasion, John Verney's fellow travellers comprised a tanner's wife, a cooper and a nursing mother, an experience that was too much for his sensitive nostrils. In 1703, Nicholas Blundell complained about being harangued by a 'disputing parson' on a journey between London and Oxford. Three years later, he wrote disparagingly about a fellow-passenger as a 'gold-digger: she 'passed for a great fortune but we suppose she is not'.[118]

With their servants and greater resources, the upper classes could minimize the inconvenience caused by the need to get to and from the staging point. On 27 August 1692 Robert Harley, then in London, informed his father that he was coming up on the Worcester coach the following Friday (2 September) and asked him if could have horses ready for him on Saturday evening when he arrived in the city. From there he and his companion, John Child, had about a fifty-five mile ride to Brampton Bryan. Later in the year he informed his father that his sister and aunt had just left on the Bridgnorth coach and that he had arranged with Mr Baker to provide a coach for them at their destination. On another occasion, probably in 1715, a chariot took Mr Garwood, then staying with Robert's son, Edward, at Wimpole Hall in Cambridgeshire, to Buntingford where he could catch the stage coach to London.[119] The population at large had fewer options but they could hire a post horse, which would get them closer to home, though perhaps not all the way. Another problem when travelling by stage coach was the early start, particularly when catching a flying coach. They regularly set out before dawn and, even if a passenger lived locally, he or she had to get up much earlier.[120] For passengers coming to town, the journey began the previous day and involved an overnight stay. Thus, when Nicholas Blundell travelled to London with his wife and friends in May 1723, the party had put up at the Coach and Horses in Chester the night before.[121]

For the social elite who ran the country, image was an important consideration. It was not enough merely to be wealthy, wealth had also to be displayed. The possession of a coach and horses enabled the owner to flaunt it in public. When coaches were first introduced, they met with a mixed reaction among the upper classes. In towns, especially London, they soon became popular, as they did among ladies in general. On their estates, however, many gentlemen contemplating the purchase of a coach, perhaps at the urging of their wife, were initially reluctant to do so. Conveyances for carrying people had long been associated with ladies, the old and the sick and to buy one might indicate weakness. This attitude gradually changed over the course of the seventeenth century as they came to appreciate the possibilites for self-advertising provided by being seen in an expensive coach pulled by equally valuable horses. No doubt, they secretly enjoyed the benefits too: they kept dry, could converse easily with their companions and could take more luggage with them. It may even have made it easier for them to commit adultery. The development of stage wagons or coaches and hackney cabs extended the facility to the middling orders. They proved so popular among them that they incurred the wrath of vested interests, mainly from people working in occupations threatened by the spread of coach traffic. The complaints of watermen, sedan operators, innkeepers, postmasters and the like were, however, to no avail and coaches continued to multiply on the roads. By the end of the seventeenth century coachmasters had established a national network of coaching services, running throughout the year and at fixed times. In the process, they conveyed large numbers of people from place to place, over short and long distances, and if passengers did not travel in complete comfort, they were at least protected from the elements.

Conclusion

This is a book about demand, specifically the ways in which early modern English society deployed horses to meet its varied needs. For most people the requirement was an economic one, for they used horses in the course of their work: to prepare the ground, pull wagons, transport packs, operate gins or carry them on business. As such, horses were assessed according to size, strength and function. However, as horses also possessed social and cultural worth, individuals were prepared to pay premium prices for fine specimens, ones which showed their owners off to advantage if they rode on them or put them between the shafts of a coach. This book therefore makes a contribution to the on-going debate about the consumer revolution that transformed the way of life of a significant proportion of the population, especially in the period after the Restoration of 1660. The lists of indicator commodities compiled by historians of consumption do not include horses perhaps because of their association with 'old' luxury and aristocratic profligacy, characterized by large houses, impressive stable blocks and strings of horses. In the late seventeenth century, moreover, commercial expansion and a burgeoning middle class created an alternative focus, one that emphasized 'commerce, utility, taste and comfort'. The 'new' luxuries, often imports or home produced versions of them, were associated with innovation in domestic life, whether functional, ritualistic or decorative. They included napery, textiles, soft furnishings and furniture; cutlery, cooking equipment, tea and coffee sets; and miscellaneous items like pictures, books, mirrors and clocks. Horses clearly do not fit in such a list but it would be wrong to exclude them from the overall account. Horses do feature in the aspirations of the middling orders, and therefore an examination of the services these animals performed provides insights into the nature of consumer behaviour at the time.[1]

Commentators on the consumer revolution emphasize the crucial role played by the middling orders in fuelling demand, their combined purchasing power stimulating the import trade in new and exotic goods and encouraging the production of these and other items at home. Incidentally, they also acquired horses and bought services that required these animals. With regard to household items, the process began among the upper classes, whose wealth, social networks and London connexions provided them with the knowledge of these new goods and the money to buy them on a regular basis. Diffusion outside the elite really began after the Restoration, mainly among the pseudo gentry and wealthy merchants and professionals living in towns. In the early eighteenth century these commodities spread much more widely, though with uneven uptake, among the middling orders in the countryside as well as in the town.[2] Within this framework, historians have sought to explain why this development took place by examining the motives of the purchasers. Among the first theories put forward was that of emulation, supporters of this view arguing that prospering members of the middling orders displayed their rising wealth and status by aping the manners of their social superiors. The weight of recent research, however, downplays this view, arguing that the middling orders were more concerned about convenience, availability and the establishment of their own cultural norms. Undoubtedly, possession of these goods did confer status but a distinction might be made between those commodities on public display and those that were not. Items, like clocks, of course, had a utilitarian function as well as social one.[3]

The upper classes certainly took the lead in improving the quality and range of horses in the country, as well as using them for non-functional social purposes. At the opening of the period *c.* 1500 England produced a limited range of horses, most of them ponies up to fourteen hands high. By 1750 a complete transformation had taken place. To a certain extent this was inevitable. As population rose in the late sixteenth and early seventeenth centuries, demand for horses not only increased but also diversified. Autonomous developments in breeding and marketing, aimed at providing horses for the population at large, would in any case have increased the number of packhorses, heavier draught animals and light saddle mounts in the country. This did happen but to an extent was only made possible by the impact of outside forces, notably the impetus given by the requirements of state and the interests of the upper classes. Where native horses were lacking in essential qualities, they imported stock from abroad that could do the job. In this respect, horses, as a commodity, conformed to the pattern exhibited amongst other sought-after consumer goods, namely the impact of imports on taste and function. Imports of Arabian, Barb and Turcoman horses provided the trade with its own exotic Eastern 'brands' and eventually its own home-produced varieties.

IMPROVEMENTS IN DRAUGHT HORSES

Initially, the motive to improve the quality of the nation's draught horses was a utilitarian one, based on increasing the strength of the animals required for the army's artillery and baggage trains. The crown took the lead. Henry VIII started the process, importing strong Flemish horses, having discovered, while campaigning abroad, that they performed much better than the ones he had brought over from England. When the elite took them up they primarily did so to pull their coaches, valuing them both for their utility and as a fashion statement, a combination that characterized many of the new commodities of the consumer revolution. Coaches demonstrably served a practical purpose, even if gentlemen of the old school were reluctant to ride in them. They kept passengers dry and clean, enabled them to talk to their fellow travellers and provided them with extra luggage space. The occupants did not suffer from saddle sores either and with the coach's rudimentary suspension, they probably travelled in a little more comfort. Horses bought for the coach often performed other practical tasks, such as preparing the ground and carting off on the estate. When past their prime, their owners sold them to farmers and carriers who employed them in these capacities full-time. For those that did not make the grade as coach horses because of some blemish, whether an ungainly action, poor conformation or slight discolouring, this was their fate anyhow. In this way, the fashion for riding in coaches had a more general effect, improving the quality of horses on the farms and roads of England. The middling orders were quick to make use of these horses. Carriers in the south-east were harnessing them to their wagons from the turn of the sixteenth century and on the region's farms yeomen were deploying them as draught horses a generation later. Their counterparts elsewhere in the country followed suit over the course of the following hundred years.

A coach and its team of horses also served as a means of ostentatious display, a mobile advertisement of the wealth and standing of the occupants, identified by the coat of arms painted or carved on the vehicle. Moreover, in the post-Restoration period the custom of visiting friends, acquaintances and one's peers in coaches linked coach ownership with changes in social behaviour that accompanied the consumer revolution. The ritual of tea drinking and the use of china cups, for instance, was similarly functional and socially innovative.[4] In the late seventeenth century some of the wealthiest members of the middling orders, especially in London, were emulating their social superiors and buying coaches. In 1679 Alexander Denton, the cousin of John Verney, spent £60 on a velvet-lined coach that had belonged to a London merchant. That the vendor realized he had transgressed an invisible social divide is indicated by his statement that 'he thinks it too fine for him and hath lately bought a second-hand chariot for £23 without harness'. By the turn of the century citizens had no such qualms and, as a result, coach ownership had expanded.[5]

Most of the middling orders made do with hackney cabs. The question is whether these people were copying the genteel lifestyle, if in a cheaper form, or were they making use of a convenient, affordable and readily available form of transport for their own purpose. The initiative for the service seems to have come from enterprising cab owners in London, but citizens of means eagerly adopted this form of transport. Contemporaries certainly thought that the rapid growth in the number of hackney coaches in London in the early seventeenth century reflected the middling orders' desire to impress and to experience the pleasure of being driven round the capital in style. On 21 April 1667, Samuel Pepys, having decided to buy a coach, admitted that he was 'almost ashamed to be seen in a hackney'. On 11 May he justified his decision by arguing that, as he was spending so much on hackney cabs, it would be cheaper to have his own coach. Significantly he added that he was 'a little dishonoured' by riding in a cab. Even so, he had a point. The regularity with which Pepys and his friends and acquaintances rode through the crowded, muddy streets of London in hackney cabs meant that the service did cost them an appreciable amount of money. It also indicated that hackney cabs performed a useful utilitarian function, in the same way that taxis do today.[6]

Hackney cabs may have been ideal conveyances for travelling around London or even for a jaunt into the countryside but they did not offer the same freedom of movement that owners of private coaches enjoyed. Apart from escalating hiring charges, they were unable to venture more than a day or two from the capital in them. This limited movement to journeys within the Home Counties.[7] In spite of earlier stage wagon services, the real advance came with the introduction of stage coaches and the establishment of a national coaching network during the course of the later seventeenth and eighteenth centuries. The first routes ran along the arterial roads out of London, but by 1750 the system had acquired numerous branch lines linking stage towns to smaller centres. By 1700, flying coaches, working a long day, enabled passengers from London to reach towns as far away as Cirencester. It is hard to overestimate the impact that the creation of a national network of coaching services had on travel in the country. While costs put them beyond the reach of the humbler members of society, the middling orders could afford to travel in stage coaches, allowing them to enjoy the benefits they provided. Operating to a regular timetable throughout the year, they brought a degree of order and certainty to long-distant transport and helped to overcome provincial isolation. Moreover, in spite of the dangers, whether in the form of potholed roads or ruffianly highwaymen, they represented a comparatively safe form of transport. Parents or guardians no longer felt obliged to send someone to accompany women, children or elderly or sick relatives, secure in the knowledge that the coach would convey them to their destination.

IMPROVEMENTS IN SADDLE HORSES

Military necessity also promoted measures to improve the quality of saddle horses. While England and Wales produced plenty of light cavalry mounts, the countries lacked sufficient horses suitable for heavily armoured men-at-arms.

Henry VIII therefore sent agents abroad to acquire them. He obtained others as part of the diplomatic process. In addition, he encouraged the upper classes to breed serviceable horses on their estates, supplementing the 'carrot' with the 'whip' of legislative action. His successors continued his policy. Over time the type of horses changed as cavalry tactics evolved. While Neapolitan coursers made ideal mounts for men-at-arms, they gave way to Spanish ginetes in the late sixteenth century, as cavalrymen became mounted pistoleers. Subsequently Gustavus Adolphus reintroduced the element of shock, but his troopers were lightly armoured, mounted on fast, nimble horses, some with eastern blood in them. In England, habitual weaknesses in the quality of the horses displayed at musters of the county militias suggest limited progress but this is to ignore the political dimension. The gentry did possess suitable horses but disliked being pressurized into making binding commitments. In the build-up to the Bishops' Wars of 1639–40 the response to Charles I's pleas for horses was poor because so many members of the elite did not want to support an unpopular monarch.

The upper classes were interested in breeding good quality saddle mounts, but they did so for their own consumerist purposes: to emphasize their status, for recreation and as an object of conspicuous consumption. Fortunately, horses that matched these requirements made suitable army mounts. So their stables, if only incidentally, contained a number of horses that could serve in the cavalry. As horsemanship was the essential mark of a gentleman, they cultivated an image of power and authority by riding fine, mettlesome mounts in public: hence the objection to sitting in coaches. For sheer size and grandeur nothing could compare with Neapolitan coursers and for this reason they lasted longer as parade animals than they did as cavalry mounts. In the early seventeenth century, however, ginetes were replacing them, as depicted in equestrian portraits of the time. For many members of the elite mere display sufficed. Some took the process further, flaunting their skills by engaging in the *manège*, the ultimate test of horsemanship. They tended to choose Neapolitan coursers and large ginetes as their mounts on account of the imposing stature, which enabled them fully to demonstrate the link between horsemanship and qualities of leadership. Apart from their stress on the emblematic quality of fine saddle horses, the upper classes influenced the composition of the nation's stock of horses by their interest in equine pursuits. Horse racing, although an exclusive activity dependent upon the gentry for the runners and riders, had a wider impact on the quality of the horses bred in the country. By the end of the sixteenth century owners were importing eastern horses and crossing them with tested home-bred racers as a means of improving the speed and stamina of their charges. Here, unusually for the elite, performance predominated over style. The racecourse test rather than consumerist considerations of colour and conformation decided which animals stood at stud. In addition owners used the stallions to cover their non-racing mares and hired them out to others, either to defray the enormous cost of maintaining a racing stud or merely because they were available. Accordingly, the number of half-bred saddle horses with eastern blood in them increased, providing a widening pool of fine mounts for the battleground or hunting field. In turn, gentlemen allowed their hunters (and militia horses), as well as their coach horses, to cover the mares of their tenantry. They also disposed of their older, less active or showy animals, at markets and fairs, offering the general public the chance to acquire an exotic, if ageing, animal in the same way that motorists today might buy a battered old Mercedes.

Reselling, which was common in the horse trade, was an important feature in the growth of consumerism. Because it enabled people to acquire sought-after commodities at prices they could not have afforded when new, it extended the market for fashionable goods. The second-hand clothing trade operated in the same way. As Lemire has remarked, 'many middling and labouring people turned to second-hand goods, some to trade and others to achieve a respectable or even a refined appearance'. The clothing that one wore, like the horse that one rode, proclaimed the person, and choice depended upon such criteria as price, fashion and utility. Because of the rapid growth of demand for second-hand clothing in the post-Restoration period, garments of all kinds flooded on to the market, just as the trade in horses expanded. In both cases much of the business passed through the hands of middlemen. For instance, servants, who had acquired cast-off clothing from their masters or mistresses sold them on to clothes dealers, that is when (or after) they did not wear them in public themselves.[8]

Naturally, the middling orders did not acquire horses (or dress up) to indulge in such aristocratic pursuits as hunting game, hawking, horse racing, jousting or riding in the *manège* ring. If sheer cost did not act as sufficient deterrent to their aspirations, the elite erected barriers to keep them out. By law the middle classes could not emulate the elite by hunting game and their inferior status and upbringing precluded them from taking part in a tournament. Some gentlemen did invite their tenantry to hunt non-game animals with them in an attempt to foster good relations in the countryside, while in places groups of people banded together to maintain a plebeian hunt to chase foxes and other vermin. Of course ordinary people attended race meetings, trailed along after a hunt and perhaps watched a tournament, but they played a supporting role, a human backdrop to the action. Even so, as spectators, they contributed to the rise of the leisure industry, a key component in the consumer revolution.[9] This is particularly noticeable in the sport of horse racing which grew rapidly in popularity after the Restoration. The number of events proliferated and a hierarchy of centres developed. Because of their income and leisure time the middling orders were prominent among those attending the races, where they went to enjoy a day out and to experience the thrill of a bet on the outcome of a race. The development of the stage coach network enabled them to travel to the larger, more prestigious meetings and their wealth allowed them to put up at a reasonable inn overnight. They learnt of events through advertisements in the *London Gazette* or, increasingly in the eighteenth century, in local newspapers. Newspapers also provided them with information on other leisure pursuits such as theatrical performances, concerts and cricket matches.[10]

If the middling orders did not participate in the *manège*, they might emulate the elite by riding for pleasure or by choice. As the mere possession of a horse conferred status, owners who kept a designated saddle mount were making a public statement of their standing. Significantly the number of mounts rose in the late seventeenth century. In contrast to the general pattern of consumption for most of the new commodities, the rise in the ownership of saddle horses was essentially a rural phenomenon, an indication of the different priorities in town and countryside. Yeomen and minor gentry had to rely on their own horses to a greater extent than did their urban counterparts, who could more readily hire a riding hack or travel in a hackney or stage coach. Lesser tradesmen and farmers viewed their horses more prosaically. If a small-scale farmer rode a plough mare to market, for instance, he did so for the sake of utility rather than as a means of 'cutting a dash'.

EXPLOITATION OF HORSES

Mankind exploited horses in numerous ways, to the extent that early modern society would not have functioned very effectively without them. Few people questioned their right to do so: after all, God had given them dominion over the whole natural world. To Christian theology, medieval scholars added notions of human distinction derived from the newly rediscovered views of classical philosophers. Aristotle's concept of a graded *scala naturae* formed the basis of the 'Great Chain of Being', an idea that exerted considerable influence from the Middle Ages down to the eighteenth century. Man occupied the highest point on the continuum, reflected in his unique qualities which distinguished him from other creatures: reason, language and the possession of a soul. Early modern philosophers however did differ in their opinions. If Descartes' mechanistic view of animals marked one end of the spectrum, others increasingly questioned the sharpness of the division. Theriophilic writers claimed that animals could reason to a certain degree, were able to communicate among themselves and, according to some, possessed a soul. They viewed horses, in particular, as intelligent, sentient creatures. People who worked with horses shared this opinion.

Changing attitudes towards animals should have had an impact on the way people treated horses, though to have any real effect they had to reach beyond the intelligentsia. This is the problem. In trying to discern what actually happened, one faces a hierarchy of evidence. The top two layers tend to deal with the problem in the abstract, though the people concerned generally had experience of horses. At the highest level there are the views of the intellectuals, many of whom possessed horses, but who were essentially writing in philosophical terms. Closer to reality were those who produced handbooks on horse management, offering advice on all aspects of the subject, including breeding, training, discipline and the treatment of injuries and diseases. They might discuss horses' qualities and attributes as well. Over time the instructions contained in these manuals displayed a softening of attitudes towards horses: horses should be cherished rather than beaten, as befitted creatures of intelligence and nobility. Primarily aimed at the gentry, these manuals also found a market among the middling orders and one that grew during the course of the seventeenth century. The books on farriery were particularly aimed at them.

The final layer of evidence provides data that is qualitatively different from the other two. It comprises information on actual practice. For the upper classes we have plenty of material in the form of diaries, commonplace books and correspondence. In general, they appear to have absorbed the advice given to them in the handbooks and to have acted accordingly. Unfortunately in certain circumstances they continued to abuse their animals. Their records also include references to the way their servants looked after their charges and here the evidence is far more damning. Collecting together scattered references from all sources it is easy to find examples of abuse committed by a wide range of people: servants, carriers, coachmen and the like. If this information is rather anecdotal, though impressive in total, toll books offer a source of quantitative data. An analysis of the nomenclature of horses according to age reveals that breeders broke in their colts and fillies earlier than was recommended. The same was broadly true (though somewhat less clear-cut) with regard to the age of weaning, covering and castration. Horses therefore tended not to receive the best start to life, though the situation could have been worse. Even so, premature training would have had an adverse effect on their health and performance in the long run. Worse still, many people worked their horses too hard too soon, wearing them out by the age of ten. In general, early modern man treated horses in an unsympathetic way, disposing of even the highest priced animals when they were of no further value, either through age or injury. Chipped teacups met the same fate.

As the main purpose of the manuals was to influence readers to follow their precepts, they did not state what actually happened but what the authors wanted to happen. Indeed, they often refer to the gap between prescription and practice. Evidence derived from the toll books reveals that many buyers and sellers, a largely middle-class group, did not fully act on the advice given in the handbooks. Perhaps they adhered to the instructions contained in the books on farriery because they provided them with information on how to cure a valuable possession. On the other hand, they might still have preferred time-honoured remedies learnt as part of a traditional oral culture. The gap between the ideal and real life was also apparent in the response to the advice given in the conduct books which provided models of behaviour in the new consumer society. Social activities such as visiting, shopping, tea-drinking and even holding a knife and fork at dinner were not always conducted according to prescription.

Glossary

almain rivet	armour comprising a corslet (q.v.) and perhaps tassets (q.v.). The plates of the sleeves are joined together with sliding rivets for ease of movement.
anthropocentrism	view that put humans as the highest organism at the centre of the natural world.
arrêt de cuirasse	a rest, which supported the heavy lance and, acting as a fulcrum, gave the knight greater control as he lowered the weapon from the vertical to the horizontal at speed. In addition, by bracing the lance against the breastplate, the knight was better able to absorb the shock of impact and keep the weapon on target.
battle	the main infantry unit of an army, traditionally divided into three: the forward, middleward and rearward battles.
bill	a pole weapon with a cutting edge and a hooked end.
bonnaght	Irish: Buan 'permanent'.
burgonet	helmet with a high crest.
casement	pill-box extension into a dry ditch from a curtain wall.
chap-fallen	dropped lower jaw.
commissary officers	in charge of supplying essential materials to an army.
corslet	back and breast plate held together with leather straps.
cuirassier	a heavy cavalryman, successor to the medieval man-at-arms, though clad in lighter, three-quarter length articulated armour.
diapente	medicine comprising five ingredients.
drag	harrow.
equity courts	courts operating alongside the common law, based on the notion of equity in individual cases rather than on precedent.
Exclusion Crisis	caused by the Whig-inspired measure in Parliament (1679–81) to exclude the Roman Catholic, James Duke of York, from the succession.
galled	chafed.

gallowglass	Irish: Gall Óglaigh 'foreign soldiers'.
garron	Irish draught horse.
gentleman-pensioner	members of the royal household with special responsibility for the provision of horses for military and ceremonial purposes. Formed the core of the heavy cavalry in wartime.
guilder	also known as a florijn, it was worth a little less than an English florin of 2s.
halberd	pole weapon incorporating an axe blade, a spear point and either a pick or a hammer head.
haler	person who pulled boats upstream.
hart	red deer.
jack	leather jacket often with steel plates sewn into the sleeves.
jade	perjorative term for a horse.
kirtle	gown.
muster	meeting of the county militia forces for review and training.
ordinary	inn providing a meal at a fixed price and time.
pain	bye-law instituted at the manor court.
palfrey	an early term for an ambling horse.
palio	horse races that took place in a number of Italian towns. Strictly speaking, the banner presented to the winner of a race.
petronel	light, unarmoured cavalryman firing a carbine.
pike	sixteen foot wooden pole weapon with a metal point.
pistole	coin worth about 17s.
pot	metal helmet.
purveyor	person who bought goods, usually at a favourable price, for the crown under warrant.
ravelin	detached triangular bastion built on the outer side of a moat.
reiving	raiding across the Anglo-Scottish border.
shildron	units of Scottish spearmen.
sumpter	pack horse normally employed by the upper classes to carry their effects.
tasset	armoured skirt to protect the thighs.
theophilia	pro-animal sentiment.
through post	comprising riders, who delivered a dispatch rather than handing it on in a relay.

tilt	barrier in the tiltyard, which separated the two riders in the joust royal.
toll	payment levied on items bought and sold at a fair or market.
twinter	two year old animal.
unbarded horse	one without armour.

Notes

Notes to Preface

1. C.H. Herford and P. and E. Simpson, eds, *Ben Jonson, III, The Poems, The Prose Works*, The Forrest, II: 'To Penshurst' (1616) (Oxford, 1947), lines 29–30.
2. C.J. Adams, *Neither Man nor Beast: Feminism and the Defense of Animals* (New York, 1994), p. 69.
3. K. Thomas, *Man and the Natural World: Changing Attitudes in England, 1500–1800* (London, 1983).
4. For example, H. Ritvo, *The Animal Estate: The English and other Creatures in the Victorian Age* (Cambridge, Massachusetts, 1987); T. Ingold, ed., *What is an Animal?* (London, 1994); J. Wolch and J. Emel, 'Bringing the Animals Back In', *Environment Planning D, Society and Space*, 13 (1995); E. Fudge et al., *At the Borders of the Human* (Basingstoke, 1999); A. Mack, ed., *Humans and other Animals* (Columbus, Ohio, 1999); E. Fudge, *Perceiving Animals: Humans and Beasts in Early Modern English Culture* (Basingstoke, 2000); C. Philo and C. Wibert, eds, *Animal Spaces, Beastly Places: New Geographies of Human-Animal Relations* (London, 2000); N. Rothfels, ed., *Representing Animals* (Bloomington and Indianapolis, Indiana, 2002); E. Fudge, ed., *Renaissance Beasts: Of Animals, Humans and Other Wonderful Creatures* (Urbana and Chicago, Illinois, 2004).
5. E. Fudge, 'A Left-Handed Blow: Writing the History of Animals', in Rothfels, *Representing Animals*, p. 80.

Notes to Chapter 1: Horse and Society

1. F.M.L. Thompson, *Victorian England: The Horse-Drawn Society* (London, 1970).
2. J. Parkes, *Travel in the Seventeenth Century* (Oxford, 1925), p. 61; TNA, SP 46/60, fol. 213. An ambler was an easy paced saddle horse.
3. George Farquhar, *The Recruiting Officer*, P. Dixon, ed. (Manchester, 1986), act 1, scene 1, lines 69–71.
4. S. Wells and G. Taylor, eds, *The Oxford Shakespeare: The Complete Works* (Oxford, 1994), *Cymbeline*, act 3, scene 2, lines 67–71.
5. A.M. Everitt, 'Farm Labourers', in J. Thirsk, ed., *The Agrarian History of England and Wales, IV, 1500–1640* (Cambridge, 1967), p. 416.

6. P. Edwards, *The Horse Trade of Tudor and Stuart England* (Cambridge, 1988), p. 7. A probate inventory comprised a list of personal goods of the deceased drawn up by appraisers, normally shortly after death.
7. J. Thirsk, *Horses in Early Modern England: For Service, for Pleasure, for Power* (Reading, 1978), p. 6.
8. Edwards, *The Horse Trade*, p. 9.
9. Society of Antiquaries, MS 129, fos 444r–48r.
10. Warwickshire Record Office, Newdigate of Arbury MSS, CR 136/V/142.
11. Thirsk, *Horses in Early Modern England*, p. 7.
12. R. Longrigg, *The English Squire and his Sport* (London, 1977), p. 88; G. Worsley, *The British Stable* (New Haven and London, 2004), p. 18.
13. Worsley, *The British Stable*, pp. 20, 38, 89, 94, 124, 134; G. Worsley, 'Country Stables and their Implications for Seventeenth Century English Architecture', *The Georgian Group Journal*, 13 (2003), pp. 114–27; J.T. Cliffe, *The World of the Country House in Seventeenth-Century England* (New Haven, 1999), p. 36, citing John Bowack, *The Antiquities of Middlesex* (1705–6), p. 48.
14. Conrad Heresbach, *Foure Bookes of Husbandrie*, trans. Barnaby Googe (London, 1577), p. 114v. The original book, entitled *Rei rusticae*, became available in English when Barnaby Googe first published it in 1570.
15. Thomas de Gray, *The Compleat Horseman and Expert Ferrier* (London, 1639), pt 2, p. 5.
16. Thirsk, *Horses in Early Modern England*, p. 7, citing TNA, SP 12/26, no. 29.
17. With additional expense for compressing the hay. *CSPD, 1702–3*, p. 14.
18. Warwickshire Record Office, Newdigate MSS, CR 136/A/20.
19. Suffolk Record Office, Blomfield MSS, HD 330/7.
20. Edwards, *The Horse Trade*, p. 4.
21. Thomas Blundeville, *The Fower Chiefyst Offices Belonging to Horsemanship* (London, 1565), fos 10v–11r; William Camden, *Britannia*, trans. Philemon Holland (London, 1610), p. 18.
22. J.W. Burns, ed., *Miscellaneous Writings of John Spreull ... 1646–1722* (Glasgow, 1882), pp. 26, 30.
23. Ibid., p. 56.
24. Peter Keen, *Description of England* (London, 1599), p. 128; 'Montgomeyshire Horses, Cobs and Ponies', *Montgomeryshire Historical Collections*, 22 (1888), pp. 19, 29; H.l. Squires and E. Rowley, eds, 'Early Montgomeryshire Wills at Somerset House', *Montgomeryshire Historical Collections*, 22 (1888), p. 284; Edwards, *The Horse Trade*, pp. 27–9.
25. Edwards, *The Horse Trade*, pp. 24–31.
26. C. Gill, ed., *Dartmoor: A New Study* (Newton Abbot, 1970), p. 171.
27. Richard Carew, *The Survey of Cornwall*, ed., F.E. Halliday (New York, 1969), p. 107.
28. Edwards, *The Horse Trade*, p. 31; TNA, E101/56/24; E101/60/24; E101/107/17; E101/107/28.
29. Edwards, *The Horse Trade*, pp. 36–8.
30. *CSPV*, II, *1509–19*, p. 51.
31. *CSPV*, VI, pt 3, *1557–58*, p. 1049.
32. *Letters and Papers of Henry VIII*, XIX, pt 1, *1544*, p. 465.

33 *L & P of Henry VIII*, XV, *1540*, p. 229.
34 D.M. Goodall, *The Foals of Epona* (London, 1988), p. 234.
35 Blundeville, *The Fower Chiefyst Offices*, fos Aii–iv.
36 *CSPV*, VI, pt 3, *1557–58*, p. 1049.
37 Richard Blome, *The Gentleman's Recreation* (London, 1686), part 2, p. 2.
38 *HMC*, 'Salisbury MSS', XIX (London, 1965), p. 23.
39 Bodleian Library, Ashmole 1621, R. Child's letter printed in Samuel Hartlib, *The Legacie* (2nd edn, London, 1652).
40 Edwards, *The Horse Trade*, p. 50.
41 Society of Antiquaries, MS 129.
42 M.M. Reese, *The Royal Office of the Master of the Horse* (London, 1976), p. 160.
43 C.M. Prior, *The Royal Studs of the Sixteenth and Seventeenth Centuries* (London, 1935), p. 74.
44 27 Henry VIII, c. 6; 33 Henry VIII, c. 5.
45 *L & P of Henry VIII*, XVII, *1542*, p. 80.
46 *CSPD, 1547–80*, p. 685.
47 Thirsk, *Horses in Early Modern England*, pp. 15–16.
48 R. Hutton, *The Royalist War Effort, 1642–1646* (London, 1982), p. 103.
49 Thirsk, *Horses in Early Modern England*, pp. 17–20.
50 Ibid., p. 17.
51 P.C.D. Brears, ed., 'Yorkshire Probate Inventories, 1542–1689', *Yorkshire Archaeological Society*, 124 (1972), pp. 3–8.
52 BL, Harleian MS 29443, fol. 3v.
53 Staffordshire Record Office, HM27/2, Edward James's Farming Accounts, 1692–1710.
54 de Gray, *Compleat Horseman*, I, pp. 1–2.
55 Derbyshire Record Office, Chandos-Pole-Gell MSS, D258/box 29/9a.
56 Warwickshire Record Office, Newdigate MSS, CR136/V/142.
57 Andrew Borde, *The Fyrst Boke of the Introduction of Knowledge* (London, 1542), chapter 8, no pagination; Blundeville, *The Fower Chiefyst Offices*, fol. 10r. This description of Flanders mares reveals what Henry VIII thought of his fourth wife, Anne of Cleves.
58 Blundeville, *The Fower Chiefyst Offices*, fos 9r–10v; *CSPD, 1568–79*, p. 429; William Cavendish, *A New Method and Extraordinary Invention to Dress Horses* (London, 1667), p. 65.
59 K. Raber and T. Tucker, 'Introduction', in K. Raber and T. Tucker, eds, *The Culture of the Horse: Status, Discipline, and Identity in the Early Modern World* (Basingstoke, 2005), p. 29.
60 Blundeville, *The Fower Chiefyst Offices*, fos 7v–8r; G. Parker, *The Military Revolution* (Cambridge, 1989), p. 69; D.M. Goodall, *A History of Horse Breeding* (London, 1977), p. 156.
61 Blundeville, *The Fower Chiefyst Offices*, fos. 9r–9v, 12r.
62 P. Edwards, *Dealing in Death: The Arms Trade and the British Civil Wars, 1638–52* (Thrupp, 2000), pp. 13, 155; F. Kitson, *Prince Rupert: Portrait of a Soldier* (London, 1994), p. 263.
63 S. Loch, *The Royal Horse of Europe: The Story of the Andalusian and Lusitano* (London, 1986), p. 80.
64 Goodall, *Horse Breeding*, pp. 150, 156–7; Blundeville, *The Fower Chiefyst Offices*, fos 7v–8r.

65 Goodall, *Horse Breeding*, p. 157.
66 Cavendish, *A New Method*, pp. 49–50.
67 A. Hyland, *The Medieval Warhorse* (Far Thrupp, 1994), pp. 55–7; Loch, *The Royal Horse*, p. 75; Goodall, *Horse Breeding*, pp. 161, 163; *CSPV*, II, *1509–19*, p. 198.
68 P. Edwards, 'The Horse Trade in Tudor and Stuart Staffordshire', *Staffordshire Studies*, 13 (2001), p. 36.
69 *L & P of Henry VIII*, XIX, pt 1, *1544*, pp. 482, 518–9; XX, pt 1, *1545*, p. 5.
70 *L & P of Henry VIII*, XXI, pt 1, *1546*, p. 303.
71 A. Dent, *Horses in Shakespeare's England* (London, 1987), p. 108; Nottingham University Library, Manuscripts Department, Middleton MSS, Mi A 81.
72 Goodall, *Horse Breeding*, p. 158; E. Tobey, 'The *Palio* Horse in Renaissance and Early Modern Italy', in K. Raber and T. Tucker, eds, *The Culture of the Horse*, pp. 71–5.
73 *CSPV*, II, *1509–19*, pp. 174–5, 179, 183, 198, 379, 389; III, *1520–26*, pp. 319, 321; *L & P of Henry VIII*, I, pt 2, *1513–14*, p. 1451.
74 *HMC*, 'Marquis of Downshire MSS', III (1938), pp. 192, 194.
75 R. Strong, *Henry, Prince of Wales and England's Lost Renaissance* (London, 2000), pp. 43–4.
76 R. Sherwood, *The Court of Oliver Cromwell* (London, 1977), p. 57.
77 N.E. McClure, ed., *The Letters of John Chamberlain*, I (Philadelphia, 1939), p. 563.
78 Nicholas Morgan, *The Perfection of Horsemanship* (London, 1609), p. 18.
79 Cavendish, *A New Method*, pp. 54–7.
80 *HMC*, 'Salisbury MSS', X (London, 1904), p. 148.
81 BL, Add. MS 33146.
82 'The Memorandum Book of Richard Cholmeley of Brandsby, 1602–1623', *North Yorkshire Record Office Publication*, 44 (1988), p. 138; J.P. Hore, *The History of Newmarket and the Annals of the Turf*, III (London, 1886), p. 352.
83 Edwards, *The Horse Trade*, p. 45.
84 Cavendish, *A New Method*, p. 58.
85 Ibid., pp. 59–60.
86 Ibid., p. 59; P. Edwards, 'The Horse Trade of the Midlands in the Seventeenth Century', *Agricultural History Review*, 27 (1979), p. 94.
87 Surrey Record Office, LM Cor 10/122.
88 Introduced in 1555 (2 and 3 Philip & Mary, c. 7) and extended in 1589 (31 Elizabeth I, c. 12); Edwards, *The Horse Trade*, pp. 55–60.
89 Edwards, *The Horse Trade*, pp. 99–103.
90 BL, Add. MSS, 33144–47, 33149; A. Fletcher, *A County Community in Peace and War: Sussex, 1600–1660* (London, 1975), pp. 44–53.
91 Staffordshire Record Office, Leveson-Gower MSS, D593/F/2/38.
92 Blome, *The Gentleman's Recreation*, pt 2, p. 2.
93 Buckinghamshire Record Office, Chester of Chicheley MSS, D/C/4/10.
94 Lincolnshire Archives Office, Massingberd of Gunby MSS, MG 5/2/7; Northamptonshire Record Office, Cartwright of Aynho MSS, C(A) 3489.
95 Edwards, 'Staffordshire Horse Trade', p. 41.

Notes to Chapter 2: Attitudes towards Horses

1. K. Thomas, *Man and the Natural World: Changing Attitudes in England, 1500–1800* (London, 1983), pp. 17, 30.
2. Genesis, 9: 2–3.
3. Imagination: animals generate mental images, derived from sensation, but these impressions can be true or false. The purpose of imagination is twofold: it forms the basis of memory and stimulates action and movement; G.E.R. Lloyd, *Aristotle: The Growth and Structure of his Thought* (Cambridge, 1968), pp. 191–2, 239–40.
4. J. Clutton-Brock, 'Aristotle, the Scale of Nature and Modern Attitudes to Animals', in A. Mack. ed., *Humans and Other Animals* (Columbus, Ohio, 1999), pp. 7–8.
5. Clutton-Brock, 'Aristotle', p. 7; A.J. Lovejoy, *The Great Chain of Being: A Study of the History of an Idea* (New York, 1960), pp. 56–62.
6. *The Philosophical Works of Descartes*, trans. E.S. Haldane and G.R.T. Ross, I (Cambridge, 1911), p. 117.
7. Ibid., I, p. 117.
8. Thomas, *Man and the Natural World*, p. 33.
9. Ibid., p. 33; J. Cottingham, 'Descartes' Treatment of Animals', in J. Cottingham, *Descartes* (Oxford, 1998), pp. 225–33.
10. Thomas, *Man and the Natural World*, p. 41.
11. S. James, ed., *Margaret Cavendish: Political Writings* (Cambridge, 2003), p. 64; Thomas Tryon, *The Country-Mans Companion* (London, 1683?), p. 1; The Lady Newcastle (Margaret Cavendish), 'The Hunting of the Hare', *Poems and Fancies* (London, 1653), p. 112.
12. Ibid., p. 112.
13. Thomas, *Man and the Natural World*, p. 124.
14. Michel de Montaigne, 'An Apology for Raymond Sebond', *The Complete Essays of Montaigne*, trans. D.A. Frame (Stanford, California, 1965), p. 331.
15. Lady Newcastle, *Poems*, p. 94.
16. Ibid., p. 105.
17. John Hildrop, *Free Thought upon the Brute-Creation: or an Examination of Father Bougeant's Philosophical Amusements* (London, 1742), pp. 6–7.
18. John Lawrence, *A Philosophical and Practical Treatise on Horses, and on the Moral Duties of Man towards the Brute Creation* (London, 1796), pp. 78, 83.
19. G. Aillaud, 'Why Look at Animals?', in J. Berger, ed., *About Looking* (London, 1980), pp. 3–4.
20. Michel de Montaigne, 'An Apology for Raymond Sebond', p. 331.
21. Bonaventure des Périers, *Cymbalum Mundi*, ed., Y. Delègue (Paris, 1995), pp. 73–4.
22. B. Cummings, 'Pliny's Literate Elephant and the Idea of Animal Language in Renaissance Thought', in E. Fudge, ed., *Renaissance Beasts: Of Animals, Humans, and other Wonderful Creatures* (Urbana and Chicago, Illinois, 2004) pp. 164–85.
23. R. Preece and D. Fraser, 'The Status of animals in Biblical and Christian Thought: A Study in Colliding Values', *Society & Animals*, 8, III (2000), p. 247.
24. Thomas, *Man and the Natural World*, p. 154.

25 Montaigne, 'Of Cruelty', *The Complete Essays*, p. 316.
26 S. Wells and G. Taylor, eds, *The Oxford Shakespeare: The Complete Works* (Oxford, 1994), *Love's Labour Lost*, act 4, scene 1, lines 34–5.
27 Lady Newcastle, *Poems*, p. 112.
28 Ibid., pp. 70–1.
29 Thomas, *Man and the Natural World*, p. 29.
30 Lady Newcastle, *Poems*, p. 59.
31 Preece and Fraser, 'Status of Animals', pp. 255–6.
32 Thomas, *Man and the Natural World*, pp. 137–9; E. Fudge, *Perceiving Animals: Humans and Beasts in Early Modern English Culture* (Basingstoke, 2000), pp. 148–9.
33 Preece and Fraser, 'Status of Animals', p. 256.
34 Cited in M. Carmill, *A View to a Death in the Morning* (Cambridge, Massachusetts, 1993), p. 98.
35 Lawrence, *Treatise on Horses*, pp. 83–4.
36 H. Erskine-Hill, *Gulliver's Travels* (Cambridge, 1993), pp. 75–7.
37 H. Ritvo, 'Border Trouble: Shifting the Line between People and Other Animals', in A. Mack, ed., *Humans and Other Animals* (Columbus, Ohio, 1999), p. 69.
38 Fudge, *Perceiving Animals*, p. 143; Fudge, *Renaissance Beasts*, pp. 2, 8–9.
39 Michael Baret, *An Hipponomie or The Vineyard of Horsemanship* (London, 1618), fol. 6.
40 John Worlidge, *Systema Agriculturae* (London, 1675), pp. 160–1.
41 John Fitzherbert, *Boke of Husbandry* (London, 1523), fos 31r–32r.
42 Baret, *Hipponomie*, fo. 6; Worlidge, *Systema Agriculturae*, pp. 160–1.
43 Leonard Mascall, *The Booke of Cattell* (London, 1587), p. 117; Gervase Markham, *Cavelarice* (London, 1607),VIII, p. 20.
44 Thomas de Gray, *The Compleat Horseman and Expert Ferrier* (London, 1639), II, pp. 1–2.
45 M. Midgley, 'Beasts, Brutes and Monsters', in T. Ingold, ed., *What is an Animal?* (London, 1994), p. 43.
46 Fudge, *Perceiving Animals*, p. 26.
47 *HMC*, 'Portland MSS', II (1893), p. 306.
48 Ibid., p. 306; J. Parkes, *Travel in the Seventeenth Century* (Oxford, 1925), p. 244; for the oxen at Susa: Montaigne, 'An Apology', p. 340.
49 Baret, *Hipponomie*, fol. 9.
50 Mascall, *The Booke of Cattell*, p. 117; Gervase Markham, *Countrey Contentments* (London, 1615), II, p. 41; Thomas Blundeville, *The Arte of Rydynge* (London, c. 1560), fos 7v, 62r–62v; Thomas Powell, *Humane Industry or, a History of Most Manual Arts* (London, 1661), p. 177.
51 A. Stewart, *Philip Sidney, a Double Life* (London, 2000), p. 132.
52 Duchess of Newcastle, *The Life of the Thrice Noble ... William Duke of Newcastle* (London, 1667), II, p. 67.
53 J.M. Shuttleworth, ed., *The Life of Edward, First Lord Herbert of Cherbury, Written by Himself* (Oxford, 1976), p. 52.
54 Erskine-Hill, *Gulliver's Travels*, p. 66.
55 Fudge, *Perceiving Animals*, pp. 102–3.
56 *HMC*, 'Rutland MSS', II (London, 1889), p. 114.

57 That is, they formed a part of the economic system. C. Levi-Strauss, *The Savage Mind* (London, 1962), pp. 205–6.
58 East Suffolk Record Office, Blomfield of Stonham MSS, HD 330/7.
59 J.J. Bagley, ed., 'The Great Diurnal of Nicholas Blundell of Little Crosby, Lancashire', II, '1712–19', *Record Society of Lancashire & Cheshire*, 112 (1970), p. 41.
60 Cumbria Record Office, Muncaster Castle MSS, D/PEN/203 Estate Account Book 1695–1708; Bagley, 'Diurnal of Nicholas Blundell', I, '1702–11', 110 (1968), pp. 84, 111, 140.
61 TNA, PROB 4/9736.
62 Richmond and District Civil Society Annual Report 1978, no.1, p. 22.
63 That is, they represented an alien or artificial form of society as viewed and organized by its members, the racing fraternity: Levi-Strauss, *The Savage Mind*, p. 208.
64 Ibid., p. 208.
65 P.R. Seddon, ed., 'Letters of John Holles, 1587–1637', I, *Thoroton Society*, Record Series, 31 (1975), p. 10.
66 Cited in M.M. Reese, *The Royal Office of the Master of the Horse* (London, 1976), p. 166.
67 J.P. Hore, *The History of Newmarket and the Annals of the Turf*, III (London, 1886), p. 55.
68 Shuttleworth, *Herbert*, p. 43.
69 Sir Thomas Elyot, *The Boke Named the Governour* (London, 1531), fol. 68v.
70 William Cavendish, *A New Method and Extraordinary Invention to Dress Horses* (London, 1667), p. 13.
71 Ibid., p. 13.
72 *Letters and Papers of Henry VIII*, II, pt 2, *1517–18*, p. 1399.
73 *CSPV*, III, *1520–26*, p. 56.
74 G.R. Batho, ed., 'The Household Papers of Henry Percy, Ninth Earl of Northumberland, 1564–1632', *Camden Society*, third series, 93 (1962), p. 64.
75 W. Jerdan, ed., 'Original Documents ... Selected from the Private Archives of his Grace the Duke of Rutland', *Camden Society*, 21 (1842), p. 28.
76 J.G. Nichols, ed., 'The Diary of Henry Machyn', *Camden Society*, 42 (1848), p. 294.
77 W.A. Leighton, 'The Early Chronicles of Shrewsbury', *Transactions of the Shropshire Archaeological Society*, 3 (1880), p. 294.
78 Robert Surtees, *The History and Antiquities of the County Palatine of Durham*, I (London, 1816), p. cxliii.
79 R. Strong, *Henry, Prince of Wales and England's Lost Renaissance* (London, 2000), p. 85.
80 D. Howarth, *Images of Rule: Art and Politics in the English Renaissance, 1485–1649* (Basingstoke, 1997), p. 141.
81 Reese, *Master of the Horse*, p. 184; G.S. Layard, *The Headless Horseman: Pierre Lombart's Engraving: Charles or Cromwell?* (London, 1922), passim.
82 Hertfordshire Record Office, Henry de Nassau MSS, D/ENa 03.
83 C.M. Prior, *The Royal Studs of the Sixteenth and Seventeenth Centuries* (London, 1935), p. 2.
84 Ibid., pp. 11, 14–15, 19–20, 39–42, 44, 74–5.
85 Gervase Markham, *How to Chuse, Ride, Traine, and Diet Both Hunting-Horses and Running Horses* (London, 1599), p. A3v.
86 E.S. De Beer, ed., *The Diary of John Evelyn* (Oxford, 1955), IV, pp. 398–9.

87 *HMC*, 'Portland MSS', V (London, 1899), p. 118.
88 D. Landry, 'The Bloody Shouldered Arabian and Early Modern English Culture', *Criticism*, 46 (2004) pp. 59–61.
89 This section is based on the theme discussed by Professor Landry, 'The Bloody Shouldered Arabian', pp. 41–69.
90 BL, Add. MS 70143, fol. 305r.
91 Landry, 'The Bloody Shouldered Arabian' p. 47; Lawrence, *Treatise on Horses*, i, p. 161.
92 Markham, *How to Chuse*, fol. A3v.
93 Landry, 'The Bloody Shouldered Arabian', p. 57.
94 *HMC*, 'Finch MSS', II (London, 1922) p. 122.
95 Landry, 'The Bloody Shouldered Arabian', p. 61.
96 Ibid., p. 52.
97 Ibid., p. 48.
98 Ibid., pp. 57–9.
99 M.M. Verney, ed., *Memoirs of the Verney Family*, IV, *1660–1696* (London, 1970), p. 376; Thomas, *Man and the Natural World*, p. 118.
100 Thomas, *Man and the Natural World*, p. 190.
101 *CSPD, Addenda, 1580–1625*, p. 138.
102 *HMC*, 'Portland', IX (London, 1923), p. 62.
103 R.A. Greenberg, ed., *Jonathan Swift: Gulliver's Travels* (New York, 1970), p. 208.
104 Cited in Thomas, *Man and the Natural World*, p. 100; W.M. Myddelton, ed., *Chirk Castle Accounts, A.D. 1666–1753* (Manchester, 1931), p. 106; J. Wake and D.C. Webster, eds, 'The Letter Books of Daniel Eaton 1725–32', *Northamptonshire Record Society*, 24 (1970–71), p. 82.
105 Thomas, *Man and the Natural World*, pp. 115–16.
106 R. Meens, 'Eating Animals in the Early Middle Ages: Classifying the Animal World and Building Group Identities', in A.N.H. Creager and W.C. Jordan, eds, *The Animal-Human Boundary* (Rochester, New York, 2002), pp. 3–18.
107 S. Pearson and M. Weismantel, 'Does "The Animal" Exist? Towards a Theory of Social Life with Animals', paper read at the conference, 'Animals in History', held at Cologne, 18–21 May 2005, pp. 7–8. I am grateful to Professors Susan Pearson and Mary Weismantel for allowing me to quote from their as yet unpublished paper.
108 E. Leach, 'Anthropological Aspects of Language: Animal Categories and Verbal Abuse', in E.H. Lenneberg, ed., *New Directions in the Study of Language* (Cambridge, Massachusetts, 1964), pp. 32–3.
109 H.G. Tibbutt, ed., 'The Letter Books 1644–45 of Sir Samuel Luke' (London, 1963), p. 29.
110 M.M. Verney, ed., *Memoirs of the Verney Family*, III, *1650–1660* (London, 1970), p. 418.

Notes to Chapter 3: The Training and Treatment of Horses

1 John Astley, *The Art of Riding* (London, 1584), p. 5.
2 Cited in C. Hill, *The World Turned Upside Down* (Harmondsworth, 1975), p. 308.

3 William Cavendish, *A New Method and Extraordinary Invention to Dress Horses* (London, 1667), pp. 31–2; J. Thirsk, *Horses in Early Modern England: For Service, for Pleasure, for Power* (Reading, 1978), p. 19; E. Graham, 'Reading, Writing, and Riding Horses in Early Modern England', in E. Fudge, ed., *Renaissance Beasts: Of Animals, Humans, and other Wonderful Creatures* (Urbana and Chicago, Illinois, 2004), p. 126; K. Raber, 'A Horse of a Different Colour: Nation and Race in Early Modern Horsemanship Treatises', in K. Raber and T. Tucker, eds, *The Culture of the Horse: Status, Discipline, and Identity in the Early Modern World* (Basingstoke, 2005), p. 227.

4 Thirsk, Horses, pp. 19–20; Graham, 'Horses in Early Modern England', pp. 125–34, especially pp. 125–7.

5 D. Neave, ed., *Winteringham 1650–1760* (Winteringham, 1984), p. 18.

6 F.W. Steer, ed., *Farm and Cottage Inventories of Mid Essex, 1635 to 1749* (Chichester, 1969), passim.

7 Northamptonshire Record Office, Westmorland MSS, Misc. Vol. 15; Warwickshire Record Office, Warwick Castle MSS, CR 1886/411; D.R. Hainsworth and C. Walker, eds, 'The Correspondence of Lord Fitzwilliam of Milton and Francis Guybon his Steward, 1697–1709', *Northamptonshire Record Society* (1990), pp. 91, 105.

8 J.J. Bagley, ed., 'The Great Diurnal of Nicholas Blundell of Little Crosby, Lancashire', I, '1702–11', *Record Society of Lancashire & Cheshire*, 110 (1968), p. 20; II, '1712–19', 112 (1970), pp. 40, 42, 133, 229, 258, 275; III, '1720–29', 114 (1972), p. 61; BL, Add. MS 70385, fos 58, 61, 109; Add. MS 70386, fol. 95.

9 R. Longrigg, *The English Squire and his Sport* (London, 1977), p. 88; J. Wake and D.C. Webster, eds, 'The Letter Books of Daniel Eaton 1725–32', *Northamptonshire Record Society*, 24 (1970–71), p. 80.

10 Staffordshire Record Office, Paget of Beaudesert MSS, D[W] 1734/3/3/276, 279: Bryan Bould, Bulleker, Hugh Cater, John Fearn, John Urlin and Vincent looked after the horses, while several outsiders were hired to break colts and carry out farriery and smithy work; G.R. Batho, ed., 'The Household Papers of Henry Percy, Ninth Earl of Northumberland (1564–1632)', *Camden Society*, third series, 93 (1962), pp. 148–64; TNA, SP 1/113 fos 148–51; M.M. Reese, *The Royal Office of the Master of the Horse* (London, 1976), pp. 138–40, 200–1.

11 Bishop Thomas Percy, *The Regulations and Establishment of the Houshold of Henry Algernon Percy, Fifth Earl of Northumberland at his Castles of Wressle and Leconsfield begun 1512* (London, 1905), p. 55; TNA, SP 12/233, no. 69.

12 Bodleian Library, Douce 0182, Collection of Ordinances and Regulations for the Government of the Royal Household, Society of Antiquaries (London, 1790), p. 202; Reese, *Master of the Horse*, pp. 138–40, 200–1; Warwickshire Record Office, CR 1886/411.

13 E. LeGuin, 'Man and Horse in Harmony', in Raber and Tucker, *Culture of the Horse*, p. 177; Astley, *The Art of Riding* (London, 1584), pp. 12, 14.

14 Thomas Blundeville, *The Fower Chiefyst Offices belonging to Horsemanship* (London, 1565), fos 17–18, 28r.

15 Cavendish, *A New Method*, p. 26; Gervase Markham, *Cavelarice*, I (London, 1607), p. 55; John Worlidge, *Systema Agriculturae* (London, 1675), p. 284; Society of Antiquaries, MS 129.

16 Conrad Heresbach, *Four Bookes of Husbandry*, trans. Barnaby Googe (London, 1577 ed.), p. 117; Cavendish, *A New Method*, p. 95; John Halfpenny, *The Gentleman's Jockey and Approved Farrier* (London, 1674), p. 92.
17 Heresbach, *Husbandry*, p. 118v; Markham, *Cavelarice*, I, p. 55; Gervase Markham, *Markhams Maister-Peece* (London, 1615), p. 222.
18 Halfpenny, *The Gentleman's Jockey*, p. 96.
19 Bagley, 'Diurnal of Nicholas Blundell, I, pp. 84–5; Staffordshire Record Office, Bagot MSS, D1721/3/194; Herefordshire Record Office, Foley MSS, FH/111/3; Lincolnshire Archives Office, Massingberd of Gunby MSS, MASS 28/1; Massingberd of Mumby MSS, MM 6/1/1; Cumbria R.O.[Carlisle], D/PEN/203.
20 Norfolk Record Office, Pratt of Ryston MSS, m/f reel 219/1, 218/7.
21 'The Memorandum Book of Richard Cholmeley of Brandsby, 1602–1623', *Yorkshire (North) Record Office Publication*, 44 (1988), p. 114.
22 Heresbach, *Husbandry*, p. 119v.
23 Blundeville, *The Fower Chiefyst Offices*, fol. 29r; Markham, *Cavelarice*, I, p. 68; Gervase Markham, *Countrey Contentments* (London, 1615), I, pp. 70–1.
24 Cholmeley of Brandsby, p. 138; Nottingham University Library, MSS Department, Middleton MSS, Mi A 71; Bagley, 'Diurnal of Nicholas Blundell', II, p. 62.
25 Cholmeley of Brandsby, p. 67; Bagley, 'Diurnal of Nicholas Blundell', I, p. 66.
26 Oxfordshire Record Office, Garsington Account Book 1625–1701, BL I/V/2. I am grateful to Dr Wendy Thwaites for this reference.
27 Cholmeley of Brandsby, p. 93.
28 Blundeville, *The Fower Chiefyst Offices*, fos 30r–30v; Markham, *Cavelarice*, I, pp. 30–2.
29 Blundeville, *The Fower Chiefyst Offices*, fos 30r–30v.
30 Markham, *Countrey Contentments*, II, pp. 37–9; Cavendish, *A New Method*, pp. 93–5.
31 Thomas Blundeville, *The Arte of Rydynge* (London, c. 1560), fol. 7v; Blundeville, *The Fower Chiefyst Offices*, fol. 30v; Markham, *Countrey Contentments*, II, p. 41.
32 Blundeville, *Arte of Rydynge*, fol. 9.
33 *CSPV*, II, *1509–19*, p. 51; Cavendish, *A New Method*, pp. 94–5.
34 S. Wells and G. Taylor, eds, *The Oxford Shakespeare: The Complete Works* (Oxford, 1994), *Venus and Adonis*, lines 419–20.
35 Markham, *Cavelarice*, I, p. 60; Blundeville, *The Fower Chiefyst Offices*, fos 29v–30r; Halfpenny, *The Gentleman's Jockey*, p. 101; Nicholas Morgan, *The Perfection of Horsemanship* (London, 1609), p. 98.
36 Halfpenny, *The Gentleman's Jockey*, p. 92; Markham, *Cavelarice*, I, pp. 73–4; Blundeville, *The Fower Chiefyst Offices*, fol. 29v; Cavendish, *A New Method*, pp. 94–5.
37 Cavendish, *A New Method*, p. 95; Markham, *Cavelarice*, I, pp. 73–4; Michael Baret, *An Hipponomie or the Vineyard of Horsemanship* (London, 1618), pp. 48–9.
38 Halfpenny, *The Gentleman's Jockey*, p. 99; Edward Topsell, *The Historie of Foure-Footed Beastes* (London, 1607), p. 302.
39 Warwickshire Record Office, Newdigate MSS, CR 136/B/1024; C.M. Prior, *Early Records of the Thoroughbred* (London, 1924), p. 129; Herefordshire Record Office, Coningsby MSS, W15/2. I am grateful to Julian Tonks for this reference; Norton Conyers Hall, Indenture, 30 September 1623. I am grateful to Sir Richard Graham for allowing me access to his family's

muniments; TNA, E 101/533/14, SP 46/83, fol. 51; Nottingham University Library, MSS Department, Newcastle of Clumber MSS, Walter to the Earl of Clare at Clare House, Drury Lane, 2 August 1662.
40 J. Fairfax-Blakeborough, *Northern Turf History*, I (London, 1949), pp. 37, 50.
41 Astley, *The Art of Riding*, pp. 56–7.
42 Staffordshire Record Office, Paget MSS, D[W] 1734/4/1/6; Herefordshire Record Office, Foley of Stoke Edith MSS, FH/111/13 Norfolk R.O., Hare of Stoke Bardolph MSS, Hare 5284.
43 Norfolk Record Office, Hare MSS, Hare 5284; Northamptonshie Record Office, Cartwright MSS, C[A] 3489.
44 *Letters and Papers of Henry VIII*, III, pt 1 *1521–23*, p. 199; Thirsk, *Horses*, pp. 11–12, 16; *HMC*, 'Pepys MSS' (London, 1911), p. 18.
45 Markham, *Countrey Contentments*, II, p. 35; Graham, 'Horses in Early Modern England', pp. 127, 130, 132–3.
46 Morgan, *Horse-manship*, p. 98.
47 Markham, *Cavelarice*, I, p. 51.
48 As this fair was being held in the spring, many of the other horses were so described and this should be borne in mind when examining the figures. Summer and autumn fairs often listed horses as 'past' a certain age or added to the age 'and advantage'.
49 Markham, *Cavelarice*, I, p. 60.
50 Norton Conyers MSS.
51 A. Hyland, *The Horse in the Middle Ages* (Thrupp, 1999), pp. 20, 28.
52 Bristol Record Office, Smyth family MSS, AC/C46/9. I am grateful to Dr Joe Bettey for this reference. Lincolnshire Archives Office, Massingberd of Mumby MSS, MM 6/1/5.
53 Cited in Longrigg, *English Squire*, p. 57.
54 Blundeville, *The Fower Chiefyst Offices*, fol. 22r; Blundeville, *Arte of Rydynge*, 9v–10r.
55 Wells and Taylor, *The Oxford Shakespeare, Henry VIII*, act 5, scene 2, lines 53–8.
56 Cholmeley of Brandsby, p. 221.
57 Hyland, *The Horse in the Middle Ages*, pp. 64–5.
58 Ibid., p. 65; Blundeville, *Arte of Rydynge*, fos 9v–10r; Astley, *The Art of Riding*, p. 6.
59 Astley, *The Art of Riding*, pp. 6–7.
60 K. Thomas, *Man and the Natural World: Changing Attitudes in England, 1500–1800* (London, 1983), p. 45; B. Boehrer, *Shakespeare among the Animals* (Basingstoke, 2002), pp. 22–4.
61 Cited in L. Stone, *Family, Sex and Marriage in England, 1500–1800* (Harmondsworth, 1979), p. 121.
62 Ibid., p. 119.
63 D. Cressy, *Education in Tudor and Stuart England* (London, 1975), pp. 90–2; D.W. Sylvester, *Educational Documents, 800–1816* (London, 1970), p. 117–19; N.E. McClure, ed., *The Letters of John Chamberlain*, I (Philadelphia, 1939), p. 400.
64 L. Pollock, *Forgotten Children: Parent-Child Relations from 1500 to 1900* (Cambridge, 1983), passim; R. O'Day, *Education and Society, 1500–1800* (Harlow, 1982), p. 201; Cressy, *Education*, pp. 90–4.
65 Thomas, *Man and the Natural World*, pp. 101, 118, 143, 154–6, 188, 190; Leonard Mascall, *The Booke of Cattell* (London, 1587), p. 117.

66 Blundeville, *Arte of Rydynge*, fol. 7v; Markham, *Countrey Contentments*, II, pp. 37–41.
67 Mascall, *Booke of Cattell*, p. 117; Blundeville, *Arte of Rydynge*, fol. 9; Markham, *Cavelarice*, II, pp. 30, 46.
68 Astley, *The Art of Riding*, p. 6; Markham, *Countrey Contentments*, II, p. 41; A. Bryant, ed., *Postman's Horn: An Anthology of Letters of Latter Seventeenth-Century England* (London, 1946), p. 168. I am grateful to Ms Janet Heskins for this reference.
69 Markham, *Countrey Contentments*, II, p. 41.
70 Blundeville, *Arte of Rydynge*, fos 63r–63v; Markham, *Cavelarice*, IV, pp. 92–3, 96.
71 Markham, *Cavelarice*, IV, p. 95.
72 Cavendish, *A New Method*, pp. 42–3, 196, 198; LeGuin, 'Man and Horse in Harmony', in Raber and Tucker, *Culture of the Horse*, pp. 181–6.
73 M.M. Verney, ed., *Memoirs of the Verney Family*, IV, *1660–1696* (London, 1970) pp. 12, 166; S.E. Whyman, *Sociability and Power in Late-Stuart England: The Cultural Worlds of the Verneys, 1660–1720* (Oxford, 1999), pp. 15–16.
74 Verney Memorials, IV, p. 169.
75 Cholmeley of Brandsby, p. 216; *HMC, Portland MSS*, V (London, 1899), p. 598; *Verney Memorials*, III, *1650–1660*, p. 195.
76 Thomas de Gray, *The Compleat Horseman and Expert Ferrier* (London, 1639), I, sig. C2.
77 M.K. Geiter and W.A. Speck, eds, *Memoirs of Sir John Reresby* (London, 1991), p. 423.
78 Thomas Tryon, *The Country-Mans Companion* (London, 1683?), pp. 2–3.
79 Moon blindness: a recurring inflammation of the eye that made a horse intermittently blind.
80 J.H. Turner, ed., *The Reverend Oliver Heywood B.A.*, IV (Brighouse, 1885), p. 134.
81 Sheffield University Library, Hartlib MSS, 31/1/64–65.
82 *Verney Memoirs*, IV, p. 169.
83 Cholmeley of Brandsby, p. 142.
84 Lady E. Newton, *Lyme Letters, 1660–1760* (London, 1925), p. 185.
85 BL, Add. MS 70385 fos 37, 40, 77.
86 Wake and Webster, 'Letters of Daniel Eaton', p. 29.
87 *HMC*, 'Duke of Rutland MSS', II (London, 1889), p. 88.
88 J.T. Cliffe, *The World of the Country House in Seventeenth-Century England* (New Haven, 1999), pp. 130–1; E.S. De Beer, ed., *The Diary of John Evelyn*, III (Oxford, 1955), pp. 112–13, 525; *HMC, Marquis of Bath MSS*, IV (London, 1968), p. 308.
89 M. Exwood and H.L. Lehmann, eds, 'The Journal of William Schellink's Travels in England, 1661–1663', *Camden Society*, 5th series, 1 (1993), pp. 32–3.
90 Halfpenny, *The Gentleman's Jockey*, p. 101.
91 Morgan, *Horse-manship*, p. 98; East Sussex Record Office, Blomfield of Stonham MSS, HD 330/7; TNA, C3/141/98.
92 Tryon, *Country-Mans Companion*, p. 3; Thomas Bedingfield, *The Art of Riding* (London, 1584), pp. 96–8; John Lawrence, *A Philosophical and Practical Treatise on Horses, and on the Moral Duties of Man towards the Brute Creation*, I (London, 1796), pp. 144–50.
93 For example: TNA, Requests 2/157/163, 2/162/16, 2/396/80; Chancery C1/1009/58, C23/141/98.
94 TNA, C1/1009/58.

95 F.J. Furnivall, ed., 'Harrison's Description of England', III, 'The Supplement', *New Shakespeare Society*, series 6, no. 8 (1881), p. 271.
96 J.E. Ward, 'John Spedding's Accounts of Horses Used in the Whitehaven Colleries etc., from 1715 Onwards', *Transactions of the Cumberland and Westmormorland Antiquarian and Archaeological Society*, 89 (1989), p. 182; Cumbria Record Office (Carlisle), Lowther MSS, D/LONS/W/unlisted.
97 D. Gerhold, *Carriers and Coachmasters: Trade and Travel before the Turnpikes* (Chichester, 2005), pp. 46–7.
98 TNA, Req 2/308/1. One carried 2½ cwts and the other 2 cwts.
99 Thomas, *Man and the Natural World*, p. 101, citing John Stow, *A Survey of ... London*, John Strype, ed., (1720), I, p. 49; BL, Lansdowne MS 38/35.
100 John Flavell, *Husbandry Spiritualized* (London, 1669), p. 206.
101 John Evelyn, *Acetaria: A Discourse of Sallets* (London, 1699), pp. 140–2.
102 Essex Record Office, Q/SR 53/30, 56/20.
103 William Horman, *Vulgaria* (London, 1519), fol. 248v.
104 James Howell, *Instructions for Forreine Travell* (London, 1642), p. 194.
105 H. Robinson, *The British Post Office: An History* (New Jersey, 1948), pp. 13–14.
106 W. Rye, 'Depositions Taken before the Mayor and Aldermen of Norwich, 1549–67', *Norfolk and Norwich Archaeological Society* (1905), p. 79.
107 *HMC*, 'Portland MSS', III (London, 1894), p. 163.
108 Thomas, *Man and the Natural World*, p. 144.
109 E. Fudge, *Perceiving Animals: Humans and Beasts in Early Modern English Culture* (Basingstoke, 2000), pp. 11–15.
110 De Beer, *John Evelyn*, III, pp. 491–2.
111 Thomas, *Man and the Natural World*, pp. 97–8.
112 De Beer, *John Evelyn*, III, pp. 491–2.
113 Warwickshire Record Office, Warwick Castle MSS, 1886/411; Hertfordshire Record Office, Wittewronge MSS, D/ELW F20; Norfolk Record Office, Pratt of Ryston MSS, NRO m/f reel 219/1); M. Reed, ed., 'Buckinghamshire Probate Inventories, 1661–1714', *Buckinghamshire Record Society*, 24 (1988), p. 181.
114 Thomas, *Man and the Natural World*, pp. 49–50, 184.
115 S. Hindle, *On the Parish? The Micro-Politics of Poor Relief in Rural England, c. 1550–1750* (Oxford, 2004), pp. 35–48; J.M. Neeson, *Commoners: Common Right, Enclosure and Social Change in England, 1700–1820* (Cambridge, 1993), pp. 5, 40, 162, 170, 181.
116 B. Howells, ed., 'A Calendar of Letters Relating to North Wales 1533–c.1700', *Board of Celtic Studies, University of Wales History and Law Series*, 23 (Cardiff, 1967), p. 202.
117 Sheffield University Library, Hartlib MSS, 31/1/64–5
118 Wells and Taylor, *The Oxford Shakespeare, The Taming of the Shrew*, act 3, scene 2, lines 49–55.
119 Thirsk, *Horses*, pp. 20–1.
120 L.H. Curth, 'Seventeenth-Century English Almanacs: Transmitters of Advice for Sick Animals', in W. de Blécourt and C. Usborne, eds, *Cultural Approaches to the History of Medicine: Mediating Medicine in Early Modern and Modern Europe* (Basingstoke, 2004), p. 59.

121 Bagley, 'Diurnal of Nicholas Blundell', I, pp. 165, 211, 218.
122 Curth, 'Almanacs', pp. 65–6; L.H. Curth, 'The Care of the Brute Beast: Animals and the Seventeenth-Century Medical Market-Place, *The Society for the Social History of Medicine*, 15, pt. 3 (2002), pp. 383, 385.
123 Staffordshire Record Office, Paget MSS, D[W] 1734/3/3/276, 279; A.C. Edwards, *John Petre, 1549–1613* (London, 1975), p. 66.
124 Curth, 'The Care of the Brute Beast', p. 383; D. Gardiner, ed., *The Oxinden Letters, 1607–1642* (London, 1933), p. 146.
125 Staffordshire Record Office, Paget MSS, D[W] 1734/3/4/177; TNA, SP 12/24, no. 59.
126 Cholmeley of Brandsby, p. 125; Bagley, 'Diurnal of Nicholas Blundell', II, p. 26.
127 Shropshire Record Office, Forester MSS, 1224/box 205, Wellington Manor Court Book 1690–1704; Warwickshire Record Office, Newdigate MSS, CR 136/B/5158.
128 Curth, 'The Care of the Brute Beast', pp. 383, 387–8; Anon., *The English Farrier or Countrymans Treasure* (London, 1636), title page; William Poole, *The Countrey Farrier* (London, 1648), p. A3; Cumbria Record Office (Carlisle), Browne MSS vol. 8, p. 3, typescript p. 59.
129 Nottingham University Library, MSS Department, 'Portland MSS', Pw V4; Cumbria Record Office (Carlisle), Lowther MSS, D/Lons/L/A1/4a.
130 J.P. Hore, *The History of Newmarket and the Annals of the Turf*, III (London, 1886), pp. 223, 287; Northamptonshire Record Office, Fitzwilliam Correpondence F[M]C 1080.
131 Elecampane was used as an expectorant and liquorice powder as a laxative.
132 Hore, *Newmarket*, III, pp. 223, 287; HMC, 'Portland MSS', III (London, 1894), p. 604; Bagley, 'Diurnal of Nicholas Blundell', III, p. 230.
133 Derbyshire Record Office, Chandos-Pole-Gell MSS, D258/box 29/44b.
134 BL, Add. MS 22149; HMC, *12th Report, Appendix part VII*, 'MSS of S.H. Le Fleming Esq. of Rydall Hall' (London, 1890), p. 382.

Notes to Chapter 4: Horse Riding and Status

1 S. Wells and G. Taylor, eds, *The Oxford Shakespeare: The Complete Works* (Oxford, 1994), *Richard III*, act 5, scene 4, lines 7–13.
2 E. Cruickshanks, *The Glorious Revolution* (Basingstoke, 2000), p. 89; HMC, 'Portland MSS', IV (1897), p. 570.
3 J.J. Bagley, ed., 'The Great Diurnal of Nicholas Blundell of Little Crosby, Lancashire', I, '1702–11', *Record Society of Lancashire & Cheshire*, 110 (1968), p. 144; III, '1720–29, 114 (1972), p. 217.
4 Ibid., I, p. 194; II, '1712–19, 112 (1970), pp. 55, 96, 259.
5 BL, Add. MSS 70385, fol. 109; 70386, fo 51.
6 Thomas Blundeville, *The Fower Chiefyst Offices belonging to Horsemanship* (London, 1565), fol. 11r.
7 See above.
8 Warwickshire Record Office, Newdigate MSS, CR136/V/142; A. Dent and D.M. Goodall, *A History of British Native Ponies* (London, 1988), p. 155.
9 P. Edwards, *The Horse Trade of Tudor and Stuart England* (Cambridge, 1988), p. 56.

10 Based on data in toll books which indicate gait for a significant proportion of the horses listed.
11 TNA, SP 46/48/fol. 78; Blundeville, *The Fower Chiefyst Offices*, fol. 6v.
12 TNA, SP 46/60, fol. 213.
13 Thomas Middleton and Thomas Dekker, *The Roaring Girl*, A. Gomme, ed. (London, 1976), act 3, scene 1, lines 62–5.
14 Staffordshire Record Office, D260/M/F/1/6/33.
15 *HMC, 9th Report*, 'Marquis of Salisbury MSS', XI (London, 1906), p. 13.
16 Worcestershire Record Office, Berkeley Family Household Account Book, b705:93/4; NLW, Sir Edward Owen MSS 73, Thomas Brereton's Accounts, 1662–3; NLW, Schedule of Powys Castle Correspondence, I, p. 12; F.G. Emmison, *Tudor Secretary: Sir William Petre at Court and Home* (London, 1961), p. 176; *HMC*, 'Duke of Rutland MSS', IV (London, 1905), p. 420; *HMC*, 'Marquis of Salisbury MSS', XI (London, 1906), p. 13; Nottingham University Library, MSS Department, Portland MSS, Pw V4–5, Accounts of Holles Family; Cumbria Record Office (Carlisle), Muncaster Castle MSS, D/PEN/202 Estate Account Book, 1660–94; Bishop T. Percy, *Earl of Northumberland's Household Book Begun 1512* (London, 1905), pp. 55, 345; TNA, Equitium Regis Accounts, E101/107/17; SP 12/233/69; C.M. Prior, *The Royal Studs of the Sixteenth and Seventeenth Centuries* (London, 1935), passim.
17 Blundeville, *The Fower Chiefyst Offices*, fos 6v, 9r; William Cavendish, *A New Method and Extraordinary Invention to Dress Horses* (London, 1667), p. 31; A. Dent and D.M. Goodall, *A History of British Native Ponies* (London, 1988), p. 158.
18 Blundeville, *The Fower Chiefyst Offices*, fos 12r–12v.
19 Richard Blome, *The Gentleman's Recreation*, II (London, 1686), p. 9; W.D. Cooper, ed., 'Letters of Henry Savile Esquire', *Camden Society* (1858), p. 160.
20 Cavendish, *A New Method*, p. 80.
21 Personal communication from Ann Hyland.
22 BL, Add. MS 70385, fol. 71.
23 Herefordshire Record Office, Coningsby MSS, W15/2. I am grateful to Julian Tonks for this reference.
24 D. Defoe, *A Tour through the Whole Island of Great Britain*, P. Rogers, ed. (Harmondsworth, 1971), p. 600.
25 Bagley, 'Diurnal of Nicholas Blundell', I, pp. 36, 162, 164, 178, 210, 214, 261; II, '1712–19', 112 (1970), p. 108.
26 Dent and Goodall, *A History of British Native Ponies*, pp. 158–9; Nottingham University Library, MSS Department, Middleton MSS, Mi A 62; Bristol Record Office, AC/C46/9; Yorkshire Archaeological Society, Leeds, DD56/J3/2, 8: Accounts of Slingsby Family; Northamptonshire Record Office, Cartwright MSS, C[A] 3489.
27 *CSPV*, VI, pt 3, *1557–58*, p. 1672.
28 R.W. Ambler and B. and L. Watkinson, eds, 'Farmers and Fishermen, The probate inventories of the ancient parish of Clee, South Humberside 1536–1742', *Studies in Regional & Local History*, IV (Hull, 1987), p. 89; D. Hey, 'The North-West Midlands, in J. Thirsk, ed., *The Agrarian History of England and Wales*, V, *1640–1750*, pt 1 (Cambridge, 1984), p. 133.
29 Lincolnshire Archives Office, INV 40/431; INV 36/760; P.A. Kennedy, Nottinghamshire Household Inventories, *Thoroton Society, Record Series*, 22 (1963), pp. 61, 102.

30 Shropshire Record Office, Shrewsbury Quarter Sessions Papers, 2212; TNA, ASSI 45/8/2/76.
31 Estimated by the number of horses, so designated, together with those linked with saddles and bridles. The analysis is based on the following sets of probate inventories: H. Thwaite, ed., 'Abstracts of Abbotside Wills 1552–1688', *Yorkshire Archaeological Society*, Record Series, 130 (1967); J. Groves, *Ashton-on-Mersey and Sale Wills*, I, *1600–1650* (Sale, 1999), II, *1651–1700* (Sale, 2000), III, *1700–1760* (Sale, 2002); E.R.C. Brinkworth and J.S.W. Gibson, eds, 'Banbury Wills and Inventories', II, '1621–1850', *Banbury History Society*, 14 (1976); J.S. Roper, ed., *Belbroughton Wills and Probate Inventories, 1539–1647* (Dudley, 1967–68); J. Groves, *Bowden Wills*, I, *1600–1650* (Sale, 1997), II, *1651–1689* (Sale, 1998), III, *1690–1760* (Sale, 1999); Ambler and Watkinson, *Clee*; J.S. Moore, ed., *Clifton and Westbury Probate Inventories, 1609–1761* (Bristol, 1981); J.S. Roper, ed., *Dudley Probate Inventories, 1544–1603* (Dudley, 1965–66); J.S. Moore, ed., *The Good and Chattels of our Forefathers: Frampton Cotterell and District Probate Inventories, 1539–1804* (Chichester, 1976); Lincolnshire Archives Office, Horbling Probate Inventories; M. Reed, ed., 'The Ipswich Probate Inventories, 1583–1631', *Suffolk Record Society*, 22 (1981); D.G. Vaisey, ed., 'Probate Inventories of Lichfield and District, 1586–1680', *Staffordshire Record Society*, fourth series, V (1969); Steer, *Mid Essex*; West Suffolk Record Office, Mildenhall Probate Inventories; P.A. Kennedy, ed., 'Nottinghamshire Household Inventories', *Thoroton Society, Record Series*, 22 (1963); M.A. Havinden, 'Household and Farm Inventories in Oxfordshire', *Oxfordshire Record Society*, 44 (London, 1965); M. Parker, ed., *All My Worldly Goods* (St Albans, 1985); J.S. Roper, ed., *Sedgeley Probate Inventories, 1614–1787* (Dudley, 1960); H.C.F. Lansberry, ed., 'Sevenoaks Wills and Inventories in the Reign of Charles II', *Kent Archaeologocal Society, Kent Records*, 25 (1988); J.S. Roper, ed., *Stourbridge Probate Inventories 1541–1558* (Dudley, 1966); Neave, *Winteringham*.
32 Steer, *Mid-Essex Inventories*, p. 150.
33 Gervase Markham, *Cheape and Good Husbandry*, I (London, 1614), p. 5.
34 Steer, *Mid-Essex Inventories*, p. 205.
35 G.H. Kenyon, 'Kirdford Inventories, 1611 to 1776', *Sussex Archaeological Collections*, 93 (1955), p. 127.
36 *CSPV*, VI, pt 2, *1557–8*, p. 1670.
37 Bagley, 'Diurnal of Nicholas Blundell', I, p. 104; II, p. 58.
38 Cavendish, *A New Method*, pp. 11, 47.
39 R. Latham and W. Matthews, eds, *The Diary of Samuel Pepys*, VII, *1666* (London, 1972), p. 162.
40 P. Cunnington and A. Mansfield, *English Costume for Sports and Outdoor Recreation* (London, 1969), p. 107. I am grateful to Ms Lindsay Smith for this reference.
41 A view expressed by Ann Hyland.
42 Wells and Taylor, *The Oxford Shakespeare, The Taming of the Shrew*, act 4, scene 1, lines 60–1.
43 A. Dent, *Horses in Shakespeare's England* (London, 1987), p. 110.
44 Neave, *Winteringham*, p. 102; Steer, *Mid-Essex*, p. 217.
45 M.M. Verney, ed., *Memoirs of the Verney Family*, III, *1650–1660* (London, 1970), p. 222.

46 Bagley, 'Diurnal of Nicholas Blundell' I, pp. 77–9, 93, 97, 111, 114, 129, 238; II, pp. 21, 23, 44–5, 68, 96, 102; III, p. 129.
47 Ibid., II, p. 129.
48 Sir W.C. and C.E. Trevelyan, eds, 'Trevelyan Papers', III, *Camden Society*, 105 (1872), p. 23.
49 Bishop T. Percy, ed., *Household of Henry Algernon Percy*, p. 345.
50 TNA, SP 12/240, no. 79.
51 F.J.C. and D.M. Hearnshaw, eds, 'Court Leet Records', I, pt 2, '1578–1602', *Southampton Record Society* (1906), pp. 228–9, 243.
52 TNA, REQ 2/413/24.
53 Fynes Moryson, *An Itinerary*, III, bk 1 (London, 1617), p. 62; TNA, REQ 2/413/24; T.D. Whitaker, ed., *The Life and Original Correspondence of Sir George Radcliffe, knight, Ll.D.* (London, 1810), p. 67.
54 Cited in J. Crofts, *Packhorse, Waggon and Post* (London, 1967) p. 87; J. Ridley, *Elizabeth I: The Shrewdness of Virtue* (New York, 1988), p. 334.
55 Crofts, *Packhorse*, p. 86, citing J. Nichols, The *Progresses, Processions and Magnicient Festivities of King James the First*, II (London, 1828), p. 458.
56 H. Robinson, *The British Post Office: An History* (New Jersey, 1948), p. 7.
57 Ibid., pp. 16–20, 64.
58 Crofts, *Packhorse*, pp. 65–6; Robinson, *Post Office*, pp. 48–9.
59 Crofts, *Packhorse*, p. 71; Robinson, *Post Office*, p. 48.
60 Crofts, *Packhorse* p. 91; *HMC, 5th Report*, appendix, p. 566.
61 Cheshire Record Office, probate wills and inventories, Richard Annion of Chester, 1666.
62 Crofts, *Packhorse*, pp. 65, 84.
63 Ibid., pp. 65, 67–8, 84.
64 Ibid., p. 69.
65 Hearnshaw, 'Court Leet Records', p. 129.
66 Robinson, *Post Office*, pp. 15, 81.
67 Rye, 'Depositions at Norwich', p. 86; Hearnshaw, 'Court Leet Records', p. 200.
68 Verney, *Memoirs*, III, p. 346
69 Warwickshire Record Office, CR 136/box B/615–25.
70 HMC, 'Portland MSS', IX (1923), p. 58; Bagley, 'Diurnal of Nicholas Blundell', I, p. 118, 278; III, p. 29, 194.
71 TNA, ASSI 45/13/1/64; ASSI 45/6/3/15.
72 TNA, REQ 2/30/38.
73 Whitaker, *Life of Sir George Radcliffe*, p. 53.
74 Henry Peacham, *The Worth of a Peny: or a Caution to Keep Money* (London, 1647), p. 30; *The Complete Essays of Montaigne*, trans. D.A. Frame (Stanford, California, 1965), p. 747.
75 CSPD, *Elizabeth I, 1598–1601*, p. 481; P.L. Ralph, *Sir Humphrey Mildmay: Royalist Gentleman* (New Brunswick, 1947), p. 68.
76 Longrigg, *English Squire*, p. 57.
77 Reese, *Master of the Horse*, p. 160.
78 Thomas Bedingfield, *The Art of Riding* (London, 1584), fol. A2v.
79 Ibid., fos Aiiv–Aiiir.

80 J.M. Shuttleworth, ed., *The Life of Edward, First Lord Herbert of Cherbury, Written by Himself* (Oxford, 1976), p. 45.
81 R. Lockyer, *Buckingham: The Life and Political Career of George Villiers, First Duke of Buckingham, 1592–1628* (Harlow, 1981), p. 11; P.R. Seddon, ed., 'Letters of John Holles, 1587–1637', I, *Thoroton Society, Record Series*, 31 (1975), p. 104.
82 R. Strong, *Henry, Prince of Wales and England's Lost Renaissance* (London, 2000), pp. 41–2.
83 Ibid., pp. 42–4; *HMC, 10th Report*, IV, 'Earl of Kilmorrey MSS' (London, 1885), p. 366.
84 Cavendish, *A New Method*, p. 6.
85 *HMC*, 'Portland MSS', II (London, 1894), p. 366.
86 De Beer, ed., *John Evelyn*, I, p. 88; Worsley, *The British Stable*, pp. 70–1; *HMC*, 'Portland MSS', V (London, 1899), p. 532.
87 Markham, *Countrey Contentments*, I, p. 35; Thomas de Gray, *The Compleat Horseman and Expert Ferrier* (London, 1639), I, fol. C2.
88 Henry Peacham, *Coach and Sedan* (London, 1636), fol. E 4v.
89 Hore, *Newmarket*, III, p. 350.
90 B. Boehrer, *Shakespeare among the Animals* (Basingstoke, 2002), pp. 24–5.
91 E. Fudge, *Perceiving Animals: Humans and Beasts in Early Modern English Culture* (Basingstoke, 2000), p. 22; Boehrer, *Shakespeare*, p. 25; C. J. Adams, *Neither Man nor Beast: Feminism and the Defense of Animals* (New York, 1994), pp. 11–12.
92 Wells and Taylor, *The Oxford Shakespeare, The Comedy Of Errors*, 2, i, line 14.
93 J. Clutton-Brock, 'Aristotle, the Scale of Nature and Modern Attitudes to Animals', in A. Mack. ed., *Humans and Other Animals* (Columbus, Ohio, 1999), p. 11.
94 S. Mendelson and P. Crawford, *Women in Early Modern England* (Oxford, 1998), pp. 32–3.
95 Wells and Taylor, *The Oxford Shakespeare, The Comedy of Errors*, act 2, scene 1, lines 16–25.
96 E. Graham et al, eds, *Her Own Life: Autobiographical Writings by Seventeenth-Century Englishwomen* (London, 1989), pp. 7–8.
97 Richard Gough, *Antiquityes and Memoyres of the Parish of Myddle* (Shrewsbury, 1875), pp. 66, 130.
98 D. E. Underdown, 'The Taming of the Scold: The Enforcement of Patriarchal Authority in Early Modern England', in A. Fletcher and J. Steventon, eds, *Order & Disorder in Early Modern England* (Cambridge, 1985), pp. 116–21; L.E. Boose, 'Scolding Brides and Bridling Scolds: Taming the Woman's Unruly Member', in I. Kamps, ed., *Materialist Shakespeare: A History* (London, 1995), p. 244.
99 M. Ingram, 'Ridings, Rough Music and the "Reform of Popular Culture" in Early Modern England', *Past & Present*, 105 (1984), pp. 79–113.
100 Boose, 'Scolding', p. 258.
101 Wells and Taylor, *The Oxford Shakespeare, The Taming of the Shrew*, act 1, scene 2, lines 254–5.
102 Ibid., *The Taming of the Shrew*, act 5, scene 2, lines 128–38.
103 Ibid., *Antony and Cleopatra*, act 1, scene 5, line 21; *Henry IV*, Part 1, act 2, scene 3, lines 97–9; Boehrer, *Shakespeare*, pp. 24–5.

104 Boehrer, *Shakespeare*, pp. 25, 45.
105 D.G. Hey, *An English Rural Community: Myddle under the Tudors and Stuarts* (Leicester, 1974), p. 226; Gough, *Myddle*, pp. 132–3.
106 Wells and Taylor, *The Oxford Shakespeare, Venus and Adonis*, lines 260, 385–6, 404–7.
107 Boehrer, *Shakespeare*, p. 71.
108 Underdown, 'Taming of the Scold', p. 118.
109 Boehrer, *Shakespeare*, pp. 91–2.

Notes to Chapter 5: The Racecourse

1 R. Longrigg, *The English Squire and his Sport* (London, 1977), pp. 20–1.
2 Hereafter designated oriental.
3 D. and S. Lysons, *Magna Britannia*, II (London, 1810), pt 2, 'Cheshire', p. 899, state 1512 as the year; J. Fairfax-Blakeborough, *Northern Turf History*, I (London, 1949), p. 171.
4 P. Borsay, *The English Urban Renaissance: Culture and Society in the Provincial Town, 1660–1770* (Oxford, 1991), pp. 180–6, 355–67.
5 Francis Drake, *Eboracum: The History and Antiquities of the City of York* (1736 repr. East Ardsley, 1978), p. 241, cited in Borsay, *Urban Renaissance*, p. 182.
6 Charles Deering, *An Historical Account of the Ancient and Present State of the Town of Nottingham* (Nottingham, 1751), p. 76.
7 13 George II, c. 19; Borsay, *Urban Renaissance*, pp. 183–4.
8 Borsay, *Urban Renaissance*, pp. 184–5; A.J. Kettle, 'Lichfield Races', *Transactions of the Lichfield and South Staffordshire Archaeological & History Society*, 6 (1964–65), p. 4.
9 Borsay, *Urban Renaissance* p. 185; Deering, *Nottingham*, p. 76.
10 S.H.A.H., ed., *Letter Books of John Hervey, First Earl of Bristol 1651 to 1750*, I (Wells, 1894), p. 323.
11 N. Russell, *Like Engend'ring Like: Heredity and Animal Breeding in Early Modern England* (Cambridge, 1986), p. 19.
12 HMC, 'Duke of Rutland MSS', I (London, 1888), p. 63; Fairfax-Blakeborough, *Northern Turf History*, II, pp. 140–3.
13 Fairfax-Blakeborough, *Northern Turf History*, I, pp. 9–10.
14 Longrigg, *English Squire*, p. 84, citing Edward Webbe, *His Trauailes* (London, 1590), no page given.
15 Thomas Heywood, *The English Traveller* (1633, repr. New York, 1973), fol. F4r.
16 Borsay, *Urban Renaissance*, p. 195; Longrigg, *English Squire*, p. 84.
17 Borsay, *Urban Renaissance*, p. 195; J.P. Hore, *The History of Newmarket and the Annals of the Turf* (London, 1886), III, p. 107.
18 Borsay, *Urban Renaissance*, pp. 194–5.
19 Ibid., p. 185.
20 Shropshire Record Office, Shrewsbury Borough Records LIX/2211.
21 Leeds Archives Department, LAD Temple Newsam MSS, TN/EL/C 19; cited in Hore, *Newmarket*, III, p. 307; William Cavendish, *A New Method and Extraordinary Invention to Dress Horses* (London, 1667), p. 60.

22 Hore, *Newmarket*, III, p. 320.
23 Lincolnshire Archives Office, Monson MSS, MON 7/Misc. Book 7/13, fol. 175.
24 Hore, *Newmarket*, III, p. 293.
25 Borsay, *Urban Renaissance*, pp. 214–15.
26 M.E. Finch, 'Some Domestic Animals in the Reigns of Elizabeth and James I', *Northamptonshire Past and Present*, 1, pt 5 (1952), p. 38.
27 Hore, *Newmarket*, I, p. 86; E.S. De Beer, ed., *The Diary of John Evelyn*, III (Oxford, 1955), pp. 114–15 and footnote 6; Hore, *Newmarket*, III, p. 316.
28 Cheshire Record Office, Farndon MSS, DCH/J/40; J.J. Bagley, ed., 'The Great Diurnal of Nicholas Blundell of Little Crosby, Lancashire', I, '1702–11', *Record Society of Lancashire & Cheshire*, 110 (1968), p. 23, II, '1712–19', 112 (1970), pp. 237–8, 266, 268, III, 1720–29, 112, 114 (1972), pp. 52, 129, 190, 193; Hore, *Newmarket*, III, pp. 300, 310–13, 318, 321, 324, 330–1.
29 Longrigg, *The English Squire*, p. 85.
30 Hore, *Newmarket*, I, p. 338; III, p. 154, citing *London Gazette*, 24–27 July 1682.
31 Borsay, *Urban Renaissance*, p. 187; Longrigg, *The English Squire* p. 55; A.P.M. Wright, 'Sport: Horse-Racing', in C.R. Elrington, ed., *A History of the County of Cambridgeshire*, V (London, 1973), p. 279.
32 Borsay, *Urban Renaissance*, pp. 187–8; Wright, 'Sport', p. 280.
33 Borsay, *Urban Renaissance*, pp. 186–7.
34 Ibid., pp. 188–190; D. Defoe, *A Tour through the Whole Island of Great Britain*, ed., P. Rogers (Harmondsworth, 1971), pp. 452, 456.
35 Borsay, *Urban Renaissance*, pp. 189, 193–4.
36 Ibid., pp. 195, 302.
37 John Cheny, *A Historical List of All Horse-Matches Run* (London, 1741), passim.
38 M.W. Jones, *The Derby* (London, 1979), p. 20; Wright, 'Sport: Horse Racing', p. 279.
39 Borsay, *Urban Renaissance*, pp. 302–5.
40 R.W. Malcolmson, *Popular Recreations in English Society, 1700–1850* (Cambridge, 1973), p. 51.
41 Borsay, *Urban Renaissance*, p. 304.
42 N. Marlow, trans., 'The Diary of Thomas Isham of Lamport', *Northamptonshire Record Society*, 17 (1955), pp. 99–100.
43 J.B. Muir, *Ye Olde New-Markitt Calendar of Matches, Results and Programs from 1619 to 1719* (London, 1892), p. 24; Hore, *Newmarket*, III, p. 44.
44 Defoe, *Tour*, p. 99.
45 De Beer, *John Evelyn*, III, p. 596.
46 S.H.A.H., ed., *Letter Books of John Hervey*, I, pp. 322, 324; S.H.A.H., *The Diary of John Hervey First Earl of Bristol 1651 to 1750 with Extracts from his Book of Expenses 1688 to 1742* (Wells, 1894), pp. 57–8.
47 *HMC, 12th Report*, 'Duke of Rutland MSS', I (London, 1888), p. 137.
48 *HMC*, 'MSS in Various Collections', IV (London, 1907), p. 229.
49 S. Wells and G. Taylor, eds, *The Oxford Shakespeare: The Complete Works* (Oxford, 1994), *Cymbeline*, act 3, scene 2, lines 68–74.
50 Hore, *Newmarket*, I, p. 352; II, p. 267; III, pp. 305, 308.
51 M.K. Geiter and W.A. Speck, eds, *Memoirs of Sir John Reresby* (London, 1991), pp. 259, 333.

52 Hore, *Newmarket*, III, pp. 319, 332; Borsay, *Urban Renaissance*, p. 177.
53 K. Thomas, *Man and the Natural World: Changing Attitudes in England, 1500–1800* (London, 1983), pp. 153–160; Borsay, *Urban Renaissance*, p. 178.
54 *HMC*, 'Portland MSS', IV (London, 1897), pp. 429, 591; Norfolk Record Office, Bradfer Lawrence MSS VI b 2.
55 Hore, *Newmarket*, II, p. 284, citing *The Travels of Cosmo III, Grand Duke of Tuscany through England 1669* (London 1821); Defoe, *Tour*, p. 168.
56 C. Abdy, *Epsom Past* (Chichester, 2001), p. 14; C. Morris, ed., *The Journeys of Celia Fiennes* (London, 1947), p. 236.
57 Borsay, *Urban Renaissance*, pp. 191–2; Defoe, *Tour*, p. 168.
58 Fairfax-Blakeborough, *Northern Turf History*, III, p. 31.
59 Borsay, *Urban Renaissance*, p. 193.
60 Hore, *Newmarket*, III, pp. 312, 315, 322, 333.
61 J. Spurr, *English Puritanism, 1603–1689* (Basingstoke, 1998), p. 72; H.N. Brailsford, *The Levellers and the English Revolution* (London, 1961), p. 122 ff.
62 Finch, 'Some Domestic Animals', p. 38.
63 Thomas, *Man and the Natural World*, p. 158; Thomas Tryon, *The Country-Mans Companion* (London, 1683), p. 1.
64 *CSPD, 1671–72*, p. 216; John Lawrence, *A Philosophical and Practical Treatise on Horses, and on the Moral Duties of Man towards the Brute Creation*, I (London, 1796), pp. 146–7.
65 J.M. Shuttleworth, ed., *The Life of Edward, First Lord Herbert of Cherbury, Written by Himself* (Oxford, 1976), p. 35.
66 C. Durston, *Cromwell's Major-Generals: Godly Government during the English Revolution* (Manchester, 2001), p. 18; *CSPD, January to October 1655*, p. 53; *CSPD, 1655–56*, p. 103.
67 Durston, *Major-Generals*, pp. 157–8, 178.
68 R. Hutton, *Charles II* (Oxford, 1989), pp. 399–400.
69 J.R. Western, *The English Militia in the Eighteenth Century: The Story of a Political Issue 1660–1802* (London, 1965), pp. 56, 62; *CSPD, 1682*, pp. 370, 389, 393; Hore, *Newmarket*, III, pp. 164–6.
70 *CSPD, 1682*, p. 393.
71 A.J. Kettle, 'Lichfield Races', *Transactions of the Lichfield and South Staffordshire Archaeological and Historical Society*, 6 (1964–5), pp. 39, 41.
72 Hore, *Newmarket*, III, pp. 332, 341.
73 Ibid., pp. 304–41.
74 D. Wilkinson, *Early Horse Racing in Yorkshire and the Origins of the Thoroughbred* (York, 2003), p. 40.
75 Ibid., pp. 50–4.
76 Bagley, 'Diurnal of Nicholas Blundell, II, p. 237; Hore, II, p. 278; J.R. Witty, 'Documents relating to Beverley and District', *Yorkshire Archaeological Journal*, 36 (1944–47), p. 119.
77 D. Laird, *Royal Ascot* (London, 1976), p. 16.
78 Wright, 'Sport', p. 280; '*HMC*, Portland MSS', VI (London, 1901), p. 89.
79 Wright, 'Sport', p. 280; Hore, *Newmarket*, I, p. 334.
80 Wright, 'Sport', p. 280; Hore, *Newmarket*, III, p. 155; Bagley, 'Diurnal of Nicholas Blundell', II, p. 237.

81   Hore, *Newmarket*, I, p. 85; Lincolnshire Archives Office, Lincoln Corporation Minute Book LI/I/I/4; De Beer, *John Evelyn*, III, pp. 114–15.
82   Wright, 'Sport', p. 280.
83   Borsay, *Urban Renaissance*, p. 305; For York, Wilkinson, *Early Horse Racing in Yorkshire*, p. 49.
84   Bagley, 'Diurnal of Nicholas Blundell, I, p. 23.
85   Wilkinson, *Early Horse Racing in Yorkshire*, p. 34.
86   Muir, *New-Markitt Calendar*, passim.
87   Hore, *Newmarket*, III, pp. 303, 310, 315.
88   Ibid., III, p. 313.
89   Ibid., II, p. 246; III, p. 154.
90   Nottingham University Library, MSS Department, Portland MSS, Ne E8.
91   Wilkinson, *Early Horse Racing in Yorkshire*, p. 52.
92   Borsay, *Urban Renaissance*, p. 182; Hore, *Newmarket*, III, pp. 306–7, 308, 310, 312, 315, 321–2, 333.
93   Cheny, *Horse-Matches Run*, passim; Hore, *Newmarket*, III, p. 248.
94   *HMC*, 'Portland MSS', V (London, 1899), pp. 325–6.
95   Defoe, *A Tour*, p. 524; S.H.A.H. *Hervey's Letter Books*, I, pp. 57–8; Nottingham University Library, MSS Department, Portland MSS, Ne E8; Hore, *Newmarket*, I, p. 86. At Hambleton the donation of a gold cup was discontinued in 1720 and replaced with 100 guineas in specie: Wilkinson, *Early Horse Racing in Yorkshire* p. 42.
96   Hore, *Newmarket*, III, pp. 299–300, 304, 314, 320, 323, 328, 331–2, 336–40.
97   Wilkinson, *Early Horse Racing in Yorkshire*, p. 36.
98   Muir, *New-Markitt Calendar*, pp. 35, 39, 43, 48, 53, 57; Wilkinson, *Early Horse Racing in Yorkshire*, p. 44.
99   E. Graham, 'Reading, Writing, and Riding Horses in Early Modern England: James Shirley's *Hyde Park* (1632) and Gervase Markham's *Cavelarice* (1607)', in E. Fudge, ed., *Renaissance Beasts: Of Animals, Humans, and other Wonderful Creatures* (Urbana and Chicago, Illinois, 2004), pp. 119–25; Hore, *Newmarket*, II, p. 128.
100 Muir, *New-Markitt Calendar*, pp. 20–58.
101 Bagley, 'Diurnal of Nicholas Blundell', passim.
102 Based on an analysis of races listed in Muir, *New-Markitt Calendar* and Hore, *Newmarket*.
103 Muir, *New-Markitt Calendar*, p. 30; Hore, *Newmarket*, III, pp. 228–9.
104 S.H.A.H., *Lord Hervey's Diary*, p. 44.
105 It had also won the plate at Crosby on 29 August, probably running three times that day, and at Knowsley Park on 1 September: Bagley, 'Diurnal of Nicholas Blundell', III, pp. 193, 195.
106 Muir, *New-Markitt Calendar*, pp. 28, 32.
107 A. Bryant, ed., *Postman's Horn: An Anthology of the Letters of the Latter Seventeenth Century England* (London, 1936), p. 170. I am grateful to Ms Janet Heskey for this reference. Hore, *Newmarket*, III, p. 333.
108 Muir, *New-Markitt Calendar*, pp. 18–19; S.H.A.H., *Lord Hervey's Diary*, pp. 14, 18.
109 Muir, *New-Markitt Calendar*, pp. 35, 39, 48.

110 Hore, *Newmarket*, III, pp. 299, 300; F.R. Raines, ed., 'The Journal of Nicholas Assheton of Downham ... 1617', *Chetham Society* (1948), p. 27.
111 Hore, *Newmarket*, I, pp. 60–1.
112 Muir, *New-Markitt Calendar*, p. 20, 28; Longrigg, *The English Squire*, p. 85.
113 Muir, *New-Markitt Calendar*, p. 38.
114 Hore, *Newmarket*, II, p. 324–5.
115 S.H.A.H., *Lord Hervey's Diary*, pp. 28, 41; S.H.A.H., *Lord Hervey's Letter Book*, I, p. 137.
116 Defoe, *A Tour*, p. 98.
117 Muir, *New-Markitt Calendar*, p. 27.
118 Marlow, 'Isham's Diary', p. 231; Bagley, 'Diurnal of Nicholas Blundell', III, p. 25.
119 See Graham, 'Reading, Writing, and Riding Horses', pp. 119–25.
120 Defoe, *A Tour*, p. 98.
121 Ibid., p. 98.
122 Wilkinson, *Early Horse Racing in Yorkshire*, p. 35; Hore, *Newmarket*, III, p. 215; *HMC*, 'Portland MSS', V (London, 1899), p. 488.
123 James Shirley, *Hyde Park* (London, 1632), fol. G4r. I am grateful to Dr Kevin de Ornellas for this reference.
124 North Yorkshire Record Office, Sir William Chaytor of Croft Hall MSS, D/Ch/C/793.
125 S.H.A.H., *Hervey's Letter Book*, I, p. 137; Muir, *New-Markitt Calendar*, p. 27.
126 Lawrence, *Treatise on Horses*, I, p. 146.
127 Thomas Blundeville, *The Fower Chiefyst Offices belonging to Horsemanship* (London, 1565), fol. 12v; E. Tobey, 'The *Palio* Horse in Renaissance and Early Modern Italy', in K. Raber and T. Tucker, eds, *The Culture of the Horse: Status, Discipline, and Identity in the Early Modern World* (Basingstoke, 2005), p. 68–9.
128 Gervase Markham, *How to Chuse, Ride, Traine, and Diet both Hunting-Horses and Running Horses* (London, 1599), fol. A3v.
129 Cavendish, *A New Method*, pp. 54, 56, 69, 73.
130 BL, Add. MS 70143, fos 179v–181v, 183v, 194r, 215v–216r, 223r, 225r–226r, 227r, 239r, 246r, 275r, 287r, 305r–305v.
131 Ibid., fos 179v–180r; D. Landry, 'The Bloody Shouldered Arabian and Early Modern English Culture', *Criticism*, 46, i (2004), p. 53.
132 C.M. Prior, *Early Records of the Thoroughbred* (London, 1924), p. 126; R. Nash, '"Honest English Breed": The Thoroughbred as Cultural Metaphor', in Raber and Tucker, *The Culture of the Horse*, pp. 248–50.
133 T.S. Willan, *Studies in Elizabethan Foreign Trade* (Manchester, 1959), p. 299.
134 Cavendish, *A New Method*, p. 69.
135 BL, Add. MS 70143, fol. 275r; R. Davis, *The Rise of the English Shipping Industry in the Seventeenth and Eighteenth Centuries* (Newton Abbot, 1962), pp. 251–2.
136 De Beer, *John Evelyn*, IV p. 398.
137 TNA, E351/1762.
138 D.M. Goodall, *A History of Horse Breeding* (London, 1977), p. 231; Hore, *Newmarket*, I, p. 71; Tobey, 'Palio Horse', pp. 74–5.
139 R. Lockyer, *Buckingham: The Life and Political Career of George Villiers, First Duke of Buckingham 1592–1628* (Harlow, 1981), p. 26; C.M. Prior, *The Royal Studs of the Sixteenth*

and Seventeenth Centuries (London, 1935), pp. 72–4; Hore, Newmarket, II, p. 54; Nash, 'Thoroughbred', pp. 249–50.
140   Hore, Newmarket, II, p. 212; Nash, 'Thoroughbred', pp. 249–50; Tobey, 'Palio Horse', p. 69.
141   Hore, Newmarket, III, p. 25; CSPD, May 1684 to 5 February 1685, p. 128. Suz, now a province of Morocco, was then an independent kingdom.
142   HMC, 'Marquis of Salisbury MSS', XIV (London, 1923), p. 177; HMC, 'Rutland MSS', I (London, 1888), p. 421.
143   Wilkinson, Early Horse Racing in Yorkshire, p. 14 for Darley; BL, Add. MS 70143, fos 225r–226r, 239r, 246r for the Dun Arabian and fos 287v, 288r, 305r for the Bloody Shouldered Arabian.
144   Wilkinson, Early Horse Racing in Yorkshire, pp. 6–7; BL, Add. MS 70386, fol. 101.
145   Gervase Markham, Cavelarice, VI (London, 1607), p. 2; Tobey, 'Palio Horse', pp. 70–1.
146   N. Russell, Heredity and Animal Breeding in Early Modern England (Cambridge, 1986), pp. 102–3.
147   Ibid., pp. 84–5, 96.
148   Cavendish, A New Method, p. 92.
149   Wilkinson, Early Horse Racing in Yorkshire, pp. 12–14.
150   Nottingham University Library, MSS Department, Pw2.325–344; Prior, Thoroughbred, pp. 29–35.
151   S.H.A.H.. Lord Hervey's Diary, p. 45.
152   Prior, Thoroughbred, pp. 125–6; Nottingham University Library, MSS Department, Pw 2/340.
153   Defoe, A Tour, p. 512.
154   Cheny, Horse-Matches Run, passim; Salop Journal, 30 July 1817, 29 July 1846.
155   Nash, 'Thoroughbred', p. 257.
156   Nash, 'Thoroughbred', p. 257; www.tbheritage.com.
157   Cited in Nash, 'Thoroughbred', p. 257.
158   HMC, 12th Report, 'MSS of Captain Stewart of Alltyrodyn, Llandyssil' (London, 1890), p. 110.
159   See activities of Sir Cuthbert Routh of Snape Hall, Bedale, in Prior, Thoroughbred, pp. 29–35.
160   Defoe, Tour, p. 400.
161   Letters and Papers of Henry VIII, 14, pt 1, 1539, pp. 425–6.
162   Prior, Thoroughbred, p. 129.

Notes to Chapter 6: Preparation for War

1   A. Young, Tudor and Jacobean Tournaments (Dobbs Ferry, New York, 1987), pp. 28, 33.
2   Letters and Papers of Henry VIII, I, pt 1, 1509–13, p. 284.
3   Young, Tudor and Jacobean Tournaments, p. 46. The coronel was a crown-like safety device.
4   James I, 'Basilicon Doron', The Workes (London, 1616), pp. 185–6.

NOTES TO PAGES 120–123

5   R. Longrigg, *The English Squire and his Sport* (London, 1977), pp. 79–80, 90; D. Landry, *The Invention of the Countryside: Hunting, Walking and Ecology in English Literature, 1671–1831* (Basingstoke, 2001), pp. 73–6.
6   R. Carr, *English Fox Hunting: A History* (London, 1976), p. 21; R. Almond, *Medieval Hunting* (Thrupp, 2003), pp. 34, 64.
7   George Gascoigne, *The Noble Arte of Venerie or Hunting* (London, 1575), p. 162.
8   Landry, *Countryside*, p. 158.
9   For hares: Gascoigne, *Venerie*, p. 162; for foxes: Sir Thomas Elyot, *The Boke Named the Governour* (London, 1531), fol. 72v.
10 Carr, *Fox Hunting*, pp. 24–5.
11 Gascoigne, *Venerie*, p. 162.
12 Elyot, *Governour*, fol. 72v; Carr, *Fox Hunting*, p. 24; J.J. Bagley, 'The Great Diurnal of Nicholas Blundell of Little Crosby, Lancashire', I, '1702–11', *Record Society of Lancashire & Cheshire* (1968), pp. 44, 120, 235 and passim.
13 E. Berry, *Shakespeare and the Hunt: A Cultural and Social Study* (Cambridge, 2001), p. 18; Longrigg, *The English Squire*, p. 76.
14 Strictly speaking, a male peregrine falcon but often used, as here, as the male of a species.
15 Almond, *Medieval Hunting*, pp. 43–6; M. Vale, *The Gentleman's Recreations* (Cambridge, 1977), p. 43; M. S. Byrne, ed., *The Lisle Letters*, I (Chicago, 1981), p. 569.
16 Almond, *Medieval Hunting*, pp. 43, 45–6; Vale, *The Gentleman's Recreations*, p. 44.
17 HMC, 'Portland MSS', II (London, 1893), p. 258.
18 Carr, *Fox Hunting*, p. 17.
19 D. G. Hey, *An English Rural Community: Myddle under the Tudors and Stuarts* (Leicester, 1974), p. 9.
20 Gascoigne, *Venerie*, p. 188.
21 Landry, *The Invention of the Countryside*, p. 12.
22 Carr, *Fox Hunting*, pp. 50–4; R. Longrigg, *The History of Foxhunting* (London, 1975), pp. 68–9; S. Rees, *The Charlton Hunt: A History* (Chichester, 1998), passim.
23 G. Marvin, 'Unspeakability, Inedibility, and the Structures of Pursuit in the English Foxhunt', in Rothfels, *Representing Animals*, p. 144.
24 Marvin, 'Foxhunt', p. 144.
25 Carr, *Fox Hunting*, pp. 35–7; Longrigg, *Foxhunting*, p. 68.
26 HMC, *12th Report*, appendix, part VII, 'MSS of S.H. le Fleming of Rydal Hall' (London, 1890), p. 16.
27 Markham, *Countrey Contentments* (London, 1615), I, p. 7.
28 S. Wells and G. Taylor, eds, *The Oxford Shakespeare: The Complete Works* (Oxford, 1994), *A Midsummer Night's Dream*, act 4, scene 1, line 122.
29 The Lady Newcastle, *Poems and Fancies* (London, 1653), p. 112.
30 Carr, *Fox Hunting*, pp. 35–7; Longrigg, *Foxhunting*, p. 68.
31 Carr, *Fox Hunting*, p. 34; Longrigg, *Foxhunting*, p. 69.
32 Carr, *Fox Hunting*, p. 70.
33 John Cheny, *A Historical List of all Horse-Matches Run* (London, 1741), 1739 race list passim.

34 Staffordshire Record Office, Leveson-Gower MSS, D 593/P/16/1/3.
35 Cheny, *Horse-Matches Run*, 1739, p. 156; G. Worsley, *The British Stable* (New Haven and London, 2004), p. 133.
36 Carr, *Fox Hunting*, p. 30; D. Landry, 'The Bloody Shouldered Arabian and Early Modern English Culture', *Criticism*, 46, I (2004), pp. 47–8.
37 C. Morris, ed., *The Journeys of Celia Fiennes* (London, 1947), p. 5.
38 Landry, 'Bloody Shouldered Arabian', pp. 44–5; Carr, *Fox Hunting*, p. 30.
39 M.W. Myddelton, ed., *Chirk Castle Accounts, A.D. 1666–1753* (Manchester, 1931), p. 156.
40 Richard Blome, *The Gentleman's Recreation*, II (London, 1686), p. 8.
41 J.P Hore, *The History of Newmarket and the Annals of the Turf*, III (London, 1886), p. 227.
42 Gascoigne, *Venerie*, p. A4r.
43 Robert Burton, *The Anatomy of Melancholy* (London, 1621), pp. 158, 339.
44 J.T. Cliffe, *The World of the Country House in Seventeenth-Century England* (New Haven, 1999); J.M. Shuttleworth, ed., *The Life of Edward, First Lord Herbert of Cherbury, Written by Himself* (Oxford, 1976), p. 35.
45 TNA, E315/414.
46 *L & P of Henry VIII*, I, pt 1, *1509–13*, p. 58; IV, pt 2, *1526–8*, pp. 1084, 2065; XIII, pt 2, *1538*, p. 87; XVIII, pt 2, *1543*, pp. 19, 139.
47 J.G. Russell, *The Field of the Cloth of Gold* (London, 1969), p. 119; *L & P of Henry VIII*, XVI, pt 1, *1540–1*, pp. 147–8, 254.
48 C. Bingham, *James VI of Scotland* (London, 1979), pp. 75–6; A. Stewart, 'Government by Beagle: The Impersonal Rule of James VI and I', in E. Fudge, *Renaissance Beasts: Of Animals, Humans, and other Wonderful Creatures* (Urbana and Chicago, Illinois, 2004), pp. 103, 106; *CSPV, 1603–7*, p. 90.
49 S.J. Houston, *James I* (Harlow, 1995), pp. 101–15; James I, 'Basilicon Doron', *The Workes* (London, 1616), p. 186.
50 Longrigg, *The English Squire*, p. 41.
51 *L & P of Henry VIII*, II, pt 1, *1515–6*, p. 561.
52 Young, *Tudor and Jacobean Tournaments*, p. 28; R. Strong, *Henry, Prince of Wales and England's Lost Renaissance* (London, 2000), p. 44.
53 Young, *Tudor and Jacobean Tournaments*, p. 184.
54 Gascoigne, *Venerie*, pp. 109–40.
55 Cited in Berry, *Shakespeare and the Hunt*, p. 72.
56 Young, *Tudor and Jacobean Tournaments*, pp. 57, 70.
57 Ibid., p. 72; R. Strong, *The Cult of Elizabeth: Elizabethan Portraiture and Pageantry* (London, 1999), p. 138.
58 Young, *Tudor and Jacobean Tournaments*, pp. 61–4.
59 Worcestershire Record Office, Account Book of Casper Henning Esq., 705:366/B.A. 2252/6(i).
60 Burton, *Melancholy*, p. 158.
61 *HMC*, 'Portland MSS', IV (London, 1897), p. 612.
62 Shropshire Record Office, Forester MSS, 1224/296.
63 Northamptonshire Record Office, Cartwright of Aynho MSS, C[A] 3489.

NOTES TO PAGES 128–133

64 Essex Record Office, Petre MSS, D/DP/Z/3716.
65 Young, *Tudor and Jacobean Tournaments*, p. 46.
66 22 & 23 Charles II c. 25; Landry, *The Invention of the Countryside*, pp. 73–4.
67 Landry, *The Invention of the Countryside*, pp. 73–4; P.B. Munsche, *Gentlemen and Poachers* (Cambridge, 1981), p. 5.
68 Munsche, *Gentlemen and Poachers*, pp. 12–13, 16–19.
69 'The Memorandum Book of Richard Cholmeley of Brandsby, 1602–1623', *Yorkshire (North) R.O. Publication*, 44 (1988), p. 75.
70 TNA, PROB 4/1675; PROB 4/2802.
71 J.S. Cockburn, ed., *Calendar of Assize Records: Kent Indictments, Charles II* (London, 1995), pp. 179, 291, 370.
72 9 George I, c. 22; Munsche, *Gentlemen and Poachers*, pp. 21–3.
73 Young, *Tudor and Jacobean Tournaments*, pp. 11–15.
74 *L & P of Henry VIII*, III, pt 1, *1521–23*, p. 307.
75 *L & P of Henry VIII*, I, pt 2, *1513–14*, p. 1451; Young, *Tudor and Jacobean Tournaments*, pp. 15–16.
76 Young, *Tudor and Jacobean Tournaments*, p. 23.
77 G. Phillips, *The Anglo-Scots Wars, 1513–1550* (Woodbridge, 1999), p. 24.
78 Young, *Tudor and Jacobean Tournaments*, p. 23.
79 J.G. Nichols, 'The Chronicle of Calais (in the Reigns of Henry VII and Henry VIII to the Year 1540)', *Camden Society*, 35 (1846), p. 190.
80 Burton, *Melancholy*, pp. 339–40.
81 Longrigg, *Foxhunting*, p. 60.
82 Landry, *The Invention of the Countryside*, pp. 108–9, 173; Marvin, 'Foxhunt', p. 150.
83 Elyot, *Governour*, pp. 69v–71v.
84 Almond, *Medieval Hunting*, p. 66; Gascoigne, *Venerie*, pp. 110, 148–9.
85 Shuttleworth, *Herbert*, pp. 46–7.
86 Gascoigne, *Venerie*, p. 110; Edward of Norwich, *The Master of Game*, W.A. & F. Baillie-Grohman, eds, (London, 1909/repr. Philadelphia, 2005), p. 23.
87 Either by hamstringing the hart, followed by a thrust into the spinal column with a sword or knife, or by plunging a sword into the heart from behind the shoulder. Almond, *Medieval Hunting*, p. 74.
88 Berry, *Shakespeare and the Hunt*, p. 24.
89 A. Clark, ed., *Aubrey's Brief Lives*, II (Oxford, 1898), p. 267.
90 P. Young and R. Holmes, *The English Civil War* (London, 1974), pp. 44–5.
91 Elyot, *Governour*, pp. 71r–71v.
92 William Higford, *Institutions of Advice to his Grandson* (London, 1658), p. 90.
93 Elyot, *Governour*, pp. 72r–72v.
94 *CSPD, 1547–80*, p. 448.
95 Elyot, *Governour*, pp. 72v–73r.
96 Berry, *Shakespeare and the Hunt*, p. 24.
97 F.G. Emmison, *Tudor Secretary, Sir William Petre at Court and Home* (London, 1961), p. 223; Longrigg, *Foxhunting*, pp. 38–9; *L & P of Henry VIII*, XVI, pt 2, *1540–41*, p. 533.
98 Elyot, *Governour*, p. 68v.

99   *HMC, 10th. report, appendix, pt IV,* 'Earl of Kilmorrey MSS' (London, 1885), p. 366.
100 William Cavendish, *A New Method and Extraordinary Invention to Dress Horses* (London, 1667), pp. 5–6.
101 Shuttleworth, *Life*, pp. 33–4.
102 *HMC*, 'Rutland MSS', IV (London, 1905), p. 426.
103 *CSPD, Charles I, 1628–29*, p. 8; Shuttleworth, *Herbert*, pp. 34–5.
104 *L & P of Henry VIII*, I, pt 1, *1509–13*, p. 379; XV, *1540*, p. 300.
105 Young, *Tudor and Jacobean Tournaments*, pp. 30–1.
106 Berry, *Shakespeare and the Hunt*, pp. 42–3; Bagley, 'Diurnal of Nicholas Blundell', I, pp. 40, 45; II, '1712–19', 112 (1970), pp. 195–6, 224.
107 Myddelton, *Chirk Castle Accounts*, p. 75; Carr, *Fox Hunting*, p. 60.
108 M.K. Geiter and W.A. Speck, eds, *Memoirs of Sir John Reresby* (London, 1991), p. 464; T.J. McCann, 'The Correspondence of the Dukes of Richmond and Newcastle 1724–1750', *Sussex Record Society*, 73 (1982–3), p. 26.
109 Young, *Tudor and Jacobean Tournaments*, p. 27.
110 Cited in Landry, *The Invention of the Countryside*, pp. 154–5.
111 Berry, *Shakespeare and the Hunt*, p. 105.
112 Cholmeley of Brandsby, pp. 26–7, 176.
113 Landry, *The Invention of the Countryside*, p. 148; Gascoigne, *Venerie*, p. 125.
114 Wells and Taylor, *The Oxford Shakespeare, 3 Henry VI*, act 2, scene 5, lines 129–30.
115 Ibid., *1 Henry VI*, act 4, scene 2, lines 45–7, 49, 51–2.
116 Ibid., *Julius Caesar*, act 3, scene 1, lines 205–7.
117 Berry, *Shakespeare and the Hunt*, pp. 31–2.
118 N.E. McClure, *The Letters of John Chamberlain*, I (Philadelphia, Pennsylvania, 1939), pp. 570–1.
119 Wells and Taylor, *The Oxford Shakespeare, Titus Andronicus*, act 2, scene 2, lines 25–6; Berry, *Shakespeare and the Hunt*, p. 35.
120 Higford, *Institutions*, pp. 69–70.
121 R.L. Smallwood and S. Wells, eds, Thomas Dekker, *The Shoemaker's Holiday* (Manchester, 1979), scene 9, lines 44–7.
122 M. Hattaway, 'Male Sexuality and Misogyny', in C.M.S. Alexander and S. Wells, eds, *Shakespeare and Sexuality* (Cambridge, 2001), pp. 108–9; Young, *Tudor and Jacobean Tournaments*, p. 18
123 Wells and Taylor, *The Oxford Shakespeare, Romeo and Juliet*, act 1, scene 1, lines 18–33.
124 Strong, *Cult of Elizabeth I*, pp. 131, 133–5, 138–40.
125 Berry, *Shakespeare and the Hunt*, p. 32; H. Hackett, *Virgin Mother, Maiden Queen: Elizabeth and the Cult of the Virgin Mary* (Basingstoke, 1995), p. 97.
126 Berry, *Shakespeare and the Hunt*, pp. 31, 41–2.
127 B. Boehrer, *Shakespeare among the Animals* (Basingstoke, 2002), p. 71; Wells and Taylor, *The Oxford Shakespeare, All's Well That Ends Well*, act 2, scene 2, lines 19–20.
128 Wells and Taylor, *The Oxford Shakespeare, As You Like It*, act 4, scene 1, lines 59–60.
129 Ibid., *The Taming of the Shrew*, act 4, scene 1, lines 177–8, 184.
130 Ibid., *The Taming of the Shrew*, act 5, scene 2, lines 54–5, 57–8.
131 Berry, *Shakespeare and the Hunt*, p. 114.

132 Young, *Tournaments*, pp. 14, 24–5.
133 Young, *Tudor and Jacobean Tournaments*, pp. 153–4; Hackett, *Virgin Mother*, p. 88.
134 *L & P of Henry VIII*, XX, pt 2, *1545*, pp. 64–5.
135 J.J. Scarisbrick, *Henry VIII* (London, 1988), pp. 445–55; P. Croft, *King James* (Basingstoke, 2003), pp. 109–110.
136 Cholmeley of Brandsby, pp. 212–13.
137 *L & P of Henry VIII*, XXI, pt 1, *1546*, p. 653; XVI, pt 2, *1541*, p. 17.
138 *L & P of Henry VIII*, XII, pt 2, *1537*, p. 479.
139 *CSPD, 1581–90*, p. 269; HMC, 'Rutland MSS', I (London, 1888), p. 492.
140 J. Payne Collier, ed., 'The Egerton Papers', *Camden Society*, 12 (1840), pp. 95, 157; Geiter and Speck, *Reresby*, pp. 45, 187 and passim.
141 McCann, 'Correspondence', pp. 24–5.
142 HMC, 'Portland MSS', III (London, 1894), p. 441.
143 Ibid., II, p. 203; Bagley, 'Diurnal of Nicholas Blundell', I, pp. 79, 166, II, pp. 144, 150.
144 Western, *The English Militia*, p. 71.

Notes to Chapter 7: The Cavalry and Early Modern Warfare

1 M. Roberts, *The Military Revolution, 1560–1660* (Belfast, 1956); C.J. Rogers, ed., *The Military Revolution Debate* (Boulder, Colorado, 1995).
2 G. Phillips, *The Anglo-Scots Wars 1513–1550* (Woodbridge, 1999), p. 17; C.J. Rogers, 'The Military Revolutions of the Hundred Years War, A Myth?', in C.J. Rogers, ed., *The Military Revolution Debate*, p. 59; G. Parker, *The Military Revolution* (Cambridge, 1989), pp. 16, 58–9, 69.
3 Ibid., p. 58.
4 Phillips, *The Anglo-Scots Wars*, p. 24.
5 Parker, *The Military Revolution*, p. 69; J. Giono, *The Battle of Pavia*, trans. A. E. Murch (London, 1965), pp. 153–5: accessed through www.derimilitari.org/RESOURCES?articles/pavia.htm.
6 S. Adams, 'Tactics or Politics? "The Military Revolution" and the Hapsburg Hegemony, 1525–1648', in Rogers, *Military Revolution*, p. 259.
7 M. Howard, *War in European History* (Oxford, 1976), p. 15; Phillips, *The Anglo-Scots Wars*, p. 22.
8 Phillips, *The Anglo-Scots Wars*, pp. 17, 19; F. Tallett, *War and Society in Early-Modern Europe, 1495–1715* (London, 1992), p. 24.
9 William Louis, his brother, John, and Maurice, son of William of Orange: Tallett, *War and Society*, pp. 24–5.
10 M. Wanklyn and F. Jones, *A Military History of the English Civil War* (Harlow, 2005), p. 28, 32–3; Tallett, *War and Society*, p. 27–8.
11 Ibid., pp. 27–28; D. Chandler, *Marlborough as Military Commander* (London, 1979), p. 64.
12 Phillips, *The Anglo-Scots Wars*, pp. 23–4; D. Featherstone, *Armies and Warfare in the Pike and Shot Era 1422–1700* (London, 1998), pp. 124–5.

13 Rogers, 'The Military Revolutions of the Hundred Years War', p. 57.
14 Phillips, *The Anglo-Scots Wars*, p. 28.
15 J. X Evans, *The Works of Sir Roger Williams* (Oxford, 1972), pp. 30–1.
16 Parker, *The Military Revolution*, p. 69; Phillips, *The Anglo-Scots Wars*, pp. 25–6.
17 Phillips, *The Anglo-Scots Wars*, pp. 25–7; Tallett, *War and Society*, p. 23; P. Young, ed., *Military Memoirs, The Civil War: Richard Atkyns* (London, 1967), pp. 24–5. I am grateful to Professor Malcolm Wanklyn for the technical information and for the reference to Atkyns.
18 Tallett, *War and Society*, p. 31.
19 Wanklyn and Jones, *A Military History*, p. 30; Adams, 'Tactics or Politics?', p. 259.
20 M. Roberts, *Gustavus Adolphus: A History of Sweden 1611–1632*, II (London, 1958), *1626–1632* (London, 1958), pp. 254–62; Tallett, *War and Society*, pp. 30–1; Wanklyn and Jones, *A Military History*, pp. 33–4.
21 N. Ahnlund, *Gustavus Adolphus the Great* (New York, 1999), pp. xvii–xviii; Roberts, *Gustavus Adolphus*, II, p. 257; J. Black, *European Warfare, 1453–1815* (Basingstoke, 1999), p. 53.
22 Rogers, 'The Military Revolutions of the Hundred Years War', pp. 68–75.
23 Parker, *The Military Revolution*, pp. 10–11.
24 C. Cruickshank, *Henry VIII and the Invasion of France* (Far Thrupp, 1994), p. 67.
25 P. Edwards, *Dealing in Death: The Arms Trade and the British Civil Wars, 1638–52* (Thrupp, 2000), pp. 13–14.
26 W.C. and C.E. Trevelyan, eds, 'The Trevelyan Papers', 3, Camden Society, 105 (1872), pp. 250–1.
27 BL, Harleian MS 6852, fol. 50.
28 Edwards, *Dealing in Death*, pp. 232–3.
29 *Letters and Papers of Henry VIII*, XIX, I, *1544*, pp. 145–6.
30 H. Miller, *Henry VIII and the English Nobility* (Oxford, 1989), pp. 133–4.
31 Ibid., pp. 134, 146–8.
32 M.C. Fissel, *English Warfare, 1511–1642* (London, 2001), pp. 133–4; L. Boynton, *The Elizabethan Militia, 1558–1638* (London, 1967), p. 161.
33 K. Sharpe, *The Personal Rule of Charles I* (New Haven and London, 1992), p. 799; T. Cogswell, *Home Divisions: Aristocracy, the State and Provincial Conflict* (Manchester, 1998), p. 258.
34 *CSPD, 1638–39*, pp. 461, 466.
35 Edwards, *Dealing in Death*, p. 158.
36 *CSPD, 1641–43*, p. 344.
37 F.P. Verney, *The Memoirs of the Verney Family*, II, *During the Civil War* (London, 1970), p. 92; Lincolnshire Archives Office, Monson MSS, MON 27/3/1; J.W.W. Bund, ed., 'Diary of Henry Townshend', II, *Worcestershire Historical Society* (1920), p. 70.
38 Edwards, *Dealing in Death*, p. 50.
39 A.R. Bayley, *The Great Civil War in Dorset, 1642–1660* (Taunton, 1910), p. 73; D.H. Pennington and I.A. Roots, eds, *The Committee at Stafford, 1643–45* (Manchester, 1957), pp. 31–2.
40 R.H.C. Davis, *The Medieval Warhorse* (London, 1989), pp. 25–6, 67.
41 Davis, *The Medieval Warhorse*, p. 67; A. Ayton, *Knights and Warhorses, Military Service and the English Aristocracy under Edward III* (Woodbridge, 1994), p. 220.

42 *CSPV*, V, *1534–54*, p. 350.
43 A. Stewart, *Philip Sidney, a Double Life* (London, 2000), p. 132.
44 R.W. Stewart, 'The English Ordnance Office: A Case-Study in Bureaucracy', *Studies in History*, 73 (Woodbridge, 1996), p. 166.
45 M. Cash, ed., 'Devon Inventories in the Sixteenth and Seventeenth Centuries', *Devon and Cornwall Record Society*, new series, 11 (1966), pp. 15–16.
46 P. Edwards, 'The Supply of Horses to the Parliamentarian and Royalist Armies in the English Civil War', *Bulletin of the Institute of Historical Research*, 68 (1995), pp. 53–4.
47 H.G. Tibbutt, ed., 'The Letter Books 1644–45 of Sir Samuel Luke', *HMC* (London, 1963), p. 225.
48 D. O'Carroll, 'Change and Continuity in Weapons and Tactics, 1594–1691', in P. Lenihan, ed., *Conquest and Resistance: War in Seventeenth-Century Ireland* (Leiden, 2001), p. 219.
49 M. Roberts, 'The "Military Revolution", 1560–1660', in Rogers, *The Military Revolution Debate*, p. 23.
50 Roberts, 'The Military Revolution', p. 23, citing Sir James Turner, *Pallas Armata* (London, 1683), p. 166.
51 Boynton, *The Elizabethan Militia*, p. 251; C.H. Firth, *Cromwell's Army: A History of the English Soldier during the Civil Wars, the Commonwealth and the Protectorate* (London, 1962), pp. 70–1.
52 Fissel, *English Warfare*, p. 50.
53 P.E.H. Hammer, *Elizabeth's Wars* (Basingstoke, 2003), pp. 140–1.
54 W.P.D. Murphy, ed., 'The Earl of Hertford's Lieutenancy Papers 1603–1612', *Wiltshire Records Society*, 23 (1969), p. 4; Hammer, *Elizabeth's Wars*, p. 141.
55 Fissel, *English Warfare*, p. 54.
56 Boynton, *The Elizabethan Militia*, p. 7.
57 Fissel, *English Warfare*, pp. 8–12; Miller, *Henry VIII*, pp. 159–60.
58 4 and 5 Philip & Mary, cc. 2, 3.
59 Boynton, *The Elizabethan Militia*, pp. 9–10; Hammer, *Elizabeth's Wars*, p. 54.
60 A. Hassell Smith, 'Militia Rates and Militia Statutes 1558–1663', in P. Clark et al, eds, *The English Commonwealth, 1547–1640* (Leicester, 1979), p. 94. Hassell Smith absolves the framers of the legislation of ill-advised conservatism, claiming that they could not have foreseen the impending revolution in methods of warfare. Not so! As is discussed at length in this chapter, change was already discernible to military planners. Even if the government had equipped the soldiers with the new weapons, the acts did not ensure that they received proper training; Hammer, *Elizabeth's Wars*, p. 98.
61 Boynton, *The Elizabethan Militia*, pp. 7, 9–10; Hammer, *Elizabeth's Wars*, pp. 52, 98.
62 Boynton, *The Elizabethan Militia*, pp. 91; Hammer, *Elizabeth's Wars*, p. 99.
63 Boynton, *The Elizabethan Militia*, pp. 96–107, 178; A. Hassell Smith, *County and Court: Government and Politics in Norfolk, 1558–1603* (Oxford, 1974), p. 129, 285, 287–9; C.L. Hamilton, ed., '"The Muster-Master" by Gervase Markham', *Camden Society*, fourth Series, 14 (1975), p. 51.
64 G.M. Fraser, *The Steel Bonnets: The Story of the Anglo-Scottish Border Reivers* (London, 1971), pp. 115–16; Durham University, Department of Palaeography and Diplomatic, Howard of Naworth MSS, 201/9.

65 Cumbria Record Office (Carlisle), Scaleby inventories.
66 *CSPD, Addenda, 1547–65*, p. 465.
67 *CSPD, Addenda, 1566–79*, p. 367.
68 Ibid., pp. 92, 335.
69 Boynton, *The Elizabethan Militia*, p. 210.
70 M.C. Fissel, *The Bishops' Wars: Charles I's Campaigns against Scotland, 1638–1640* (Cambridge, 1994), p. 193; Boynton, *The Elizabethan Militia*, p. 240.
71 Boynton, *The Elizabethan Militia*, p. 246.
72 Fissel, *The Bishops' Wars*, pp. 4–5, 79.
73 Fissel, *The Bishops' Wars*, p. 206.
74 Ibid., p. 24; Edwards, *Dealing in Death*, p. 19.
75 Fissel, *The Bishops' Wars*, p. 213.
76 Ibid., p. 27.
77 Ibid., pp. 27–8.
78 R.B. Manning, *Swordsmen: The Martial Ethos in the Three Kingdoms* (Oxford, 2003), p. 17; A. Woolrych, 'Cromwell as a Soldier', in J. Morrell, ed., *Oliver Cromwell and the English Revolution* (Harlow, 1990), p. 93.
79 Fissell, *The Bishops' Wars*, pp. 78–82.
80 Edwards, *Dealing in Death*, p. 182; Fissel, *The Bishops' Wars*, pp. 81–2.
81 Edwards, *Dealing in Death*, p. 191; P. Lenihan, *Confederate Catholics at War, 1641–49* (Cork, 2001), pp. 44–5.
82 J.R. Western, *The English Militia in the Eighteenth Century, The Story of a Political Issue 1660–1802* (London, 1965), pp. 12–15.
83 J. Childs, *The Army of Charles II* (London, 1976), pp. 218, 220.
84 Western, *The English Militia*, pp. 15–16.
85 Ibid., pp. 17–18, 22.
86 Ibid., p. 22.
87 Ibid., p. 15.
88 Childs, *Charles II's Army*, for Scotland, pp. 196–7; for Ireland, pp. 203–4.
89 Ibid., pp. 22–3.
90 Western, *The English Militia*, pp. 39–44.
91 Childs, *Charles II's Army*, pp. 196–203.
92 Boynton, *The Elizabethan Militia*, p. 93.
93 Hammer, *Elizabeth's Wars*, p. 99.
94 *CSPV*, V, *1534–54*, p. 548.
95 Blunderville, *The Arte of Rydynge*, preface.
96 Boynton, *The Elizabethan Militia*, pp. 77–8; *CSPD, Addenda, 1566–79*, p. 75.
97 Boynton, *The Elizabethan Militia*, pp. 78–81.
98 See above; TNA, SP 12/136/42; *CSPD, Addenda, 1547–80*, p. 685.
99 TNA, SP 12/136/4.
100 TNA, SP 12/136/42; SP 12/137/17.
101 J. Goring and J. Wake, eds, 'Northamptonshire Lieutenancy Papers and Other Documents, 1580–1614', *Northamptonshire Record Society*, 27 (1975), pp. xviii–xix; *HMC*, 'Rutland MSS', I (London, 1888), p. 153; Boynton, *The Elizabethan Militia*, p. 86.

102 In 1586 the government attempted to get justices of the peace to supply petronels: one from each magistrate and a second from those who served on the quorum. Firth, *Cromwell's Army*, p. 111, n. 2; Boynton, *Militia*, pp. 87–8.
103 Boynton, *The Elizabethan Militia*, p. 228.
104 Hassell Smith, 'Militia Rates', p. 105; B.W. Quintrell, ed., 'The Maynard Lieutenancy Book, 1608–1639', *Essex Historical Documents*, 3, pt 1 (Chelmsford, 1993), pp. 19–20; Boynton, *The Elizabethan Militia*, p. 228.
105 *Acts of the Privy Council, 1617–19* (London, 1929), p. 118; Hassell Smith, 'Militia Rates', p. 105.
106 Boynton, *The Elizabethan Militia*, p. 229.
107 Ibid., pp. 151, 246, 248.
108 A. Fletcher, *A County Community in Peace and War: Sussex 1600–1660* (London, 1975), p. 185; Quintrell, 'The Maynard Lieutenancy Book', II, p. 189.
109 Boynton, *The Elizabethan Militia*, pp. 252–3.
110 *CSPD, 1638–39*, p. 325; Sharpe, *Charles I*, p. 800.
111 Edwards, *Dealing in Death*, p. 158; *CSPD, 1638–9*, p. 387.
112 Edwards, *Dealing in Death*, p. 28.
113 Ibid., p. 160.
114 G. Robinson, 'Horse Supply in the English Civil War, 1642–1646' (unpublished University of Reading Ph.D. Thesis, 2001), p. 51.
115 Edwards, *Dealing in Death*, pp. 162–3.
116 Ibid., p. 161.
117 P. Edwards, *The Horse Trade of Tudor and Stuart England* (Cambridge, 1988), pp. 77 ff.
118 BL, Thomason Tracts E2621/6, p. 260.
119 University College of North Wales Library, Bangor, Baron Hill MS 328.
120 C.V. Wedgwood, *The King's War, 1641–1647* (London, 1958), pp. 368, 370.
121 Robinson, *Horse Supply*, pp. 238–42.
122 Ibid., p. 34.
123 TNA, E101/107/27–8. Usually an individual parish but at times in groups of two or three.
124 *L & P of Henry VIII*, I, pt 1, *1509–13*, p. 929; Cruickshank, *Invasion of France*, p. 61.
125 *L & P of Henry VIII*, I, pt 2, *1513–14*, p. 1226.
126 Cruickshank, *Henry VIII and the Invasion of France*, p. 62.
127 *L & P of Henry VIII*, XIX, pt 1, *1544*, pp. 146–7.
128 *L & P of Henry VIII*, XIX, pt 1, *1544*, pp. 203, 544–5.
129 Ibid., p. 545.
130 *Calendar of State Papers Ireland, 1599–1600*, p. 17.
131 Ibid., pp. 17–18, 229.
132 Edwards, *Dealing in Death*, pp. 223–4.
133 National Archives of Scotland, Hamilton MSS, GD406/1/10491.
134 Edwards, *Dealing in Death*, pp. 158–9; Northamptonshire Record Office, Finch-Hatton MSS, F(M)C 275.
135 TNA, WO 49/68, fos 33–4.
136 Edwards, *Dealing in Death*, p. 228.
137 *CSPD, 1641–43*, pp. 408, 459.

138 National Library of Wales, Crosse of Shaw Hill MSS, no. 1106.
139 Edwards, *Dealing in Death*, p. 230; TNA, SP 28/29/I, fol. 331.
140 Edwards, *Dealing in Death*, pp. 228–30.
141 Ibid., p. 240.
142 TNA, SP28/28, III; SP28/30, IV; SP28/38, III; SP28/140, VII passim.
143 Chandler, *Marlborough*, p. 73.
144 Ibid., p. 130.
145 Tallett, *War and Society*, p. 58; John Millner, *A Compendious Journal of the Marches, Famous Battles, Sieges and other Note-worthy, Heroical, and Ever Memorable Actions of the Triumphant Armies, of the Ever-Glorious Confederate High Allies* (Uckfield, 2004), p. 96.
146 Fissel, *English Warfare*, pp. 282–93.
147 Shropshire Record Office, Attingham Park MSS, 112/74, 76.
148 Miller, *Henry VIII*, pp. 141–2; Cruickshank, *Henry VIII and the Invasion of France*, p. 69.
149 Reputedly the Wars of the Roses decimated the country's stock of large mounts. D.M. Goodall, *A History of Horse Breeding* (London, 1977), p. 158.
150 Cruickshank, *Henry VIII and the Invasion of France*, pp. 146, 165.
151 Ibid., p. 67.
152 Fissel, *English Warfare*, p. 11; Miller, *Henry VIII*, p. 159.
153 Cruickshank, *Henry VIII and the Invasion of France*, pp. 72–3.
154 *CSPV*, II, *1509–19*, pp. 174–5, 179, 198, 379; *L & P of Henry VIII*, I, pt 2, *1513–14*, p. 1451; II, pt 1, *1515–16*, p. 120, II, pt 2, *1517–18*, p. 1180.
155 Fissel, *English Warfare*, p. 4; D. Starkey, 'Intimacy and Innovation: The Rise of the Privy Chamber, 1485–1547', in D. Starkey et al, *The English Court from the Wars of the Roses to the Civil War* (London, 1987), pp. 86–90; Phillips, *The Anglo-Scots Wars*, pp. 158–9.
156 Miller, *Henry VIII*, p. 159.
157 Ibid., pp. 158–9.
158 Cruickshank, *Henry VIII and the Invasion of France*, p. 176.
159 Phillips, *The Anglo-Scots Wars*, pp. 115–30.
160 Miller, *Henry VIII*, p. 159; Phillips, *The Anglo-Scots Wars*, pp. 158–9, 176.
161 Phillips, *The Anglo-Scots Wars*, pp. 126–8; Fissel, *English Warfare*, pp. 21–3.
162 Fraser, *The Steel Bonnets*, passim; Phillips, *The Anglo-Scots Wars*, pp. 125–6.
163 Ibid., p. 152, citing Hamilton Papers, I, xvi.
164 Ibid., pp. 186, 197.
165 *CSPD, Addenda, 1566–79*, pp. 121, 123.
166 Ibid., p. 123.
167 C. Falls, *Elizabeth's Irish Wars* (London, 1996), p. 39.
168 Boynton, *The Elizabethan Militia*, p. 84; 'Order for the Mustering of Demi-Lances and Light Horsemen on Mousehold near Magdalen Chapel, 1584', *Norfolk Archaeology*, 1 (1849), pp. 21–2; Firth, *Cromwell's Army*, p. 111, n. 2; Boynton, *The Elizabethan Militia*, pp. 87–8; TNA, WO 49/20, fol. 119; 26, fol. 80.
169 Firth, *Cromwell's Army*, p. 8.
170 TNA, WO 49/30, fos 104, 144v; WO 49/20, fol. 86.
171 TNA. WO 49/19–26 passim; Firth, *Cromwell's Army*, p. 8.
172 G. Roberts, ed., 'Diary of Walter Yonge, Esq.', *Camden Society* (1847), pp. 16–18.

173 Boynton, *The Elizabethan Militia*, pp. 170–1.
174 Fissel, *English Warfare*, pp. 151, 163–4, 167.
175 Ibid., p. 145; J.S. Nolan, *Sir John Norreys and the Elizabethan Military World* (Exeter, 1997), pp. 99, 144, 177, 185, 283 n. 28.
176 Ibid., pp. 210, 217, 222, 224.
177 J. McGirk, *The Elizabethan Conquest of Ireland* (Manchester, 1997), p. 61.
178 Ibid., pp. 64–5; Fissel, *English Warfare*, pp. 103–4.
179 Falls, *Elizabeth's Irish Wars*, p. 39.
180 TNA, WO 49/26, fos 55v, 80.
181 McGurk, *Irish Wars*, pp. 231–2.
182 Fissel, *English Warfare*, pp. 233–5; Falls, *Elizabeth's Irish Wars*, pp. 305–7; O'Carroll, 'Weapons and Tactics', pp. 230–1.
183 J.M. Hill, *Celtic Warfare, 1595–1763* (Edinburgh, 1986), pp. 23–4; O'Carroll, 'Weapons and Tactics', p. 222.
184 Blunderville, *The Fower Chiefyst Offices*, fos 10v–11r.
185 O'Carroll, 'Weapons and Tactics', pp. 227–8.
186 Fissel, *English Warfare*, p. 256.
187 Boynton, *The Elizabethan Militia*, p. 238.
188 *HMC*, 'Salisbury MSS', XXII (London, 1971), pp. 142–3.
189 R.W. Stewart, 'War and Government in the Channel and Beyond', in M.C. Fissel, *War and Government in Britain, 1598–1650* (Manchester, 1991), p. 113.
190 Fissel, *English Warfare*, pp. 257–8.
191 Edwards, *Dealing in Death*, pp. 6, 13.
192 Firth, *Cromwell's Army*, pp. 116–17.
193 Ibid., p. 11; C.H. Firth, 'The Raising of the Ironsides', in I.R. Christie, ed., *Essays in Modern History* (London, 1968), p. 139.
194 Edwards, *Dealing in Death*, pp. 6–7; Firth, *Cromwell's Army*, p. 118.
195 Edwards, *Dealing in Death*, pp. 6–7.
196 J.L. Malcolm, 'Caesar's Due: Loyalty and King Charles 1642–1646', Royal Historical Society, *Studies in History*, 38 (1983), pp. 99–105.
197 Edwards, *Dealing in Death*, p. 1.
198 Malcolm, 'Caesar's Due', pp. 96–7, 99, 103–4.
199 Edwards, *Dealing in Death*, p. 165.
200 Ibid., p. 166
201 O'Carroll, 'Weapons and Tactics', pp. 235, 244. At Benburb the Confederates defeated the Scottish covenanting army, similarly short of horses.
202 Wanklyn and Jones, *A Military History*, pp. 269–74; J. Barratt, *Cavaliers: The Royalist Army at War 1642–1646* (Thrupp, 2000), pp. 20–32.
203 A. Woolrych, 'Cromwell as a Soldier', in J. Morrell, ed., *Oliver Cromwell and the English Revolution* (Harlow, 1990), pp. 100–1.
204 J. Childs, 'The Williamite War, 1689–1691', in T. Bartlett and K. Jeffery, eds, *A Military History of Ireland* (Cambridge, 1996), pp. 189–90.
205 Ibid., p. 192; R. Doherty, *The Williamite War in Ireland, 1688–1691* (Dublin, 1998), p. 25.

206 Doherty, *The Williamite War*, pp. 25, 214; For horses: personal communication from Dr Lenihan.
207 Doherty, *The Williamite War*, pp. 50, 119–20.
208 Ibid., pp. 56, 60–2.
209 Ibid., pp. 72–3, 77, 83–4.
210 Ibid., pp. 174–9; Childs, 'Williamite War', pp. 193, 195, 201, 207.
211 Chandler, *Marlborough*, pp. 71–2.
212 Ibid., p. 91.
213 Ibid., pp. 91, 147.
214 Ibid., p. 176.
215 A.H. Burne and P. Young, *The Great Civil War* (Moreton-in-Marsh, 1998), p. 11; Wanklyn and Jones, *A Military History*, pp. 29–30.
216 Ibid., p. 12.
217 P. Young and R. Holmes, *The English Civil War: A Military History of the Three Civil Wars* (London, 1974), p. 49; Edwards, *Dealing in Death*, p. 99; Fissel, *The Bishops' Wars*, pp. 54–9.
218 Burne and Young, *The Great Civil War*, pp. 103–7.
219 Chandler, *Marlborough*, p. 93.
220 *CSPV*, VI, pt 3, *1557–58*, p. 1049.
221 Robinson, *Horse Supply*, p. 12.
222 Edwards, *The Horse Trade*, p. 50.
223 Edwards, *Dealing in Death*, p. 183.

Notes to Chapter 8: Work Horses

1 J. Langdon, 'The Economics of Horses and Oxen in Medieval England', *Agricultural History Review*, 30 (1980), pp. 31–40, 158–64, 175; John Fitzherbert, *Boke of Husbandrie* (London, 1523), fol. 4v.
2 A. Young, *General View of the Agriculture of Hertfordshire* (1804/repr. Newton Abbot, 1971), pp. 199–212.
3 E. Kerridge, 'The Agrarian Development of Wiltshire, 1540–1640' (unpublished London University PhD thesis, 1951), p. 127; R.W. Chell, 'Agriculture and Rural Society in Hampshire *circa* 1600' (unpublished Leicester University MPhil thesis, 1975), p. 65; J.C.K. Cornwall, 'The Agrarian History of Sussex, 1560–1640' (unpublished London University MA thesis, 1953), pp. 94–5; C.W. Chalklin. *Seventeenth-Century Kent* (London, 1965), p. 104; Lambeth Palace Library, Surrey Probate Inventories.
4 W. Harwood Long, 'Regional Farming in Seventeenth-Century Yorkshire', *Agricultural History Review*, 8 (1960), pp. 106–7; J. Thirsk, *English Peasant Farming* (London, 1957), pp. 88, 175; E. Kerridge, *The Agricultural Revolution* (London, 1967), p. 68.
5 Kerridge, *Agricultural Revolution*, pp. 74, 77, 79, 89; HMC, 'Portland MSS', II (London, 1893), p. 266.
6 P. Edwards, *The Horse Trade of Tudor and Stuart England* (Cambridge, 1988), pp. 35–6.
7 D. Fleming, 'A Local Market System: Melton Mowbray and the Wreake Valley, 1549–1720' (unpublished Leicester University PhD thesis, 1980), p. 38; J. Goodacre, *The Transformation*

of a Peasant Economy: Townspeople and Villagers in the Lutterworth Area, 1500–1700 (Aldershot, 1994), p. 84; M.A. Havinden, 'Household and Farm Inventories in Oxfordshire', *Oxfordshire Record Society*, 44 (London, 1965), p. 38.
8 E. Kerridge, *Agricultural Revolution*, pp. 86, 91; S. Porter, 'An Agricultural Geography of Huntingdonshire, 1610–1749' (unpublished Cambridge University MLitt thesis, 1973), p. 70.
9 Cornwall, *The Agrarian History of Sussex*, pp. 94–5; G.H. Kenyon, 'Kirdford Inventories 1611 to 1776', *Sussex Archaeological Collections*, 93 (1955), pp. 107, 109, 111; Lambeth Palace Library, Surrey Probate Inventories; J.M. Harding, *Charlwood Inventories* (Charlwood, 1976), pp. 109–10.
10 J. Thirsk and J.P. Cooper, *17th Century Economic Documents* (Oxford, 1972), p. 179.
11 Kerridge, Agricultural Revolution, p. 119; M. Cash, ed., 'Devon Inventories in the Sixteenth and Seventeenth Centuries', *Devon and Cornwall Record Society*, new series, 11 (1966), passim; William Marshall, *Rural Economy of the West of England*, I (1796/repr., Newton Abbot, 1970), p. 116.
12 G.E. Mingay, 'Farming Techniques', in G.E. Mingay, ed., *The Agrarian History of England and Wales*, VI, *1750–1850* (Cambridge, 1989), p. 289.
13 J. Langdon, 'Horse Hauling: A Revolution in Vehicle Transport in Twelfth- and Thirteenth-Century England?', *Past & Present*, 103 (1984), p. 55.
14 P.A Kennedy, ed., 'Nottinghamshire Household Inventories', *Thoroton Society*, Record Series, 22 (1963), passim; Harding, *Charlwood Inventories*, p. 107; Kerridge, 'Wiltshire', p. 127.
15 D. Hey, *Packmen, Carriers and Packhorse Roads: Trade and Communications in North Derbyshire and South Yorkshire* (Leicester, 1980), pp. 28, 92–4, 96–7; P. Edwards, *Dealing in Death: The Arms Trade and the British Civil Wars, 1638–52* (Thrupp, 2000), pp. 223, 233.
16 Normally 240 lbs but at Kendal 256 lbs. D. Gerhold, 'Packhorses and Wheeled Vehicles in England, 1550–1800', *Journal of Transport History*, third series, 14 (1993), pp. 11–12; For Kendal c. 1692, Cumbria Record Office (Kendal), WQ/01 Order Book 1669–96.
17 Gerhold, 'Packhorses', pp. 9–17; J. Chartres, 'Road Carrying in England in the Seventeenth Century: Myth and Reality', *Economic History Review*, second series, 30 (1977), pp. 83–4.
18 Gerhold, 'Packhorses', p. 18.
19 T. Barker and D. Gerhold, *The Rise and Rise of Road Transport, 1700–1990* (Basingstoke, 1993), p. 40.
20 Ibid., pp. 20, 40.
21 Ibid., p. 35.
22 M.J.T. Lewis, 'Early Wooden Railways', *Antiquity*, 48 (1974), p. 87.
23 J.U. Nef, *The Rise of the British Coal Industry*, I (New York, 1932; reprint, 1972), p. 89.
24 P.R. Edwards, 'The Farming Economy of North-East Shropshire in the Seventeenth Century' (unpublished Oxford University DPhil thesis, 1976), p. 197; D.G. Hey, 'The Rural Metalworkers of the Sheffield Region', *Leicester University, Department of English Local History Occasional Papers*, second series, 5 (Leicester, 1972), p. 15; A.M. Everitt, 'The Marketing of Agricultural Produce', in J. Thirsk, ed., *The Agrarian History of England and Wales*, IV, *1500–1640* (Cambridge, 1967), p. 508.

25 D Rollison, *The Local Origins of Modern Society: Gloucestershire, 1500–1800* (London, 1992), p. 50.
26 T.S. Willan, *The Inland Trade* (Manchester, 1976), p. 25.
27 M. Exwood and H. Lehmann, eds, 'The Journal of William Schellink's Travels in England 1661–1663', *Camden Society*, fifth series, 1 (1993), p. 78; T.S. Willan, *River Navigation in England, 1600–1750* (London, 1964), pp. 100–2.
28 Horses had to be fed when not in use, whereas halers were hired by the day.
29 Willan, *River Navigation*, pp. 101–2.
30 R. Galloway, *Annals of Coal Mining and the Coal Trade*, I (London, 1898; Newton Abbot, reprint, 1971), p. 249.
31 Lewis, 'Railways', pp. 89–91.
32 Ibid., pp. 91–3.
33 Ibid., pp. 95–7.
34 Everitt, 'Marketing', p. 493; Kerridge, *Wiltshire*, p. 280.
35 R. Fieldhouse and B. Jennings, *A History of Richmond and Swaledale* (Chichester, 1978), p. 171; C.B. Robinson, ed., 'Rural Economy in Yorkshire in 1641, Being the Farming and Account Books of Henry Best of Elmeswell in the East Riding', *Surtees Society*, 33 (1857), pp. 99–100.
36 D.O. Pam, 'Tudor Enfield: The Maltmen and the Lea Navigation', *Edmonton Hundred Historical Society Occasional Paper*, new series, 18 (ND) p. 3; BL, Lansdowne MS 32, no. 40.
37 F. Hull, 'Agriculture and Rural Society in Essex, 1560–1640' (unpublished London University PhD thesis, 1950), p. 219; Hey, *Packmen*, p. 72.
38 P. Edwards, 'The Development of Dairy Farming on the North Shropshire Plain in the Seventeenth Century', *Midland History*, 4 (1978), pp. 184–7.
39 Edwards, *The Horse Trade*, p. 117.
40 P.J. Bowden, *The Wool Trade in Tudor and Stuart England* (London, 1971), p. 81.
41 B.C. Jones, 'Westmorland Pack-Horse Men in Southampton', *Transactions of the Cumberland and Westmorland Antiquarian and Archaeological Society*, new series, 59 (1960), pp. 65–83.
42 C. Morris, ed., *The Journeys of Celia Fiennes* (London, 1947), p. 246.
43 Nef, *British Coal Industry*, I, pp. 101, 382, II, p. 142; R.W. Malcolmson, 'A Set of Ungovernable People: the Kingswood Colliers in the Eighteenth Century', in J. Brewer and J. Styles, eds, *An Ungovernable People: The English and their Law in the Seventeenth and Eighteenth Centuries* (London, 1983), p. 98.
44 Lichfield Joint Record Office, probate inventories, 20 November 1604, Wombridge.
45 Willan, *Inland Trade*, pp. 12–13.
46 Chartres, 'Road Carrying', p. 78.
47 According to D. Gerhold, 'The Growth of the London Carrying Trade, 1681–1838, *Economic History Review*, second series, 41 (1988), pp. 395–6, *The Merchants and Traders Necessary Companion* of 1715 appears to be a lightly amend version of *The Traveller's and Chapman's Daily Instructor* of 1705.
48 Barker and Gerhold, *Road Transport*, pp. 27–9.
49 TNA, PROB 4/7440; PROB 4/335; Barker and Gerhold, *Road Transport*, p. 20; Hey, *Packmen*, p. 213.

50 Shropshire Record Office, Shrewsbury Records, Quarter Sessions Papers, 2228.
51 Gerhold, 'Packhorses', p. 3; Edwards, *The Horse Trade*, p. 4; Hey, Packmen, pp. 121, 125, 205; G.E. Mingay, 'The Midlands', in J. Thirsk, ed., *The Agrarian History of England and Wales*, V, *1640–1750* (Cambridge, 1984), pt 1, p. 126.
52 Somerset R.O., CQ 3/1/34, fol. 42; Richard Gough, *Antiquityes and Memoyres of the Parish of Myddle* (Shrewsbury, 1875), p. 93; North Yorkshire Record Office, Calendar of Quarter Sessions Papers, QSB 1710.
53 Thirsk and Cooper, *17th Century Economic Documents*, p. 188.
54 Everitt, 'Marketing', p. 579.
55 E.H.B. Harbin, ed., *Quarter Sessions Records for the County of Somerset*, II, 1625–1639, Somerset Record Society (1908), p. 117. I am grateful to Neil Howlett for this reference.
56 Hey, *Packmen*, p. 88.
57 North Yorkshire Record Office, Calendar of Quarter Sessions Papers, QSB 1707, Easter 1707.
58 D. Gerhold, *Carriers and Coachmasters: Trade and Travel before the Turnpikes* (Chichester, 2005), p. 61.
59 D. Gerhold, *Road Transport before the Railways: Russell's London Flying Waggons* (Cambridge, 1993), pp. 8, 11, 17, 33–4.
60 C. Jackson, ed., 'Yorkshire Diaries and Autobiographies in the Seventeenth and Eighteenth Centuries', II, *Surtees Society*, 77 (1883), p. 23.
61 Edwards, *Dealing in Death*, p. 140; J. de L. Mann, *The Cloth Industry in the West of England from 1640 to 1880* (Gloucester, 1987), p. 4.
62 Edwards, *Dealing in Death*, p. 229.
63 Thomas Blundeville, *The Fower Chiefyst Offices belonging to Horsemanship* (London, 1565), fol. 13r.
64 Gervase Markham, *Cheape and Good Husbandry*, I (London, 1614), p. 5.
65 The argument remains valid, even if some of these animals served as saddle mounts.
66 N. Penney, ed., *The Household Account Book of Sarah Fell of Swarthmoor Hall, 1673–78* (Cambridge, 1920), pp. 339, 409.
67 Durham Record Office, Quarter Sessions Records, 1695 bundle.
68 Gerhold, *Carriers and Coachmasters*, p. 4.
69 John Stow, *A Survey of London*, ed., C.L. Kingsford (1908; reprint, Oxford, 1971), I, p. 84; II, p. 282. The road version was a little heavier.
70 Sir H. Ellis, ed., 'Norden's Description of Essex', *Camden Society* (1840), p. xii; also Gerhold, 'Packhorses', pp. 3–4; Stow, *London*, II, p. 282, footnote 840.
71 Thirsk and Cooper, *Economic Documents*, p. 179; J. Crofts, *Packhorse, Waggon and Post: Land Carriage and Communications under the Tudors and Stuarts* (London, 1967), pp. 7–8; Hey, *Packmen*, p. 93; Chartres, 'Road Carrying', pp. 73–94.
72 For references to the sets of probate inventories used, see n. 27, chapter 3, Saddle Horses.
73 Steer, *Mid-Essex*, p. 84 for John George.
74 H.C.F. Lansberry, ed., 'Sevenoaks Wills and Inventories in the Reign of Charles II', *Kent Archaeol. Society, Kent Records*, 25 (1988).
75 M. Parker, *All My Worldly Goods* (St Albans, 1985); M. Reed, ed., 'Buckinghamshire Probate Inventories, 1661–1714', *Buckinghamshire Record Society*, 24 (1988). This is a selected list.

76 S. Porter, 'Farm Transport in Huntingdonshire 1610–1749', *Journal of Transport History*, third series, 3 (1982), pp. 35–45, especially pp. 38, 43–4; Goodacre, *Lutterworth*, p. 196; Thirsk and Cooper, *Economic Documents*, p. 179.
77 Goodacre, *Lutterworth*, p. 196.
78 R. Plot, *The Natural History of Oxfordshire* (London, 1677), p. 257.
79 M.A. Havinden, 'The Rural Economy of Oxfordshire 1580–1730' (unpublished Oxford University BLitt thesis, 1961), pp. 204–6; As Havinden notes, 'There was hardly a yeoman in George I's reign who did not possess at least one wagon, in contrast to the situation at the Restoration when even the wealthiest yeomen were without them'. M.A. Havinden, 'Agricultural Progress in Open-Field Oxfordshire', in W.E. Minchinton, ed., *Essays in Agrarian History*, I (Newton Abbot, 1968), pp. 158–9.
80 Lincolnshire Archives Office, Horbling Probate Inventories; D. Neave, ed., *Winteringham, 1650–1760* (Winteringham, 1984), passim.
81 R. Plot, *Natural History of Staffordshire* (London, 1686), p. 354.
82 D. G. Vaisey, ed., *Probate Inventories of Lichfield and District 1586–1680*, Staffordshire Record Society, fourth series, V (1969), p. 280.
83 P. Edwards, 'Agriculture, 1540–1750', *The Victoria History of Shropshire*, IV, Agriculture (Oxford, 1989), pp. 149–50.
84 J.S. Moore, ed., *The Goods and Chattels of our Forefathers: Frampton Cotterell and District Probate Inventories, 1539–1804* (Chichester, 1976), no. 182, p. 144.
85 Hey, *Packmen*, p. 93.
86 J. Groves, ed., *Ashton-on-Mersey and Sale Wills, II, 1651–1700* (Sale, 2000); III, *1701–1760* (Sale, 2002).
87 H. Thwaite, ed., 'Abstract of Abbotside Wills, 1552–1688', *Yorkshire Archaeological Society*, 130 (1968).
88 Blundeville, *The Fower Chiefyst Offices*, fol. 12v.
89 Ibid., fol. 12v.
90 J. Thirsk, 'Farming Techniques', in Thirsk, *The Agrarian History*, IV, p. 192.
91 Blundeville, *The Fower Chiefyst Offices*, fos, 9r–10v.
92 TNA, REQ 2/188/6.
93 Edwards, *The Horse Trade*, p. 36.
94 Edwards, *Dealing in Death*, pp. 229–30.
95 Richard Blome, *The Gentleman's Recreation*, p. 10.
96 As the data on Rothwell indicates.
97 TNA, PROB 4/1528; Lincolnshire Archives Office, LCC Wills, 1692/i/31. Inventory valuations follow market prices but usually at a lower level: J. and N. Cox, 'Valuations in Probate Inventories', pt 2, *Local Historian*, 17, II (1986), pp. 85–100.
98 Hertfordshire Record Office, Henry de Nassau MSS, D/ENa 05, 07–08, 019, 025; TNA, E 351/1750, 1752, 1763; Leicestershire Record Office, Finch MSS, DG 7/1/19a.
99 D. Defoe, *A Tour through the Whole Island of Great Britain*, ed. P. Rogers (Harmondsworth, 1971), p. 409.
100 Ibid., p. 255.
101 F.G. Emmison, 'Jacobean Household Inventories', *Bedfordshire Record Society*, 20 (1938), pp. 65, 70. Hawnes may be Haynes near Bedford.

102 J. Thirsk, 'Agrarian History, 1540–1950', in W.G. Hoskins and R.A. McKinley, eds, *Victoria History of the County of Leicestershire*, II (Oxford, 1954), p. 222.
103 F.W. Steer, ed., *Farm and Cottage Inventories of Mid Essex, 1635 to 1749* (Chichester, 1969), p. 84.
104 Reed, 'Buckinghamshire Inventories', no. 18, p. 48; Goodacre, *Lutterworth*, p. 118; Herefordshire Record Office, probate of Thomas Sheinton of Chelmarsh, 30 July 1745.
105 Sheffield University Library, Hartlib MS 31/1/64–5.
106 Nottingham University Library, MSS Department., Portland MSS, Pw V4–5; N. Marlow, trans., The Diary of Thomas Isham of Lamport, *Northamptonshire Record Society*, 17 (1955), p. 99; *HMC*, 'Portland MSS', VI (London, 1901), p. 100.
107 Hull, *Essex*, p. 228.
108 J.F. Larkin and P.L. Hughes, eds, *Stuart Royal Proclamations*, I, *James I, 1603–25* (Oxford, 1973), no. 174, pp. 396–7; no. 231, pp. 551–3.
109 J.A. Chartres, *Internal Trade in England, 1500–1700* (London, 1977), p. 40; Hey, *Packmen*, p. 96; Crofts, *Packhorse*, pp. 7–8; Gerhold, 'Packhorses', p. 4.
110 Gerhold, 'Packhorses', p. 4.
111 J.C. Jeaffreson, *Middlesex County Records*, 2 (1887), pp. 159, 166.
112 Hull, *Essex*, p. 234.
113 Jeaffreson, *Middlesex County Records*, 2, p. 173.
114 TNA, STAC 8/30/11.
115 *Acts of the Privy Council, 1621–23* (London, 1932), p. 338.
116 Hey, *Packmen*, pp. 96–7; Gerhold, *Carriers and Coachmasters*, p. 64; *HMC*, 'House of Lords, 1714–18' (London, 1977), pp. 524–7.
117 Willan, *The Inland Trade*, p. 3.
118 Chartres, 'Road Carrying', p. 87; Hey, *Packmen*, pp. 91–102.
119 W. Albert, *The Turnpike Road System in England, 1663–1840* (Cambridge, 1972), p. 17; Chartres, *Inland Trade*, p. 41.
120 Chartres, *Inland Trade*, p. 41; Barker and Gerhold, *Road Transport*, p. 37.
121 Defoe, *A Tour*, pp. 429ff.
122 D. Gerhold, 'Productivity Change in Road Transport Before and After Turnpiking, 1690–1840', *Economic History Review*, 49 (1996), pp. 504, 511.
123 Galloway, *Coal Mining*, I, pp. 168, 178–9.
124 Morris, *Celia Fiennes*, pp. 181–2.
125 J.E. Ward, 'John Spedding's Accounts of Horses Used in the Whitehaven Colleries etc., from 1715 Onwards', *Transactions of the Cumberland and Westmormorland Antiquarian and Archaeological Society*, 89 (1989), p. 182; D.R. Hainsworth, ed., 'The Correspondence of Sir John Lowther of Whitehaven, 1693–1698: A Provincial Community in Wartime', *Records of Social and Economic History*, new series, 7 (1983), p. 43.
126 J.C., *The Compleat Collier* (1708).
127 Nottingham University Library, MSS Department, Middleton MSS, Mi A 78.
128 TNA, C2/Jas. I/F4/53; R.A.S. Redmayne and L.F. Salzman, 'Industries: Coal Mining', W. Page, ed., *The Victoria History of the County of Warwickshire*, II (London, 1908), p. 221; A.W.A. White, 'Men and Mining in Warwickshire', *Coventry and North Warwickshire History Pamphlets*, 7 (Coventry, 1970), p. 9.

129 Galloway, *Coal Mining*, I, pp. 239–41.
130 Ward, 'John Spedding's Accounts', pp. 181, 183.
131 Nottingham University Library, MSS Department, Middleton MSS, Mi A 71.
132 Hainsworth, 'Sir John Lowther's Correspondence', p. 20.
133 Ibid., pp. 357, 446.
134 J.C., *Compleat Collier*, p. 12.
135 Nottingham University Library, MSS Department, Middleton MSS, Mi A 71, 77–78; Ward, 'John Spedding's Accounts', p. 183.
136 *HMC*, 'Portland MSS', II (London, 1893), p. 306.
137 City of Chester Record Office, Assembly Book, 1624–85, fol. 176v; *HMC*, 'Portland MSS', II, 'Thomas Baskerville's Journeys in England temp. Car. II', p. 291.
138 Lincolnshire Archives Office, Horbling Probate Inventories, INV 6/142; INV 10/3; INV33/321, 361; INV 65/60, 120; INV 75/2; INV 96/103; INV 102/149; INV 130/428; INV 175/480.
139 Parker, *Worldly Goods*, p. 55.
140 Goodacre, *Lutterworth*, p. 145; Thirsk and Cooper, *Economic Documents*, p. 179.
141 Hertfordshire Record Office, Wittewronge MSS, D/ELW F18, 20–21, 23.
142 A.C. Edwards, *John Petre, 1549–1613* (London, 1975), p. 62.
143 J. Wake and D.C. Webster, eds, 'The Letter Books of Daniel Eaton, 1725–32', *Northamptonshire Record Society*, 24 (1970–71), p. 132.
144 Ibid., p. 133.
145 L.P. Wenham, ed., *Roger Strickland of Richmond: Jacobite Gentleman, 1680–1745* (Northallerton, 1982), pp. 52–101.
146 F.J. Furnivall, ed., *Harrison's Description of England*, pt 2, *The Third Book* (London, 1878), p. 4.
147 J. Parkes, *Travel in the Seventeenth Century* (Oxford, 1925), p. 241.
148 Society of Antiquaries, MS 12, lines 8523–34.
149 Norton Conyers MSS; Hertfordshire Record Office, Henry de Nassau's Accounts, D/ENa 07.
150 Yorkshire Archaeological Society, Records Department, Leeds, Clifford of Skipton Castle MSS, DD 121/bundle 36A/3; Shropshire Record Office, Kilmorrey MSS, 946/B360.
151 M.M. Myddelton, ed., *Chirk Castle Accounts, A.D. 1666–1753* (Manchester, 1931), p. 214.
152 For example: *Acts of the Privy Council, 1617–19* (London, 1929), p. 214.
153 Furnivall, *Harrison's Description*, pt 2, *The Third Book*, p. 4. Described as 'carewares'.
154 'The Memorandum Book of Richard Cholmeley of Brandsby, 1602–1623', *North Yorkshire R.O. Publication*, 44 (1988), p. 22; J.J. Bagley, ed., 'The Great Diurnal of Nicholas Blundell of Little Crosby, Lancashire', *Record Society of Lancashire and Cheshire* (1970), I, '1702–11', 110 (1968), pp. 139, 221, 225, 263, 297–98; II, '1712–19', 112 (1970), pp. 19, 30–31, 61, 65, 72, 97.

Notes to Chapter 9: Coach and Horses

1 R. Straus, *Carriages and Coaches* (London, 1912), p. 53.

2   *HMC*, 'Rutland MSS', IV (London, 1905), p. 289.
3   *CSPV, III 1520–26*, p. 50.
4   Straus, *Carriages and Coaches*, pp. 111, 139–41.
5   J. Crofts, *Packhorse, Waggon and Post* (London, 1967), p. 118; S.E. Whyman, *Sociability and Power in Late-Stuart England: The Cultural Worlds of the Verneys 1660–1720* (Oxford, 1999), p. 102; Straus, *Carriages and Coaches*, pp. 119, 139–40; P. Edwards, *The Horse Trade of Tudor and Stuart England* (Cambridge, 1988), p. 10; A. MacGregor, 'Horsegear, Vehicles and Stable Equipment at the Stuart Court: A Documentary Archaeology', *Archaeological Journal*, 153 (1996), pp. 34–51.
6   R. Latham and W. Matthews, eds, *The Diary of Samuel Pepys*, VIII, *1667* (London, 1974), pp. 289–90.
7   Ibid., IX, *1668–69* (London, 1976), pp. 332–3, 335, 337, 342, 345, 352.
8   University College of North Wales Bangor, Library, Mostyn Letters, vol. IV, no. 54; general comment on transition, Straus, *Carriages and Coaches*, pp. 111, 116.
9   J. Munby, 'Les Origines du coche', in D. Reytier, ed., *Voitures, chevaux et attelages du XVIe au XIXe Siècle* (Paris, 2000) pp. 76–7. 'il est significant que celui-ci ne possède pas de caisse suspendue', 'Les origines du coche', p. 77; E. Coczian-Szentpeteri, 'L'èvolution du Coche ou l'histoire d'une invention hongroise', in Reytier, *Voitures*, p. 86. 'La différence avec le "kocsi" consiste dans les essieux directement reliés à la caisse au moyen d'un système de suspension'.
10 Coczian-Szentpeteri, 'L'évolution du coche', pp. 85–9.
11 Straus, *Coaches*, pp. 66, 70, 76.
12 Ibid., Straus, *Carriages and Coaches*, p. 75.
13 D. Gerhold, *Carriers and Coachmasters: Trade and Travel before the Turnpikes* (Chichester, 2005), p. 65.
14 Straus, *Carriages and Coaches*, pp. 109–46.
15 J. Parkes, *Travel in the Seventeenth Century* (Oxford, 1925), p. 71n.
16 John Cooke, Greene's *Tu Quoque: or The Cittie Gallant* (1614), act 1, scene 6, line 522–3.
17 *HMC, 6th Report*, Appendix, 'MSS of Sir Richard Graham' (London, 1877), p. 326.
18 MacGregor, 'Horsegear', pp. 34–8.
19 I. Richefort, 'Différent usages des carosses de Louis XIV', in D. Reytier, *Voitures*, pp. 297–8. 'Ces carosses royals délaissèrent les progrès techniques qui se multipliaient …'
20 A. Clark, ed., *Aubrey's Brief Lives*, II (Oxford, 1898), p. 267; Thomas Nash, *Quaternio* (London, 1633), pp. 31–2.
21 N.E. McClure, *The Letters of John Chamberlain*, I (Philadelphia, Pennsylvania, 1939), p. 499.
22 T.T. Lewis ed., 'Letters of Lady Brilliana Harley', *Camden Society*, first series, 58 (1854), p. 134.
23 Crofts, *Packhorse*, p. 122; TNA, E134/7 William III, Easter, no. 3, Shropshire.
24 F.G. Emmison, *Tudor Secretary, Sir William Petre at Court and Home* (London, 1961), p. 206.
25 A.C. Edwards, *John Petre, 1549–1613* (London, 1975), p. 67.
26 P. Edwards and C. Gibson, eds, *The Plays and Poems of Philip Massinger* (Oxford, 1976), act 2, scene 2, lines 108–13.

27 L. Stone, 'The Residential Development of the West End of London in the Seventeenth Century', in B.C. Malament, ed., *After the Reformation* (Philadelphia, Pennsylvania, 1980), p. 77.
28 Whyman, *Sociability and Power*, p. 87.
29 M.K. Geiter and W.A. Speck, eds, *Memoirs of Sir John Reresby* (London, 1991), p. 214.
30 C. Morris, ed., *The Journeys of Celia Fiennes* (London, 1947), p. 337.
31 C. Jackson, ed., 'Yorkshire Diaries and Autobiographies in the Seventeenth and Eighteenth Centuries', II, *Surtees Society*, 77 (1883), p. 115; Whyman, *Sociability and Power*, p. 100.
32 M.M. Verney, *The Memoirs of the Verney Family*, III, *1650–1660* (London, 1970), p. 192.
33 Michel de Montaigne, 'Of Coaches', *The Complete Essays of Montaigne*, trans. D.A. Frame (Stanford, California, 1965), p. 687.
34 Clark, *Aubrey's Brief Lives*, II, p. 267.
35 Verney, *Memoirs*, III, pp. 255–6.
36 R. Davies, 'The Life of Marmaduke Rawdon of York', *Camden Society*, old series, 85 (1863), p. 88.
37 *HMC*, 'Portland MSS', VI (London, 1901), pp. 81–147.
38 A. Dent, *Horses in Shakespeare's England* (London, 1987), p. 51.
39 *HMC*, 'Lord De L'Isle and Dudley MSS', I (London, 1925), p. 265.
40 Ibid., VI, *Sidney Papers, 1626–98* (London, 1966) p. 437.
41 Hertfordshire Record Office, Henry de Nassau MSS, D/ENa 05.
42 McClure, *Letters of John Chamberlain*, I, pp. 433–4.
43 BL, Harleian MS 7660, fos, 30, 34.
44 *HMC*, 'Portland MSS', III (London, 1894), p. 606.
45 Whyman, *Sociability and Power*, p. 102.
46 Henry Peacham, *Coach and Sedan* (London, 1636), p. F1r–v; Latham and Matthews, *Pepys*, IX, *1668–9*, p. 352.
47 University College of North Wales Bangor, Library, Mostyn Letters, vol. 4, no. 54. St Sepulchre's is the parish which includes the Smithfield.
48 TNA, PROB 4/21162; PROB 4/7324; the Smithfield was located in the parish of St Sepulchre.
49 G.S. Thomson, *Life in a Noble Household, 1641–1700* (London, 1937), p. 54; Warwickshire Record Office, Warwick Castle MSS, CR 1886/411.
50 J.J. Bagley, 'The Great Diurnal of Nicholas Blundell of Little Crosby, Lancashire', *Record Society of Lancashire & Cheshire*, I, '1702–11', 110 (1968), p. 97, III, '1720–29', 114 (1972), pp. 92, 151.
51 Edwards, *John Petre*, p. 68
52 Warwickshire Record Office, Warwick Castle MSS, CR1886/413.
53 Ibid., CR 1886/411.
54 McClure, *Letters of John Chamberlain*, II, p. 621.
55 Bagley, 'Diurnal of Nicholas Blundell', I, pp. 198, 257, 298, 306, II, '1712–19', 112 (1970), pp. 48, 243, III, pp. 2, 24, 77, 185–6, 199; Edwards, *The Horse Trade*, pp. 10–11.
56 Hertfordshire Record Office, Wittewronge MSS, D/ELW F20; Derbyshire Record Office, D258/47/22. I am grateful to Dr Stephen Porter for this reference.
57 J. Wake and D.C. Webster, eds, 'The Letter Books of Daniel Eaton, 1725–32', *Northamptonshire Record Society*, 24 (1970–71), p. 37.

58   Richard Blome, *The Gentleman's Recreation* (London, 1686), p. 10.
59   Gerhold, *Carriers and Coachmasters*, p. 115; Wake and Webster, 'The Letters of Daniel Eaton', p. 22.
60   Norton Conyers MSS; Hertfordshire Record Office, Henry de Nassau MSS, D/Ena 05, 07, 08, 025.
61   *HMC*, 'Hastings MSS', I (London, 1928), p. 373.
62   G. Ornsby, ed., 'Household Books of Lord Willian Howard of Naworth Castle', *Surtees Society*, 68 (1878), p. 272.
63   *HMC, 12th Report*, 'Coke MSS', I (London, 1888), p. 247; Hertfordshire Record Office, Henry de Nassau MSS, D/ENa 019.
64   *HMC, 11th Report*, pt 4, 'Marquis of Townshend's MSS' (London, 1887), p. 203.
65   Nicholas Morgan, *The Perfection of Horse-manship* (London, 1609), p. 18.
66   BL Add. MS 32697, fol. 12. I am grateful to Dr Joe Bettey for this reference.
67   *HMC, 11th Report*, Appendix, pt 5 (London, 1887), p. 127.
68   G.S. Thomson, *Life in a Noble Household, 1641–1700* (London, 1937), p. 54; Buckinghamshire Record Office, Chester of Chicheley MSS, D/C/4/8.
69   North Yorkshire Record Office, Cholmeley/Strickland MSS, ZCG/IV/5/2/6; Hertfordshire Record Office, Henry de Nassau MSS, D/ENa 07–08.
70   Hertfordshire Record Office, Wittewronge MSS, D/ELW F20.
71   Latham and Matthews, *Pepys's Diary*, IX, *1668–9*, p. 384.
72   Peacham, *Coach and Sedan*, p. E4; Blome, *The Gentleman's Recreation*, pt 2, p. 2.
73   Edwards, *The Horse Trade*, pp. 19, 95, 98. Estate records recording the purchase or sale of coach horses at the Smithfield include Craven (Montgomeryshire), National Library of Wales, Powis Castle Correspondence, I, p. 5; Hervey (Suffolk), S.H.A.H., *The Diary of John Hervey First Earl of Bristol 1651 to 1750 with Extracts from his Book of Expenses 1688 to 1742* (Wells, 1894), p. 122; Massingberd of Mumby (Lincolnshire), Lincolnshire Archives Office, MM 6/1/5; Master (Kent), [–] Dalison, trans., Expense Book of James Master Esq: pt 4, *Archaeologia Cantiana*, 18, 1889, p. 2; Pelham (Sussex), BL, Add. MSS 33144–45; and Slingsby (Yorkshire), Leeds Archives Office, DD 56/J3/7. Estate records merely referring to London include Brooke (Warwickshire), Warwickshire Record Office, Warwick Castle MSS, CR 1886/411; Massingberd of Mumby, as above; Monson (Lincolnshire), Lincolnshire Archives Office, MON 10/1/A/14; Pelham, BL, Add. MS 33146; Petre [Essex] Essex Record Office, D/DP/A55; Strathmore (Durham), Durham Record Office, V 606.
74   Edwards, *The Horse Trade*, pp. 22–4, 34–8.
75   Hinkley Fair: Newdigate (Warwickshire), Warwickshire Record Office, CR 136/V/142; Leicester Fair: Finch (Rutland), Leicestershire Record Office, DG 7/1/19a, 22; Bradford (Staffordshire), Staffordshire Record Office, Bradford MSS, account book 1716–47; Lutterworth Fair: Holles (Nottinghamshire), Nottingham University Library, MSS Department, Pw V4; Fotheringhay Fair: Vane (Northamptonshire), Northamptonshire Record Office, Westmorland (Apethorpe), Misc. Vol. 4; Oundle Fair: Rockingham (Kent), Lincolnshire Archives Office, Monson MSS MON 10/1/A/19; Northampton Fair: Boteler (Bedfordshire), Bedfordshire Record Office, PO 3; Brooke (Warwickshire), Warwickshire Record Office, Warwick Castle MSS, CR 136/V/142; Cartwright (Northamptonshire), Northamptonshire Record Office, C(A) 3489; Chester (Buckinghamshire), Buckinghamshire Record Office, D/C/4/8; Finch (Rutland),

Leicestershire Record Office, DG 7/1/19a–b; Manners (Leicestershire), *HMC*, 'Rutland MSS', IV, p. 550; Massingberd of Gunby (Lincolnshire), Lincolnshire Archives Office, MG 5/2/7–8; Massingberd of Mumby (Lincolnshire), Lincolnshire Archives Office, MM 6/1/4; Pratt (Norfolk), Norfolk Record Office, NRO m/f reel 218/7; Rockingham (Kent), Lincolnshire Archives Office, MON 10/1/A/18; Rushout (Gloucestershire), Worcestershire Record Office, Bulk Accession 4221, Ref. 705:66/51(vi); Toke (Kent), E.C. Lodge, ed., *The Account Book of a Kentish Estate, 1616–1704* (London, 1927), p. 391; Vane (Northamptonshire), Westmorland (Apethorpe) Misc. Vol. 4; Verney (Buckinghamshire), M.M. Verney, ed., *Memoirs of the Verney Family*, IV, *1660–1696* (London, 1970), p. 54; Rothwell Fair: Finch (Rutland), Leicestershire Record Office, DG 7/1/19a; Hatcher (Lincolnshire), Joan Thirsk, *English Peasant Farming* (London, 1957), p. 176.

76   Hertfordshire Record Office, Henry de Nassau MSS, D/Ena 07; Northamptonshire Record Office, MTM 595.

77   William Cavendish, *A New Method and Extraordinary Invention to Dress Horses* (London, 1667), p. 59.

78   *HMC*, 'Duke of Buccleuch and Queensberry MSS', II (London, 1903), p. 164; D. Defoe, *A Tour through the Whole Island of Great Britain*, ed., P. Rogers (Harmondsworth, 1971), p. 406.

79   Warwickshire Record Office, Warwick Castle MSS, CR 1886/411; Buckinghamshire Record Office, Chester MSS, D/C/4/8; Hertfordshire Record Office, Wittewronge MSS, D/ELW/F 21.

80   *HMC*, 'Portland MSS', III (London, 1894), p. 61; Warwickshire Record Office, Warwick Castle MSS, CR 1886/411.

81   Surrey History Centre, Loseley MSS, LM Cor 10/122.

82   Warwickshire Record Office, Warwick Castle MSS, CR 1886/411; Bagley, 'Diurnal of Nicholas Blundell', III, p. 184; Northamptonshire Record Office, Cartwright of Aynho MSS, C[A] 3489.

83   Northamptonshire Record Office, Cartwright of Aynho MSS, C(A)3489.

84   Lincolnshire Archives Office, Massingberd of Gunby MSS, MG 5/2/7.

85   Lincolnshire Archives Office, Massingberd of Gunby MSS, MG 5/2/1; Warwickshire Record Office, Earl of Northampton MSS., CR 556/275.

86   Warwickshire Record Office, Warwick Castle MSS., CR1886/411; Thomson, *Noble Household* (1937) pp. 204–5.

87   A. MacGregor, 'The Royal Stables: A Seventeenth-Century Perspective', *Antiquaries Journal*, 76 (1996), pp. 186, 188.

88   Lincolnshire Archive Office, Massingberd of Mumby MSS, MM 6/1/5.

89   Whyman, *Sociability and Power*, p. 60.

90   This section is based on D. Gerhold, *Carriers and Coachmasters*. I am extremely grateful to him for providing me with a copy of a transcript of his book before publication.

91   Taylor, *The World runnes on Wheels*, fol. E4; F. Moryson, *Itinerary* (London, 1617), p. 62.

92   Gerhold, *Coaches and Coachmasters*, p. 80; F.P. Verney, *The Memoirs of the Verney Family*, I (London, 1970), p. 109; Straus, *Carriages and Coaches*, p. 88 states 1625 but this allows too little time for the huge expansion, satirized by Peacham, to occur.

93   Peacham, *Coach and Sedan*, p. F1r.

94   Nash, *Quaternio*, pp. 31–2; John Taylor, *The World Runnes on Wheels* (London, 1623), fol. B1v.

95 Ibid., fos, A3–4.
96 Verney, *Memoirs*, I, p. 110; Whyman, *Sociability and Power*, p. 236, n. 65.
97 H. Robinson, *The British Post Office: An History* (New Jersey, 1948), pp. 67–8; Whyman, *Sociability and Power*, pp. 101–2; TNA, SP29/319, no. 201.
98 TNA, SP 29/319, nos 200, 202, p. 6.
99 Moryson, *Itinerary*, p. 62.
100 TNA, SP 29/319, no. 200, p. 1.
101 Gerhold, *Coaches and Coachmasters*, pp. 83–4, 112.
102 Ibid., pp. 85, 112.
103 Ibid., p. 79.
104 TNA, SP 29/319, no. 201; Robinson, *Post Office*, p. 68.
105 Gerhold, *Coaches and Coachmasters*, p. 81.
106 Ibid., pp. 88–9; Crofts, *Packhorse*, p. 127.
107 Gerhold, *Coaches and Coachmasters*, pp. 115–16.
108 Ibid., p. 117.
109 TNA, PROB 4/9736.
110 Lincolnshire Archives Office, Massingberd of Mumby MSS, MM 6/1/5; Oxford tolls.
111 J. Thirsk and J. Cooper, eds, *17th Century Economic Documents* (Oxford, 1972), pp. 379–87.
112 Gerold, *Coaches and Coachmasters*, p. 88.
113 Crofts, *Packhorse*, pp. 129–31; TNA, SP 29/319/200, fol. 2.
114 M.Y. Ashcroft, *Sir William Chaytor (1639–1721)*, North Riding County Record Office Publications, 33 (1983), p. 148.
115 Edward Chamberlayne, *Angliae Notitia: or the Present State of England* (London, 1671), pt 2, pp. 405–6.
116 Davies, *Rawdon*, p. 70; Bagley, 'Diurnal of Nicholas Blundell', III, p. 105.
117 W.M. Myddelton, ed., *Chirk Castle Accounts, A.D. 1666–1753* (Manchester, 1931), p. 355.
118 Whyman, *Sociability and Power*, p. 102; Bagley, 'Diurnal of Nicholas Blundell', I, pp. 35, 114.
119 *HMC*, 'Portland MSS', III (London, 1894), pp. 498, 506; BL, Add. MS 70440 no foliation.
120 Crofts, *Packhorse*, pp. 127–8.
121 Bagley, 'Diurnal of Nicholas Blundell', III, p. 105.

Notes to Conclusion

1 M. Berg and E. Eger, *Luxury in the Eighteenth Century: Debates, Desires and Delectable Goods* (Basingstoke, 2003), pp. 9, 65; M. Berg and H. Clifford, eds, *Consumers and Luxury: Consumer Culture in Europe 1650–1850* (Manchester, 1999), pp. 63–9; M. Overton et al, *Production and Consumption in English Households, 1660–1750* (London, 2004), pp. 116, 120, 166.
2 L. Weatherill, *Consumer Behaviour & Material Culture in Britain 1660–1750* (London, 1996), pp. 166–89; Overton et al, *Production and Consumption*, pp. 162, 166–7.
3 Overton, *Production and Consumption*, p. 120; Weatherill, *Consumer Behaviour*, pp. 187, 189.
4 Overton, *Production and Consumption*, pp. 166–7; Berg and Eger, *Luxury*, p. 13.

5   S.E. Whyman, *Sociability and Power in Late-Stuart England: The Cultural World of the Verneys, 1660–1720* (Oxford, 1999), p. 104.
6   F. Dabhoiwala, 'The Construction of Honour, Reputation and Status in Late Seventeenth and Early Eighteenth Century England', *Transactions of the Royal Historical Society*, sixth series, VI (1996), p. 203; R. Latham and W. Matthews, *The Diary of Samuel Pepys*, VIII (London, 1974), pp. 174, 209.
7   Fynes Moryson, *An Itinerary* (London, 1617), pp. 61–2.
8   B. Lemire, 'Introduction: Dress, Culture and the English People', *Dress, Culture and Commerce: The English Clothing Trade Before the Factory, 1660–1800* (London, 1997), pp. 2–3.
9   J.H. Plumb, 'Commercialisation and Society', in N. McKendrick et al, *The Birth of a Consumer Society: The Commercialisation of Eighteenth-Century England* (London, 1983), pp. 265–85.
10 Ibid., pp. 273, 280.

Bibliography

MANUSCRIPT SOURCES

1: NATIONAL REPOSITORIES

Bodleian Library
Ashmole 1621.

British Library
Add. MSS 22149, 32697, 33144–47, 33149, 70143, 70385–86, 70440.
Harleian MSS 6852, 27660, 29443.
Penkridge fair toll books, 1558, 1579, 1640, Egerton MS 3008, fos 2v–22v.
Thomason Tracts E2621/6.

Lambeth Palace Library
Surrey Probate Inventories.

Society of Antiquaries
MS 12, lines 8523–34.
MS 129.

The National Archives
Assize: ASSI 45/6/3/15; ASSI 45/8/2/76; ASSI 45/13/1/64.
Chancery: C1/1009/58; C2/Jas. I/F4/53; C3/141/98; C23/141/98.
Declared Accounts: E 315/414; E 351/1750; E 351/1752; E 351/1762; E 351, 1763.
Exchequer, Special Commissions: E134/7 William III, Easter, no. 3, Shropshire.
Equitium Regis Accounts: E 101/56/24; E 101/60/24; E 101/107/17; E 101/107/27–28; E 101/533/14.
Probate Records: PROB 4/335; PROB 4/1528; PROB 4/1675; PROB 4/2802; PROB 4/7324; PROB 4/7440; PROB 4/9736; PROB 4/21162.

Requests: REQ 2/30/38 ; REQ 2/157/163; REQ 2/162/16; REQ 2/188/6; REQ 2/308/1; REQ 2/396/80; REQ 2/413/24.
State Papers: SP 12/24, no. 59; SP 12/136/4; SP 12/136/42; SP 12/137/17; SP 12/233/69; SP 12/240, no. 79; SP 28/28, III; SP 28/29, I, fol. 331; SP28/30, IV; SP28/38, III; SP28/140, VII; SP 29/319, nos 200–2; SP 46/48/fol. 78; SP 46/60, fol. 213; SP 46/83.
War Office: WO 49/19–26; WO 49/30, fos 104, 144v; WO 49/68, fos 33–34.

National Archives of Scotland
Hamilton MSS, GD406/1/10491.

National Library of Wales
Crosse of Shaw Hill MSS, no. 1106.
Mostyn Letters, vol. IV, no. 54.
Powis Castle Correspondence, I.
Schedule of Powys Castle Correspondence, I, p. 12.
Sir Edward Owen MSS 73, Thomas Brereton's Accounts, 1662–3.

2. LOCAL REPOSITORIES

Beccles Town Hall
Beccles market toll books, 1571–3, 1674–1710, Rix Div. IV, Markets and Fairs.

Bedfordshire Record Office
Boteler MSS, PO 3.

Birmingham Reference Library
Sutton Coldfield fair toll books, 1750–9, Ref. 80–82.

Bristol Record Office
Bristol market toll books, 1705–14, 1735–58, xerox copy of documents not in B.R.O., 52.
Smyth family MSS, AC/C46/9.

Buckinghamshire Record Office
Chester of Chicheley MSS, D/C/4/8, 10.

Chester City Record Office
Assembly Book, 1624–85, fol. 176v.
Toll books (market), 1658–1723, Sheriffs's Toll Books SBT/1.
Toll books (fair), c. 1567–79, Sheriffs's Toll Books SBT/2.

Cheshire Record Office
Farndon MSS, DCH/J/40.
Probate will, Richard Annion of Chester, 1666.

Cumbria R.O.(Carlisle)
Browne MSS vol. 8.
Carlisle fair toll books, 1631–4, 1653–4, Ca/4/152–5.
Lowther MSS, D/Lons/L/A1/4a; D/LONS/W/unlisted.
Rosley Hill fair toll books, 1649–50, Cockermouth Castle, Leconfield MSS, D/Lec/323.

Cumbria Record Office (Kendal)
WQ/01 Order Book 1669–96.
Muncaster Castle MSS, D/PEN/202–3, Estate Account Books 1660–94 and 1695–1708.
Probate inventories: Scaleby parish.

Derby Reference Library
Derby fair toll books, 1638–61, 1677, late 17th century, 1697–1700.

Derbyshire Record Office
Chandos-Pole-Gell MSS, D258/box 29/9a, 44b; D258/47/22.

Devon (East) Record Office
Hartland market toll books, 1615–73, Hartland Borough Records, 1201 A/B1.

Devon (North) Athenaeum, Barnstaple
Barnstaple fair toll books, 1628–65, 3973, 4143.

Devon (West) Record Office
Plymouth market toll books, 1590–1606, Plymouth Corporation Records, W89.

Dudley Reference Library
Dudley fair toll book, 1702–10, Dudley Estate Collection, Misc. Box.

Durham Record Office
Quarter Sessions Records, 1695 bundle.
Strathmore MSS, V 606.

Durham University, Department of Palaeography and Diplomatic
Howard of Naworth MSS, 201/9.

Essex Record Office
Blackmore fair toll book, 1679, D/DB M154.
Clopton Diary, 1648–52.
Hatfield Broadoak fair toll books, 1644–59, D/DHt M50.
Petre MSS, D/DP/A55; D/DP/Z/3716.
Quarter Sessions Records: Q/SR 53/30, 56/20.

Folger Shakespeare Library, Washington DC
Market Bosworth fair toll books, 1603–32, MS.V.b.165.

Herefordshire Record Office
Coningsby MSS, W15/2.
Foley MSS, FH/111/3; FH/111/13.
Leominster fair toll books, 1556–7, Leominster Borough Records, Bailiffs' Accounts 8.
Probate inventories: Thomas Sheinton of Chelmarsh, 30 July 1745.

Hertfordshire Record Office
Henry de Nassau MSS, D/ENa 03, 05, 07–08, 019, 025.
Wittewronge MSS, D/ELW F20–21, 23.

Kidderminster Reference Library
Kidderminster fair toll book, 1694–1711, KID 352/No. 1455.

Lancashire Record Office
Clifton of Lytham MSS, DDCl/399.

Leeds Archives Department
LAD Temple Newsam MSS, TN/EL/C 19.
Ripley fair toll books, 1708, 1721–30, 1773–7, Ingilby MSS, 3117–18.

Leicestershire Record Office
Finch MSS, DG 7/1/19a–b; 22.
Hallaton fair toll books, 1720–8, DE 339/350–53.
Leicester fair toll book, 1598, Leicester Borough Records, BR III/8/41.

Lichfield Joint Record Office
Eccleshall fair toll books, 1691–2, B/A/2/123307.
Probate inventories.

Lincolnshire Archives Office
Lincoln Corporation Minute Book LI/I/I/4.
Massingberd of Gunby MSS, MASS 28/1, MG 5/2/1, 7–8.
Massingberd of Mumby MSS, MM 6/1/4–5; MM 6/1/1.
Monson MSS, MON 7/Misc. Book 7/13, fol. 175; MON 10/1/A/14, 18, 19; MON 27/3/1.
Probate inventories: Horbling parish.

Much Wenlock Guildhall
Much Wenlock fair toll books, 1632–8, transcript of toll books 1632–8.

Norfolk Record Office
Bradfer Lawrence MSS VI b 2.
Hare of Stoke Bardolph MSS, Hare 5284.
Pratt of Ryston MSS, m/f reel 219/1, 218/7.

Northamptonshire Record Office
Boughton Green fair toll book, 1627, ZA 2455.
Cartwright of Aynho MSS, C(A) 3489.
Finch-Hatton MSS, F(M)C 275.
Fitzwilliam Correpondence F(M)C 1080.
Rothwell horse fair c. 1684–1721, MTM 595.
Westmorland MSS, Misc. Vols 4, 15.

Norton Conyers Hall
Graham Family MSS.

Nottinghamshire Record Office
Nottingham fair toll books, 1634–64, CA 1504–5.

Nottingham University Library, Manuscripts Department
Middleton MSS, Mi A/62, 71, 78, 81.
Newcastle of Clumber MSS, Walter to the Earl of Clare at Clare House, Drury Lane, 2 August 1662.
Portland MSS, Ne E8; Pw2.325–344; Pw V4–5.

Oxfordshire Record Office
Banbury fair toll books, 1753–67, B.B. VIII/vii/1.
Garsington Account Book 1625–1701, BL I/V/2.

Oxford Reference Library
Oxford market toll book, 1673–1745, Oxford City Records, F.4.4.

Portsmouth Record Office
Portsmouth market toll books, 1623–63, Sessions Book 1598–1638, CE 1/4.

Sheffield University Library
Hartlib MSS, 31/1/64–65.

Shropshire Record Office
Attingham Park MSS, 112/74, 76.
Bridgnorth fair and market toll books, 1631, 1644–1720, 1767–78, Bridgnorth Corporation Records 4001/Mar/1/268–71.
Forester MSS, 1224/296.
Kilmorrey MSS, 946/B360.
Ludlow fair toll books, 1646–9, 1687–95, Ludlow Corporation Records 356/Box 297, 356/32/Box 466.
Shrewsbury Borough Records LIX/2211.
Shrewsbury fair and market toll books, Shrewsbury Borough Records, 2645–68.
Shrewsbury Quarter Sessions Papers, 2212, 2228.

Somerset Record Office
Taunton fair toll books, 1621–39, 1667, 1671, 1674, 1686–97, DD/SP 341.
White Down fair toll books, 1637–49, DD/HI By 53.

Staffordshire Record Office
Bagot MSS, D1721/3/194.
Bradford MSS, account book 1716–47.
Brewood fair toll books, 1661–2, 1683, Giffard MSS, D590/435/1–3.
Edward James's Farming Accounts, 1692–1710, HM27/2.
Leveson-Gower MSS, D593/F/2/38; D 593/P/16/1/3.
Paget of Beaudesert MSS, D[W] 1734/3/3/276, 279; D[W] 1734/3/4/177; D[W] 1734/4/1/6.
Persehouse MSS, D260/M/F/1/6/33.
Rugeley fair toll books, 1767–88, D603/X/1/8.
Stafford fair toll books, 1614–15, Matthew Craddock's Commonplace Book, D 1287/10/2.

Shakespeare Library, Stratford-upon-Avon
Stratford-upon-Avon fairs toll books, 1602, 1646, Misc. Docts V, VII, XIV.

Suffolk (East) Record Office
Blomfield MSS, HD 330/7.

Suffolk (West) Record Office
Probate Inventories: Mildenhall.

Surrey Record Office
Loseley MSS, LM Cor 10/122.

University College of North Wales Library, Bangor
Baron Hill MS 328.

Walsall Town Hall
Walsall fair toll books, 1628–c. 1636, WTC II/40/1–15.

Warwickshire Record Office
Newdigate of Arbury MSS, CR 136/A/20; CR 136/V/142; CR 136/B/1024; CR 136/B/5158.
Earl of Northampton MSS, CR 556/275.
Warwick Castle MSS, CR 1886/411–12.
Warwick fair toll books, 1651–6, 1684–93, Warwick Borough Records, W 13/1.

Winchester Cathedral Library
Winchester fair toll books, 1620–1, 1623, 1625, 1647–8, Calendars of Cathedral Papers + date.

Worcester Guildhall
Worcester toll books: fair (1552–64), market (1635–56), Worcester Corporation Archives.
View of Frankpledge, vol. 1, Liber Recordum.

Worcestershire Record Office
Berkeley Family Household Account Book, b705:93/4/B.A. 845.
Casper Henning Esq., account book, 705:366/B.A. 2252/6(i).
Rushout MSS, 705:66/51(vi)/B.A. 4221.

Yorkshire (North) Record Office
Sir William Chaytor of Croft Hall MSS, D/Ch/C/793.
Cholmeley/Strickland MSS, ZCG/IV/5/2/6.
Quarter Sessions Papers, Calendar: QSB 1707, 1710.

Yorkshire Archaeological Society, Leeds
Clifford of Skipton Castle MSS, DD 121/bundle 36A/3.
Slingsby MSS, DD56/J3/2, 7, 8.

PRINTED PRIMARY SOURCES

Acts of the Privy Council: 1617–19, 1621–23.
Ambler, R.W. and B. and L. Watkinson, eds, 'Farmers and Fishermen, The probate inventories of the ancient parish of Clee, South Humberside 1536–1742', *Studies in Regional & Local History*, IV (Hull, 1987).
Anon., Collection of Ordinances and Regulations for the Government of the Royal Household, Society of Antiquaries (London, 1790).
Anon., 'Montgomeyshire Horses, Cobs and Ponies', *Montgomeryshire Historical Collections*, 22 (1888).
Ashcroft, M.Y., *Sir William Chaytor* (1639–1721), North Riding County Record Office Publications, 33 (1983).
Bagley, J.J., ed., 'The Great Diurnal of Nicholas Blundell of Little Crosby, Lancashire': I, '1702–11', *Record Society of Lancashire & Cheshire*, 110 (1968); II, '1712–19', 112 (1970); III, '1720–29', 114 (1972).
Batho, G.R., ed., 'The Household Papers of Henry Percy, Ninth Earl of Northumberland, 1564–1632', *Camden Society*, third series, 93 (1962).
Brears, P.C.D., ed., 'Yorkshire Probate Inventories, 1542–1689', *Yorkshire Archaeological Society*, 124 (1972).
Brinkworth, E.R.C. and J.S.W. Gibson eds, 'Banbury Wills and Inventories', II, '1621–1850', *Banbury History Society*, 14 (1976).
Bryant, A., ed., *Postman's Horn: An Anthology of Letters of Latter Seventeenth-Century England* (London, 1946).
Bund, J.W.W., ed., 'Diary of Henry Townshend', II, *Worcestershire Historical Society* (1920).
Burns, J.W., ed., *Miscellaneous Writings of John Spreull ... 1646–1722* (Glasgow, 1882).
Byrne, M.S., *The Lisle Letters*, I (Chicago, 1981).
Calendars of State Papers Domestic: 1581–90; 1598–1601, 1628–29; 1638–39; 1641–43; January to October 1655, 1655–56; 1671–72; 1682, May 1684 to 5 February 1685, 1702–3.
Calendars of State Papers Domestic Addenda: 1547–80; 1547–65; Addenda, 1566–79; Addenda, 1580–1625.
Calendar of State Papers Ireland, 1599–1600.
Calendars of State Papers Venetian, II, *1509–19*; III, *1520–26*; V, *1534–54*; VI, pt 3, *1557–58*; XV, *1540*.

BIBLIOGRAPHY

Carew, Richard, *The Survey of Cornwall*, ed., F.E. Halliday (New York, 1969).

Cash, M., ed., 'Devon Inventories in the Sixteenth and Seventeenth Centuries', *Devon and Cornwall Record Society*, new series, 11 (1966).

Clark, A., ed., *Aubrey's Brief Lives*, II (Oxford, 1898).

Cockburn, J.S., ed., *Calendar of Assize Records: Kent Indictments, Charles II* (London, 1995).

Cooper, W.D., ed., 'Letters of Henry Savile Esquire', *Camden Society* (1858), p. 160.

Dalison, trans., Expense Book of James Master Esq: pt 4, *Archaeologia Cantiana*, 18, 1889.

Davies, R., 'The Life of Marmaduke Rawdon of York', *Camden Society*, old series, 85 (1863).

Dixon, P., ed., *George Farquhar's The Recruiting Officer* (Manchester, 1986).

De Beer, E.S., ed., *The Diary of John Evelyn*, 6 vols (Oxford, 1955).

Defoe, D., *A Tour through the Whole Island of Great Britain*, ed., P. Rogers (Harmondsworth, 1971).

de Montaigne, Michel, *The Complete Essays of Montaigne*, trans. D.A. Frame (Stanford, California, 1965).

des Périers, Bonaventure, *Cymbalum Mundi*, ed., Y. Delègue (Paris, 1995).

Edward of Norwich, *The Master of Game*, W.A. and F. Baillie-Grohman, eds, (London, 1909/repr. Philadelphia, 2005).

Edwards, A.C., *John Petre, 1549–1613* (London, 1975).

Edwards, P. and. C. Gibson, eds, *The Plays and Poems of Philip Massinger* (Oxford, 1976).

Ellis, Sir H., ed., 'Norden's Description of Essex', *Camden Society* (1840).

Emmison, F.G., 'Jacobean Household Inventories', *Bedfordshire Record Society*, 20 (1938).

Evans, J.X., *The Works of Sir Roger Williams* (Oxford, 1972).

Exwood, M. and H.L. Lehmann, eds, 'The Journal of William Schellink's Travels in England, 1661–1663', *Camden Society*, 5th series, 1 (1993).

Furnivall, F.J., ed., 'Harrison's Description of England', III, 'The Supplement', *New Shakespeare Society*, series 6, no. 8 (1881).

Geiter, M.K. and W.A. Speck, eds, *Memoirs of Sir John Reresby* (London, 1991).

Goring J. and J. Wake, eds, 'Northamptonshire Lieutenancy Papers and Other Documents, 1580–1614', *Northamptonshire Record Society*, 27 (1975).

Gough, Richard, *Antiquityes and Memoyres of the Parish of Myddle* (Shrewsbury, 1875).

Groves, J., ed., *Ashton-on-Mersey and Sale Wills*, I, *1600–1650* (Sale, 1999), II, *1651–1700* (Sale, 2000), III, *1700–1760* (Sale, 2002).

Groves, J., ed., *Bowden Wills*, I, *1600–1650* (Sale, 1997), II, *1651–1689* (Sale, 1998), III, *1690–1760* (Sale, 1999).

Hainsworth, D.R., ed., 'The Correspondence of Sir John Lowther of Whitehaven, 1693–1698: A Provincial Community in Wartime', *Records of Social and Economic History*, new series, 7 (1983).

Hainsworth, D.R. and C. Walker, eds, 'The Correspondence of Lord Fitzwilliam of Milton and Francis Guybon his Steward, 1697–1709', *Northamptonshire Record Society* (1990).

Haldane, E.S. and G.R.T. Ross, trans, *The Philosophical Works of Descartes*, I (Cambridge, 1911).

Hamilton, C.L., ed., '"The Muster-Master" by Gervase Markham', *Camden Society*, fourth series, 14 (1975).

Harbin, E.H.B., ed., *Quarter Sessions Records for the County of Somerset*, II, 1625–1639, *Somerset Record Society* (1908).

Harding, J.M., *Charlwood Inventories* (Charlwood, 1976).

Havinden, M.A., ed., 'Household and Farm Inventories in Oxfordshire', *Oxfordshire Record Society*, 44 (London, 1965).

Hearnshaw, F.J.C. and D.M., eds, 'Court Leet Records', I, pt 2, '1578–1602', *Southampton Record Society* (1906).

Herford, C.H. and P. and E. Simpson, eds, *Ben Jonson*, III, *The Poems, The Prose Works. The Forrest*, II: 'To Penshurst' (1616) (Oxford, 1947).

Heywood, Thomas, *The English Traveller* (1633/ repr. New York, 1973).

Historical Manuscripts Commission:
  6th Report, Appendix, 'MSS of Sir Richard Graham' (London, 1877).
  10th Report, IV, 'Earl of Kilmorrey MSS'.
  11th Report, pt 4, 'Marquis of Townshend's MSS'.
  11th Report, Appendix, pt 5.
  12th Report, 'Coke MSS', I.
  12th Report, 'MSS of Captain Stewart of Alltyrodyn, Llandyssil'.
  12th Report, Appendix, part VII, 'MSS of S.H. Le Fleming Esq. of Rydall Hall'.
  'Bath MSS', IV.
  'Buccleuch and Queensberry MSS', II.
  'De L'Isle and Dudley MSS', I, VI.
  'Downshire MSS', III.
  'Finch MSS', II.
  'House of Lords, 1714–18'.
  'MSS in Various Collections, IV.
  'Pepys MSS'.
  'Portland MSS', II–VI, IX.
  'Rutland MSS', I–II, IV.
  'Salisbury MSS', X–XI, XIV, XIX, XXII.

Jackson, C., ed., 'Yorkshire Diaries and Autobiographies in the Seventeenth and Eighteenth Centuries', II, *Surtees Society*, 77 (1883).

James, S., ed., *Margaret Cavendish: Political Writings* (Cambridge, 2003).
Jerdan, W., ed., 'Original Documents ... Selected from the Private Archives of his Grace the Duke of Rutland', *Camden Society*, 21 (1842).
Kennedy, P.A., ed., Nottinghamshire Household Inventories, *Thoroton Society, Record Series*, 22 (1963).
Kenyon, G.H., 'Kirdford Inventories, 1611 to 1776', *Sussex Archaeological Collections*, 93 (1955).
Lansberry, H.C.F., ed., 'Sevenoaks Wills and Inventories in the Reign of Charles II', *Kent Archaeologocal Society, Kent Records*, 25 (1988).
Larkin, J.F. and P.L. Hughes, eds, *Stuart Royal Proclamations*, I, *James I, 1603–25* (Oxford, 1973).
Latham, R. and W. Matthews, eds, *The Diary of Samuel Pepys*, VII, *1666* (London, 1972); VIII, *1667* (London, 1974); IX, *1668–69* (London, 1976).
Leighton, W.A., ed., 'The Early Chronicles of Shrewsbury', *Transactions of the Shropshire Archaeological Society*, 3 (1880).
Letters and Papers of Henry VIII, I, pt 1, *1509–13*; I, pt 2, *1513–14*; II, pt 1, *1515–16*; II, pt 2, *1517–18*; III, pt 1, *1521–23*; IV, pt 2, *1526–8*; XII, pt 2, *1537*; XIII, pt 2, *1538*; XIV, pt 1, *1539*; XV, *1540*; XVI, pt 1, *1540–1*; XVI, pt 2, *1541*; XVII, *1542*; XVIII, pt 2, *1543*; XIX, pt 1, *1544*; XX, pt 1, *1545*; XX, pt 2, *1545*; XXI, pt 1, *1546*.
Lewis T.T., ed., 'Letters of Lady Brilliana Harley', *Camden Society*, first series, 58 (1854).
Lodge, E.C., ed., *The Account Book of a Kentish Estate, 1616–1704* (London, 1927).
Marlow, N., trans., 'The Diary of Thomas Isham of Lamport', *Northamptonshire Record Society*, 17 (1955).
McCann, T.J., 'The Correspondence of the Dukes of Richmond and Newcastle 1724–1750', *Sussex Record Society*, 73 (1982–3).
McClure, N.E., ed., *The Letters of John Chamberlain*, 2 vols (Philadelphia, 1939).
Middleton, Thomas and Thomas Dekker, *The Roaring Girl*, ed., A. Gomme (London, 1976).
Midgley, M., 'Beasts, Brutes and Monsters', in T. Ingold, ed., *What is an Animal?* (London, 1994).
Millner, John, *A Compendious Journal of the Marches, Famous Battles, Sieges and other Note-worthy, Heroical, and Ever Memorable Actions of the Triumphant Armies, of the Ever-Glorious Confederate High Allies* (Uckfield, 2004).
Moore, J.S., ed., *The Good and Chattels of our Forefathers: Frampton Cotterell and District Probate Inventories, 1539–1804* (Chichester, 1976).
Moore, J.S., ed., *Clifton and Westbury Probate Inventories, 1609–1761* (Bristol, 1981).

Morris, C., ed., *The Journeys of Celia Fiennes* (London, 1947).
Muir, J.B., *Ye Olde New-Markitt Calendar of Matches, Results and Programs from 1619 to 1719* (London, 1892).
Myddelton, W.M., ed., *Chirk Castle Accounts, A.D. 1666–1753* (Manchester, 1931).
Neave, D., ed., *Winteringham 1650–1760* (Winteringham, 1984).
Newton, Lady E., *Lyme Letters, 1660–1760* (London, 1925).
Nichols, J.G., 'The Chronicle of Calais (in the Reigns of Henry VII and Henry VIII to the Year 1540)', *Camden Society*, 35 (1846).
Nicholas, J.G., ed., 'The Diary of Henry Machyn', *Camden Society*, 42 (1848).
'Order for the Mustering of Demi-Lances and Light Horsemen on Mousehold near Magdalen Chapel, 1584', *Norfolk Archaeology*, 1 (1849).
Ornsby, G., ed., 'Household Books of Lord Willian Howard of Naworth Castle', *Surtees Society*, 68 (1878).
Parker, M., ed, *All My Worldly Goods* (St Albans, 1985).
Penney, N., ed., *The Household Account Book of Sarah Fell of Swarthmoor Hall, 1673–78* (Cambridge, 1920).
Pennington, D.H. and I.A. Roots, eds, *The Committee at Stafford, 1643–45* (Manchester, 1957).
Percy, Bishop Thomas, *The Regulations and Establishment of the Houshold of Henry Algernon Percy, Fifth Earl of Northumberland at his Castles of Wressle and Leconsfield begun 1512* (London, 1905).
Prior, C.M., *Early Records of the Thoroughbred* (London, 1924).
Prior, C.M., *The Royal Studs of the Sixteenth and Seventeenth Centuries* (London, 1935).
Quintrell, B.W., ed., 'The Maynard Lieutenancy Book, 1608–1639', *Essex Historical Documents*, 3 (Chelmsford, 1993).
Raines, F.R., ed., 'The Journal of Nicholas Assheton of Downham ... 1617', *Chetham Society* (1948).
Reed, M., ed., 'The Ipswich Probate Inventories, 1583–1631', *Suffolk Record Society*, 22 (1981).
Reed, M., ed., 'Buckinghamshire Probate Inventories, 1661–1714', *Buckinghamshire Record Society*, 24 (1988).
Richmond and District Civil Society Annual Report (Richmond, 1978).
Roberts, G., ed., 'Diary of Walter Yonge, Esq.', *Camden Society* (1847).
Robertshaw, W., ed., 'Notes on Adwalton Fair', *Bradford Antiquary*, new series, 5 (1927).
Roper, J.S., ed., *Sedgeley Probate Inventories, 1614–1787* (Dudley, 1960).
Roper, J.S., ed., *Dudley Probate Inventories, 1544–1603* (Dudley, 1965–66).
Roper, J.S., ed., *Stourbridge Probate Inventories 1541–1558* (Dudley, 1966).

Roper, J.S., ed., *Belbroughton Wills and Probate Inventories, 1539–1647* (Dudley, 1967–68).

Robinson, C.B., ed., 'Rural Economy in Yorkshire in 1641, Being the Farming and Account Books of Henry Best of Elmeswell in the East Riding', *Surtees Society*, 33 (1857).

Rye, W., 'Depositions Taken before the Mayor and Aldermen of Norwich, 1549–67', *Norfolk and Norwich Archaeological Society* (1905), p. 79.

Seddon, P.R., ed., 'Letters of John Holles, 1587–1637', I, *Thoroton Society*, Record Series, 31 (1975).

S.H.A.H., ed., *Letter Books of John Hervey, First Earl of Bristol 1651 to 1750* (Wells, 1894).

S.H.A.H., *The Diary of John Hervey First Earl of Bristol 1651 to 1750 with Extracts from his Book of Expenses 1688 to 1742* (Wells, 1894).

Shuttleworth, J.M., ed., *The Life of Edward, First Lord Herbert of Cherbury, Written by Himself* (Oxford, 1976).

Smallwood, R.L. and S. Wells, eds, Thomas Dekker, *The Shoemaker's Holiday* (Manchester, 1979).

Squires, H.L. and E. Rowley, eds, 'Early Montgomeryshire Wills at Somerset House', *Montgomeryshire Historical Collections*, 22 (1888).

Statutes: 27 Henry VIII, c. 6; 33 Henry VIII, c. 5; 2 and 3 Philip & Mary, c. 7; 4 and 5 Philip & Mary, cc. 2, 3; 31 Elizabeth I, c. 12; 22 & 23 Charles II c. 25; 9 George I, c. 22; 13 George II, c. 19.

Steer, F.W., ed., *Farm and Cottage Inventories of Mid Essex, 1635 to 1749* (Chichester, 1969).

Stow, John, *A Survey of ... London*, ed., John Strype, 1720.

Surtees, Robert, *The History and Antiquities of the County Palatine of Durham*, I (London, 1816).

Sylvester, D.W., *Educational Documents, 800–1816* (London, 1970).

'The Memorandum Book of Richard Cholmeley of Brandsby, 1602–1623', *North Yorkshire Record Office Publication*, 44 (1988).

Thirsk, J. and J.P. Cooper, *17th Century Economic Documents* (Oxford, 1972).

Thwaite, H., ed., 'Abstracts of Abbotside Wills 1552–1688', *Yorkshire Archaeological Society*, Record Series, 130 (1967).

Tibbutt, H.G., ed., 'The Letter Books 1644–45 of Sir Samuel Luke' (London, 1963).

Trevelyan, Sir W.C. and C.E., eds, 'Trevelyan Papers', III, *Camden Society*, 105 (1872).

Turner, J.H., ed., *The Reverend Oliver Heywood B.A.*, IV (Brighouse, 1885).

Vaisey, D.G., ed., 'Probate Inventories of Lichfield and District, 1586–1680', *Staffordshire Record Society*, fourth series, V (1969).

Wake J. and D.C. Webster, eds, 'The Letter Books of Daniel Eaton 1725–32', *Northamptonshire Record Society*, 24 (1970–71).
Wells, S. and G. Taylor, eds, *The Oxford Shakespeare: The Complete Works* (Oxford, 1994).
Wenham, L.P., ed., *Roger Strickland of Richmond: Jacobite Gentleman, 1680–1745* (Northallerton, 1982).
Whitaker, T.D., ed., *The Life and Original Correspondence of Sir George Radcliffe, knight, Ll.D.* (London, 1810).
Witty, J.R., 'Documents relating to Beverley and District', *Yorkshire Archaeological Journal*, 36 (1944–47).
Young, Arthur, *General View of the Agriculture of Hertfordshire* (1804/repr., Newton Abbot, 1971).
Young, P., ed., *Military Memoirs, The Civil War: Richard Atkyns* (London, 1967).

CONTEMPORARY TEXTS

Anon., *The English Farrier or Country-mans Treasure* (London, 1636).
Astley, John, *The Art of Riding* (London, 1584).
Baret, Michael, *An Hipponomie or The Vineyard of Horsemanship* (London, 1618).
Bedingfield, Thomas, *The Art of Riding* (London, 1584).
Blome, Richard, *The Gentleman's Recreation* (London, 1686).
Blundeville, Thomas, *The Arte of Rydynge* (London, c. 1560).
Blundeville, Thomas, *The Fower Chiefyst Offices Belonging to Horsemanship* (London, 1565).
Borde, Andrew, *The Fyrst Boke of the Introduction of Knowledge* (London, 1542).
Burton, Robert, *The Anatomy of Melancholy* (London, 1621).
Cavendish, Margaret (The Lady Newcastle), *Poems and Fancies* (London, 1653).
Cavendish, Margaret (Duchess of Newcastle), *The Life of the Thrice Noble ... William Duke of Newcastle* (London, 1667).
Cavendish, William, *A New Method and Extraordinary Invention to Dress Horses* (London, 1667).
Chamberlayne, Edward, *Angliae Notitia: or the Present State of England* (London, 1671).
Cheny, John, *A Historical List of All Horse-Matches Run* (London, 1741).
Cooke, J., *Greene's Tu Quoque: or The Cittie Gallant* (1614).
Deering, Charles, *An Historical Account of the Ancient and Present State of the Town of Nottingham* (Nottingham, 1751).

de Gray, Thomas, *The Compleat Horseman and Expert Ferrier* (London, 1639).
Elyot, Sir Thomas, *The Boke Named the Governour* (London, 1531).
Evelyn, John, *Acetaria: A Discourse of Sallets* (London, 1699).
Fitzherbert, John, *Boke of Husbandrie* (London, 1523).
Flavell, John, *Husbandry Spiritualized* (London, 1669).
Gascoigne, George, *The Noble Arte of Venerie or Hunting* (London, 1575).
Halfpenny, John, *The Gentleman's Jockey and Approved Farrier* (London, 1674).
Hartlib, Samuel, *The Legacie* (2nd edn, London, 1652).
Heresbach, Conrad, *Foure Bookes of Husbandrie*, trans. Barnaby Googe (London, 1577).
Higford, William, *Institutions of Advice to his Grandson* (London, 1658).
Hildrop, John, *Free Thought upon the Brute-Creation: or an Examination of Father Bougeant's Philosophical Amusements* (London, 1742).
Horman, William, *Vulgaria* (London, 1519).
Howell, James, *Instructions for Forreine Travell* (London, 1642).
James I, 'Basilicon Doron', *The Workes* (London, 1616).
J.C., *The Compleat Collier* (1708).
Keen, Peter, *Description of England* (London, 1599).
Lawrence, John, *A Philosophical and Practical Treatise on Horses, and on the Moral Duties of Man towards the Brute Creation* (London, 1796).
Markham, Gervase, *How to Chuse, Ride, Traine, and Diet Both Hunting-Horses and Running Horses* (London, 1599).
Markham, Gervase, *Cavelarice* (London, 1607).
Markham, Gervase, *Cheape and Good Husbandry* (London, 1614).
Markham, Gervase, *Countrey Contentments* (London, 1615).
Markham, Gervase, *Markhams Maister-Peece* (London, 1615).
Marshall, William, *Rural Economy of the West of England*, I (1796/repr., Newton Abbot, 1970).
Mascall, Leonard, *The Booke of Cattell* (London, 1587).
Morgan, Nicholas, *The Perfection of Horse-manship* (London, 1609).
Moryson, Fynes, *An Itinerary* (London, 1617).
Nash, Thomas, *Quaternio* (London, 1633).
Peacham, Henry, *Coach and Sedan* (London, 1636).
Peacham, Henry, *The Worth of a Peny: or a Caution to Keep Money* (London, 1647).
Plot, R., *The Natural History of Oxfordshire* (London, 1677).
Plot, R., *Natural History of Staffordshire* (London, 1686).
Poole, William, *The Countrey Farrier* (London, 1648).
Powell, Thomas, *Humane Industry or, a History of Most Manual Arts* (London, 1661).
Shirley, James, *Hyde Park* (London, 1632).

Taylor, John, *The World Runnes on Wheels* (London, 1623).
Topsell, Edward, *The Historie of Foure-Footed Beastes* (London, 1607).
Tryon, Thomas, *The Country-Mans Companion* (London, 1683?).
Worlidge, John, *Systema Agriculturae* (London, 1675).

SECONDARY SOURCES

Abdy, C., *Epsom Past* (Chichester, 2001).
Adams, C.J., *Neither Man nor Beast: Feminism and the Defense of Animals* (New York, 1994).
Adams, S., 'Tactics or Politics? "The Military Revolution" and the Hapsburg Hegemony, 1525–1648', in C.J. Rogers, ed., *The Military Revolution Debate* (Boulder, Colorado, 1995).
Ahnlund, N., *Gustavus Adolphus the Great* (New York, 1999).
Aillaud, G., 'Why Look at Animals?', in J. Berger, ed., *About Looking* (London, 1980).
Albert, W., *The Turnpike Road System in England, 1663–1840* (Cambridge, 1972).
Almond, R., *Medieval Hunting* (Thrupp, 2003).
Ayton, A., *Knights and Warhorses, Military Service and the English Aristocracy under Edward III* (Woodbridge, 1994).
Barker, T. and D. Gerhold, *The Rise and Rise of Road Transport, 1700–1990* (Basingstoke, 1993).
Barratt, J., *Cavaliers: The Royalist Army at War 1642–1646* (Thrupp, 2000).
Bayley, A.R., *The Great Civil War in Dorset, 1642–1660* (Taunton, 1910).
Berg, M. and H. Clifford, eds, *Consumers and Luxury: Consumer Culture in Europe 1650–1850* (Manchester, 1999).
Berg, M. and E. Eger, *Luxury in the Eighteenth Century: Debates, Desires and Delectable Goods* (Basingstoke, 2003).
Berry, E., *Shakespeare and the Hunt: A Cultural and Social Study* (Cambridge, 2001).
Bingham, C., *James VI of Scotland* (London, 1979).
Black, J., *European Warfare, 1453–1815* (Basingstoke, 1999).
Boehrer, B., *Shakespeare among the Animals* (Basingstoke, 2002).
Boose, L.E., 'Scolding Brides and Bridling Scolds: Taming the Woman's Unruly Member', in I. Kamps, ed., *Materialist Shakespeare: A History* (London, 1995).
Borsay, P., *The English Urban Renaissance: Culture and Society in the Provincial Town, 1660–1770* (Oxford, 1991).
Bowden, P.J., *The Wool Trade in Tudor and Stuart England* (London, 1971).
Boynton, L., *The Elizabethan Militia, 1558–1638* (London, 1967).
Brailsford, H.N., *The Levellers and the English Revolution* (London, 1961).

Burne, A.H. and P. Young, *The Great Civil War* (Moreton-in-Marsh, 1998).
Carmill, M., *A View to a Death in the Morning* (Cambridge, Massachusetts, 1993).
Carr, R., *English Fox Hunting: A History* (London, 1976).
Chalklin. C.W., *Seventeenth-Century Kent* (London, 1965).
Chandler, D., *Marlborough as Military Commander* (London, 1979).
Chartres, J.A, 'Road Carrying in England in the Seventeenth Century: Myth and Reality', *Economic History Review*, second series, 30 (1977).
Chartres, J.A., *Internal Trade in England, 1500–1700* (London, 1977).
Childs, J., *The Army of Charles II* (London, 1976).
Childs, J., 'The Williamite War, 1689–1691', in T. Bartlett and K. Jeffery, eds, *A Military History of Ireland* (Cambridge, 1996).
Cliffe, J.T., *The World of the Country House in Seventeenth-Century England* (New Haven, 1999).
Clutton-Brock, J., 'Aristotle, the Scale of Nature and Modern Attitudes to Animals', in A. Mack.' ed., *Humans and Other Animals* (Columbus, Ohio, 1999).
Coczian-Szentpeteri, E., 'L'èvolution du Coche ou l'histoire d'une invention hongroise', in D. Reytier, ed., *Voitures, chevaux et attelages du XVIe au XIXe Siècle* (Paris, 2000).
Cogswell, T., *Home Divisions: Aristocracy, the State and Provincial Conflict* (Manchester, 1998).
Cottingham, J., 'Descartes' Treatment of Animals', in J. Cottingham, *Descartes* (Oxford, 1998).
Cressy, D., *Education in Tudor and Stuart England* (London, 1975).
Crofts, J., *Packhorse, Waggon and Post* (London, 1967).
Cruickshank, C., *Henry VIII and the Invasion of France* (Far Thrupp, 1994).
Cruickshanks, E., *The Glorious Revolution* (Basingstoke, 2000).
Cummings, B., 'Pliny's Literate Elephant and the Idea of Animal Language in Renaissance Thought', in E. Fudge, ed., *Renaissance Beasts: Of Animals, Humans, and other Wonderful Creatures* (Urbana and Chicago, Illinois, 2004).
Cunnington, P. and A. Mansfield, *English Costume for Sports and Outdoor Recreation* (London, 1969).
Curth, L.H., 'The Care of the Brute Beast: Animals and the Seventeenth-Century Medical Market-Place', *The Society for the Social History of Medicine*, 15, pt 3 (2002).
Curth, L.H., 'Seventeenth-Century English Almanacs: Transmitters of Advice for Sick Animals', in W. de Blécourt and C. Usborne, eds, *Cultural Approaches to the History of Medicine: Mediating Medicine in Early Modern and Modern Europe* (Basingstoke, 2004).

Dabhoiwala, 'The Construction of Honour, Reputation and Status in Late Seventeenth and Early Eighteenth Century England', *Transactions of the Royal Historical Society*, sixth series, VI (1996).

Davis, R., *The Rise of the English Shipping Industry in the Seventeenth and Eighteenth Centuries* (Newton Abbot, 1962).

Davis, R.H.C., *The Medieval Warhorse* (London, 1989).

Dent, A., *Horses in Shakespeare's England* (London, 1987).

Dent, A. and D.M. Goodall, *A History of British Native Ponies* (London, 1988).

Doherty, R., *The Williamite War in Ireland, 1688–1691* (Dublin, 1998).

Durston, C., *Cromwell's Major-Generals: Godly Government during the English Revolution* (Manchester, 2001).

Edwards, P., 'The Development of Dairy Farming on the North Shropshire Plain in the Seventeenth Century', *Midland History*, 4 (1978).

Edwards, P., 'The Horse Trade of the Midlands in the Seventeenth Century', *Agricultural History Review*, 27 (1979).

Edwards, P., *The Horse Trade of Tudor and Stuart England* (Cambridge, 1988).

Edwards, P., 'Agriculture, 1540–1750', *The Victoria History of Shropshire*, IV, *Agriculture* (Oxford, 1989).

Edwards, P., 'The Supply of Horses to the Parliamentarian and Royalist Armies in the English Civil War', *Bulletin of the Institute of Historical Research*, 68 (1995).

Edwards, P., *Dealing in Death: The Arms Trade and the British Civil Wars, 1638–52* (Thrupp, 2000).

Edwards, P., 'The Horse Trade in Tudor and Stuart Staffordshire', *Staffordshire Studies*, 13 (2001).

Emmison, F.G., *Tudor Secretary: Sir William Petre at Court and Home* (London, 1961).

Erskine-Hill, H., *Gulliver's Travels* (Cambridge, 1993).

Everitt, A.M., 'Farm Labourers', in J. Thirsk, ed., *The Agrarian History of England and Wales, IV, 1500–1640* (Cambridge, 1967).

Everitt, A.M., 'The Marketing of Agricultural Produce', in J. Thirsk, ed., *The Agrarian History of England and Wales*, IV, *1500–1640* (Cambridge, 1967).

Fairfax-Blakeborough, J., *Northern Turf History* (London, 1949).

Falls, C., *Elizabeth's Irish Wars* (London, 1996).

Featherstone, D., *Armies and Warfare in the Pike and Shot Era 1422–1700* (London, 1998).

Fieldhouse, R. and B. Jennings, *A History of Richmond and Swaledale* (Chichester, 1978).

Finch, M.E., 'Some Domestic Animals in the Reigns of Elizabeth and James I', *Northamptonshire Past and Present*, 1, pt 5 (1952).

Firth, C.H., *Cromwell's Army: A History of the English Soldier during the Civil Wars, the Commonwealth and the Protectorate* (London, 1962).

Firth, C.H., 'The Raising of the Ironsides', in I.R. Christie, ed., *Essays in Modern History* (London, 1968).

Fissel, M.C., *The Bishops' Wars: Charles I's Campaigns against Scotland, 1638–1640* (Cambridge, 1994).

Fissel, M.C., *English Warfare, 1511–1642* (London, 2001).

Fletcher, A., *A County Community in Peace and War: Sussex, 1600–1660* (London, 1975).

Fraser, G.M., *The Steel Bonnets: The Story of the Anglo-Scottish Border Reivers* (London, 1971).

Fudge, E. et al., *At the Borders of the Human* (Basingstoke, 1999); A. Mack, ed., *Humans and Other Animals* (Columbus, Ohio, 1999).

Fudge, E., *Perceiving Animals: Humans and Beasts in Early Modern English Culture* (Basingstoke, 2000).

Fudge, E., 'A Left-Handed Blow: Writing the History of Animals', in N. Rothfels, ed., *Representing Animals* (Bloomington and Indianapolis, Indiana, 2002).

Fudge, E., ed., *Renaissance Beasts: Of Animals, Humans and Other Wonderful Creatures* (Urbana and Chicago, Illinois, 2004).

Galloway, R., *Annals of Coal Mining and the Coal Trade* (London, 1898/repr. Newton Abbot, 1971).

Gerhold, D., 'The Growth of the London Carrying Trade, 1681–1838', *Economic History Review*, second series, 41 (1988).

Gerhold, D., *Road Transport before the Railways: Russell's London Flying Waggons* (Cambridge, 1993).

Gerhold, D., 'Packhorses and Wheeled Vehicles in England, 1550–1800', *Journal of Transport History*, third series, 14 (1993).

Gerhold, D., 'Productivity Change in Road Transport Before and After Turnpiking, 1690–1840', *Economic History Review*, 49 (1996).

Gerhold, D., *Carriers and Coachmasters: Trade and Travel before the Turnpikes* (Chichester, 2005).

Gill, C., ed., *Dartmoor: A New Study* (Newton Abbot, 1970).

Giono, J., *The Battle of Pavia*, trans. A. E. Murch (London, 1965).

Goodacre, *The Transformation of a Peasant Economy: Townspeople and Villagers in the Lutterworth Area, 1500–1700* (Aldershot, 1994).

Goodall, D.M., *A History of Horse Breeding* (London, 1977).

Goodall, D.M., *The Foals of Epona* (London, 1988).

Graham, E. et al, eds, *Her Own Life: Autobiographical Writings by Seventeenth-Century Englishwomen* (London, 1989).

Graham, E., 'Reading, Writing, and Riding Horses in Early Modern England: James Shirley's *Hyde Park* (1632) and Gervase Markham's *Cavelarice*

(1607)', in E. Fudge, ed., *Renaissance Beasts: Of Animals, Humans, and other Wonderful Creatures* (Urbana and Chicago, Illinois, 2004).

Greenberg, R.A., ed., *Jonathan Swift: Gulliver's Travels* (New York, 1970).

Hackett, H., *Virgin Mother, Maiden Queen: Elizabeth and the Cult of the Virgin Mary* (Basingstoke, 1995).

Hammer, P.E.H., *Elizabeth's Wars* (Basingstoke, 2003).

Harwood Long, W., 'Regional Farming in Seventeenth-Century Yorkshire', *Agricultural History Review*, 8 (1960).

Hassell Smith, A., *County and Court: Government and Politics in Norfolk, 1558–1603* (Oxford, 1974).

Hassell Smith, A., 'Militia Rates and Militia Statutes 1558–1663', in P. Clark et al, eds, *The English Commonwealth, 1547–1640* (Leicester, 1979).

Hattaway, M., 'Male Sexuality and Misogyny', in C.M.S. Alexander and S. Wells, eds, *Shakespeare and Sexuality* (Cambridge, 2001).

Havinden, M.A., 'Agricultural Progress in Open-Field Oxfordshire', in W.E. Minchinton, ed., *Essays in Agrarian History*, I (Newton Abbot, 1968).

Hey, D.G., 'The Rural Metalworkers of the Sheffield Region', *Leicester University, Department of English Local History Occasional Papers*, second series, 5 (Leicester, 1972).

Hey, D.G., *An English Rural Community: Myddle under the Tudors and Stuarts* (Leicester, 1974).

Hey, D.G., *Packmen, Carriers and Packhorse Roads: Trade and Communications in North Derbyshire and South Yorkshire* (Leicester, 1980).

Hey, D.G., 'The North-West Midland', in J. Thirsk, ed., *The Agrarian History of England and Wales*, V, *1640–1750* pt 1 (Cambridge, 1984).

Hill, C., *The World Turned Upside Down* (Harmondsworth, 1975).

Hill, J.M., *Celtic Warfare, 1595–1763* (Edinburgh, 1986).

Hindle, S., *On the Parish? The Micro-Politics of Poor Relief in Rural England, c. 1550–1750* (Oxford, 2004).

Houston, S.J., *James I* (Harlow, 1995).

Howard, M., *War in European History* (Oxford, 1976).

Howarth, D., *Images of Rule: Art and Politics in the English Renaissance, 1485–1649* (Basingstoke, 1997).

Hore, J.P., *The History of Newmarket and the Annals of the Turf*, 3 vols (London, 1886).

Howells, B., ed., 'A Calendar of Letters Relating to North Wales 1533–c.1700', *Board of Celtic Studies, University of Wales History and Law Series*, 23 (Cardiff, 1967).

Hutton, R., *The Royalist War Effort, 1642–1646* (London, 1982).

Hutton, R., *Charles II* (Oxford, 1989).

Hyland, A., *The Medieval Warhorse* (Far Thrupp, 1994).
Hyland, A., *The Horse in the Middle Ages* (Thrupp, 1999).
Ingold, T., ed., *What is an Animal?* (London, 1994).
Ingram, M., 'Ridings, Rough Music and the "Reform of Popular Culture" in Early Modern England', *Past & Present*, 105 (1984).
Jeaffreson, J.C., ed., *Middlesex County Records*, 2 (1887).
Jones, B.C., 'Westmorland Pack-Horse Men in Southampton', *Transactions of the Cumberland and Westmorland Antiquarian and Archaeological Society*, new series, 59 (1960).
Jones, M.W., *The Derby* (London, 1979).
Kerridge, E., *The Agricultural Revolution* (London, 1967).
Kettle, A.J., 'Lichfield Races', *Transactions of the Lichfield and South Staffordshire Archaeological & History Society*, 6 (1964–5).
Kitson, F., *Prince Rupert: Portrait of a Soldier* (London, 1994).
Laird, D., *Royal Ascot* (London, 1976).
Landry, D., *The Invention of the Countryside: Hunting, Walking and Ecology in English Literature, 1671–1831* (Basingstoke, 2001).
Landry, D., 'The Bloody Shouldered Arabian and Early Modern English Culture', *Criticism*, 46 (2004).
Langdon, J., 'The Economics of Horses and Oxen in Medieval England', *Agricultural History Review*, 30 (1980).
Langdon, J., 'Horse Hauling: A Revolution in Vehicle Transport in Twelfth- and Thirteenth-Century England?', *Past and Present*, 103 (1984).
Layard, G.S., *The Headless Horseman: Pierre Lombart's Engraving: Charles or Cromwell?* (London, 1922).
Leach, E., 'Anthropological Aspects of Language: Animal Categories and Verbal Abuse', in E.H. Lenneberg, ed., *New Directions in the Study of Language* (Cambridge, Massachusetts, 1964).
LeGuin, E., 'Man and Horse in Harmony', in K. Raber and T. Tucker, eds, *The Culture of the Horse: Status, Discipline, and Identity in the Early Modern World* (Basingstoke, 2005).
Lemire, B., 'Introduction: Dress, Culture and the English People', *Dress, Culture and Commerce: The English Clothing Trade Before the Factory, 1660–1800* (London, 1997).
Lenihan, P., *Confederate Catholics at War, 1641–49* (Cork, 2001).
Levi-Strauss, C., *The Savage Mind* (London, 1962).
Lewis, M.J.T., 'Early Wooden Railways', *Antiquity*, 48 (1974).
Lloyd, G.E.R., *Aristotle: The Growth and Structure of his Thought* (Cambridge, 1968).
Loch, S., *The Royal Horse of Europe: The Story of the Andalusian and Lusitano* (London, 1986).

Lockyer, R., *Buckingham: The Life and Political Career of George Villiers, First Duke of Buckingham, 1592–1628* (Harlow, 1981).

Longrigg, R., *The History of Foxhunting* (London, 1975).

Longrigg, R., *The English Squire and his Sport* (London, 1977).

Lovejoy, A.J., *The Great Chain of Being: A Study of the History of an Idea* (New York, 1960).

Lysons, D. and S., *Magna Britannia* (London, 1810).

MacGregor, A., 'Horsegear, Vehicles and Stable Equipment at the Stuart Court: A Documentary Archaeology', *Archaeological Journal*, 153 (1996).

MacGregor, 'The Royal Stables: A Seventeenth-Century Perspective', *Antiquaries Journal*, 76 (1996).

Malcolm, J.L., 'Caesar's Due: Loyalty and King Charles 1642–1646', Royal Historical Society, *Studies in History*, 38 (1983).

Malcolmson, R.W., *Popular Recreations in English Society, 1700–1850* (Cambridge, 1973).

Malcolmson, R.W., 'A Set of Ungovernable People: the Kingswood Colliers in the Eighteenth Century', in J. Brewer and J. Styles, eds, *An Ungovernable People: The English and their Law in the Seventeenth and Eighteenth Centuries* (London, 1983).

Mann, J. de L., *The Cloth Industry in the West of England from 1640 to 1880* (Gloucester, 1987).

Manning, R.B., *Swordsmen: The Martial Ethos in the Three Kingdoms* (Oxford, 2003).

Marvin, G., 'Unspeakability, Inedibility, and the Structures of Pursuit in the English Foxhunt', in N. Rothfels, ed., *Representing Animals* (Bloomington and Indianapolis, Indiana, 2002).

McGirk, J., *The Elizabethan Conquest of Ireland* (Manchester, 1997).

Meens, R., 'Eating Animals in the Early Middle Ages: Classifying the Animal World and Building Group Identities', in A.N.H. Creager and W.C. Jordan, eds, *The Animal-Human Boundary* (Rochester, New York, 2002).

Mendelson, S. and P. Crawford, *Women in Early Modern England* (Oxford, 1998).

Midgley, M., 'Beasts, Brutes and Monsters', in T. Ingold, ed., *What is an Animal?* (London, 1994).

Miller, H., *Henry VIII and the English Nobility* (Oxford, 1989).

Mingay, G.E., 'Farming Techniques', in G.E. Mingay, ed., *The Agrarian History of England and Wales*, VI, *1750–1850* (Cambridge, 1989).

Munby, J., 'Les Origines du coche', in D. Reytier, ed., *Voitures, chevaux et attelages du XVIe au XIXe Siècle* (Paris, 2000).

Munsche, P.B., *Gentlemen and Poachers* (Cambridge, 1981).

Murphy, W.P.D., ed., 'The Earl of Hertford's Lieutenancy Papers 1603–1612', *Wiltshire Records Society*, 23 (1969).

Nash, R., '"Honest English Breed": The Thoroughbred as Cultural Metaphor', in K. Raber and T. Tucker, eds, *The Culture of the Horse: Status, Discipline, and Identity in the Early Modern World* (Basingstoke, 2005).

Neeson, J.M., *Commoners: Common Right, Enclosure and Social Change in England, 1700–1820* (Cambridge, 1993).

Nef, J.U., *The Rise of the British Coal Industry* 2 vols (New York, 1932/repr., 1972).

Nolan, J.S., *Sir John Norreys and the Elizabethan Military World* (Exeter, 1997).

O'Carroll, D., 'Change and Continuity in Weapons and Tactics, 1594–1691', in P. Lenihan, ed., *Conquest and Resistance: War in Seventeenth-Century Ireland* (Leiden, 2001).

O'Day, R., *Education and Society, 1500–1800* (Harlow, 1982).

Overton, M. et al, *Production and Consumption in English Households, 1600–1750* (London, 2004).

Pam, D.O., 'Tudor Enfield: The Maltmen and the Lea Navigation', *Edmonton Hundred Historical Society Occasional Paper*, new series, 18 (ND).

Parker, G., *The Military Revolution* (Cambridge, 1989), p. 69.

Parkes, J., *Travel in the Seventeenth Century* (Oxford, 1925).

Payne Collier, J., ed., 'The Egerton Papers', *Camden Society*, 12 (1840).

Pearson S. and M. Weismantel, 'Does "The Animal" Exist? Towards a Theory of Social Life with Animals', paper read at the conference, 'Animals in History', held at Cologne, 18–21 May 2005.

Phillips, G., *The Anglo-Scots Wars, 1513–1550* (Woodbridge, 1999).

Philo, C. and C. Wibert, eds, *Animal Spaces, Beastly Places: New Geographies of Human-Animal Relations* (London, 2000).

Plumb, J.H., 'Commercialisation and Society', in N. McKendrick et al, *The Birth of a Consumer Society: The Commercialisation of Eighteenth-Century England* (London, 1983).

Pollock, L., *Forgotten Children: Parent-Child Relations from 1500 to 1900* (Cambridge, 1983).

Preece, R. and D. Fraser, 'The Status of animals in Biblical and Christian Thought: A Study in Colliding Values', *Society & Animals*, 8, III (2000).

Raber, 'A Horse of a Different Colour: Nation and Race in Early Modern Horsemanship Treatises', in K. Raber and T. Tucker, eds, *The Culture of the Horse: Status, Discipline, and Identity in the Early Modern World* (Basingstoke, 2005).

Ralph, P.L., *Sir Humphrey Mildmay: Royalist Gentleman* (New Brunswick, 1947).

Redmayne, R.A.S. and L.F. Salzman, 'Industries: Coal Mining', W. Page, ed., *The Victoria History of the County of Warwickshire*, II (London, 1908).

Reese, M.M., *The Royal Office of the Master of the Horse* (London, 1976).
Richefort, I., 'Différent usages des carosses de Louis XIV', in D. Reytier, ed., *Voitures, chevaux et attelages du XVIe au XIXe Siècle* (Paris, 2000).
Ridley, J., *Elizabeth I: The Shrewdness of Virtue* (New York, 1988).
Ritvo, H., *The Animal Estate: The English and other Creatures in the Victorian Age* (Cambridge, Massachusetts, 1987).
Ritvo, H., 'Border Trouble: Shifting the Line between People and Other Animals', in A. Mack, ed., *Humans and Other Animals* (Columbus, Ohio, 1999).
Roberts, M., *The Military Revolution, 1560–1660* (Belfast, 1956).
Roberts, M., *Gustavus Adolphus: A History of Sweden 1611–1632*; II, *1626–1632* (London, 1958).
Roberts, M., 'The "Military Revolution", 1560–1660', in C.J. Rogers, *The Military Revolution Debate* (Boulder, Colorado, 1995).
Robinson, H., *The British Post Office: An History* (New Jersey, 1948).
Rogers, C.J., ed., *The Military Revolution Debate* (Boulder, Colorado, 1995).
Rogers, C.J., 'The Military Revolutions of the Hundred Years War, A Myth?', in C.J. Rogers, ed., *The Military Revolution Debate* (Boulder, Colorado, 1995).
Rollison, D., *The Local Origins of Modern Society: Gloucestershire, 1500–1800* (London, 1992).
Rothfels, N., ed., *Representing Animals* (Bloomington and Indianapolis, Indiana, 2002).
Russell, J.G., *The Field of the Cloth of Gold* (London, 1969).
Russell, N., *Like Engend'ring Like: Heredity and Animal Breeding in Early Modern England* (Cambridge, 1986).
Scarisbrick, J.J., *Henry VIII* (London, 1988).
Sharpe, K., *The Personal Rule of Charles I* (New Haven and London, 1992).
Sherwood, R., *The Court of Oliver Cromwell* (London, 1977).
Spurr, J., *English Puritanism, 1603–1689* (Basingstoke, 1998).
Starkey, D., 'Intimacy and Innovation: The Rise of the Privy Chamber, 1485–1547', in D. Starkey et al, *The English Court from the Wars of the Roses to the Civil War* (London, 1987).
Stewart, A., *Philip Sidney, a Double Life* (London, 2000).
Stewart, A., 'Government by Beagle: The Impersonal Rule of James VI and I', in E. Fudge, *Renaissance Beasts: Of Animals, Humans, and other Wonderful Creatures* (Urbana and Chicago, Illinois, 2004).
Stewart, R.W., 'War and Government in the Channel and Beyond', in M.C. Fissel, *War and Government in Britain, 1598–1650* (Manchester, 1991).
Stewart, R.W., 'The English Ordnance Office: A Case-Study in Bureaucracy', *Studies in History*, 73 (Woodbridge, 1996).

BIBLIOGRAPHY

Stone, L., *Family, Sex and Marriage in England, 1500–1800* (Harmondsworth, 1979).

Stone, L., 'The Residential Development of the West End of London in the Seventeenth Century', in B.C. Malament, ed., *After the Reformation* (Philadelphia, Pennsylvania, 1980).

Straus, R., *Carriages and Coaches* (London, 1912).

Strong, R., *The Cult of Elizabeth: Elizabethan Portraiture and Pageantry* (London, 1999).

Strong, R., *Henry, Prince of Wales and England's Lost Renaissance* (London, 2000).

Tallett, F., *War and Society in Early-Modern Europe, 1495–1715* (London, 1992).

Thomas, K., *Man and the Natural World: Changing Attitudes in England, 1500–1800* (London, 1983).

Thirsk, J., 'Agrarian History, 1540–1950', in W.G. Hoskins and R.A. McKinley, eds, *Victoria History of the County of Leicestershire*, II (Oxford, 1954).

Thirsk, J., *English Peasant Farming* (London, 1957).

Thirsk, J., 'Farming Techniques', in Thirsk, *The Agrarian History of England and Wales*, IV, *1500–1640* (Cambridge, 1967).

Thirsk, J., *Horses in Early Modern England: For Service, for Pleasure, for Power* (Reading, 1978).

Thompson, F.M.L., *Victorian England: The Horse-Drawn Society* (London, 1970).

Thomson, G.S., *Life in a Noble Household, 1641–1700* (London, 1937).

Tobey, E., 'The *Palio* Horse in Renaissance and Early Modern Italy', in K. Raber and T. Tucker, eds, *The Culture of the Horse: Status, Discipline, and Identity in the Early Modern World* (Basingstoke, 2005).

Underdown, D.E., 'The Taming of the Scold: The Enforcement of Patriarchal Authority in Early Modern England', in A. Fletcher and J. Steventon, eds, *Order & Disorder in Early Modern England* (Cambridge, 1985).

Vale, M., *The Gentleman's Recreations* (Cambridge, 1977).

Verney, F.P., *The Memoirs of the Verney Family, During the Civil War*, two vols (London, 1970).

Verney, M.M., ed., *Memoirs of the Verney Family*: III, *1650–1660*, IV, *1660–1696* (London, 1970).

Wanklyn, M. and F. Jones, *A Military History of the English Civil War* (Harlow, 2005).

Ward, J.E., 'John Spedding's Accounts of Horses Used in the Whitehaven Colleries etc., from 1715 Onwards', *Transactions of the Cumberland and Westmormorland Antiquarian and Archaeological Society*, 89 (1989).

Weatherill, L., *Consumer Behaviour & Material Culture in Britain 1660–1750* (London, 1996).

Wedgwood, V.H., *The King's War, 1641–1647* (London, 1958).
Western, J.R., *The English Militia in the Eighteenth Century: The Story of a Political Issue 1660–1802* (London, 1965).
White, A.W.A., 'Men and Mining in Warwickshire', *Coventry and North Warwickshire History Pamphlets*, 7 (Coventry, 1970).
Whyman, S.E., *Sociability and Power in Late-Stuart England: The Cultural Worlds of the Verneys, 1660–1720* (Oxford, 1999).
Wilkinson, D., *Early Horse Racing in Yorkshire and the Origins of the Thoroughbred* (York, 2003).
Willan, T.S., *Studies in Elizabethan Foreign Trade* (Manchester, 1959).
Willan, T.S., *River Navigation in England, 1600–1750* (London, 1964).
Willan, T.S., *The Inland Trade* (Manchester, 1976).
Wolch, J. and J. Emel, 'Bringing the Animals Back In', *Environment Planning D, Society and Space*, 13 (1995).
Woolrych, A., 'Cromwell as a Soldier', in J. Morrell, ed., *Oliver Cromwell and the English Revolution* (Harlow, 1990).
Worsley, G., 'Country Stables and their Implications for Seventeenth Century English Architecture', *The Georgian Group Journal*, 13 (2003).
Worsley, G., *The British Stable* (New Haven and London, 2004).
Wright, A.P.M., 'Sport: Horse-Racing', in C.R. Elrington, ed., *A History of the County of Cambridgeshire*, V (London, 1973).
Young, A., *Tudor and Jacobean Tournaments* (Dobbs Ferry, New York, 1987).
Young and R. Holmes, *The English Civil War: A Military History of the Three Civil Wars* (London, 1974).

THESES

Chell, R.W., 'Agriculture and Rural Society in Hampshire *circa* 1600' (unpublished Leicester University MPhil thesis, 1975).
Cornwall, J.C.K., 'The Agrarian History of Sussex, 1560–1640' (unpublished London University MA thesis, 1953).
Edwards, P.R., 'The Farming Economy of North-East Shropshire in the Seventeenth Century' (unpublished Oxford University DPhil thesis, 1976).
Fleming, D., 'A Local Market System: Melton Mowbray and the Wreake Valley, 1549–1720' (unpublished Leicester University PhD thesis, 1980).
Havinden, M.A., 'The Rural Economy of Oxfordshire 1580–1730' (unpublished Oxford University BLitt thesis, 1961).
Hull, F., 'Agriculture and Rural Society in Essex, 1560–1640' (unpublished London University PhD thesis, 1950).
Kerridge, E., 'The Agrarian Development of Wiltshire, 1540–1640' (unpublished London University PhD thesis, 1951).

Porter, S., 'An Agricultural Geography of Huntingdonshire, 1610–1749' (unpublished Cambridge University MLitt thesis, 1973).

Robinson, G., 'Horse Supply in the English Civil War, 1642–1646' (unpublished Reading University PhD Thesis, 2001).

Index

Administration, assizes, 29, 62, 75
   Equity courts, 75, 187, 188, 201, 202
   Privy Council, 7, 160, 162, 166, 172, 174–5, 202, 229
   quarter sessions, 62, 75, 201
Albrighton, 114
Aleppo, 31, 110, 111, 112, 116, 121
Alington, Lady, 215
Alva, duke of, 10
animals, agency, 18, 31, 117, 119
   attitudes towards, xi–xii, 17–22, 241–2
   attributes, 17–19, 21
   meat, 5, 17, 18, 33–4, 119, 128, 132
   treatment of, 18, 20–1, 61, 62–6, 241
animal species
   antelope, 121
   bears, 61
   birds, 13, 19, 20
   boar, 120, 131, 143
   cats, 19
   cattle, 13, 25, 203
   deer, 120, 121, 127, 129, 131, 133, 136, 143
   dogs, 7, 12, 13, 19, 31, 61, 97, 120, 121, 122, 128, 129, 131, 135, 136, 144
   foxes, 120, 122–3, 131, 240
   game birds, 120, 121, 129
   hares, 120, 121, 129
   monkeys, 61
   oxen, 1, 33, 149, 183–6, 191, 201–2, 206
   pigs, 75
   rabbits, 120, 121, 129
   vermin, 119, 120, 122–23, 240
Annion, Richard, innkeeper, of Chester, 79
ap Owen, Hugh, 134

Archer, Ezekial, warrener, of Mickleham (Surrey), 129
Ariès, Philippe, 51
Aristotle, 17
Arnold, Nicholas, of Highnam (Gloucs.), 9
Atkins, Captain, 148

Bagot family of Blithfield (Staffs.), 41
   Colonel, 9
   Sir Robert, 8
Ball, Edward, 123
Banbury, 33
Banks, John, 112
Barry, Richard, of Farnsfield (Notts.), 75
Barton, Owen, gent, 215
Bateman, Thomas, wheelwright, 167
Baynes, Richard, wool stapler, of Newport (Shrops.), 189–90
Bayning, Lord, 151
Baynton, Sir Edward, 56
Bear Garden, Southwark, 61
Bedale (NRY), 114
Bedfordshire, 6, 189, 199–200
Bennet, Charles, 2nd earl of Tankerville, 142
Benthall, Mr, 16
Best, Henry, 189
Blackwell Hall, London, 190
Blomfield family of Stonham, 5, 25, 57
Blundell family of Little Crosby (Lancs.)
   Frances, of Little Crosby, 69–70, 76, 77
   Nicholas, 25, 37, 40, 63–5, 66, 69, 74, 77, 80, 93, 101, 102, 105, 108, 120, 134, 142, 219, 220, 231, 232
   William, 102
Bohemia, 217

Bolt, Richard, queen's bowyer, 172
Boorne, William, warrener, of Weybridge (Surrey), 129
Boteler, Edward, rector of Winteringham (Lincs.), 37
Bourchier, Henry, earl of Essex, 127
Bowes, Raphe, 142
Box Hill warren (Surrey), 129
Brandon, Charles, duke of Suffolk, 127
Brass, William, of Richmond (NRY), 189
Bristol, 190
Brittany, 173
Browne, Benjamin, of Troutbeck (Cumb.), 64
Brudenell family of Deene (Northants.)
    Anna, countess of Shrewsbury, 96
    Sir Edmund, 161
    George, 3rd earl of Cardigan, 206
    James, 220
Buckinghamshire, 165, 196, 201, 216
Bulkeley, Captain Humphrey, 164
Bullinger, Heinrich, 21
Burdett, Walter, of Foremark (Derbys.), 52
Bury St Edmunds (Suffolk), 218
Butler, James, 1st duke of Ormond, 14, 176
Butler, Richard, 134
Byerley, Captain Robert, of Middridge (Durham), 113

Calais, 130
Calverley, Sir Walter, of Esholt (WRY), 216
Calvin, Jean, 20, 21
Cambridge, 78
Cambridgeshire, 189
Capel family, Lord Arthur, 167, Sir Giles, 127
Carew, Sir George, 127
Carey, Sir Robert, 78
Carleton, Sir Dudley, 82, 214, 220
Carr, Sir Robert, earl of Somerset, 214
carriers, 1, 2, 55, 60, 75, 78, 167, 183, 186, 189, 190, 191–4, 197, 198, 201–3, 237, 242
    distances travelled, 191
    status, 191–2
carriers, individuals
    Barnes, Robert, of Lincoln, 198

Jonathan Beadnall of Stokesley NRY), 192,
Robert Beechcroft, of Norwich, 199
Margaret Carter of Mitcham (Surrey), 198
Thomas Chatteris of Harrington (Northants.), 206–7
William Claroe of Worcester, 191
Edith Doddington (badger) of Bishop's Hull (Som.), 192
John Exeter of Shenfield (Essex), 206
Thomas Hobson of Cambridge, 78
John Jollett of Kingsbury (Som.), 192
Jones, of Romford (Essex), 206
Silvester Keene, of Minety (Wilts.), 191
Richard Maddocks of Myddle (Shrops.), 192
Joseph Naylor of Rothwell (WRY), 192
James Nonneley of Derby, 191
Thomas Priestley of Soyland (WRY), 193
carters, 1, 22, 38, 52, 164, 166–8
Cartwright, Thomas, of Aynho (Northants.), 44, 128
Caryll, John, 142
Cavendish family
    Henry, 2nd duke of Newcastle, 134, 142, 216
    Margaret, duchess of Newcastle, 18, 19, 20
    William, 1st duke of Newcastle, 11, 13, 14, 28, 36, 39, 42, 46, 48, 53, 71, 76, 83, 110, 111, 112, 124, 133, 152
Cecil family
    Mildred, wife of Lord Burghley, 215
    Robert, earl of Salisbury, 14, 71, 112
    William, Lord Burghley, 132, 172, 173
    William, Lord Cranbourne, 112
Chain, John, coachman, of Oxford, 229
Chaloner, Sir Thomas, 7
Chamberlain, John, 13, 51, 137, 214–15, 218, 220
Charles VII, king of France, 212
Chartres, John, 186, 190–1
Chatsworth (Derbys.), 114
Chaytor, Lady Peregrina, of Croft (NRY), 230–1
Cheshire Plain, 189

INDEX

Chester, 59, 70, 71, 81, 89, 93, 101, 115, 190, 205
Chester family of Chicheley (Bucks)
    Sir Anthony, 16
    Sir John, 223
children, treatment of, 51
Chiswick (Middx.), 4
Cholmeley, Mr Francis, 28
Cholmeley, Nathaniel, of Whitby (NRY), 223
Cholmeley, Richard, of Brandsby (NRY), 14, 41, 50, 55, 129, 135, 208
Cholmondeley, Lord, 93
Christian IV, king of Denmark, 12
Churchill, John, duke of Marlborough, 168, 179, 180
Clary, Richard, yeoman, of Writtle (Essex), 76
Cleveland, 6
Clifford family
    Francis, 4th earl of Cumberland, 208
    Henry, 5th earl of Cumberland, 151, 164
Clifton, Mr, 134
Clifton, Sir Gervase, of Clifton (Notts.), 142
Clipston Park, 134, 142
coach types
    coach, 213–14, 218, 219
    calash, 212
    caroch, 213–14
    chariot, 212, 218, 219
    hackney, 211, 226–7, 232, 237, 238, 241
    private, 211, 213, 214–17, 218–20, 237, 238
    stage, 211, 228–31, 232, 241
    wagon, 212, 228
coaches, 1, 38, 76, 98, 116, 211ff
    attitudes towards, 214–17, 232, 237, 239
    benefits, 213, 215, 216, 226–7, 228–9, 237, 238
    features, 212, 213
    imports, 213, 217–18
    interior, 1, 214, 216, 219–20
    origins, 212–13
    value, 211, 212, 215, 216, 217–18
coaching services, 226–32
    coachmasters, 57

    coachmen, 56–7
    compared with riding, 230–1
    distances travelled, 228–9
    fares, 228, 231
    network, 228–9, 238
    number of hackney coaches, 227
    opponents, 227, 229–30, 232–3
    regulation, 227
coachmakers, 1, 213, 218–19
coachmen, 216, 218, 226
coalfields, 60
coalfields, individual
    Cumberland, 204
    Flintshire, 204
    Kingswood Chase, 190
    Northumberland and Durham, 187
    Nottinghamshire, 188, 204
    Shropshire, 188, 190
    Staffordshire, 204
    Warwickshire, 190, 204
coalpits, drainage of, 204–5
cockfighting, 97, 99
Coczian-Szentpeteri, Elisabeth, 212–13
Compton, William, earl of Northampton, 83, 133, 162
Coningsby, Fitzwilliam, 43, 74
conspicuous consumption, 3, 69, 88, 90–1, 108, 127–8, 211, 213, 215, 216, 220, 231, 235, 237
consumer revolution, 235–43
    explanations, 236
    horses and, 236
    'new' goods, 235
    social rituals, 216, 237
Cornwall, 6
Cornwallis, Lord, 83
Cotswolds, 184
coursing, 97, 120, 121, 140
Cowdray, 121
Cressett, John, lawyer, 229
Crofts, Christopher, 220
Cromwell, Oliver, 13, 29–30, 33, 99, 111, 158, 176, 177
Cromwell, Thomas, 7, 141

Dacre, Lord Thomas, 171
Darley family
   Richard, of Aldby Park, 113
   Thomas, 112
Dartmoor, 6
Delamere, Lord, 100
de la Rue, Arnold, 80
de Discancour, Monsieur, riding master, 82
de Gamboa, Captain Pedro, 171
de Montaigne, Michel, 18, 20, 82, 216–17
Denton family
   Alexander, 237
   Sir Edmund, 216
   Dr William, 34, 54, 216
Descartes, René, 17–18, 19, 241
D'Ewes, Simon, of Stowlangcroft (Suffolk), 218
Devon, 187
Doncaster (WRY), 101, 102, 189
Ducie, Sir William, 57

East Anglia, 186
   fens, 150, 198
   light soil areas, 184
East Midlands, 186
Eaton, Daniel, land agent, 33, 56, 206, 220, 221
Edwards, Thomas, land agent, 134
Ellesmere, 215
Ely, 205
Emden, count of, 13
Enniskillen, 178
Epsom, 216
Essex, 189, 195, 200, 201
Evelyn, John, 30, 56, 60, 62, 83–4, 96
Exeter, 190

Fairfax, General Sir Thomas, 177
Fane, Charles, 3rd earl of Westmorland, 37
farm vehicles, 1, 3, 183, 186, 195–7, 200,
   changes, 195–7, 237
farming, 2
   customs, 63
   drainage, 197
   enclosure, 62, 122, 156, 183

   equipment, 1, 83, 183–6
   practices, 6, 183, 184–5
Fauconberg, Lord, 151
Fell, Sarah, of Swarthmoor Hall, 195
Fentyman, Thomas, warrener, 129
Fetcham (Surrey), 33
Field of the Cloth of Gold, 28, 30, 130, 135
Finch, Heneage, 1st earl of Nottingham, 31
Finet, Sir John, 12
fishing, 129
Fitzwilliam, Lord William, of Milton
   (Northants.), 37, 66
Fleming, Daniel, of Rydal Hall (Westmor.), 66
Flintshire, 204
Foley family, of Stoke Edith (Herefs.), 41, 44
Forester, Francis, 128
Foubert, Monsr., riding master, 83
Fox, Sir Stephen, 4
Francis, 2nd earl of Godolphin, 114
Francis I, king of France, 28, 135
Fudge, Erica, xii, 21

Gaer, Sir Robert, 96
Gale, John, agent, 205
Garsington (Oxon.), 41
Gell, Sir John, 9, 66
Gentlemen-pensioners, 9, 170
George, John, yeoman, of Writtle (Essex),
   195, 200
Gerhold, Dorian, 186–7, 190–1
Goare, Robert, queen's purveyor of timber,
   172
Gonzaga family of Mantua, 6, 11, 12, 111
Gorges, Edward, 50
great chain of being, 17
Greenwich, 119, 127
Greville family of Warwick Castle, 37, 62, 219,
   220, 225, 226
Grisone, Frederico, riding master, 35, 50, 82
Gustavus Adolphus, king of Sweden, 146, 148,
   179, 239

Hale, Sir Matthew, 32
Hamilton, George, 1st earl of Orkney, 179

INDEX

Hampden, John, 164
Hampshire, 201, downs, 184
Hampton Court (Midx.), 30, 50
Hare family of Stow Bardolph (Norf.), 44
Harley family of Brampton Bryan (Herefs.)
    Lady Brilliana, 215
    Colonel, Sir Edward, 215
    Edward, 2nd earl of Oxford, 38, 101, 187, 200–1, 217, 218, 231
    Nathaniel, 31, 110, 111, 112, 121
    Sir Robert, 215
    Robert, 1st earl of Oxford, 30, 54, 66, 83, 128, 232
    Robert, son of Edward 'Auditor' Harley, 121
    Thomas, 61
Hastings family
    Henry, 3rd earl of Huntingdon, 162, 180
    Henry, 5th earl of Huntingdon, 151, 221
Hatfield Chase (WRY), 133
hawking, 9, 38, 94, 97, 119, 121, 125–6, 128, 134, 135–6, 141, 142
    birds of prey, 121, 128, 135–6, 140, 142, 143, 240
    costs, 128
    gifts, 141–2
    ritual, 127
Hawkins, Richard, 78
Helmsley (NRY), 97, 122
Henry II, king of France, 130
Henry IV, king of France, 83, 173
Henry, Lord Maltravers, governor of Calais, 130
Herbert family
    Edward, Lord Herbert, 24, 82, 99, 125, 131, 133
    Henry, 2nd earl of Pembroke, 93
Hertfordhire, 6, 189
Hesilrige, Sir Arthur, 148, 175
Hesketh, Mrs, of Rufford (Lancs.), 76
Hesse, landgrave of, 13
Hewitt, Mr, 14

Heywood, Oliver, clergyman, 55
Hobart, Isaac, land agent, 38, 55, 56, 70, 112
Hoby, Sir Philip, 213, 215
Holdsworth, Robert, yeoman, of Clee (Lincs.), 75
Holles family, 200
    Denzil, 223
    John, 2nd earl of Clare, 43, 66
    John, 4th earl of Clare and 3rd duke of Newcastle, 43, 113–14
    Sir John, 27, 32, 80, 83
    Thomas Pelham-Holles, duke of Newcastle, 134, 142
Holy Roman Emperors
    Charles V, 30, 141, 166, 170
    Rudolf II, 7
Home Counties, 186, 195, 198, 238
Hooke, Robert, 212, 218
Horbling (Lincs.), 3, 205
horsemanship, 3, 27–28, 29, 69, 82, 83–4, 90, 95–6, 125, 132, 152, 163, 170, 217, 239
horses
    acquisition and disposal, 12, 223
        costs, 16, 111, 222, 225
        export, 7–8, 156, 161
        gifts, 12, 13, 30, 111, 117
        import, 9, 10, 12, 13, 14, 28–9, 31, 110–14, 116, 165–6, 170, 180
        markets and fairs, 5, 14–15, 81, 115, 164, 224
        plunder, 165, 167
        privately, 14, 15, 115, 223–4
        purveyance, 165–6
        resale, 240
        theft, 81
    aged, 32–4, 49, 57, 58–9
    ailments, 33, 54, 55, 57–8, 60, 62, 63–6, 223, 224, 242
        farriers, 1, 4, 38, 63, 64, 65, 66
        horse leeches, 1, 61, 64, 65, 66
        treatment, 63–6, 243
    appearance, 6, 9, 10, 14, 16, 57
    attitudes towards, xi–xii, 19, 21, 22ff, 52, 63, 66–7

horse (*continued*)
  attributes of, 19, 22–4, 25–7, 31–2, 39, 242
  breeding, 3, 4, 8, 9, 10, 12, 14, 15, 38, 89, 91, 112–14, 160–1, 170, 239, 242
    circles, 9, 14, 16
    covering, 39–41, 46, 48
    gelding, 41, 46–7
    grounds, 4, 15
    weaning, 38–9, 46
  breeds
    Arabian, 11, 13, 30–2, 71, 89, 90, 110–14
    Barb, 10, 11, 13, 14, 30, 89, 90, 110–14
    Corsican, 12
    Danish, 10, 221, 223
    Dutch, 10, 14, 198, 199, 221
    fen, 6, 15, 150, 198, 199
    Flemish, 9, 10, 11, 12, 14, 150, 165–6, 170, 180, 198, 221, 236–37
    French, 12
    Friesian, 10, 221
    Galloway, 5, 74, 112, 176, 195, 230
    German, 10, 11, 198, 221
    hill and moorland, 6, 15
    Hungarian, 11
    Irish hobby, 5, 12, 71, 74, 77, 112, 176
    Montgomeryshire merlin, 5
    Neapolitan and other coursers, 9, 11, 13, 28, 30, 64, 77, 112, 152, 211, 212, 239
    Oldenburg, 10
    Polish, 12
    Sardinian, 12
    Savoyard, 12
    Spanish, 10, 11, 14, 24, 29, 30, 71, 74, 239
    Suffolk punch, 6, 184, 197–8
    thoroughbred, 31–2, 89, 110, 111, 112–14, 239
    Turcoman, 10, 11, 14, 71, 89, 90, 110, 112–13, vale, 6, 14, 15
    Yorkshire, 15, 91, 114, 124, 164
  dealers, 1, 4, 13, 14, 15, 16, 114, 164, 168, 198, 199, 207, 224, 240

equids
  asses, 55, 183, 200
  mules, 1, 22, 38, 61, 77
fodder, 1, 15, 37, 75, 168
  cost, 4–5, 16, 81, 184
  grazing, 37, 75
function
  ceremonial, 11, 27–8, 30
  coach, 3, 10, 12, 14, 16, 25, 37, 59, 77, 142, 199, 215, 220–5, 232, 237, 240
    costs, 229
    criteria, 220–1, 224
    size of team, 220
    value, 220, 221, 223, 229
  draught, 1, 3, 6, 7, 10, 12, 14, 16, 59, 75, 183–6, 187, 188, 190, 194, 197–201, 207, 221, 235
    on the farm, 14, 37, 39, 183–6, 199–200, 208, 235
      oxen, comparison with and move from, 1, 183–86, 206
    on the road, 186, 187, 188, 191, 198–9, 200–1
      compared with packhorses, 186–7, numbers kept, 191–2
  hunters, 3, 7, 13, 16, 53, 69, 70, 84, 121, 123, 124, 128, 132, 136, 142, 217, 240
  manège, 11, 24, 30, 69, 82–4, 88
  pack, 1, 60, 60, 187, 189, 192, 235
  post, 78–81
  racing, 7, 12, 16, 25–7, 31, 44, 69, 88, 89ff, 123, 224, 239
  saddle, 2–3, 6, 7, 11, 12, 13, 14, 16, 21, 23, 34, 37, 55, 56, 59, 60, 69, 70, 74, 75, 77, 92, 217, 224, 240
  sumpter, 77, 207
  tournament, 127
  war, 3, 6, 8, 9, 11, 69, 70, 88, 124–5, 132, 133, 240
    cavalry, 145, 151–2, 156, 160–3, 164–5, 169, 171, 172, 175, 217
    cavalry horse shortages, 151, 161, 162, 164, 169, 173, 175, 176, 180–1, 197, 238

INDEX

draught, 6–7, 145, 149–50, 165–8, 170, 179, 180, 236
  poor quality and shortage of draught horses, 165–6, 170, 180
work, 1, 23, 25, 60, 75, 203–6, 235
  gins, 1, 60, 203–6, 235
gaits, 9, 10, 30, 49–50, 70–4, 76, 80, 194, 223
iconic, 3, 27–32, 33, 69, 82, 84, 88, 95, 113, 117, 135, 239
markets and fairs, 14–16
  Amesbury (Wilts.), 225
  Ashbourne (Derbys.), 225
  Banbury (Oxon.), 225
  Biggleswade (Beds.), 225
  Boughton Green (Northants.), 198
  Bristol, 81, Carlisle (Cumb.), 46, 48, 74
  Chester, 59, 70, 71, 81
  Derby, 14, 71,
  Dunstable (Beds.), 198, 225
  Eccleshall (Staffs.), 46
  Fotheringhay (Northants.), 224
  Hinckley (Leics), 224
  Kidderminster (Worcs.), 59
  Leighton Buzzard (Beds.), 15, 225
  Lenton (Notts.), 14
  Leicester, 224
  Lichfield (Staffs.), 16
  Malton (NRY), 14, 92
  Market Bosworth (Leics.), 47, 48
  Market Harborough (Leics.), 14, 224
  Melton Mowbray (Leics.), 14
  Northampton, 14, 56, 222, 224, 225
  Nottingham, 14, 71
  Oundle (Northants.), 224
  Oxford, 59
  Penkridge (Staffs.), 16, 47, 70, 115
  Plymouth (Devon), 81
  Portsmouth (Hants.), 81
  Ripon (WRY), 14, 92
  Rothwell (Northants.), 14, 224
  Rugeley (Staffs.), 16
  Shrewsbury, 15, 47, 70
  Smithfield (London), 164, 198, 207, 224
  Stafford, 16
  Stratford-on-Avon (Warwicks.), 47
  Uppingham (Ruts.), 224
  Warwick, 46
meat, 33, 184
  man aversion to, 5, 3–34
names, 14, 15, 23, 24–7, 242
quality, 6–8, 9, 10, 12, 13, 14, 25, 30–1, 69, 70, 74, 80, 84, 110, 164, 220–6, 239
Rearing, areas, 6, 15
tack, 12, 16, 35, 50–1, 52, 75, 77, 79, 88, 111, 124
  harness makers, 1
  lorimers, 1
  saddlers, 1, 12, 124
training of, 5, 19, 23, 41–6, 48–9, 85, 133–4, 199–200, 242
  horse breakers, 43, 44, 50
treatment of, 1, 18, 20–1, 31, 32–4, 35–7, 39, 41, 50ff, 99, 109–10, 116–17, 242
  grooms, 24, 38, 56, 92, 101, 115
value, 5, 9, 13, 24, 28, 30, 54, 55, 62, 70, 75, 110, 115, 128, 142, 152, 153, 194–5, 198, 200, 207–8, 225
Howard family
  Frances, 214
  Thomas, Lord Howard, 161
  Sir Thomas, 112
  Thomas, 3rd duke of Norfolk, 7, 166
  Thomas, 4th duke of Norfolk, 29
  William, Lord Howard of Naworth, 221
Hungary, 212–13, 217
hunting, 1, 7, 20, 38, 54, 94, 97, 119, 120–4, 125–6, 128, 130–1, 132, 134, 135–6, 139, 140, 141, 142, 143, 240
  costs, 128
  diplomacy, 141
  exclusivity, 128–9
  game, 120, 121–2, 127, 128, 129, 131, 133, 136, 143
  game laws, 62
  hounds, 7, 12, 97, 120, 121, 122–3, 128, 129, 131, 132, 135, 136, 144
  huntsmen, 128, 131, 135, 143

hunting (*continued*)
  par force hunting, 120, 137
  politics, 142
  ritual, 127, 131
  vermin, 121, 122–3, 131
  virility, 143
hunts, 123, 128
  Charlton Hunt, 122, 131, 142
  Chirk Castle, 124, 134
  Cliveden, 122
  Helmsley, 122
  Uppark, 122
Huntingdonshire, 196

Ireland, 81, 114, 135

Jackson, Henry, 152
James, Edward, of Kinvaston (Staffs.), 9, 16
Jockey Club, 114
Jones, Frank, 177
Jonson, Ben, xi, 125

Kendal (Westmor.), 190
Kenilworth (Warwicks.), 141
Kent, 201
  downs, 184
Kermond, William, land agent, 225
Keswick (Cumb.), 190
Kilmorrey, Lord, 208
Kingston, Sir William, 127
Kirkham, William, 77
Kocs (Hungary), 213

La Broue, Salomon de, riding master, 83, 134
Ladislas, V, king of Hungary
Lancashire, 189
Lane, Captain, 9
Leach, Edmund, 33
Leconfield Castle (ERY), 38
Lee, Sir Henry, the queen's champion, 138, 141
Leedes, Edward, of North Milford (WRY), 113
Legh, Peter, of Lyme Park (Ches.), 55

legislation, 8, 62, 70, 79, 90, 94, 95, 115, 116, 128–9, 154, 180, 192, 202, 203, 239
Leicestershire, 185, 190, 196, 199, 200
Lennox, Charles, 2nd duke of Richmond, 134, 142
Leslie, Alexander, covenanter commander, 158
Leveson-Gower family
  Gower, Lord, 123
  Sir John, 9
  Sir William, 15
Levi-Strauss, Claude, 25–7
Lichfield (Staffs.), 916, 90, 100
Lincolnshire, 196
  fens, 6, 15, 196, 198
  wolds, 184
Lippincotte, Arthur, Esquire, 152
litters, 211, 212, 216
Liverpool, 69
Lombart, Pierre, engraver, 30
London, 5, 60, 78, 82, 94, 186, 190, 198, 214, 215, 216, 218, 226, 227, 237, 238
Louis XIV, king of France, 179, 214
Low Countries, 36, 157, 163, 166, 173, 174
Lowther family, 60, 151, 204–5
Lucy, Sir Thomas, 24
Lundy, Colonel Robert, 178
Luke, Sir Samuel, Scoutmaster-General, 153
Lyme Regis, 172
Lyttelton family of Hagley Hall (Worcs.)
  Sir John, 74
  Sir Thomas, 43

MacCarthy, Justin, viscount Mountcashel, 178
Macclesfield, Lord, 100
Maidwell, Lewis, riding master, 83
Malmesbury (Wilts.), 48
Malton (WRY), 92, 101, 189
Man and the natural world, xi, 17, 20, 21, 52, 66, 85, 135, 136, 241
Manchester, 102, 189, 190
Manchester, Lord, 56

manège, 11, 24, 69, 82–4, 119, 121, 127, 133, 134, 143, 239, 240
Manners family, earls of Rutland, 25, 97, 127, 134, 142, 160, 211
Mansell, Sir Edward, 224
manuals on horse management, 9, 36, 54, 57, 63–5, 66–7, 85, 242
markets and fairs (non-horse references), 192
    Beverley (ERY), 189
    Bristol, 189
    Chertsey (Surrey), 57
    Malton (NRY), 189
    Pocklington (ERY), 189
    Richmond (NRY), 189
    Shaftesbury (Dors.), 188
    Warminster (Wilts.), 189
    Whitchurch (Shrops.), 92
Marseilles, 112
Mary of Hungary, 12, 166
Massingberd family, of Gunby (Lincs.), 41, 226
Massingberd family, of Mumby (Lincs.), 41, 50, 226, 229
Masters, Mr, 14
Maudant, John, 1st earl of Peterborough, 151
Meens, Robert, 33
Merchant Taylors' Hall, London, 214
Metcalf, William, Esquire, 124
Middlesex, 5, 189
Middleton, Lord, 41
Mildmay, Sir Humphrey, 82
Molyneux, Lord, of Sefton (Lancs.), 102, 134
Monck, General George, 175
Monmouth, duke of, 100
Montague, Lord, 13
Moore, William, yeoman, of Winteringham (Lincs.), 77
More, Andrew, hackneyman, of London, 78
More family of Loseley (Surrey), 15
Morgan, Mr John, 231
Morocco, 111
Morton, Sir Thomas, 163
Mostyn, Thomas, of Gloddaeth (Caernvs.), 212, 218

Munby, Julian, 212
Musgrave, Sir William, 171
Myddle (Shrops.), 122
Myddleton family of Chirk Castle (Denbs.), 33, 124, 134, 208, 231–2

Naples, 11
Napper, Sir Gerrard, 152
Nassau family, 146
nets, 132
Newark (Notts.), 193
Newcastle-upon-Tyne, 166, 188, 169, 207
Newdigate family of Arbury (Warwicks.)
    Sir John, 5, 43
    Sir Richard, 3, 9–10, 70, 80
New Forest (Hants.), 6
Newton, Sir John, 92
Newton, Toney (Wilts.), 124
Nicholson, hackneyman, of London, 80
Nonsuch Palace (Surrey), 126
Norfolk, 6
Norreys, Sir John, 173
Norris, Lord, 82
Northamptonshire, 165, 190, 201, 206
North Downs, 184
North, Roger, 23

O'Neill, Owen Roe, confederate general, 158
Ottoman Empire, 111, 116
Oumbler, William, gent, of Hedon (ERY), 81
Overton, Richard, 21
Oxford, 59, 78, 99
Oxfordshire, 6, 185, 190, 196, 201
Oxinden family
    Henry, of Barham, 64
    Henry, of Deane, 64

Paget family, 44, 64
    Thomas, 3rd Lord Paget of Beaudesert, 38
Paris, 84, 218
parks, 7, 8, 30, 37, 62, 104, 120, 122, 128, 129, 132, 134, 136, 141, 142, 161, 216
Peak District, 6, 189, 203

Pelham family of Halland
  Sir John, 14
  Sir Thomas, 15, 66
Penn, Sir William, 212
Pennines, 6
Pennington family, of Muncaster Castle, 25, 41
Pepys, Samuel, 212, 218, 238
Pershouse, Richard, 71
Percy family
  Algernon, 10th earl of Northumberland, 14, 15
  Henry, 9th earl of Northumberland, 28, 38
  Henry Algernon, 5th earl of Northumberland, 38, 77, 151
Petre family, 64, 128, 133, 206, 215, 219
Philip II, king of Spain
Pigeon, Mr, 134
Pinner, William, yeoman, of Loughton (Essex), 200
Plaxton, Reverend George, 123
Pluvinel, Antoine de, riding master, 82, 83
poaching, 129
Pollock, Linda, 51
Pomerania, 217
Poole, Sir James, 102, 134
Potton (Beds.), 60
Povey, Mr, 212, 218
Pratt, Sir Roger, of Ryston Hall (Norf.), 41, 62
Preston, Elizabeth, duchess of Ormond, 84
Pruce, John, land agent, 226
Pugliano, Jon Pietro, riding master, 23, 152
Pulver Fen (Suffolk), 37
Putto, John, miller, of Writtle (Essex), 75
Pye, Lady, 98

race meetings, 89, 93–5
  Abingdon (Berks.), 92, 100
  Aughton Moor (Lancs.), 105
  Barnet (Herts.), 91
  Beverley (ERY), 101, 102
  Bungay (Suffolk), 98
  Burford (Oxon.), 99–100
  Chester, 89, 93, 101, 115
  Childwall (Lancs.), 105
  Crosby Marsh (Lancs.), 105, 108
  Croydon (Surrey), 94, 102
  Doncaster (WRY), 101, 102
  Durham, 100, 103
  Edinburgh, 95
  Epsom, 91–2, 94, 95, 98, 100, 101, 102
  Forest of Delamere (Ches.), 100
  Gatherley Moor (NRY), 89, 97
  Great Crosby (Lancs.), 93, 101, 102, 105
  Halifax (WRY), 95
  Hambleton (WRY), 44, 91, 92, 101, 106
  Harlestone (Northants.), 93, 99
  Hurley (Berks.), 107
  Ireland, 114
  Kiplingcotes (ERY), 91
  Lichfield (Staffs.), 90, 100
  Lilly Hoo (Kent), 97, 98, 103
  Lincoln, 97, 103
  Liverpool, 107
  Manchester, 102
  Melksham (Wilts.), 107
  Newcastle under Lyme (Staffs.), 123
  Newmarket (Suffolk), 31, 90, 92, 94, 96, 97, 98, 99–100, 101, 102, 103, 104, 105, 107, 108, 114, 115
  Malton (NRY), 92, 101
  Nottingham, 90, 94, 98, 103, 104, 109
  Ormskirk (Lancs.), 93, 103, 105
  Prees (Shrops.), 92, 97
  Quainton Meadow (Bucks.), 96, 100
  Richmond (NRY), 97, 103, 104
  Ripon (WRY), 92, 97, 100, 103
  Rothwell (Northants.), 108
  Salisbury (Wilts.), 93, 102
  Saltby (Lincs.), 92
  Shrewsbury, 98
  Stamford (Lincs.), 102
  Swaffham (Norf.), 97, 98
  Tunbridge Wells (Kent), 92
  Wales, 95
  Wallasey (Ches.), 91, 92, 106

Winchester (Hants.), 94, 101, 103
Windsor (Berks.), 94, 102
York, 98, 101, 103, 104, 109, 114
racing, 89ff, 121, 239, 240
   cheating, 109
   distances, 101–3, 105, 114
   gambling, 55, 91, 92, 95, 96, 97, 101, 108, 109, 115
   opposition to, 99
   organization, 91, 92, 93, 101, 102
   politics, 99–100, 117
   private courses, 91, 93, 105
   prizes, 44, 90, 93, 94, 96, 102, 103, 104, 106, 115, 124
   riders, 90, 96, 97, 107, 109–10, 116
   stands, 102
   types of races, 90, 94, 95, 96, 97, 102–8, 114, 116, 123, 124–5
Radcliffe, Sir George, 81
Radcliffe, Thomas, 3rd earl of Sussex, 172
Rawdon, Marmaduke, 217, 231
recreational facilities, 91–2, 93, 96, 98, 102, 116, 134
Reresby family of Thrybergh Hall (WRY)
   Sir George, 9
   Sir John, 134, 142, 216
retinue, 28–9
Reynal, Sir Carew, 71
Reynolds, William, queen's fletcher, 172
Richmond (NRY) 97, 103, 104, 189, 207, 220
Richmond (Surrey), 78, 188
riding, 2–3, 23, 55, 56, 60, 71, 74, 75, 76, 81, 124, 241
   dangers, 69–70, 96
   distances, 2
   hackney, 61, 69, 78–81, 88
   pillion, 69, 76–7, 216
   post, 59, 61, 78–9, 80
riding schools
   Bolsover Castle (Derbys.), 83
   Ludlow Castle (Shrops.), 83, 133
   Wolferton (Norf.), 83
Ripon (WRY), 14, 92, 97, 100, 103

Ripon, Treaty of, 157
Roberts, Michael, 145, 149
Rogers, Clifford J, 145
Roth, Sir Thomas, 60
Routh, Cuthbert, of Dinsdale (Durham), 113
Rowley, Thomas, horse dealer, 15
Roxwell (Essex), 37, 195
royal family, 3, 4, 8, 93
   Anne, 101, 199, 223
   Anne of Denmark, 218
   Prince Arthur, 130
   Charles I, 13, 27, 29, 30, 83, 111, 132, 141, 143, 151, 157, 175, 176, 180, 213, 239
   Charles II, 54–5, 89, 94, 97, 99–100, 102, 107, 108, 111, 114, 117, 122, 130, 159, 169, 226
   Edward VI, 8, 127
   Edward of Norwich, duke of York, 131
   Elizabeth I, 8, 10, 30, 38, 64, 78, 82, 121, 127, 133, 138–9, 140–1, 171, 173, 180, 213
   Frederick, Elector Palatine, 12, 175, 218
   George, Prince, of Denmark, 223
   Henrietta Maria, 214
   Henry VI, 150
   Henry VII, 140, 150
   Henry VIII, 3, 6–7, 8, 10, 12, 16, 28, 30, 79, 111, 121, 126, 127, 128, 130, 134, 140, 141, 149, 151, 165–6, 170, 171, 180, 207, 221, 236, 239
   Henry Fitzroy, 134
   Henry, Prince of Wales, 13, 27, 29, 44, 78, 83, 126, 127, 128, 131–2, 143
   James I, 8, 13, 30, 78, 93–4, 97, 102, 120, 126, 132, 156, 157, 174, 175, 213, 221
   James II, 25, 27, 94, 122, 169, 177, 213
   Margaret Tudor, 211
   Mary I, 8, 213
   Richard III, 69
   Rupert, Prince, 11, 176, 177
   William III, 69, 106, 107, 108, 117, 178–9, 199, 221

royal household officials
   Equerry, Robert Terrett, 143
   Gentlemen of the Horse
      Sir Richard Graham, 207–8, 221
      Sir William Villiers, 24–5, 223
   Keeper of the Stables, Sir Stephen Fox, 223
   Masters of the Horse
      Sir Anthony Browne, 38
      Robert Devereux, 2nd earl of Essex, 36, 93, 127
      Robert Dudley, 1st earl of Leicester, 32, 44, 82, 132, 133, 141, 218
      Henry de Nassau, 30, 198, 208, 221, 224
      George Villiers, 1st duke of Buckingham, 8, 83, 111
      George Villiers, 2nd duke of Buckingham, 96, 122, 223
   Master of the Wardrobe, William Feilding, 1st earl of Denbigh, 213–14
   Racing Master, Mr Tregonwell Frampton, 107, 108
   Riding Masters
      Robert Alexander, 50, 82
      Pierre Antoine Bourdin, seigneur de St Antoine, 29, 83
      Claudio Corte, 82
   Studmasters
      James Darcy, 114, 220
      John Fenwick, 115
      Thomas Pulleine, 30, 113
Royal Society, 213
Russell family
   Mr, 223
   John, 4th duke of Bedford, 100
   William, 1st duke of Bedford, 219, 226
Russell, George, Esq., 62
Ryle, Francis, of Edingale (Staffs.), 75

St Albans, 79, 196, 205
Sadler, Raphe, 141, 171
Saint-Ruth, Marshal, 178
Salt, Mr, 9
Sarsfield, Patrick, earl of Lucan, 178

Savidge, Lord, 142
Schellink, William, 57
Scotland, 5, 94
   trade in horses with, 5
Scudamore family, 69, 137
Sedley, John, 127
Semple, Robert, 57
Sevenoaks area (Kent), 196
Seymour, Edward, earl of Hertford and duke of Somerset, 170, 171
Sheffield, Lord, 32, 80
Sheffield, Sir John, 112
Sheinton, Thomas, yeoman, of Chelmarsh (Shrops.), 200
shooting, 124, 129
Shrewsbury, 15, 29, 47, 70, 98, 190
Shropshire, 6, 189, 197
Sidney family
   Sir Philip, 23, 152
   Sir Robert, 137
Skippon, Philip, Sergeant-Major-General of Foot, 168
Skipton Castle (WRY), 164, 167
Smyth, Sir Hugh, 50
social class
   elite, 3, 15–16, 23, 35, 44, 54, 55, 63–4, 69, 80, 82, 88, 90–1, 93, 94, 95, 102, 108, 112, 114, 115, 116, 120, 122, 125–9, 150–3, 206, 211–12, 220, 227, 231–2, 235–6, 237, 239, 242
   lower orders, 2–3, 62, 89, 95, 102, 108, 116, 128, 240
   middling orders, 2–3, 74–5, 88, 89, 94, 95, 98, 102, 108, 116, 129, 153, 226, 232, 235–6, 237, 240–1, 242
Somerset, 6, 187, 190
   Levels, 6, 198, 100
Somerset, duchess of, 57
Somerset, Henry, marquis of Worcester, 152
Southampton, 78, 80, 190
South Downs, 184
Southwell (Notts.), 6
Spain, 10, 13, 174

Special Commission for the Increase and Breed of Horses 1580, 8, 160–1, 180
Spedding, John, land agent, 60
stables, 1, 3–4, 37, 38, 43, 55, 56, 60, 70, 80, 84, 92–3, 114, 115, 151, 161
   staff, 1, 3–4, 38, 41, 64
   wage bill, 38
Stafford, Lord, 83
Staffordshire, 189, 197, 199
standard of living, 2–3
status symbol, 2–5, 14, 27, 29, 33, 52, 69, 80, 88, 253, 211, 214, 215, 216, 220, 227, 238, 239
Staveley, Ninian, Esq., of Ripon Park (WRY), 9
Stewkeley, Will, 54
Strickland, Sir Roger, of Richmond (NRY), 207
studs, 14, 55, 83–4, 100, 101, 112, 113, 114, 115, 124, 151
   crown, 6, 12, 30, 39, 44, 48, 50, 170
   Italian, 12
   Mantuan, 11, 12, 28
   Spanish, 11–12
   staff, 44
Suffolk, 6
Surrey, downs, 184
   weald, 185
Sussex, downs, 184
   weald, 185
Suz, king of, 111
Syer, Mr, 134

Talbot, George, 4th earl of Shrewsbury, 151
Tangier, 111
Tempest, Sir John, 29
Temple, Sir Richard, 218
Thomas, Keith, xi–xii, 18, 52
Thompson, Michael, 1
Toobey, Robert, hackney coachman, 25
tournament: 119–20, 121, 126–7, 128, 130, 134, 135, 137–9, 140, 240
   Accession Day tilts, 138
   costs, 127
   diplomacy, 140

Eglinton Tournament, 121
foot matches, 119
iconography, 137–9, 140, 143
joust royal, 119, 120, 129, 134, 137, 143
ritual, 127
running at the ring, 119, 127
tiltyards, 119, 126
tourney, 119
virility, 137–8
weapons, 119, 126
Trafford, Mr, 134
transport by road, 2, 6, 70, 188ff.
   carrier services, 1, 78, 186, 187, 189–95, 228
   dangers, 193
   drivers, 191
   loads, 186, 187, 201, 202
   middlemen, 192
   networks, 190, 195
   packhorse teams, 1, 60, 75, 187, 189, 190, 192–5, 207
   packmen, 1, 192
   repair of roads, 202–3
   turnpikes, 203
   vehicles, 1, 10, 165–8, 187, 188, 189, 195, 201–3, 207, 237
   wagonways, 188
transport by water, 1, 111, 187–8, 208–9
   barges, 187
   halers, 188
   river ports, 187
   rivers, 188–9, 196, 207
transported goods, 183, 183, 187–9, 191, 192, 206–7
Tufton, John, 2nd earl of Thanet, 151
Tuke, Brian, Master of the Posts, 79
Turner, Sir James, 153
Tutbury, 12, 50
Talbot, Richard, earl of Tyrconnell, 177

urban cultural renaissance, 93
Uvedale, John, 7

Van Dyck, Anthony, 29
van Hulst, coachmaker, 218

Vavasour, Mr Henry, 54
Vaudemont, count of, 13
Verney family of Middle Claydon
   Edmund 54, 55, 80, 151, 157
   John, 216, 237
   Sir Ralph, 34, 54, 55, 77, 216, 217

Wales, 5, 6, 95
   South, 187
Walker, William, yeoman, of Lichfield (Staffs.), 197
Wallenstein, Albrecht von, 148
Walsingham, Sir Francis, 142
Wanklyn, Malcolm, 177
warfare
   allies, 166, 168, 170
   arms and equipment
      armour, 127–8, 130, 146, 152, 156, 159, 170, 172, 175, 179
      artillery and baggage trains, 145, 150, 165–8, 169–70, 180, 236
      edge weapons
         axes, 171, 172, 174
         bows and arrows, 132, 133, 146, 147, 170, 174
         crossbows, 132, 143
         daggers, 143, 156, 172, 174
         socket bayonets, 147
         swords, 119, 147, 149, 156, 159, 171, 172, 173, 174, 175, 176, 179
      firearms, 132, 133, 145, 146, 156, 174, 175
         calivers, 146, 172
         carbines, 159, 171, 172, 175–6, 179
         harquebuses, 146, 147, 175
         muskets, 145, 153, 159, 171, 172
         petronels, 172
         pistols, 145, 148, 149, 153, 159, 171, 172, 173, 175, 176, 179
      munitions, ammunition, 168
         cartridges, 147
         gunpowder, 134, 145, 149
         match, 134
      ordnance, 145, 148, 149, 168, 169, 179, 180
         field pieces, 149, 179
         gunners, 170
      pole weapons, bills, 171, 172
         lance, 119, 126, 130, 137, 143, 146, 171, 172, 175
         pike, 145, 153, 159, 171, 174
         pole, 146
      shields
         bucklers, 174
         targe, 119, 174
      throwing weapons
         darts, 174
         javelin, 132, 147
         spears, 119, 146, 156, 172
   weaponry
      imports, 158, 181
   battles, abroad
      Agincourt, 146
      Bicocca, 146
      Blenheim, 179
      Cadiz, 175
      Cassel, 146
      Cerignola, 146
      Coutras, 148
      Crecy, 146
      Ivry, 148
      La Rochelle, 175
      Laupen, 146
      Lützen, 148
      Marignano, 146
      Mons-en-Pévèl, 146
      Pavia, 146
      Poitiers, 146
      Ramilles, 179
      Ravenna, 146
      Zutphen, 139, 173
   battles, in Britain
      Armada, 151
      Aughrim, 178
      Bannockburn, 146
      Benburb, 176
      Boyne, 178

Edgehill, 132, 177
Flodden, 170, 171
Grantham, 177
Kinsale, 174
Marston Moor, 177
Naseby, 176
Newburn, 179–80
Newbury I, 177
Newbury II, 180
Newtonbutler, 178
Pinkie Clough, 171
Ross, 150
Roundway Down, 148
conflicts within Britain
　English Civil Wars, 9, 33, 151–3, 163–5, 169, 175, 180–1, 186, 193, 195
　　composition of armies, 175–6
　Ireland, 150, 157
　　composition of armies, 173–4, 176, 177–8
　　Confederacy, 169
　　O'Neill's Rebellion, 166, 172
　　Williamite War, 177–9
　Northern Rising, 151, 160, 171–2
　Scotland, 151, 157, 159
　　Bishops' War, 166, 169, 175, 180, 239
　　border tenure, 156
　　composition of Scottish army, 171, 175, 176, 179
　　Flodden campaign, 170
　　'Hot Trod', 155–6
　　Pinkie Clough campaign, 171
Council of War, 134, 150, 166, 176
drill, 146, 147, 174, countermarch, 146–7
Engagement, 151
Finance, 167–8, 170
Foot, 145, 146, 159, 169, 171, 172, 175, 177, 179
　archers, 146, 169, 171, 172
　billmen, 169, 171, 172
　dragoons, 147, 153, 175
　halberdiers, 146
　harquebusiers, 146, 172

musketeers, 147, 148, 171, 172
pikemen, 146, 147, 171, 172
fortifications, 149
Horse, 132, 133, 143, 145, 146, 147, 152, 159, 173, 175, 178, 179, 239
　cuirassiers, 153, 175, 176
　demi-lances, 148, 172, 173, 175, 180
　heavy horse, 130, 132, 145, 146, 148, 152, 169, 170, 171, 173, 174, 180
　light horse, 147, 152–3, 162, 170–1, 172, 174, 179, 180
　mounted harquebusiers, 171, 175
　petronels, 162, 172, 175, 179
　tactics, 145, 147, 148–9, 152, 153, 171–2
Legislation
　Assize of Arms, 154,
　Commission of Array, 157
　Marian Acts, 154, 156–7
　Militia Acts 1662–63, 158–9
　Militia Ordinance, 157
　Statute of Winchester, 154
lieutenancy, 29, 142–3, 153–4, 155, 157, 159, 162, 166
mercenaries, 170, 171
military revolution, 145, 146–50, 173
　Britain
　　agents of change, 158, 169, 170, 171
　　archaic armies, 169, 170, 180, 181
　　modernization, 155, 158–9, 171, 172, 173, 174–5, 181
　　slow rate of adoption, 145, 169, 171, 172–3, 181
　militia, 3, 153–9
　counties
　　Caernarvonshire, 173
　　Devon, 163
　　Derbyshire, 159–60, 162
　　Dorset, 161
　　Essex, 159, 162, 163
　　Hampshire, 161
　　Kent, 173
　　Leicestershire, 160, 162
　　Lincolnshire, 163
　　Middlesex, 161

warfare, military revolution, counties
   (*continued*)
      Norfolk, 159, 162
      Northamptonshire, 161, 166
      Nottinghamshire, 160
      Surrey, 161
      Warwickshire, 162
      Yorkshire, 160
   finances, 157, 159, 160, 163
   Foot, 154, 159, 163, 173, 174
      foreign service, 154, 173
   Horse, 154, 159–65, 173
   localism, 158
   muster masters, 155, 157, 158, 163, 169, 181
   shortcomings, 154–5, 157, 159–63
      Horse, 154, 159–65, 174
      struggle to control, 157–8
      training, 155, 157, 159–60, 162
      veterans stiffen ranks, 158
      weaponry, 154
   musters, 151, 154, 160, 161, 162, 172
   noble contingents, 150–1
   Propositions, 151, 152, 163–4
   standing army, 159, 169, 181
   tactics, 11, 145, 148, 169, 173, 177, 179, 239
   Wars
      Thirty Years War, 158, 162, 175
      War of the Grand Alliance, 168, 179
warrens, 129, 136
Warwickshire, 6, 190
Watson, Sir Lewis, 137
Webb, John, yeoman, of Writtle (Essex), 75
Welbeck (Notts.), 55, 56, 112
Welsh Border, 190
Wentworth, Thomas, earl of Strafford, 158

Wesley, John, 21
West Country vales, 185
Wharton family
   Lord Thomas, 171
   Lord William, 223
Whyman, Susan, 54
Willoughby, Lord, 12, 13–14, 204
Wiltshire: 193, 195, 196, 201
   downs, 206
   north, 185
Windsor Forest, 133
Winteringham (Lincs.), 37, 196
Wittewronge, Sir John, of Rothamstead (Herts), 62, 206, 220, 224
Woking (Surrey), 126
women
   and coaches, 215–16, 232
      control of, 84–7, 138, 139–40
   and hunting, 134, 136, 143
   at race meetings, 95–8, 116
   riding, 76, 84
   sexual metaphors, 86–7, 136–7, 139–40
Woodstock (Oxford), 141
Wootton, John, painter, 31
Worcester, 205
Worcestershire, 6
Worsley, Giles, 124
Wressell Castle (ERY), 38
Writtle (Essex), 37, 195
Wynn, Maurice, of Wynnstay Hall (Montgs.), 63

Xenophon, 39, 131

Yetminster (Dors.), 3
Yorkshire, 15, 91, 114, 124, 160, 164, 203
   wolds, 184